TO Scan

all

104

BULL'S EYE INVESTING

**Targeting Real Returns
in a Smoke and Mirrors Market**

John Mauldin

WILEY

John Wiley & Sons, Inc.

To Eunice, who keeps me on target

———————————

ISBN 0-471-65543-0

Printed in the United States of America.

10   9   8   7   6   5   4   3   2   1

Contents

Acknowledgments

There are so many people who have been a big part of making this book possible. Words cannot express my gratitude to those who graciously allowed me to intrude upon their busy schedules when I needed data, statistics, feedback, and comments. A work of this size and scope is clearly not from just my own limited resources.

There were a number of people whose ideas directly contributed to significant parts of this book. Rob Arnott, Ed Easterling, James Montier, and Michael Alexander all contributed important ideas and in some cases the basic ideas for whole chapters and sections.

I regularly read a number of writers whose ideas permeate this book as they have helped shape my thinking. I am especially grateful to my friends and fellow analysts Bill Bonner, Art Cashin, Dennis Gartman, Bill King, Richard Russell, and Greg Weldon for their daily commentaries.

I regularly read and should note the work and writings of Martin Barnes, Peter Bernstein, Lord Alex Bridport and Roy Damary in Geneva, Chuck Butler, Mark Faber, Bill Gross, Gary Halbert, Michael Lewitt, Paul McCulley, Gary North, Barry Ritholtz, Stephen Roach, Gary Shilling, Steve Sjuggerud, and Porter Stansberry.

I should note that none of these writers is responsible for any of the errors, wrong notions, or failed forecasts in the book. Those are all mine.

I mention a number of important books and newsletters in Appendix A that have helped me in my thinking and may be of value to you.

Thanks to my editor at Wiley, Debra Englander, for bearing with me through busted deadlines and working with me even when the book came in at twice the size. I have to mention my associate Harry Ward, who helped with the research, writing, and all the hard work of doing graphs, checking facts, getting permission for quotes, and so on. Thanks to

Wayne Anderson for his editing help and to my daughter and assistant Tiffani for handling the details, and even more so to my bride (and favorite Canadian export) Eunice who keeps the operations flowing.

Many thanks to Jon Sundt, Matt Osborne, and Bob Amedeo at Altegris Investments, with whom I partner on the investment business side of my life, for letting me be absent for long periods, which probably cost them far more money than I will ever get in royalties.

Mike Casson, my e-letter publisher at Investor Insights, gets a special thanks as his hard work has made it possible for me to have such a large Internet readership and exposure.

Many readers offered thoughtful comments, suggestions, and criticisms, and I am grateful to all of you.

Introduction

"Would you tell me, please, which way I ought to go from here?"
"That depends a good deal on where you want to get to," said the Cheshire Cat.
"I don't much care where—" said Alice.
"Then it doesn't matter which way you go," said the Cat.
"—so long as I get somewhere," Alice added as an explanation.
"Oh, you're sure to do that," said the Cat, "if you only walk long enough."

—Lewis Carroll, *Alice's Adventures in Wonderland*

Every hunter knows that you don't shoot where the duck is, but where the duck is going to be. You've got to "lead the duck." If you aim where the duck is at the moment you shoot, you will miss your target (unless the duck is flying very slowly or is very close!).

Bull's Eye Investing simply attempts to apply that same principle to investing. In this book, I hope to give you an idea of the broad trends that will be evident for the remainder of the decade and help you target your investments to take advantage of these trends.

Successful investing for the period 2004 through 2010 will require you to do things differently than you did in the 1980s and 1990s. We started the last bull market with high interest rates, very high inflation, and low stock market valuations. All the elements were in place to launch the greatest bull market in history.

Now we're in the opposite environment. The stock market has high valuations, interest rates have nowhere to go but up, the dollar is dropping, and the twin deficits of trade imbalance and government debt stare us in the face.

Which way is the stock market going? Which way are bonds going? Gold? Real estate? Where should I invest?

Wall Street and the mutual fund industry say, "The market is going up; you should buy stocks and now is the time to buy. You can't time the markets, so you should buy and hold for the long term. Don't worry about the short-term drops. And my best advice is to buy my fund."

The folks on Wall Street are in the business of selling stocks because that is how they make their real money. Whether the shares are sold directly or are packaged in mutual funds or as initial public offerings (IPOs) or in wrap accounts or in variable annuities or in derivatives, these folks primarily want to sell you some type of equity (stock), preferably today. Unfortunately, the vast majority of investors believe these pitches and don't know there are better investment alternatives.

Their advice—buy what they sell—has been the same every year for a century. And it has been wrong about half the time. There are long periods of time when stock markets go up or sideways and long periods of time when markets go down or sideways.

These cycles are called secular bull and bear markets. ("Secular" as used in this sense is from the Latin word *saeculum*, which means a long period of time.) Each cycle has different types of good investment opportunities. We are currently in just the first few innings of a secular bear market. The problem for Wall Street is that the products brokers primarily sell do not do well in secular bear markets. So they have to tell you that things will get better so you should buy now. Or they advise you to "have patience, and please give us more of your money."

In secular bull markets investors should focus on investments that offer *relative returns*. By that I mean we should look for stocks and funds that will perform better than the market averages. The benchmark by which you measure your investment strategy is the broad stock market. If you "beat the market," you are doing well. Even though there will be losing years, staying invested in quality stocks will be a long-term winner.

In secular bear markets, that strategy is a prescription for disaster. If the market goes down 20 percent and you go down only 15 percent, Wall Street proclaims your performance to be "winning." But you are still down 15 percent.

In markets like those we face today, the essence of Bull's Eye Investing is to focus on *absolute returns*. Your benchmark is a money market fund. Success is measured in terms of how much you make above Treasury bills. In secular bear markets, success is all about controlling risk and carefully and methodically compounding your assets.

Some will say, as they say each year, that the bear market is over: that this book is writing about ancient history. But history teaches us that is not the case. Secular bear markets can have drops much bigger than we have already seen, and last for up to 17 years. The shortest has been eight years. They have never been over when valuations have been as high as they are today.

Investors who continue to listen to the siren song of Wall Street will be frustrated at best, in my opinion, as the research I present clearly shows we have a long way to go in this bear market cycle. For those who plan to depend on their stock market investments for retirement within a decade, the results could be particularly devastating.

Bull's Eye Investing is not, however, some gloom and doom book. Despite what Wall Street wants you to believe, there is no connection between how the economy will do and how the stock market will perform. As we will see, the economy should be fine, with just the usual corrections sandwiched between periods of growth. The world as we know it is not coming to an end. It is merely changing, as it always has. There are numerous possibilities for investment growth in a secular bear market. They just don't happen to be in the standard Wall Street fare.

What I hope to do is give you a road map to the future by looking at how and why markets have behaved in the past. We will debunk many of the myths and "scientific studies" used by Wall Street to entice investors into putting their money into buy-and-hold, relative return investments. The Wall Street insiders, not surprisingly, use theories, statistics, and so-called facts that are blatantly biased and in many cases just plain wrong. When the market goes down, they just shrug their shoulders like Chicago Cubs (or my own Texas Rangers) fans and say, "Wait till next year. And buy some more, please."

Basically, in the first half of the book I am going to teach you how to fish, and in the second half I am going to tell you where the fish are. I would politely suggest that you not skip the first half of the book—do not turn to the last part simply looking for the quick investment fix. If you don't understand what is happening in the economy and world markets, you will not have confidence in your investment strategy and you'll end up chasing the latest hot investment, which is usually a prescription for pain in any type of market.

Here's how this book is organized:

First, we look at what history teaches us about the potential for stock market returns over the rest of this decade. We examine six major (and very different) ways to look at the stock market. As a quick preview, the evidence is heavily weighted to suggest that at the end of this cycle the stock market will not be too far from where it is today. The historical and mathematical analysis of bubbles also suggests that we could see the stock market drop much further before beginning the next bull market.

We examine several of Wall Street's favorite sales tools, the famous Ibbotson study,* Jeremy Siegel's *Stocks for the Long Run*, and Modern Portfolio Theory (MPT), and see why you should exercise extreme caution when they are used in a sales presentation.

We then look at why the economy can do just fine and stock markets still can fall: It all has to do with the expectation for earnings and the value investors put on those future earnings.

Most analysts track a simple bear market from peak to trough (top to bottom). Bear markets (or 20 percent plus corrections) can happen in secular bull periods (think 1987 or 1998), just as bull markets (20 percent plus up reversals) can happen in secular bear markets (think 2000, 2001, 2002, 2003). Analysts also view a secular bear market as the lengthy period over which the market makes a top, enters into a decisive down phase, and then once again returns to the old high.

I suggest that we view a secular bear market a little differently, as the period in which the price-earnings (P/E) ratio goes from very high to quite low. It is in these periods of low valuation that we can once again begin to confidently put our money back into stocks, as the rubber band is getting ready to snap back. Of course, Wall Street folks will trot out all sorts of studies that show that stocks are always undervalued and you should buy today. They did so in 2000, 2001, and 2002, and 2003. They are doing so as this book is written and published. They are wrong, and we will examine why they're wrong.

That means earnings are important, and thus a few chapters focus on earnings. We see why Wall Street analysts are so consistently wrong (by about 50 percent per year too much), what the prospects for real earnings growth are, and how to put it all into perspective.

Next, we look at risk. As I've said, investing in secular bear markets is all about controlling risk. I believe this chapter is one of the most important in the book, but it may also be the most fun.

We discuss the most common mistakes investors make and how to avoid them. Statistics show that investors do not do as well as the funds or stocks they invest in, and we look at the causes. We examine why today's hot fund is likely to be tomorrow's loser, and what types of funds you should be looking for in this market.

We look at the future, including the demographics of the baby boomer generation, and how it will impact our investment potential. We analyze the direction of interest rates, deflation, and inflation. Then we examine

---

*Roger G. Ibbotson and Rex A. Singuefield, "Stocks, Bonds, Bills, and Inflation: Simulations of the Future (1976–2000)," *Journal of Business*, Vol. 49, Issue 3 (1976), pp. 313–338.

the world economy and the dollar and see if we can find a potential winning theme (we do!).

The consequences of these economic problems will require some painful adjustments from those who do not make the effort to protect themselves. I show you where and how to turn problems into opportunities by seeking absolute returns in turbulent markets.

After the first section, the book focuses on specific types of investments. After telling you why we are in a secular bear market for stocks, Chapters 16 through 18 explain precisely how to invest in stocks today. Ironically, in a secular bear market, the little guy has a big advantage over the larger institutions and funds. There are great opportunities in the stock market if you know where to look. During the last secular bear market, companies like Microsoft and Intel were launched. I show you a simple way to find the hidden gems sought after by the savviest investors.

Then we look at the world of fixed income investments. The rules are changing, and what worked in the 1980s and 1990s will in all likelihood be a losing proposition for the remainder of this decade.

We then analyze what are, in my opinion, some of the better potential sources of absolute returns: certain types of hedge fund styles. We look at how Wall Street has rigged the market against small investors getting the best deals. The richest investors and largest institutions with the best-paid advisors choose these high-fee, unregulated private investments because they deliver better risk-adjusted performance than one-way buy-and-hold mutual funds. We show you how to find and gain access to these private funds, and how to use some of their strategies in your own portfolios.

Finally, we take a more thorough look at the future, and why you should be optimistic. In 1974, only a few people saw the changes and opportunities that computers, telecommunications, and the Internet would bring. The world was bemoaning the losses of basic American industry as jobs were being lost to world competition.

Today, we find ourselves once again faced with serious competition for American jobs. Our core seems to be slipping away, as the market doesn't respond. The world sees us in a much different light than just a few years ago. Few notice the new revolutions that are happening in small firms and research departments that will form the basis for the next wave of American prosperity because we haven't even begun to imagine the ways in which the next waves of change will affect us.

Will there be winners and losers in this process? Of course. Anytime there are periods of upheaval and great change, there are always those who benefit from the change and those who suffer. I will try to show you how you can position yourself to be a winner.

There is a centuries-long, if not millennia-long, pattern to these cycles. Good markets are followed by bad markets, which are again followed by good markets. They are as predictable as winter and summer. These cycles have been happening since the Medes were trading with the Persians. While no one can predict the exact day winter weather will arrive, it is a pretty good bet that winter will come. You can prepare for winter just as you plan for summer. As investors, you can be successful if you understand the economic and investment seasons we are in and plan your investments accordingly.

So, let's get you started on your way to successful Bull's Eye Investing.

Car Wreck, Traffic Jam, or Freeway? 1

New Era economists, mutual fund managers, and sell-side investment advisors constantly argue that the stock market freeway is now finally wide open, with more lanes being built daily! Today is always a good time to buy (and hold!), and besides, the market always goes up over the long run. Don't worry about the short term!

These avant-garde investors throw out a wide range of reasons reassuring us that **this time the apparently high valuations in the stock market are really different** from the past high valuations, which always ended in serious corrections and decade-long secular bear markets. Furthermore, they contend all recessions in the future will be mild and short, such as the one we experienced in 2001. Therefore, the bull market of the 1990s should soon resume.

Investors are presented with so-called facts and convincing studies that interpret them. Armed with this analysis, it is easy to contend that the Dow Jones Industrial Average is going to reach 36,000 or 100,000 in the next few years, as soon as it catches its breath. The primary reasoning of these New Era cheerleaders, it seems to me, is circular logic. They tell us that investors should now see the stock market to be as safe as bonds. This means more and more investors will continue to invest in the stock market, driving up stock prices until the returns approach those of bonds. Because earnings will soon resume growing as fast as they did in the last decade (any quarter now!), we will see continued high growth in the markets even after we have driven the markets to these new bondlike valuations. This is because Peter Lynch tells us that earnings drive the stock market. Presumably ever-increasing earnings will drive the stock market to ever-increasing new highs.

These same people thought we would avoid a recession in 2001 because

Alan Greenspan was lowering interest rates. These people are cheerleaders who can pose a serious danger to your investment portfolio. I will teach you how to detect and avoid cheerleaders in later chapters.

Their circular logic is enticing. It seemed to be true throughout the 1990s. *We want it to be true because if it were we would have a clear road to riches.* Simply save 10 to 15 percent per year, let it compound in a Roth IRA or annuity earning 15 percent, and you'll be on your way to retiring at a beachfront haven for the good life. If you save more, you can retire early.

But it flies in the face of centuries of human experience and the preceding century of modern stock market investing. I think it has the potential to be a siren song that lures hopeful investors onto a very rocky shore. *Please understand me: I am not simply spreading doom and gloom. I think it is possible to save and invest and retire happily.* The trick is to make sure you have the right approach. To say this as directly as possible: *The recent era of profitable buy-and-hold stock market investing, using index funds and chasing high-growth large-cap stocks, has ended, and will not come our way again for many years. Until then, we need to change our investment habits to adjust with the times.*

As we look at dozens of studies, reports, and essays, you will see that the evidence is overwhelming. Achieving your retirement dreams is possible, but not by using the stock market freeway of the cheerleading crowd.

The road less traveled is safer and far more certain. Let me give you the map.

Secular Bear Markets

The next few chapters make the case that we are in something called a secular bear market. As mentioned, a secular bear market is loosely defined as a long period of years or even decades when stock prices are either flat or falling (think Japan today or the United States from 1966 to 1982). Historically and classically defined, secular bear markets are as short as eight years or as long as 17.

My contention, and I think the clear lesson of history, is that we will be in this environment for a long time, and that the key to successful investing will be to acknowledge this factor and invest in the types of stocks, funds, and other investments that do well in a secular bear market, while avoiding those which history has shown us to have less opportunity for success in this type of period.

Understanding the nature of the investment environment and investing accordingly are critical to your success as an investor. But before I can tell you how to invest in a secular bear market, you need to understand for yourself what these cycles are and why and how they happen.

Rules of Engagement

Investors have been taught a philosophy of investment called Modern Portfolio Theory (MPT), which has seemed to work quite well for decades. It is belief in this theory that prompts leading investor gurus to tell us to take a deep breath and to remain calm while our portfolios are down 40 percent. It is this theory, or what is really a twisted version of it, that allows brokers to tell you to buy and hold large-cap stocks with high P/E ratios (or whatever investment they are pushing), even as the stocks tumble. There is much to be learned from this philosophy, but I think it is at the root of much of the pain individual investors have been feeling these past few years.

The rules of engagement for warfare have changed. I think it is fair to say that our nation, if not much of the world, has realized that. The end of the Cold War and the beginning of the War on Terrorism have changed the manner in which we deal with those who would attack our nation. What would have been unthinkable only a few years ago is now promoted as necessary and wise by (almost) all parts of the political equation. It is clear that our military leaders are hoping to avoid the most costly and typical of all military mistakes: using the tactics of the last war to fight the current war.

I am going to suggest that the rules of engagement, as it were, for investing have changed as well. What worked for the 1980s and 1990s will now frustrate those who want to use the old investing rules to fight the next investment war. If you do not see and adjust to these changes, you will not be happy with your investment returns over the next decade.

Jumping Ahead

Future stock market returns are likely to be severely below those of recent decades and the expectations of investors. This book looks at a variety of studies and ways to understand the stock market. These views come from different premises, but they all arrive at the same conclusion: They demonstrate a very high probability that we will be in an extended period of low or negative returns, or what is called a secular bear market. (Later chapters show a whole new way to look at bear markets: one that will also give us some idea of when to actually get back in the market.)

During such a market, investors will not be able to invest in mutual funds and have a rising tide raise their funds. Index funds, despite what the fund companies may advertise, will not perform well. Equity mutual funds will increasingly be seen as bad investments. You might think this has already happened, but we are nowhere near the level of antipathy toward mutual funds that we will see in a few years and after the next few recessions. As future recessions reduce the time horizons of investors and as investors demand more immediate rewards, stock prices will continue to slide and the net asset values of mutual funds will continue to drop.

Most investors will react by chasing the latest hot fund in a desperate bid to recapture some of their losses. We will see later that this is the worst thing you can do.

So let's first look at the old rules, then survey the new territory and see if we can begin to identify some new guidelines to help us during the current cycle.

It all started in 1952 when Dr. Harry M. Markowitz wrote a series of brilliant essays for which he received the Nobel Prize in economics. His work is the foundation for Modern Portfolio Theory, which has since come to be the dominant model for investment professionals.

Put simply, Markowitz said you can reduce the overall volatility of your portfolio by diversifying your investments among a group of noncorrelating asset classes. When one asset class (such as stocks) is going down, your diversification into bonds and real estate would help hold the value of your portfolio steady.

Markowitz mathematically demonstrated how it is possible for you to combine diverse types of assets that, in and of themselves, could be quite risky and volatile, and the combination portfolio would have lower volatility and more consistent returns than the individual investments. While this seems intuitive today, it was quite novel in 1952.

At that time, it was assumed that since investors picked stocks because of the expectation of future returns, if they could truly know what those future returns would be, they would buy only the one stock or investment that would deliver the highest return.

Of course we don't know the future, so we diversify. MPT says if we diversify into different asset classes with different risk characteristics that do not have a statistical correlation with each other, and which have shown to be good investments over long periods of time, that total portfolio return would be smoother.

If we diversify into bonds, stocks, real estate, timber, oil, and so on over time our portfolio will grow and grow more smoothly than if we concentrate in one market. The key words are "over time."

Markowitz and his followers created a Greek alphabet soup of statistical measures to describe risk. Alpha, beta, gamma, delta, and their statistical cousins help analysts determine the past risk of an investment. MPT then shows professionals how to combine these investments into one portfolio with desired risk/reward characteristics. The Capital Asset Pricing Model shows us how to combine stocks into efficient indexes to achieve the lowest possible risk given their expected return.

We then are told that the market is completely efficient, and that the prices of stocks immediately reflect everything that is knowable and relevant about them. Thus, it is impossible to beat the market.

All of these analytical tools are very useful, and Modern Portfolio Theory has become the sine qua non, the gold standard of investing, especially for large institutions. No one gets fired for properly using MPT as the basis for managing large institutional money.

For the past 50 or so years it has demonstrably worked, more or less. There are hundreds of studies that illustrate the superiority of portfolios constructed with MPT.

But there are three catches to Modern Portfolio Theory that make all the difference in the world. These are three things you typically do not hear at investment sales presentations.

The first is that you have to give Modern Portfolio Theory time. Lots of time. Decades of time.

If you invested in the S&P 500 in 1966, it was 16 years before you saw a gain, and 26 years before you had inflation-adjusted gains. If you invested in the 1950s or in 1973, your gains came more quickly. If you invested in 1982 or late 1987, your gains in only a few years were spectacular. And let's not forget 1999. However, the years 2000 through 2002 were not so kind. While 2003 saw the market rally, if the market were to post similar gains for the next two to three years, valuation levels would be higher than at the peak of the recent stock market bubble.

You could make the same type of risk/reward analysis for every market: bonds, stocks, international markets, real estate, oil, and so on. They all have ups and downs and over time, they come back. Betting on America has been good.

For institutions with a 25 to 30 year time horizon, the ups and downs are annoying, but manageable. With a diversified portfolio, some holdings may decline while others perform well. In recessions, the asset mix is altered, perhaps with a slightly higher percentage of bonds, but the portfolio always contains some stocks since the institution is not attempting to time the market.

Positively, Absolutely Relative

Modern Portfolio Theory is what many investment professionals use to push their clients into a relative value game. If the market (stocks, bonds, real estate, etc.) goes down 15 percent and your portfolio is down only 12 percent, you have beaten the market and done your job. You tell your investors that they should stay with you and that in fact you deserve more of their money. If your clients are institutions, they are likely to comply.

This is one reason why you constantly hear "buy and hold" from investment professionals. It is why they want you to have a high percentage of stocks in your investment portfolio. They can trot out all sorts of studies that show that stocks are the best investment over the long term. Typically, the long term begins with a good year, but with a long enough time frame you can make a case beginning with almost any year.

"In the long run," said John Maynard Keynes, "we are all dead."

What works for institutions may not work for individuals. Most individuals do not have an extended period of years to wait for an investment to come back. How many of you are willing to let a mutual fund or an asset class go for years and years with poor performance? How many years will you stick with a technology fund that has been going down for several years? Those managers will always tell you now is the best time to buy, just as they did six months ago, one year ago, and two years ago. There is never a time to sell a fund. Every dip is just a prelude to a new high. Modern Portfolio Theory says so. Just give me time.

But study after study (we shall later view a few of them) say investors do not give them time. With remarkable consistency over many decades, investors get frustrated and buy high and sell low. Study after study shows investors, buying and selling in an attempt to boost their returns, make only a small percentage of what mutual funds make.

The plain fact is that individuals have different time frames and different needs than institutions, but have been talked into using a strategy that is psychologically opposite to their instincts. Many investors have told me they wish they had followed their intuition or their research to exit the markets in 2000 but were talked out of it by their brokers or advisors.

In a secular bear market you will not win if you're following an investment strategy that requires a 25-to-40-year time frame when your personal time frame is only a few years. Investing with a philosophy that is built on relative returns, rather than the absolute returns your instinct says you want, is a prescription for disappointing and possibly even disastrous results.

If you are following the Wall Street cheerleaders you have, whether you know it or not, bought into a rigged version of Modern Portfolio Theory. The problem is not the theory. The problem is the way it can be used by those who want to sell you something. You don't know the entire game plan and end up taking the worst parts at the wrong time.

In early 2003, I had the pleasure of talking with Nobel Prize economist Dr. Harry Markowitz. He spoke at the Global Alternative Investment Management (GAIM) conference, a rather large conference focused primarily on hedge funds.

The Correlations Change

Markowitz gives us the next two catches to using MPT. The first insight came during his presentation. He reprised a speech he gave in 2002 on the 50th anniversary of the publication of his groundbreaking work. He went through the history of how Modern Portfolio Theory came to be. Buried in the slide on the discussion on noncorrelation was the point that in the 1980s the world assumed that there was no correlation between the U.S. and international stock markets. International stock markets were considered a separate asset class and were marketed as such.

Now we know that the correlation between the two stock market classes is quite high. World markets have all tanked at the same time in the past few years. The diversification "protection" an investor got from investing offshore in 1980 has disappeared. Markowitz's point was that if you attempt to diversify, it is important that the markets you diversify into don't actually move together.

That was what caused the spectacular failure of Long-Term Capital Management in 1998. That fund, led by Nobel Prize economists, profited for years by making a highly leveraged bet that the interest rates on bonds would converge. In 99 out of 100 years, that is the case. They believed they were diversified because they held bonds in scores of different nations. Their theory was that even if the 100-year flood happened in Russia, if you had only a small amount of your capital in Russia, you were protected.

What they discovered too late was that in times of stress the world has become so connected that there is no benefit to diversifying among countries. They went down in flames, drowning in the flood that spread to the rest of the world.

Markowitz, in his work, allowed for correlations to change over time. When Wall Street uses the theory it does not. Wall Street does not want to be involved in "market timing." The advisors simply say use such and such a fixed correlation portfolio, and over time things will even out. They wait for their correlation studies to become fatally flawed, and then change them after the fact. By then customers have lost their shirts, but they will be shown the new studies that indicate what they *should* have done.

It's All about Assumptions

The third catch is best illustrated from a private conversation I had with Dr. Markowitz. There was more than one eye raised in the lobby as this very charming elder statesman and educator, deprived of his chalkboard, enthusiastically began to draw graphs in the air to illustrate his answers. He was kind enough to draw the graphs backward so that they could be "viewed" correctly from my position. (I must admit to not following the differential equations he jotted in the air.)

I then asked a question about his views on how Wall Street has used his theory. He replied that he thought it had done a reasonable job in helping institutions diversify. I brought up the point that Wall Street had used his work to justify buy-and-hold policies that were not helping small investors.

"Aahh," he replied, "it all depends on what assumptions about future returns you use."

And therein lies the rub. Wall Street and mutual funds use various studies to show rather large returns for the stock market. Stay fully invested and you can eventually grow rich. Many pension funds assume 9 percent to 10 percent returns on their total investment portfolios. Since 30 percent or more of their funds are in bonds, this means they assume they will be getting at least 12 percent or more each year from stocks.

Just like the managers of Long-Term Capital Management, investors are told if they diversify into different classes of stocks, they will do just fine: Buy some large-cap, mid-cap, and small-cap stocks. Buy both value and growth portfolios. Throw in a few international markets. You will be shown how a diversified portfolio will reduce your risk against the total market.

It is the right way to measure when the market is going up, but in a secular bear market, it simply means that your entire stock portfolio will move down as surely as one that is not as fully diversified. Perhaps it will move down less, but is that supposed to comfort you?

Instead of looking for relative returns as suggested by these proponents of Modern Portfolio Theory, savvy investors need to look for investments that offer the potential for absolute returns. Instead of riding the markets up and down over the next decade, they should try to find ways to make some money in all markets.

In essence, successful investors will use an alternative to (or maybe it is better to say a variation of) Modern Portfolio Theory that will work better for individual investors. They will still diversify among asset classes, but instead of choosing something in every possible asset class and holding for decades, they will carefully choose asset classes that either are below historical value or demonstrate the ability to produce returns apart from market fluctuations.

Simply investing large portions of your personal net worth in a one-way directional bet on the stock market because some theory says you must be fully invested in the market at all times is neither practical nor rational for investors with time horizons of less than 30 years, especially when those 30 years are at the beginning of a secular bear market.

Given the high probability that the current decade will produce very small gains in stock portfolios, it makes sense for investors to seek investment strategies that yield absolute returns irrespective of stock and bond market direction.

But their consultants and investment advisors will trot out studies to show why high expectations for stock market returns are realistic. Let's start going over these arguments in detail.

Lies, Damned Lies, and Statistics

As the saying goes, there are lies, damned lies, and statistics. Using past performance as a guide, what your return over the next decade will be all depends on when you start and when you end your study. Using a 70-year study (such as the Ibbotson study) to predict future returns is worthless, as none of us will ever invest in an index fund for 70 years. Further, it is misleading to suggest such a statistical relationship will hold for any future 10-year period. It is clear that there have been long periods of history when the market did not grow at all, let alone 10 percent.

Mean Lean Reversion Machine

Fifty percent of all doctors graduated in the bottom half of their classes. Two plus two is four. Trees do not grow to the sky. *And markets always come back to the trend.*

We are going to look at several studies using radically different methodologies that all suggest that this is not the decade in which we will see above-average returns from the stock market. In fact, they all suggest it is much more likely we will see flat to very low returns from the stock market. It's important you understand why I suggest you look to other investment strategies (value investing, income investing, and hedge funds in particular) for the remainder of this decade.

There is a considerable debate about the relationship between earnings and dividends and stock prices. Many investment analysts try to draw a direct connection between price-earnings (P/E) ratios and stock prices. If P/Es go too high, the argument goes, then either earnings have to go up or prices have to come down. They quote the historical averages as something approaching the correct values.

However, it seems to me that if there were a true connection, then the wild swings we see should not be happening. If investors knew that the stocks would always come back to these magical numbers, what rational person would invest if they were too high or not margin themselves to the teeth (borrow money to buy stocks) if they were too low?

Is there a historical connection between prices and earnings? Yes, there is. But is there something—some second factor—between prices and earnings that governs their relationship? I believe there is, and it is this second piece of information that is the real connection between earnings and stock prices. It is the piece that market analysts are reluctant to talk about, because it cannot be quantified or put into a simplistic equation.

Would that it were that easy. Life would be much simpler if we could only know what the correct price for any given stock is.

We can look for some answers in two important chapters in Yale professor Robert Shiller's must-read book, *Irrational Exuberance*. Shiller clearly demonstrates that when broad market indexes go above P/E ratios of 23 or so, investors essentially get no return over the next 10 years. The markets return to trend.

Shiller's chapter entitled "Efficient Markets, Random Walks, and Bubbles" puts this in perspective. In it he charts the connection between current dividends and current stock prices. What is so powerful is his chart where he shows the growth of dividends over the past 130 years (see Figure 1.1). It is a very smooth line with a gradually increasing slope. Then he overlays stock prices onto the graph. As you might expect, stock prices jump all over the place.

As a student of the markets, I was surprised by the following:

> The wiggles [changes] in stock prices do not in fact correspond very closely to wiggles in dividends. Recall that between the stock market peak in September 1929 and the bottom in June 1932, when the stock market fell 81% as measured by the real S&P Index, real dividends fell only 11%. Between the stock market peak in January 1973 and the bottom in December 1974, when the stock market fell 54% as measured by the real S&P Index, real dividends fell only 6%. And there are many other such examples. . . .
>
> In sum, stock prices have a life of their own; they are not simply responding to earnings or dividends. Nor does it appear that they are determined only by information about future earnings or dividends.[1]

Look at Shiller's chart. You can see that big short-term stock market movements were not in fact justified by what actually happened to dividends later.

If there were a short- or medium-term fundamental relationship between stock prices and dividends, then stocks should not have risen as

Real S&P Index Values

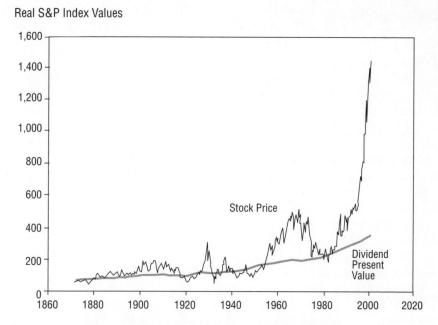

Figure 1.1   Stock Price and Dividend Present Value, 1871–2000
Source: Robert J. Shiller, *Irrational Exuberance* (Princeton, NJ: Princeton University Press, 2000), p. 186.

much as they did in the 1920s or 1960s or in 1999. Nor should they have fallen as much as they did in the 1930s or 1970s. There was very little fluctuation in dividends (relatively speaking) and enormous volatility in stock prices.

The Missing Link: Investor Sentiment

I have long argued that investor sentiment is the key to understanding stock prices. Therefore, expect to read a good deal in this book about studies that examine the psychology of investing.

Shiller's book is a good starting point. He explores the psychology of the preceding century of booms and outlines the reasons for the recent one and the reasonableness of expecting a continuation of this boom.

Don't Worry! Be Happy!

The New Era economists argue that we are now smarter than our fathers. I understood this implicitly when I was in my twenties. (As the father of seven kids, six of whom are older than 15, I now have serious doubts as to the veracity of my youthful hubris.)

In the past, we are told, our emotional forebears invested without the understanding of the markets that we now have. They didn't understand that markets will always and eventually go up if only you buy and hold and do not worry about corrections and other temporary phenomena. Now that we grasp how the markets work, we should be better off than our poor parents and grandparents.

Plus, now that we understand the causes of recessions and such, the Federal Reserve can make sure there are no major market disturbances to interrupt the onward and upward nature of the market. Look at October 1987 and October 1998. Didn't the Fed step in and save us when we were on the brink of disaster? In 2001 we experienced only a slight recession. Soon, we are told, we will return to a new bull market era.

(Unless you had invested in Internet stocks, which everyone now agrees were overpriced anyway. *Now* they tell us we should have gotten out with our triple-digit capital gains at the first sign of real trouble. So I guess the rule is that buy and hold works except for fad stocks. Then the rule is pump and dump.)

I have read many studies showing the links between earnings and prices. You can make a pretty good case if you pick and choose your data carefully. My contention, however, is that in the short term earnings in and of themselves are not *causal* in nature. It just appears that way as long as earnings and the stock market are going the same direction. It is like two cars going along the freeway. Are they part of a family group driving together or are they simply going in the same direction for a while before one takes a different path?

Shiller's work says no: *Emotion drives the stock market.* Maybe not for cold-blooded economic rationalists like you and me, but Shiller convincingly kills the rational market theory by pointing out that the rest of the investors in the world are not like you and me.

(Sure, a negative earnings announcement will usually drive a stock down. But is there any rational reason a *one-time* 10 percent earnings miss should cause a 25 to 35 percent or more drop in stock price? The earnings reports are just high-powered jet fuel for emotional investors. It gives them something to talk about.)

Let me now go to Shiller's first chapter, where he uses a scatter chart (shown in Figure 1.2) that economists and statisticians love to show the

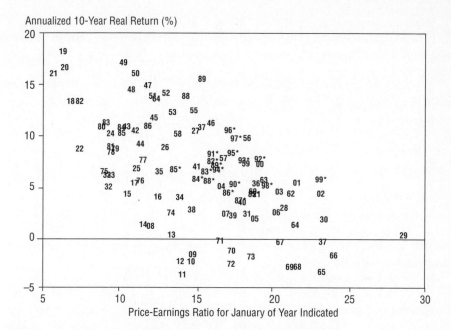

Figure 1.2   Price-Earnings Ratio as Predictor of 10-Year Returns
Note: Scatter diagram shows last two digits of 19XX; * for 18XX.
Source: Robert J. Shiller, *Irrational Exuberance* (Princeton, NJ: Princeton University Press, 2000), p. 11.

relationship between price-earnings ratios and the returns that investors got over the next 10 years. Basically, the higher the P/E the less the stock market return.

Here are some quotes from this chapter and then comments:

> Long-term investors would be well advised, individually, to stay mostly out of the market when it [the P/E ratio] is high, as it is today, and get into the market when it is low. . . .
>
> Suffice it to say that the diagram suggests substantially negative returns, on average, for the next ten years. . . .
>
> Times of low dividends relative to stock price in the stock market as a whole tend to be followed by price *decreases* (or smaller than usual increases) over long horizons, and so returns tend to take a *double* hit at such times, from both low dividend yields and price decreases. Thus the simple wisdom—that when one is not getting much in dividends relative to the price one pays for stocks it is not a good time to buy stocks—turns out to have been right historically.[2]

I do not believe that Shiller is saying that low dividend yields and high P/E ratios cause low returns. He just simply points out the historical connection. The cause is much more basic and has to do with a mix of human emotions: *hope, envy, greed, fear, desire, and dreams and aspirations.*

The problem is not the Steady Eddy investors—people who buy and hold and forget. But they are not the majority of the market. *Even institutions and mutual funds that talk piously about investing for the long run move in and out of stocks on a constant basis, taking profits and looking for value.*

Shiller writes for many chapters about bubbles and what causes them. But it all boils down to human emotion and how investors feel about the future.

Why are times of high P/E ratios and low dividend yields followed by a decade of poor or negative returns? *Because trees don't grow to the sky.* There are limits. And eventually enough investors begin to realize this and take their money off the table.

In 2000, I wrote about a study that asserted investors should expect returns from the major tech stocks like Microsoft, Cisco Systems, and Intel to continue. I pointed out that these stocks simply could not deliver returns throughout the next 10 years like they had in the prior 10 unless these few companies by themselves became larger in market capitalization than the rest of the entire U.S. economy.

These are great companies with wonderful futures. But they were great companies with very high stock prices relative to earnings. At some point, enough investors realize the emperor is naked and the stock drops back to reality or at least stops growing. As investors realize this price action is possible for stocks of great companies they begin to worry about the prices of other similar companies. The connecting dot to a general lowering of prices is the "worry factor," not the price-earnings ratio. It is the expectation of future profits. *And when investors become more worried about future losses than expectant of potential gains, the bull market is over.*

And that is what happened. We entered into a bear market phase. The key question to ask is: When will it be over?

Increasingly, in secular bear markets, investors get fed up with no growth and look for other opportunities. For the big investors there are hedge funds, which have the potential to generate 10 to 15 percent growth without a lot of volatility. They will migrate there. The current growth rate is not as thrilling as the 30 to 50 percent growth in technology stocks in the 1990s, but it is better than no growth. For smaller investors, there are alternatives, as we will see.

But this takes money out of the stock market. Each investor who leaves takes a marginal bite out of the stock market. At some point the bull dies, and the market corrects. This correction is normally done over many years, interspersed with numerous large rallies, as we see in later chapters. Shiller's work and many other studies like it show that the market does not correct to the average but, just as it went up too high, it tends to go back down too low.

The Real Link between Age and the Markets

There is one more study on P/E ratios worth reviewing. Many people (including myself) have written about the connections between the age demographics of the population and the stock market. I don't buy into Harry Dent's theory espoused in his book *The Roaring 2000s*[3] that the stock market is going up until the baby boomers start to retire in 2007.

But he's right in saying there is a strong correlation between age and buying and saving (investing) preferences. Dent's mistake is in assuming that boomers will be saving until 2007, and therefore that the stock market will be going up as well. There is a certain appealing logic to this, but unfortunately there is no statistical correlation. As Robert Arnott's study shows us in Chapter 10, the actual underlying correlation for much of the apparent connection between the boomer generation and the stock market can be found in the proportions of children, workers, and retirees.

But as we analyze P/E ratios in this chapter, let's look at a rigorous academic study that shows a further strong correlation between age demographics and the price-earnings ratio. This paper is by three rather well known economics professors writing for the Cowles Foundation at Yale University.[4] (John Geanakoplos from Yale, Michael Magill from University of Southern California, and Martine Quinzii from the University of California, Davis).

The importance of this study is not that it gives us some new and startling conclusion. It corresponds quite well with research and observations by Michael Alexander in his book *Stock Cycles* (more on him in Chapter 4), among other writers. What this paper presents is a model of how and why the changes in the age demographics influence stock market prices. It takes us from the world of anecdotal or inferential evidence into the more solid statistical basis for prediction. It moves us from the intuitively obvious (guessing) to a place where we can be more confident about our assumptions. When combined with the half dozen other studies I have written about on this topic, it makes me much more comfortable that my opinion that we are in a long-term secular bear market is accurate.

The Predictability of Randomness

Quoting from the study's Introduction (with my added emphasis):

> The results that we obtain strongly support the view that *changes in demo-graphic structure induce significant changes in security prices*—and in a way that is robust to variations in the underlying parameters. When we parametrize the model to U.S. data, we obtain variations in the price-earnings ratios which approximate those observed in the United States over the last 50 years, and in line with recent work of Campbell and Shiller (2001),[5] *the model supports the view that a substantial fall in the price-earnings ratio is likely in the next 20 years.* For the 40 year cycle in population pyramids gives rise to a 40 year cycle in equity prices—and *the prices, although random, have a strong predictable component.*[6]

Essentially, the authors create a fairly complex mathematical model of the economy. They note that based on earlier studies, there is a demonstrable difference between how young workers spend and invest and how older workers spend and invest. Further, there are differences in income. The authors take into account business cycle shocks, output fluctuations, and how much risk tolerance or aversion each generation has.

> Because the typical lifetime income of an individual is small in youth, high in middle age, and small or nonexistent in retirement, agents [that's us] typically seek to borrow in youth, invest in equity and bonds in middle age, and live on this middle-age investment in their retirement.[7]

This is a well-known life cycle of an investor, but it has an important role to play. In simpler terms, the authors divide the various age groups and generations into "cohorts." They vary the birth rate of each cohort to show baby booms and baby busts. The ratio between middle-aged generations or cohorts and young generations is something they call a MY ratio (for middle-young). When you factor all the variables, apply different sets of economic assumptions, subject the model to "shocks" (such as the 1973 oil crisis), and so forth, the outcome is still the same: *There is a strong correlation between the ratio of middle-aged to young workers and the price-earnings ratio.*

This implies that the relative size of the middle-aged and young cohorts, which can be summarized in the medium-young cohort ratio, plays an important role in determining the behavior of the equilibrium prices on the bond and equity markets.

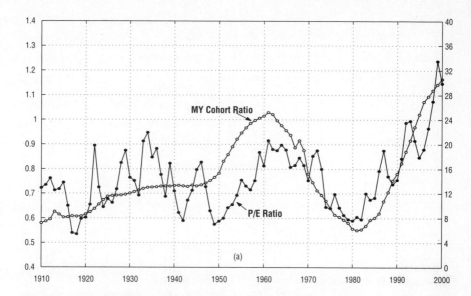

Figure 1.3A   Real S&P Price-Earnings Ratio and MY Cohort Ratio
Source: John Geanakoplos, Michael Magill, and Martine Quinzii, "Demography and the Long-Run Predictability of the Stock Market," Cowles Foundation for Research in Economics at Yale University, Paper no. 1380 (August 2002), p. 26. Available from http://cowles.econ.yale.edu/P/cd/d13b/d1380.pdf.

Indeed, when you overlay the authors' MY ratio with the P/E ratio on a chart, it appears that the MY ratio is now the trend to which the P/E ratio is invariably brought back. See Figures 1.3A and 1.3B.

Thus the model predicts that the P/E ratio will drop from the current 25 to 30 or so to somewhere between 5 and 16 in the next 20 years. The wide range is because of different assumptions. If you make fairly optimistic assumptions, you get 16. If you are pessimistic, your assumptions might lead to the model showing 5. But a drop to 16 is still a very dramatic one.

This is different than simply saying, as Robert Shiller does, that P/E ratios always revert to the historical mean, which is about 15. This paper suggests there is a fundamental reason for that reversion to the mean: the age ratio between generations.

You can read the paper for yourself at http://cowles.econ.yale.edu/P/cd/d13b/d1380.pdf.

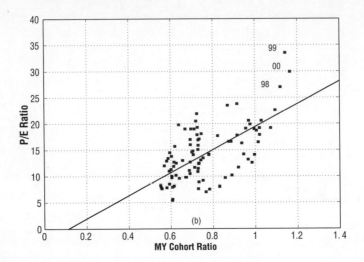

Figure 1.3B   Regression of P/E Ratio on MY Cohort Ratio
Source: John Geanakoplos, Michael Magill, and Martine Quinzii, "Demography and the Long-Run Predictability of the Stock Market," Cowles Foundation for Research in Economics at Yale University, Paper no. 1380 (August 2002), p. 26. Available from http://cowles.econ.yale.edu/P/cd/d13b/d1380.pdf.

Sideways to Down for 20 Years?

Now, let's look at some implications. Later chapters show that average actual corporate profits grow roughly in line with gross domestic product (GDP) plus inflation (or less). That has been about 6 percent. That means profits double every 12 years. Let's take an optimistic view that the economy is going to continue to rebound substantially this year and the P/E ratio of 2004 S&P core earnings will be 25 (more on what core earnings are in later chapters), rather than the previous year's 30 plus (a very optimistic assumption, by the way).

That means that if the P/E ratio drops to 16, it will be 8 to 10 years before the market permanently rises from today's levels. You don't even want to do the numbers for what happens if the P/E ratio drops to 5.

Will the market go up this year or next year? The model is not that precise. As numerous studies show, the price movements from one year to the next are pretty random. Even in secular bear markets, the stock markets rise in 50 percent of the years. All this paper tells us is that sometime over the next 15 to 20 years, there is going to be a fundamental shift to the downside in the average P/E ratio. This means that either the market moves sideways for a very long time until the P/E ratios come into line or that the market drops, perhaps significantly, at some point.

In other parts of this book I suggest it is likely that markets will move down in concert with future recessions during secular bears. It is reasonable to assume that we will have several recessions over the next 15 years, so one could expect a long-drawn-out secular bear. This isn't a pretty picture for index fund investors and buy-and-hold investors. But it is also a market with different types of opportunity for more nimble investors and those with a willingness to think outside of the buy-and-hold box.

Now let's look at an analysis of bubbles by one of the great investment managers of all time and how buy-and-hold enthusiasts bend statistics to support their case.

Faith versus History

I n the 17 years from the end of 1964 to the end of 1981, the Dow Jones Industrial Average gained exactly one-tenth of 1 percent (see Figure 2.1). In the bull market that followed from 1982 to the peak in March 2000, the Dow rose from 875 to 11,723, a spectacular rise of 1,239 percent or over 13 times from the starting point (see Figure 2.2).

We all remember what a difficult time that first period was. There were three recessions, oil shocks, Vietnam, stagflation, the collapse of the Nifty Fifty, Watergate, short-term interest rates rising to 18 percent, gold at $800, and very high inflation.

"Bad news on the doorstep" seemed to be the theme of the period.

Compare that to the subsequent period. Tax cuts and lowering interest rates fueled a boom in the stock market and the economy. Computers invaded our lives, making us more productive. By the end of the period, even Alan Greenspan was extolling the virtues of technology-led productivity growth. Inflation became a nonfactor, and mortgage rates dropped almost as fast as our property values rose. The Internet promised new ways to prosper. Peace seemed to be breaking out, and government budgets ran to surpluses.

It stands to reason, doesn't it, that the economy did poorly during the long bear market period and far better during the bull market?

You would think that, but the reality is far different. Gross domestic product (GDP) actually grew 373 percent from 1964 through 1981. During the period from 1982 until the beginning of 2000, the economy grew only 196 percent, or about half of the earlier period (see Figure 2.3).

Even if you take out the effects of inflation, you find the economy grew almost identically in both periods. In the first period (a total of 17 years) real GDP growth was 74 percent, and the second (a total of 18 years) GDP

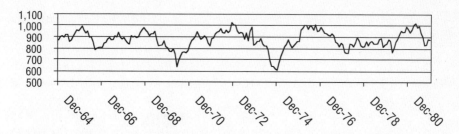

Figure 2.1   Dow Jones Industrial Average, December 1964–December 1981
Raw data obtained from Yahoo! Finance.

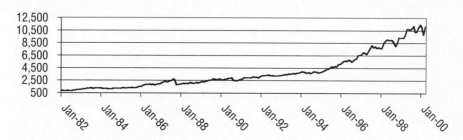

Figure 2.2   Dow Jones Industrial Average, January 1982–March 2000
Raw data obtained from Yahoo! Finance.

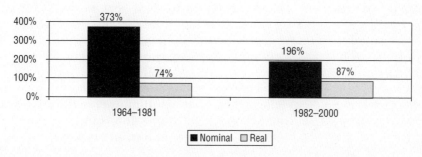

Figure 2.3   Gross Domestic Product Growth, January 1982–March 2000

was slightly higher at 87 percent. Yet if you take into account inflation, you didn't see a profit in your 1966 buy-and-hold portfolio of Dow stocks in 1982; you had to wait another 10 years, until 1992, for an inflation-adjusted return.

Yet, if you listen to many advisors and analysts today, you should be buying stocks because the U.S. economy is growing, or at least getting ready to grow. "It is always a bad idea," we are told, "to bet against the U.S. economy."

This strategy would be valid if the economy was the main driver of stock market prices. The economy more than doubled in real terms from the end of 1930 through 1950. Yet stocks prices were roughly the same after 20 years!

A reasonable analysis of the links between stock markets and the economy shows that stock markets do tend to go down before and during recessions, but they do not always go back to new highs after recessions.

Investors are told to invest for the long run. "It is impossible to time the market" is the mantra of mutual fund managers everywhere, even as they buy and sell stocks in a feverish frenzy, trying to improve their performance. They can trot out studies that show that long-term investors always do better, even as the churn rate of professional managers is far beyond that of ordinary average investors.

I believe most of these studies are grossly misleading, and are now doing great damage to the retirement prospects of entire generations. In fact, the advice that traditional money managers proffer is precisely the wrong strategy for a secular bear market.

Secular Bear Markets

The perceived wisdom is that a bear market is when stocks go down by 20 percent or more. However, trying to time bear markets can be a very tough task. In the recent 18-year bull market, there were several occasions when stock markets dropped by 20 percent or more (think 1987 and 1998, as just two examples), only to spring back quickly to even loftier heights. Investors were rewarded for being patient, and many became used to large swings. Their advisors, and the managers of mutual funds they bought, kept telling them that new highs were around the corner. Each drop in the market was a buying opportunity. Corporations churned out ever more glowing earnings projections as a reason for increasingly high valuation multiples.

Then the music stopped in the first quarter of 2000. It was downhill for almost the next three years. But you would not know that to listen to the pronouncements of the sell-side investment community. (By "sell-side" I mean those firms and funds that want you to give them money for their management. Investors are the buy side of the transaction.)

Even after $7 trillion disappeared from equity valuations over the past three years, each new low is greeted as the bottom, and the brokers and mutual fund managers find ever more reasons for you to give them your money today! Bear markets, we are told, do not last forever (true). The economy is out of recession and growing (true), and thus you should get into the market today (preferably into whatever they are selling) before the next big run-up begins (maybe not so true).

Staying in the market was precisely the right strategy for the 1980s and 1990s. It was the wrong strategy for 1966–1981. It was the right strategy for 2003. It was the wrong strategy for 2000–2002. How do you know what strategy is right for today?

Throughout this book I use the terms "secular bear market" and "secular bull market." These phrases have nothing to do with religion (although there are people who do appear to worship bull markets, or at least sacrifice a lot of money in the hope of making one appear).

The Latin word for an age or era of time is *saeculum*. When economists use the term secular, they are generally indicating time periods of longer length, much like the concept of generations when thinking of the lives of people.* The Collins Dictionary says "secular" can mean lasting for a long time or occurring slowly over a long period of time and can also be associated with astronomical time periods.

Since 1800, traditional analysis suggests there have been seven secular bull markets and seven secular bear markets (see Figure 2.4). The average real return in a secular bear market is 0.3 percent[†] (even in a falling market investors receive dividends). The average return during a bull market cycle is 13.2 percent.

Not coincidentally, this averages out to the 6.7 percent the Ibbotson study (among many others) tells us that stock investments return over the long haul. The average length of bear markets is almost 14 years, and for

---

*The brilliant Neil Howe, co-author of *The Fourth Turning* (Broadway Books, 1997), wrote me this note to help our understanding of "secular." I pass it on to you: "The word secular does come from the Latin *saeculum* (plural, *saecula*), but this does not mean cycle. It means age or era. In some of the romance languages it has literally come to mean century (in French, *siècle*; or in Italian, *secolo*), though in English we use another Latin-derived word that means "one hundred" (*centum*). Originally, the word *saeculum* seems to have referred to the length of a long human life, and may have been borrowed by the Romans from the Etruscans. We make use of this word and concept in *The Fourth Turning*, as you may recall. We call our entire rhythm of four turnings (i.e., four generations or phases of life) a full-life saeculum, which typically lasts 80–100 years. The word cycle comes from an entirely different Greek root, *kyklos*, which means wheel or rotation or cycle."

†From a study by Michael Alexander in his book *Stock Cycles* (iUniverse.com, 2000).

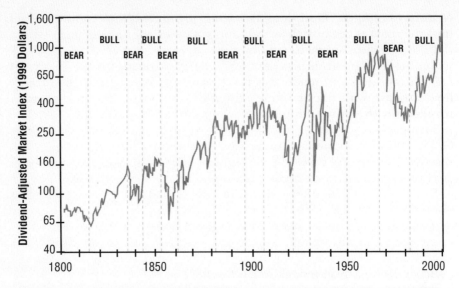

Figure 2.4 The Dividend-Adjusted Stock Index (in Constant Dollars) for 1802–1999
Source: Michael A. Alexander, *Stock Cycles: Why Stocks Won't Beat Money Markets over the Next Twenty Years* (Lincoln, NE: iUniverse.com, Inc., 2000), p. 37.

bull markets is almost 15 years. The average complete cycle of a combined secular bull and bear market is 28 years.

If you invested in a 10-year period contained within a secular bear market in the past, especially at the beginning, your real returns were quite likely to be close to zero. And that is with the historical advantage of dividends averaging 4 to 5 percent or more. In today's world of dividends that are less than 2 percent, if this secular bear market should last another 10 years, staying even will be a hard row to hoe.

Within each secular bull or bear market, there are often intermediate bull and bear markets. These are shorter-term in nature, but still are significant moves up or down. In a secular bull market, each market correction fails to get to previous lows and moves on to new highs. In a secular bear, each rally fails before it gets to the last high mark, and then stumbles down to even deeper depths.

Blind Dogs and Janus Managers

In secular bull markets, buy and hold works, as well as momentum investing, sector rotation, and a host of strategies designed to take advantage of a rising market. Blind dogs and Janus managers make money in bull markets. That is because the wind is at the back of the market.

In secular bear markets, making a profit from these strategies becomes much more difficult, if not impossible. Money managers, whom I track for a living and who made significant and steady returns in the 1990s, now languish with flat or losing returns. In the 1990s, there were many managers with nimble strategies who significantly beat the market while reducing risk.

Alas, these same managers are still reducing risk, but they clearly need a bull market to give investors the returns. The number of managers who are doing well is a much smaller list.

In secular bull markets, strategies that emphasize relative returns work well. They are a disaster in secular bear markets. In secular bear markets, you want your investment portfolio to be positioned in investment programs that emphasize absolute returns and have sound risk control policies.

Bonds, dividends, income-producing partnerships, certain types of hedging strategies, and covered call option selling would be examples of absolute return strategies. Will these give you 10 to 15 percent a year? Not likely, but they will outperform stock market investments that are going down or sideways.

Owning stocks in a secular bear market requires great skill in stock selection. I am perfectly willing to concede that there are hundreds of stocks that will double over the next few years. The problem is that there will be thousands of stocks that will drop by 50 percent. Choose wisely. (In Chapters 16 to 18, I'll offer strategies on how do so.)

How do you know if we are in a secular bear market? Unfortunately, there is no one indicator that can provide a trustworthy clue.

To be statistically significant, there should be a large number of "data points" with a given indicator that we use to verify its reliability. A poll that interviews only 10 people has little meaning, while one that has a thousand random interviews is far more reliable. Since there were only seven full bull and bear cycles in the past 200 years, we simply do not have enough data to be absolutely sure of any one indicator.

But we are not entirely lost at sea. If you combine the findings of a number of studies, each of which approaches the problem of predicting the future direction of the market from a different point and concludes that we have entered a long-term secular bear market, the evidence is overwhelming.

We will be looking at these studies and more in the next few chapters: the traditional view of price to earnings value offered by Robert Shiller in *Irrational Exuberance*; the economic growth and earnings studies by the National Bureau of Economic Research; the long wave cycle analysis of

Michael Alexander in *Stock Cycles*; the risk premium analysis by Robert Arnott; the trend analysis of Jeremy Grantham; an absolutely critical study of stock market cycles by Ed Easterling; different demographic analyses by both Arnott and Casscells; the writings of Warren Buffett; and the research on the dollar and the economy by Stephen Roach and his team at Morgan Stanley; and a lot more.

Most of these studies are by essentially mainstream analysts. They are not bears by trade. I should also note that one common denominator is that none of them make their living selling long-only stocks or mutual funds. All of these studies point to a lengthy period of time in which U.S. stocks, on average, will underperform even money market funds paying only 2 percent.

Phony Analysis

You've probably gotten solicitations from various investment newsletters about investing in the stock market. The pitch often shows that even if you started just as the secular bear market began in 1966 or 1974 and invested on the worst day each year, you would be so much farther ahead than someone who started to invest in the stock market only in 1982, even if he invested at the best possible time each year.

Therefore, the reasoning goes, you should not worry about the ups and downs of the markets and should instead invest for the long term. However, we don't live in the long term, and the baby boom generation, in particular, needs to worry about money in the next few years, not in 30 years.

If you started in 1966 to put your money in simple money markets or better yet in other absolute return vehicles based on the analysis we outline in later chapters, and then switched in the late 1970s (far ahead of the absolute bottom in value!), today you would be way ahead of investors who blindly invested in the stock market.

Can you time secular bull and bear markets? I think the answer is roughly yes. Picking the day or even the month would be impossible, but coming within a year or so is quite reasonable. And that simple, though imprecise, edge would give an investor a huge advantage over any buy-and-hold strategy.

Are We at the Bottom?

For the rest of this secular bear market, you are going to see numerous studies and analyses that purportedly show that we have reached the bottom of the bear market, and *now* is the time to buy. Certainly such prognostications were numerous throughout 2003.

These studies will largely be built around the potential for the economy to grow, with the conclusion that profits are going to grow as well, and therefore the stock market will rebound.

Don't be misled. There is no one-to-one correlation between rising profits and a growing economy and a rising stock market. You can have a bear market, even as the economy grows and as profits rise. It has happened many times in the past.

In August 2000, I wrote extensively about a 1996 Federal Reserve Bank of New York study* that showed that an inverted yield curve (when short-term rates are higher than long-term rates) is the single most reliable predictor of recessions. Recessions appear roughly a year after an inverted yield curve.

Since stock markets drop 43 percent on average during a recession, I cautioned that it might be a good time to start getting out of the stock market. I remember that when the Fed started to cut rates in January 2001, after the market had dropped, many writers started to say you had to get back in the market. Study after study appeared that showed how much stocks went up after the Fed began to cut interest rates.

I wrote a series of articles on the Fed versus History. If you thought the Fed could keep us out of recession, you would be a bull. If you thought History would prevail, you should stay out of the market. I bet on History. Time has shown that History won that fight. History is a tough opponent. Betting against History is usually a losing proposition.

Faith versus History

Today, there is another struggle going on. I think History clearly shows that we will be in a secular bear market for at least the next 7 to 10 years. The shortest secular bear cycle to date was eight years. Coming off the biggest bubble in our history, it is hard to think we can shake off the effects in just a few years.

Faith is required to invest in this market. You have to ignore high valuations, accounting issues, a Muddle Through Economy, and all the myriad issues surrounding a secular bear market. You have to believe that two

---

*Arturo Estrella and Frederic S. Mishkin, "The Yield Curve as a Predictor of U.S. Recessions," *Federal Reserve Bank of New York: Current Issues in Economics and Finance*, Vol. 2, No. 7 (June 1996).

centuries of trends are suddenly of no value. You have to believe that we are in a new economic era. You have to have Faith that this time, things really are different.

It's not that you can't make money investing in stocks. Very experienced stock analysts may do quite well. But the large majority of investors will get hurt. This includes large pension funds that feel they must allocate 70 to 80 percent of their assets to stocks.

You need to be convinced that the stock you are buying can fight upstream. Buying a stock simply because it looks cheap is not enough. Global Crossing and WorldCom were cheap two years ago. They are even cheaper today.

Either that, or you have to ignore all of the issues mentioned above. You invest simply because you hope that you will get back to even. It is not unlike going to Las Vegas. Some of you will win at the tables, but most of you will lose. In a secular bear market, just as in Vegas, the odds are stacked against you.

History tells us that either this market has a long way to go on the downside or it will go sideways for an even longer period of time, waiting for the valuations to come back to trend.

The stock markets always come back to trend. The market is nothing if it is not a lean, mean reversion machine. In the past, this has usually meant large drops in valuations, especially from the highs set during the preceding bubble. We will get to see what it does this time.

Now let's look at the very diverse studies and analyses that will lead us to the conclusion we are in a secular bear market. After you learn which way the wind is blowing, then you will know which way to set your sails. You will learn how to invest successfully. You will find there are a lot more investment possibilities than a buy-and-hold index fund in your future.

The Trend Is Your Friend
(Until It Isn't)

3

Jeremy Grantham is a highly respected money manager and analyst, in fact almost a guru in the investment industry. His firm, Grantham, Mayo, Van Otterloo (GMO) Advisors, manages $54 billion. Grantham is a famous deep value investor. He was taking his clients out of stocks in 1998 and 1999 (and even earlier) when—by his calculations—the value in traditional stock portfolios simply got out of line.

Grantham's investment theory is that over time investment classes come back to the average. When asset classes are well above trend he avoids them, and when they are well below trend he buys them. While it can take a long time for some classes to revert to the trend, this style is successful if you have time and patience. Grantham has been very successful at simply investing for the long term using history as his guide.

As a student of history, I like his approach because you are able to get on the right side of long-term trends. You will miss bubble tops and get in too soon on irrational bottoms, but patience and time will see you rewarded. We are going to look at three separate pieces of received wisdom from Grantham that have great relevance for today. One is from an article in *Barron's* in 2001, another from an appearance/debate with Professor Jeremy Siegel (of Yale University), author of *Stocks for the Long Run* and a major proponent of buy and hold. (We also dissect Siegel's arguments.) Then we turn to Grantham's recent thoughts on the current market situation.

In an interview in Barron's,[1] Grantham notes that his firm researched every bubble for which they could find data, including stocks, bonds, commodities, and currencies—28 bubbles in all. They defined a bubble as "a 40-year event in which statistics went well beyond the norm, a two-standard-deviation event."

According to Grantham, "Every one of the 28 went back to trend, no exceptions, no new eras, not a single one that we can find in history. The broad U.S. market today is still in bubble territory at 26 times earnings."

Let me repeat for emphasis: with no exceptions, bubbles and markets will come back to trend.

Then he turns that research on the recent stock market bubble. He notes that the long-term average P/E for the stock market is 14. Prior to 9/11, he thought the markets would come back to about 17½, rather than the historic average, in recognition that the world was seen as a safer place at that time. He also thought the fall to lower levels would be more graceful.

If the P/E trends down gracefully, as Grantham asserts, then that means 10 years from now the market will essentially be where it is today. There are clear historical precedents for this.

In fact, that is exactly what Robert Shiller said in his book, *Irrational Exuberance*. He points out that no stock market at the P/E levels we have seen for the past few years has ever returned anything to buy-and-hold index investors after 10 years. Period. No exceptions.

Grantham's contention is that we are still in a bubble. Even though the market had come down a lot as of 2001, he felt then it had further to fall:

Great bear markets take their time. In 1929, we started a 17-year bear market, succeeded by a 20-year bull market, followed in 1965 by a 17-year bear market, then an 18-year bull. Now we are going to have a one-year bear market? It doesn't sound very symmetrical. It is going to take years. We think the 10-year return from this point is negative 50 basis points [a basis point is one one-hundredth of a percentage point] after inflation. We take inflation out to make everything consistent. . . . When a cycle or bubble breaks it so crushes people's euphoria that they become absolutely prudent for the balance of their careers. I've been talking to older people who went through a wipeout and my best guess is about 95 percent of the people who have been through a bubble breaking never speculate in that asset class again.[2]

Ben Stein, actor, lawyer, and money maven, and co-author of the very readable *Yes, You Can Time the Market!*, tells it another way:

Philip DeMuth, the noted investment psychologist, puts it in a thought-provoking way. As DeMuth sees it, investors who lost big in the tech debacle often cannot bring themselves to sell because that would mean final recognition of their folly in getting in on the wrong side of that bubble. Not only that, but if they sold after colossal losses and the stocks did by some miracle rebound, they would be suicidal. Thus, they refrain from selling because of a combination of fear that they will be wrong again and denial of the finality of the end of the bubble. Through the prisms of fear or just plain self-delusion, investors see hope and keep on buying—a hold is the same as a buy, as Roy Ash taught me long ago—and the market stays at startlingly high levels relative to historic norms. Unless the law of reversion to the mean has been repealed—always a risky bet—these investors, myself included, are likely to feel more pain.[3]

For those interested, Grantham believes that there are good opportunities available. He likes bonds, real estate investment trusts (REITs), timber, hedge funds, value stocks, and emerging markets.

Grantham's views are consistent with a study by Hussman Econometrics.[4] The firm calculated that S&P earnings have grown at an average of 5.7 percent (including inflation) over the past 40 years. Even if the New Era hallucinations were reality—that is, even if the virtual productivity gains became real ones—these researchers suggest there is no reason to think that competition would allow higher rates of profit growth in the future.

What happens next? Rather than another decade of 15 percent per year growth in stock prices, "a more probable outlook," says the Hussman team, "is that earnings will grow at a long-term rate of 5.7 percent annually and that at the end of 10–20 years the price/record earnings multiple of stocks will be about 15. . . . Stocks will be about 13 percent below current levels a decade from now. Add in dividends and you're looking at zero total return over a decade."

It could be worse, Hussman points out. The total return from 1965 to 1982 was minus 20 percent. "If you are interested in long-term returns," continues the Hussman team, "it is madness to try to squeeze 9 percent out of a market which is priced to deliver zero."[5]

For the past two years, I have been invited to speak at the National Endowments and Foundations Symposium on the prospects for the economy and the markets for the coming year. Interestingly, when I spoke at this conference in early 2002, I was soundly taken to task by some pension/investment consultants for suggesting that the stock market would drop for a third straight year, even as the economy would Muddle Through.

"You must," I remember one consultant who came after me saying, "have a 22 percent exposure to large-cap growth stocks." I was dismissed as some kind of troglodyte bear brought in to amuse the locals, as this person noted the long list of large clients and the solid pedigree of his firm. How could such a company with so many analysts and PhDs be wrong? I note that I was asked back the next year and they were not. Perhaps the reason was that his advice cost his clients another 20 percent. Of course, they made some of their losses back in 2003, but following the advice of the consultants, they will ride out the next drop.

Investing by Committee

If you think you have been having investment problems, pity the average endowment and pension fund. Their investments are run by committee, and they hire consultants to give them advice on how to allocate their investments. Typically, these consultants are rearview mirror advisors, with tons of charts and graphs showing how if you simply stick with your stocks for the long run, you will do just fine. They trot out the famous Ibbotson study to prove their point. They show what a blend of various stock indexes will do. You must stay in the markets at all times is their basic advice. They tinker with the blends from time to time, but rarely suggest anything but long-only strategies. In many respects, they are like the typical broker you know, except they deal with larger numbers.

These endowments are pressed to give up more and more money for their causes, as the need is always great, yet the funds they manage have been shrinking. There were some shell-shocked trustees at this conference, and they are a little more wary of whose advice they take. Not surprisingly, consultants willing to think out of the box are being listened to more and more. There are consultants and advisors who can point to good results for their clients over the past years. (If you are an endowment or pension fund, write me and I will suggest a few.)

Take a Risk, You Get Fired

Before we move on, Mark Yusko from the University of North Carolina made some very interesting points about the consultant problem at the conference. First, he noted that most consultants and managers have a strong incentive to not take risks, where risk is defined as doing something different than the herd of other consultants. If you suggest something different and you are wrong, you lose your job. If you suggest sticking with the standard line, you can blame the market and point out that everybody else had problems as well; you keep your job.

This was perfectly illustrated later by Grantham. As I mentioned earlier, he was taking his clients out of stocks in 1998 and 1999 (and even earlier), as by his calculations the value in traditional stock portfolios was simply out of line.

He told us he lost 40 percent of his accounts during this period, which is a staggering number, since he managed $20 billion at the time. His large pension fund investors demanded that he keep up with other managers, and he refused, based on his sense of value. Now these funds wish they had stayed, as Grantham has beaten the socks off his competitors. As a result, his money under management has grown to $54 billion.

How painful must it have been, though, to lose that much business during the latter stages of the bubble. It is a testimony to his character that he stood by his belief in value even as his income went down. But the clients that stayed also need to be commended, as it is hard to sit out the dot-com bubble while your peers are participating. I remember the articles about how Warren Buffett just didn't get it.

There are some outstanding endowments and pension funds, as well as consultants, that have done well in this environment. They took the risk of being more conservative and today they have been rewarded. They are the exception, however.

The second point Yusko made that I found interesting was that 85 percent of portfolio performance came from asset allocation and only 15 percent from actual stock picking prowess. Intuitively this makes sense, and is in line with a previous study by Brinson, Hood, and Beebower (1986).*

What he means is that the more important decision for large (and small) investors to make about their portfolios is in which asset classes to be positioned. How much in real estate? Gold? Bonds? Stocks? Hedge funds? Actual stock picking improves portfolio performance only marginally, as large funds must buy larger stocks more representative of the market in general.

While stock picking clearly could make a much bigger impact on smaller individual portfolios, the principle is the same. If you allocate a large portion of your portfolio to stocks, you are subject to the whims of the markets: If you have the bulk of your assets in stocks and they go up, you do well; but if you ride it down, you have the opposite result. Making the decision as to what percentages of your portfolio to devote to particular asset classes has a huge impact on your overall return.

Bull versus Bear, Siegel versus Grantham

The highlight of the conference was a debate between the ever bullish Professor Jeremy Siegel of Wharton and the currently bearish on U.S.

---

*Gary P. Brinson, L. Randolph Hood, and Gilbert Beebower, "Determinants of Portfolio Performance," *Financial Analysts Journal* (July–August 1986).

stocks Jeremy Grantham of GMO Advisors. In Siegel's book *Stocks for the Long Run,* the bible for buy-and-hold investing, he points out that since stocks return 6 to 7 percent after inflation (his figures, not mine) over the long run, which is far better than bonds, you must be in stocks and ignore the ups and downs. Siegel assumes that you're paying attention to which stocks you own, but the point is that you must own them, and preferably index funds for diversification.

To his credit, he did write a very prescient piece in March 2000 in the *Wall Street Journal* called "A Sucker's Bet" about the overpriced Nasdaq stocks, pointing out that no investor had ever made money long-term on a large-cap stock with a P/E ratio of 100, and listed nine stocks that currently fit that description (Cisco, Yahoo!, AOL, etc.).

For Siegel, it is always time to buy stocks. Today you should buy because at current market values he believes stocks are likely to rise 6 to 7 percent per year over the decade, and thus will be back to new highs at the end of that time. Seven percent a year for 10 years means the market doubles. He bases this view on his study, which shows that after the market has dropped 40 percent, the subsequent five-year real returns have averaged 8.6 percent, and have never been negative.

Furthermore, he points out the market is underpriced based on his definition of value. You must ignore the current year earnings. To get a true picture, he maintains, you must look at a five-year average of reported earnings. This drops the current P/E ratio to only 17.4.

Then he argues that the market will not go back down to the historic average P/E of 14.6 because markets are more liquid, there won't be any economic disasters, and investors are smarter than they have been in the past.

The correct P/E ratio that smarter investors will adopt in the future is somewhere in the low 20s.

Then he talks about the new S&P core earnings standard, which will give investors confidence. (See Chapter 8 on earnings for a thorough explanation.) Standard & Poor's tells us that true core trailing earnings for the S&P 500 for the year of 2002 was roughly $23.75 after deducting for options expenses, pension costs, and other real-world costs, not the reported $45 that companies would have investors believe. At the time of the speech, true core earnings were $20.79. For the 12 months ending December 2003 core earnings were an even $42, which means the P/E is 27,* as the market is at 1,139, on the day I write.

---

*You can go to www2.standardandpoors.com/spf/xls/index/SP500EPSEST.XLS and see the pro forma, reported, and core earnings for the S&P 500, both historic and projected.

Even if one assumes that the market will finally return to an equilibrium P/E level of 22, that would make the market overpriced as of February 2004, yet Siegel would counsel to buy because he believes that earnings will continue to rise. In fairness, since that speech the market has risen along with earnings. Yet, as we see in Chapters 5 and 6, we are nowhere near historical averages. One has to assume that "this time its different" to believe that a return to the mean will not happen.

Cooking the Data Books

Let's analyze what I feel is a flaw in Siegel's main proposition. First, why should we use five-year operating earnings? Frankly, we now know much of the operating numbers were of the EBIH variety (earnings before interest and hype). As we will see in later chapters, there is reason to believe that earnings have been overstated by at least 30 percent from what more realistic core earnings would have been. Real earnings are what matter, and by Siegel's own admission the market is going to start using S&P core earnings as the gold standard for evaluating profits.

With today's P/E ratio using S&P core trailing earnings at around 27, using a five-year average for S&P core earnings suggests a P/E of 35.

If Siegel is right that investors are now smart enough to know that P/E ratios should be over 20, then that means the market is roughly one-third higher than his proposed new trend level, with some serious room on the downside. If markets go back to historical trend, then they are overvalued by 50 percent. If they drop below trend, as they normally do, then a serious correction is coming.

Siegel makes the assumption earnings will grow well above GDP plus inflation. However, he presents no evidence that earnings can grow over a period of multiple years in such dramatic fashion. The S&P 500 is populated with large companies for which consistent 15 to 20 percent growth on the entire index is possible only in go-go growth years. We are in the Muddle Through Economy, and that type of growth is going to be tough. In Chapter 8 we show that S&P 500 earnings grew less than 4 percent for the 15 years from 1988 to 2003. This is a far cry from 15 percent.

Why pick on Siegel, who is a fine scholar and all-around nice guy? Because such predictions are always with us, seemingly coming from all corners. Overly optimistic assumptions are a continual source of misplaced investor confidence and future problems.

How to Spot a Market Cheerleader

I go through the exercise of examining Siegel's arguments because they are a prime example of the contortions that market cheerleaders and advocates of a buy-and-hold philosophy do to justify their beliefs. If the data doesn't justify your belief, then find something that does. If current P/E ratios don't work, then create five-year smoothed ratios, using earnings levels from previous years that won't be repeated for many years. Don't tell your readers that it usually takes five to six years for companies to get back to new earnings highs after a recession. Don't mention that earnings growth in the boom years barely kept up with inflation!

Could the market decide to rise from here and never return? Of course, anything is possible. But history, as Grantham will now tell us, says it is not likely.

Jeremy Grantham took the stage after Siegel spoke, and immediately set the tone with the remark, "Investors are not smart."

Grantham is not a congenital bear. He simply looks for investment classes that are below trend and buys them, and sells them when they get above trend. Sometimes he buys too early and sometimes he sells too early, but he believes in the dictum that markets always come back to trend. As I repeat often, markets are a mean, lean reversion machine. Grantham is right. **Markets always come back to trend.**

Let me briefly repeat the concepts from Grantham expressed earlier in this chapter, as they are crucial to your understanding of how to invest in the current market conditions.

Grantham presents us with the benefits of his research into bubbles. He has looked at every bubble for which he could find data. His research goes back years and years and includes stocks, bonds, commodities, and currencies. He has found 28 bubbles. He defines a bubble as a 40-year event in which statistics go well beyond the norm, a two-standard-deviation event. Every one of the 28 went back to trend—no exceptions, no new eras, not a single one that we can find in history.

He then argues that the broad U.S. market today, as it was in 2001, is still in bubble territory, as it has not come back to trend.

Let me repeat for emphasis: with no exceptions, bubbles and markets will come back to trend.

Grantham notes that many markets and bubbles not only come back to trend, but go down right on past the trend line.

What is trend for the U.S. markets? He gives us four measures. Based on dividend yield, the market is overvalued by 50 percent. Based upon Tobin's Q (the market value of a firm's assets divided by their replacement value) the market is too high by 31 percent. The price of stocks to the 10-year average of real earnings is too high by 31 percent and as a function of market cap to GNP the market would need to come down by 45 percent to get back to trend. Mind you, this is in late 2002. The numbers would be worse in the first quarter of 2004.

The trend line for P/E is slightly under 15. Grantham thinks you could see this trend rise to 17.5 over time, as he does agree the markets are now more liquid and we live in somewhat safer times. But this would mean the market would need to drop substantially to come back to trend. How much depends on whether you use core earnings, pro forma earnings, and forward or trailing earnings. But they all suggest the need for a substantial correction.

Notice that Grantham uses a 10-year average of real earnings instead of Siegel's five years of reported earnings. The longer time frame takes out the effect of the very high four years immediately prior to 2001, and thus does not "curve fit" the data to fit a desired outcome.

It is important for Siegel and other cheerleaders, if they want to maintain any type of credibility, to look for some way to suggest that stocks are fairly valued, as Grantham's next data shows. If you can't find a reason that stocks are at fair value, then you would logically be forced to acknowledge the effects of trend reversion and an overvalued market.

What Will the Stock Market Return over 10 Years?

Grantham breaks down historic P/E ratios into five levels, or quintiles, from level (or quintile) 1, which represents the 20 percent of years with the cheapest values (lowest P/E ratios) in history right on through the fifth quintile, which represents the 20 percent of years with the most expensive values.

What kind of returns can you expect 10 years after these periods, on average? Interestingly, the first two quintiles, or cheapest periods, have identical returns: 11 percent. That means when stocks are cheap, you should get 10 percent over the next 10 years. The last, or most expensive period, sees a return over 10 years of zero percent. See Figure 3.1.

We are in a period that would easily rank among the most expensive periods.

This basically squares with data from Professor Robert Shiller of Yale, mentioned earlier. It is very public, and all cheerleaders are aware of it. To ignore it, they must show why "this time it's different."

In order for Siegel to predict, as he did, that stocks will return 6 to 7 percent over the next 10 years, he must show that values lie between the second and third quintiles—or that investors will somehow start putting

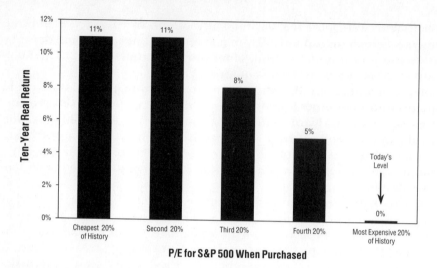

Figure 3.1 Quintiles of Market Average P/E to Predict 10-Year Returns: 20 Percent of the Time, Stocks Return 0 Percent Real over 10 Years
Source: GMO, Standard & Poor's. Data: 1925–2001.

more value on stocks, and thus a floor on the market. He attempts to show current fair value by creating a five-year smoothed average, and then argues that this time, investors are smarter and will not do as they have done in the past secular bear markets, which is to take stock valuations well below the historic average.

The problem is that the average overrun of the trend in a secular bear market is 50 percent, which is why stocks get so undervalued. By that, I mean stock market valuations do not stop at the trend. They tend to drop much lower. For Siegel to be right, we would have to see something that has never happened before. Stocks would need to drop to values 25 percent higher than the long-term historical average and no further.

Grantham spent considerable time showing different valuation models at the conference, and all suggest the same thing: There is still more downside.

This is not to suggest Grantham does not find value—he just does not find it in the U.S. stock markets. He likes Treasury inflation-protected securities (TIPS), REITs, emerging-market debt, market-neutral hedge fund strategies, and international small-cap value and small-cap growth stocks, which show historical signs of being undervalued. He is willing to invest in these markets and be patient, believing they will return to the average values and continue higher, and then he will sell and look elsewhere for value. He is also a big fan of timber, which he shows has done well in every market environment.

It's also worth noting that he shows how a portfolio with the ability to short overvaluations will make anywhere from 2 percent to 4 percent more, depending on the risk taken, than long-only portfolios. That squares with my studies and observations. It is why I believe that certain styles of hedge fund investing will become more available over this decade, as the public at large will demand it. When long-only portfolios return basically nothing for 10 years, and long-short stock portfolios show solid absolute returns that are decent, portfolio envy will overcome the lobbying interests of the mutual fund industry, and hedge funds will be available to the general public.

So what does Grantham think about the prospects for the market in 2004? Sitting on $54 billion of client money, he does not think much of the U.S. stock market. Quoting from an interview by a *Bloomberg News* columnist in the *Rocky Mountain News*:

The recovery may be "the greatest sucker rally in history," he says, with a "black hole" awaiting the markets in 2005. . . . "By the end of this year, we will have battened down the hatches as tightly as we can," Grantham says. "With any luck, 2005 and 2006 will be such a bloodbath we'll get it all out of the way quickly. . . . The market loves comfort—stable growth, stable low inflation, strong profit margins," he says. "All these things mean revert. Things are pretty good now. There is plenty of room for all these variables to move against you. If you want to make money, you buy when things are bad."[6]

Catching the Next Wave 4

Stock Market Cycles

In order to adjust our investment strategies and portfolios, it would be helpful if we could get some idea of what the future will look like. In fact, by reviewing the past we can become more successful investors.

We can find clues in *Stock Cycles* by Michael Alexander that accurately predicted what happened to the stock market after 2000, with serious implications for 2004 and beyond.

Let's jump to the conclusion first: Alexander's work shows that using past stock market cycles to predict the performance of the stock market during one particular year is not a certainty. Statistically, from almost any starting point and using price movements alone to make your prediction, you have about a 50–50 chance of the market going up or down. Even in the years that comprise a secular bear market cycle, the market goes up 50 percent of the time, and often quite substantially.

But there are certain long-term cycles that are not random, and the probabilities of those repeating are very high. As you would expect, the techniques of successful investing change somewhat dramatically from pattern to pattern and cycle to cycle. The trick, of course, is to figure out where you are in the cycle.

I have long been suspicious of stock market cycle theory, especially Long Wave theory. Long Wave (or Kondratieff Wave) theory says the economy and markets repeat every 56 to 60 years, with discernible periods marking the changing cycles. I readily concede that there are seemingly repeatable past patterns, but there are not enough data points to satisfy my need for any type of statistical certainty. This is an interesting theory that tells you where you have been and where you are going, but does not tell you with any certainty when you will get there or where you are at present.

I remember, as will many readers, how followers of the Kondratieff Wave predicted the end of the economic world in the late 1980s. Obviously, this gloom and doom scenario did not occur.

Too many analysts try to make Kondratieff Wave theory a precise predictive model. They do not look at the underlying fundamentals that cause the cycles.

It is like watching two people seemingly walking the same way in a large city. Maybe they are friends and are walking together. They could be total strangers either going to the same destination or getting ready to part ways on the next block. Until you know who they are and where they are going, using their past travels to predict future events is simply guessing.

It is one thing to use the stars, as the ancients did, to construct a calendar to predict seasons, planting times, and weather patterns. It is another to use the stars to predict personal fortunes. One methodology has a basis in fundamentals whereas astrology simply notices patterns that, like much stock market analysis, may have no connection or can be manipulated for personal benefit.

Alexander provides, at least for me, the missing link between the patterns in long wave stock cycles and the underlying economic fundamentals. He shows us, as it were, a logical connection between the positions of the stars and the seasons.

Alexander does not contend these cycles are as precisely predictable as the spring equinox. Rather, he suggests that when the underlying fundamental conditions occur, we can look for springlike conditions. Just as you plant certain types of crops and plants in spring and certain types in winter, there are some investments that do better in their respective parts of the stock cycle. Carrying the analogy further, it is easier to grow your portfolio in economic spring than in economic winter. You have a much wider variety of "plants" from which to choose in spring.

You can plant spring crops during the winter, but you're going to have to wait until spring to see them come up. It can be a long, cold winter in the meantime.

To help us see what part of the cycle we are in, Alexander first describes several types of stock cycles and then he looks at why these cycles may occur.

First, Alexander takes a purely statistical view of the stock market, looking for repeating patterns. For his purposes, a period when the stock market performs above trend is good and when it performs below trend is bad. Is there any pattern?

It turns out the only statistically valid nonrandom cycle he can find is a 13-year cycle. Since 1800, there have been 15 alternating good and bad cycles of 13 years, from stocks being undervalued to being overvalued and back again. There was one period when instead of reversing the pattern continued for an additional (and exact) 13 years. The year 2000 was a 13-year peak in his model. There is a probability of only 3.9 percent that this pattern is random.

The data suggests that index investors have little hope for capital gains over the 13 years following 2000. Buy-and-hold investors will probably be better off in money market funds, just as they were in 1966 and 1929.

(Please note that these 13-year periods are not bull and/or bear market cycles. Rather, they are periods when stock markets either outperformed or underperformed the longer-term trend, which is different from the description of price performance in Table 4.1 later in the chapter or the valuation model suggested in Chapters 5 and 6.)

Simply based on this statistical model, Alexander concludes that there is a 75 percent chance of a negative capital gains return for index fund investors over the next 20 years. However, returns in any one-year period are essentially random. Even in overvalued markets, the odds are essentially even that an index fund will outperform a money market fund for a 12-month period.

"Given today's low dividends and high valuations, a money market fund is, on average, a better investment over the next 5–20 years than the S&P 500 index. . . . In the case of overvalued markets (like today), holding for longer time periods, even up to 20 years, does not increase your odds of success," wrote Alexander in 2000, prior to the bursting of the dot-com bubble.[1]

Let me stop here and say that Alexander is not saying to avoid the stock market. He is simply pointing out, consistent with the theme of this book, that buy-and-hold index investing will not work in this current cycle. Simply picking any old mutual fund and expecting a rising tide to raise your boat will have only a random chance of success in any given year during this cycle. You have to change your investment strategy if you want to succeed.

In his Chapter 3, Alexander looks at the historical cycle of bull and bear markets. First, he points out that stocks have returned about 6.8 percent per year in real returns (adjusted for inflation) over the past 200 years, but about 4.6 percent or two-thirds of the 6.8 percent has come from dividends. The remainder corresponds to the real annual growth in GDP over that time. A National Bureau of Economic Research study that we will discuss in Chapter 8 on earnings demonstrates this very point.

The stock market does not grow faster than the economy. If it goes too high or too low, it *always* comes back to trend.

But stock prices fluctuate dramatically. There have been seven secular bear markets and seven secular bull markets since 1802. (See Table 4.1.) These are periods of at least 8 and up to 20 years when stocks are either generally rising or falling over the entire period. There are, of course, bear market rallies and bull market corrections, but the long-term trend is still either up or down.

If you were in the stock market during the 95 years of the bear market cycles, you achieved only a 0.3 percent annual average rate of return. If you picked the 105 years of the bull market cycles, you made a 13.2 percent rate of return. *Your actual returns for any one 10-year period would be totally dependent on when you made your initial investment.* The cycle length from peak to peak is 28 years on average.

Is there some model we can use to look at the overall cycle to help us determine the reason for the dramatic price movements? Here Alexander provides a new way to look at price fluctuations.

He looks at a ratio he calls P/R, or price to resources. "Resources are simply the things (plant, equipment, technical knowledge, employee skills, market position, etc.) available to the business owner to produce a profit. R is essentially retained earnings, or that portion of profits used to invest in the business to grow the business."[2]

While P/R (like P/E or price to earnings) is not particularly useful for predicting individual company or industry performance, a clear pattern develops when looking at the market as a whole. P/R peaks at bull market tops and rebounds at bear market bottoms.

But the fluctuations in resources do not appear to be as volatile as the fluctuations in earnings. That is because while earnings may swing wildly

Table 4.1 Repeating Cycles in the Stock Market

Secular Bear Markets			Secular Bull Markets		
Period	Duration	Real Return	Period	Duration	Real Return
1802–1815	13	2.8%	1815–1835	20	9.6%
1835–1843	8	−1.1%	1843–1853	10	12.5%
1853–1861	8	−2.8%	1861–1881	20	11.5%
1881–1896	15	3.7%	1896–1906	10	11.5%
1906–1921	15	−1.9%	1921–1929	8	24.8%
1929–1949	20	1.2%	1949–1966	17	14.1%
1966–1982	16	−1.5%	1982–2000	18	14.8%
Overall	**95**	**0.3%**	**Overall**	**103**	**13.2%**

Source: Michael A. Alexander, *Stock Cycles: Why Stocks Won't Beat Money Markets over the Next Twenty Years* (Lincoln, NE: iUniverse.com, Inc., 2000), p. 38.

from one year to the next, actual resources (R) are not subject to such wild swings.

Management continues to use current resources and invest in new resources in an effort to increase the business, even in recessions. Plus, resources tend to accumulate over time. Companies with large resources can weather tough economic conditions better and can come back more quickly.

Over time, there is a direct relationship between earnings and resources. As the resources of a company or nation accumulate and are put to work, the company or nation becomes more prosperous, and earnings increase. **If a nation (or its businesses) fails to increase its resources, the ability of those resources to produce a profit will decrease over time. That means earnings will decrease.**

The collective P/R ratio is the estimate of the value investors put on the ability of an economy to produce earnings. With this understanding, it now gets interesting, at least for me.

Understanding Stock Market Behavior

Earnings, we are told, are what drive the price of a stock. But real (inflation-adjusted) earnings growth for the period 1965–1982 was roughly the same as for 1982–1999, yet we all know that the S&P 500 had significantly different results. The first period was one of no stock price growth, and the latter saw growth of over 1,200 percent.

What was the difference? Clearly, it was how investors perceived the relative value of the earnings. In a period of high inflation, earnings growth of 6 to 7 percent is not all that impressive. In today's low inflation environment it is.

"Since the Civil War cycle there have been two effects of inflation," Alexander says. "First, inflation reduces the value the market places on earnings, resulting in a flat trend, rather than a rising trend in the index. Secondly, the effect of the cheapening dollar makes the real value of the index fall even further. As a result, P/R falls to extremely low levels during inflationary bear markets."[3]

(Please notice Alexander makes a connection between a falling dollar and market levels. We will show later why we should expect a falling dollar for the next few years.)

When inflation ends, you get the benefit of the old earnings growth and new growth, giving the market a double boost. **Investors become very optimistic about earnings growth and adjust their future value of stocks accordingly.** But as I have often asserted, trees cannot grow to the sky. For

200 years, the overall market has not grown much faster than the growth in GDP. This is a crucial point you need to keep in mind.

Now we enter a period when the expectations of earnings growth cannot match reality. The stock market must come back to trend, which can be a painful adjustment for some investors. Alexander notes,

> The situation is very similar to 1929. The effect of both the monetary conditions and a very optimistic assessment of the earnings growth still to come are priced into the index. This is shown by the extraordinarily high level of P/R. We should expect the current monetary cycle to be followed by a "real" cycle. [More later.] It should start with a secular bear market in which lower earnings growth will be the problem, not inflation.[4]

Growing Pains

The goal of every business is to grow its income and to grow its income at a faster rate over time. The income you get for the money you invested, or the profit you generate from a given level of resources, is called the rate of return (ROR).

However, there appear to be very real upper limits on both the absolute value of and the growth of the ROR that can be achieved for a given level of resources. This ROR fluctuates over time, just as P/E and P/R do. Why wouldn't ROR growth be constant, as many firms want? Why can't ROR just grow every year, as market cheerleaders on TV constantly predict?

What appears to happen over time is that either firms, in a moment of optimism, build too much capacity or resources and the ROR drops as capacity utilization drops or firms invest too little and thus the growth of ROR is self-limiting.

Managers simply cannot know the exact amount of future resources needed. They can do their best to make very intelligent guesses, but in the end there is usually either too much or too little resources.

It is a difficult job. Too much resources and you don't get a reasonable return. You use resources that cannot be easily reallocated to some more productive use. Too little and you invite competition or give up market share. Further, that nasty thing called competition makes it possible for a lot of businesses to build capacity for the same market, all hoping to increase their business and market share. Then you end up with too much capacity and no ability to raise prices. Computers, oil, soybeans, and ships are all examples. The list is endless. Supply and demand works. The business cycle is real.

In the telecommunications industry, management decided the world needed large amounts of fiber-optic cable. We now use less than 5 percent of the capacity of that new cable. Clearly, the industry overbuilt. But the firms that supplied equipment for that expansion also assumed that the future would look like the past and built large factories capable of manufacturing massive amounts of fiber-optic cable equipment. The overcapacity went right down the food chain.

The 1990s were characterized by the growth of capacity in almost every industry, including mature industries like agriculture, shipping, mining, retailing, and so on. We now have a new level of total resources available to U.S. businesses and the world. But since economic growth and profits do not grow faster than GDP, whatever growth we do have will be spread over a larger amount of resources.

This means the rate of return of resources will be smaller than it has been for the preceding 10 years. It follows that the growth of earnings will be smaller as well.

Expansions and Expectations

One of the great charts in *Stock Cycles* shows the relationship between the length of economic expansions and the expectations investors have for the stock market. The longer we think economic expansions will last, the more we are willing to pay for earnings that will compound at 15 percent forever. Every time we come to a period like the one we are in today, we are told that this time it is different.

If earnings truly could compound at 15 percent forever, a P/E ratio of 25 would not be illogical. But earnings cannot grow faster than GDP. Period. **Earnings will come back to trend.**

To repeat: This is because we build (or invest in) too much resources for a given market or technology. The potential profit is spread over a greater amount of resources, and earnings growth suffers.

Long Waves Explained (Finally)

Alexander then jumps to the long wave cycle. Greatly simplifying, the theory says that there are two sets of stock market cycles in each economic long wave. You have a bull and bear market cycle that is mostly influenced by monetary policy and events and is then followed by a bull and bear market cycle that is mostly influenced by real events such as earnings and economic performance.

Applying the theory, Alexander then says:

The extraordinary gains in recent years result from investors discounting future earnings growth over longer periods of time. This makes the market extraordinarily leveraged to the economy. . . . The average length of economic expansions was shorter during the 1970s than . . . either before or since. The [coming cycle] could also be characterized by short business cycles like in 1883–1896 rather than a lengthy slump like in the Depression. Shortened expansions would gradually shift the market from a future-oriented to a present-oriented valuation scheme, resulting in a contraction in P/E. The result would be a secular bear market as the valuations slowly adjust, even though economic growth might be fairly good. This, of course, is what is predicted to be imminent by P/R."[5]

Alexander shares my concern, which I mentioned previously, about the lack of connection between the long wave theory and the actual economy. But he has found a connection that not only provides the missing link, but when taken to its logical conclusion offers some very exciting prospects for future investments.

The economists Joseph Schumpeter and Gerhard Mensch both tried to establish a theoretical base for the long wave based on bursts of innovation. More recently, Harry Dent, author of *The Roaring 2000s,* has expanded on their work, and Alexander uses Dent's terminology to put forth his own new thoughts.

The importance of this process is straightforward. If you agree with Alexander's logic, then you will have "two largely independent, periodic phenomenon that we can use to characterize the changing economic environment that brings about the stock cycle."[6]

Dent sees the innovation cycle being comprised of four periods: the innovation period, the growth boom, the shakeout, and the maturity boom. Alexander calls the end of the maturity boom the economic peak, which is the time when the economic impact of the new innovation has been completely played out.

Basically, a new process or technology such as the cotton gin, telephone, electricity, airplanes, computers, and so on is invented. Following a period of innovation, there is a rapid growth of the "New Economy." Not surprisingly, there is too much capacity built and a number of companies falter.

During the shakeout, there is another process going on. We see a second innovation phase of the mature technology. Companies that create innovations now see a second growth boom prior to the final maturing seen in the economic peak. The new technology finally reaches it logical and technical growth limits and succumbs to the inevitable force of economic gravity. At maturity, a technology is limited to the growth in the overall economy. Think railroads and electricity.

Now we come to the best part of Alexander's work. He believes there have been nine different innovation cycles beginning in the early 1500s. While work similar to his has been done before, Alexander is the first (to my knowledge) to relate these cycles to their importance to the overall economy: What proportion of the growth in GDP did these innovations contribute?

Over time, as the innovation becomes mature and new innovations come on the scene, the talk is of the "New Economy" changing the world and replacing the "Old Economy." But eventually even the "new new thing" becomes mature and plays a less significant part in the growth of the economy as even newer innovations appear. It is a repetitive cycle. It is no different than what we see today. The cycles and phases are eerily the same.

There seems to be a relationship between the Long Wave and the innovation cycle that apparently has worked well enough for previous cycles over about 500 years. Alexander notes that the information economy seems to have come about 17 years later than the average 53 years. Thus, rather than being mature in the 1980s, it was just beginning. If nothing else, that explains why the Long Wave theorists were wrong when they predicted a huge bear market crash in the 1980s.

There is nothing magical about a Long Wave of 53 or 56 years. What is important is the innovation cycle. That is what influences the economy. Analysts who used the Kondratieff or Long Wave as a time prediction tool were wrong. The usefulness of the Long Wave is to help us analyze the basic nature of the underlying economy and how the innovation cycle is affecting the economy.

Thus, Long Wave theory can help us know what to expect at the end of the innovation period. It cannot predict the exact timing, but the general shape of things to come is apparent.

Finally, Alexander writes of Harry Dent's projection that the long boom will last until 2007, which corresponds to the baby boom generation: "Dent's alignment of generations and the spending wave with his phases of the innovation wave seems to break down after going back more than one cycle."[7] The significance of this observation will become obvious when we discuss retirement issues in Chapter 10.

Something New This Way Comes!

The implications of the innovation cycle bring to mind the following. First, investing in stocks at the end of the cycle is going to be difficult. Growth slows down and stocks are overvalued relative to the growth potential. Slowly the realization seeps into the minds of investors that the "new new thing" is slowly becoming commonplace.

Electricity was once the rage. Railroads were seen as the invention that would change the world forever. Both did change the world dramatically but now seem rather prosaic. Airlines, radio, television, and the automobile all had their boom and bust cycles.

In a few years, investors will realize that information technology stocks simply do not have the growth potential they once had. While there will be some astounding winners among companies who develop some dramatic innovations, the large companies simply cannot find the markets to compound at 20 to 40 percent. As we will see in later chapters, compounding at 10 percent for any length of time is very hard for large companies.

The second implication is the far more exciting: *Something new this way comes!*

There is another innovation cycle coming in our future. There will be another opportunity to get in at the beginning of a new industry that will change the world as profoundly as electricity, computers, or the telephone.

The trick is we do not yet know what it is. Smart minds predict that it will be in the area of nanotechnology or biotech. It could be fusion power or a new type of propulsion system for cars. Or it could be something that is simply not on anyone's radar screen at the moment.

The world is changing ever more rapidly. Knowledge is compounding at faster and faster rates. As freedom and capitalism expand over the world, there will be millions more inventors and businesses trying to develop the next new thing. The process is inherently messy, but the one thing we can be confident of is that the process will continue.

I should point out that there is nothing in the process that says it has to be about 53 to 60 years between each creation of a new product that drives an innovation cycle. That next new thing could be invented tomorrow and begin to have amazing effects on the world markets within a short time, or it may be a decade or two or three before that happens.

The question then becomes, how do we as investors recognize it? My friend Mark Ford, who writes the daily e-letter *Early to Rise* composed the following review, and I pass it on to you with a few comments at the end. (I'll admit I'm biased and believe *ETR* is a must-read. You can get it at www.earlytorise.com/SuccessStrategies.htm.) This will give you some idea of how to recognize the next new new thing when it comes.

The Deviant's Advantage: Why You Need to Know the Future

In *The Deviant's Advantage,*[8] authors Ryan Mathews and Watts Wacker argue that you can predict the future (and thereby enjoy explosive, exponential success) by recognizing a pattern that has characterized most major changes. This pattern starts on the Fringe and moves gradually toward the center of social convention.

Almost everything that is now extremely popular, the authors argue, was once on the Fringe. To see the future, you must keep your eye on

Fringe developments. As really weird stuff gradually becomes less weird, your attention sharpens. Once a trend passes to a certain stage of popularity, you move in and seize it. By "owning" a Fringe product that is about to become mainstream, you give yourself the best chance you'll ever have of becoming rich and famous.

The trend from Fringe to mainstream has four stages. The outer rim (the Fringe) is the stage in which individual innovators come up with weird, off-the-wall, antisocial ideas. Most of these ideas die of their own accord. A few are taken up by limited audiences of believers. This is the second stage, the Edge. To society at large, ideas at the Edge seem odd, even freaky. But to the true believers, they are sacred.

Most Edge ideas stay at the Edge, but some develop a wider base of followers. They then move into the Realm of the Cool. At that stage, the ideas that were once vilified by the press are now given credence as interesting abnormalities. The mainstream media still don't like them, but the offbeat press is positive.

Every so often, something that is in the Realm of the Cool catches fire. Suddenly, it becomes The Next Big Thing. Major media talk about it. Influential people consume it. The Next Big Thing becomes an icon for marketers. They let the mainstream buying public know it's cool.

There is then, of course, a mad rush to buy The Next Big Thing. The demand is so high that specialty manufacturers can no longer keep up with the demand. This is the stage at which Fortune 500 companies buy up the product and put it on shelves at Wal-Mart or on the menu at McDonald's.

The communicating vehicle for the Fringe is the original deviant who created it. At the Edge, it is promoted by word of mouth—the proselytizing of the apostles. As the following grows, word gets around at events and in special stories in secondary media outlets. Then, as it becomes The Next Big Thing, the major media promote it. At the final stage, it becomes a mainstay for the advertising and marketing world. Here is where it enjoys its greatest triumph and its last hurrah.

How do you take advantage of this information? Whatever you do, whatever you sell, there is a range of ideas out there that span this entire gamut. The products you are most aware of are ones that are heavily marketed and advertised. They're fully accepted by society. They are almost de rigueur. Basing your business on this stage is not a very good idea. By the time a product reaches the point at which it becomes social convention, it is awash in a ton of publicity and promotion—most of it by savvy professionals who know how to sell. This is a market where victory goes to the strongest and the strongest usually have the most money, size, cash flow, and contacts.

If you don't want to compete at that level (and you probably shouldn't), you need to concentrate your efforts on the next level: The Next Big Thing. By giving special attention to all The Next Big Things vying for competition in your marketplace (and there are usually a half-dozen), you may be able to identify one that is going to become social convention. If you can do that correctly, and get into the selling of that product before anyone else does, you stand a chance of having enormous success.

In focusing on The Next Big Thing, you should keep your eye on the Realm of the Cool—an area of great creativity and motion. Having a reasonably good acquaintance with what people in that world are saying, doing, and thinking about will give you a much-better-than-average chance to predict which Next Big Thing will enter into the Realm of the Cool. Keep abreast of what is happening at the Edge. Although a good deal of it will never go any further than the Edge, some of it will cause a stir and develop an enthusiastic alternative marketplace. If you can get a sense for what is just about to enter the Realm of the Cool, you'll be well positioned to make a lot of money fast when your idea moves from that level to the mainstream.

The biggest money, the greatest fame, and the greatest thrills come from being at the helm of that transition.[9]

Let me be very clear. When I tell you that the stock market is not a fun place to be in a secular bear market, that you should avoid index funds and most equity mutual funds, that does not mean I do not think there is a great deal of opportunity to be had by investing in exciting businesses and the stock of those businesses.

Most investors expect the rising tide of the market to deliver their profits. In a secular bear cycle, the tide is not rising, but falling. Yes, the tide will eventually rise, but it will be a long time before it does.

Investing in stocks in this part of the cycle requires a great deal of work. It is not something the vast majority of people can do by combing through data. You must come to know your investments intimately. Think Warren Buffett. Buy stock in a company because you want part of the profits or the potential for future profits, and buy only if you understand the business model and have confidence in the management.

In Chapters 16 to 18 we are going to look at some principles to help you do just this.

Into the Matrix: History's Guide to Realistic Expectations

*T*he next two chapters (5 and 6) are co-authored with Ed Easterling, president
of Crestmont Holdings, LLC. Ed Easterling is a colleague of mine in the
world of investment management and financial market analysis. He is an
expert on Texas-based hedge funds and has both institutional and high-net-worth
individual clients. He has developed a series of graphics to show his clients what
they should expect from the financial markets and from simple stock market returns
over the next decade.

This research into stock market and economic cycles will give us insight into how
secular bear markets actually work. It will also give us a clue as to how to invest in
stocks even in a secular bear market cycle. Understanding this material will also
make you a more confident investor.

**We will make the case that it is more useful to analyze stocks during sec-
ular bear markets in terms of *value* than in terms of *price*.** This is a critical
point for you to grasp as you read this chapter. In earlier chapters we used
stock price to determine secular cycles. In this chapter when we refer to
secular bull and bear markets we will be looking first at the stock market in
terms of the rise and fall of valuation or P/E ratios and secondarily at the
price returns within those periods. Thus, the charts and tables in this
chapter may have different beginnings and endings for the cycles than
those that reference the work of other analysts in preceding chapters.

Further, we show that volatility and frequent large rallies are the norm
and not the exception, thus giving the astute investor some terrific opportunities. Finally, we will make a connection between inflation, interest
rates, and stocks that will give us further indications of the direction of
the stock and bond markets in the coming decade.

If the cycles of the past century continue to repeat, most of the first decade (or more) of this century will experience a secular bear market—an extended period of generally down or sideways and choppy stock market conditions. The subsequent decade (or longer) should experience a secular bull market—an extended period of generally upward and exciting market conditions.

These periods in the past have been the result of market valuation cycles represented by the P/E ratio. The valuation cycles have resulted from generally longer-term trends in inflation toward and away from price stability. The short-term, somewhat random, market gyrations are the result of then current circumstances and market forces wrestling stock prices around the gravity line of the broader cyclical trend. **These cycles generally take a generation to work their way through the investor public, have significant magnitudes of becoming undervalued and overvalued, and have significant implications for the way investors should approach each of these periods.**

Secular Bear Markets by the Numbers

Would you like to live in paradise? There's a place where the average daily temperature is 66 degrees, rain occurs on average once every five days, and the sun shines most of the time.

Welcome to Dallas, Texas. As most know, the weather in Dallas wouldn't qualify as climate paradise. The summers begin their ascent almost before spring arrives. On some days, the buds nearly wilt before turning into blooms. During the lazy days of summer, the sun frequently stokes the thermometer into triple digits, often for days on end. There are numerous jokes about the devil, hell, and Texas summers.

Once winter is in full force, some days are mild and perfect golf weather. Yet others present frigid temperatures, snow, and the occasional ice storm. It's good for business at the local auto body shops, though it makes for sleepless nights for the insurance companies. Certainly the winters don't match the wind chills of Chicago or the blizzards of Buffalo, but the climate in Dallas is far from paradise as its seasons ebb and flow.

For the year, though, the average temperature is paradise.

Contrary to the studies that show investors they can expect 7 percent or 9 percent or 10 percent by staying in the market for the long run, the stock market isn't paradise, either. Like Texas summers, the stock market often seems like the anteroom to investment hell.

While historically the average investment returns over very long terms of times have been some of the best available, the seasons of the stock market tend to cycle with as much variability as Texas weather. The extremes and the inconsistencies are far greater than most people realize.

Let's examine the range of variability to truly appreciate the strength of the storms.

In the 103 years from 1900 through 2002, the annual change for the Dow Jones Industrial Average resulted in a simple average gain of 7.2 percent per year. During that time, 63 percent of the years reflected positive returns and 37 percent had negative returns. Only five of the years ended with changes between +5 percent and +10 percent—less than 5 percent of the time. Most of the years were far from average—many were sufficiently dramatic to drive an investor's pulse into lethal territory.

As shown in Table 5.1, almost 70 percent of the years were double-digit years, when the stock market either increased or decreased by more than 10 percent. To move out of "most" territory, the threshold increases to 16 percent—half of the past 103 years end with the stock market index either up or down more than 16 percent!

Read those last two paragraphs again. The simple fact is that the stock market rarely gives you an average year. The wild ride makes for those emotional investment experiences.

The stock market can be a very risky place to invest. The returns are highly erratic; the gains and losses are often inconsistent and unpredictable. The emotional responses to stock market volatility mean that most investors do not achieve the average stock market gains, as other studies presented elsewhere in this book clearly illustrate.

Not understanding how to manage the risks of the stock market, or

Table 5.1   Dow Jones Industrial Average: Dispersion of Annual Stock Market Returns, Percent of Years (1900–2002)

Range	103 Years Frequency
<–10%	21%
–10% to +10%	31%
>+10%	48%

Range	103 Years Frequency
<–16%	16%
–16% to +16%	50%
>+16%	34%

Copyright 2003, Crestmont Research (www.CrestmontResearch.com).

even what the risks actually are, investors too often buy high and sell low based on raw emotion. They read the words in the account opening forms that the stock market presents a significant opportunity for a loss and that the magnitude of the loss can be quite significant. But they focus on the research that says, "Over the long run, history has overcome interim setbacks and has delivered an average return of 10 percent including dividends"—or whatever the current number du jour is, and ignoring bad stuff like inflation, taxes, and transaction costs.

The 20-Year Horizon

But how long is the "long run"? Investors have been bombarded for years with the quip that one should invest for the "long run." This has indoctrinated investors' thinking to ignore the realities of stock market investing because of the "certain" expectation of ultimate gains.

This faulty line of thinking has spawned a number of pithy principles, including: "No pain, no gain," "You can't participate in the profits if you are not in the game," and our personal favorite: "It's not a loss until you take it."

These and other platitudes are often brought up as reasons to leave your money with the current management, in spite of recent large losses. Cynically restated: Why worry about the swings in your life savings from year to year if you're supposed to be rewarded in the "long run"? But what if history does not repeat itself, or if you don't live long enough for the long run to occur?

For many, the "long run" is about 20 years. We work hard to accumulate assets during the formative years of our careers, yet the accumulation for the large majority of us seems to become meaningful somewhere after midlife. We seek to have a confident and comfortable nest egg in time for retirement. For many, this will represent roughly a 20-year period.

As reflected in Figure 5.1 and Table 5.2, there have been 84 20-year periods since 1900. The first 20-year period began with the two decades from 1900 to 1919. Each rolling 20-year period was evaluated through the most recent one from 1983 to 2002. Though most have generated positive returns before dividends and transaction costs, half produced compounded returns of less than 4 percent. Less than 10 percent generated gains of more than 10 percent.

Notice that there were only nine periods when 20-year returns were above 9.6 percent. Table 5.3 shows all nine. What you will notice is that eight out of nine times were all associated with the recent stock market bubble, and all eight represent a doubling, tripling, or even quadrupling

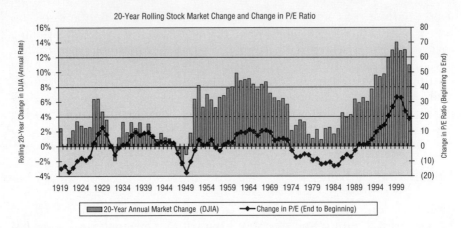

Figure 5.1   Returns over 20-Year Periods Vary Significantly, Affected by the Starting P/E Ratio
Copyright 2003, Crestmont Research (www.CrestmontResearch.com).

of P/E ratios. Prior to the bubble, there was no 20-year period that delivered 10 percent annual returns.

Every period of above 9.6 percent market returns started with low P/E ratios. *Every one.* And while not a consistent line, you will note that as annual 20-year returns increase, there is a general decline in the initial P/E ratios. If we wanted to do some detailed analysis, we could begin to ex-

Table 5.2   Twenty-Year Periods Ending 1919–2002 (84 Periods)

| Decile | Market Change by Decile Range | | Average Change | Average P/E |
	From	To		
1	−2.6%	1.0%	−0.4%	17
2	1.0%	1.7%	1.4%	13
3	1.8%	2.4%	2.1%	17
4	2.5%	3.0%	2.6%	16
5	3.2%	3.9%	3.4%	15
6	4.2%	6.0%	5.2%	17
7	6.2%	6.6%	6.4%	14
8	6.6%	7.8%	7.2%	14
9	8.0%	9.4%	8.7%	11
10	9.6%	14.0%	11.6%	10

Copyright 2003, Crestmont Research (www.CrestmontResearch.com).

Table 5.3   Nine Periods of 20-Year Returns over 9.6 Percent

Beginning Year	Ending Year	Annual ROR	Beginning P/E	Ending P/E
1975	1994	9.6%	10.9	20.5
1977	1996	9.7%	11.5	25.9
1942	1961	9.9%	12.2	20.5
1983	2002	10.9%	7.3	25.9
1978	1997	11.9%	10.4	31.0
1981	2000	12.8%	8.8	41.7
1979	1998	12.9%	9.4	36.0
1982	2001	13.0%	8.5	32.1
1980	1999	14.0%	8.9	42.1

plain the variation from this trend quite readily. For instance, the period beginning with 1983 was the lowest initial P/E ratio, but was also associated with the two-year-old secular bear market, which was beginning to lower 20-year return levels.

In all cases, throughout the years, the level of returns correlates very highly to the trend in the market's P/E ratio. The P/E ratio is the measure of valuation as reflected by the relationship between the prices paid per share to the earnings per share (EPS). Higher returns are associated with periods during which the P/E ratio increased and lower or negative returns resulted from periods during which the P/E ratio declined.

This may be the single most important investment insight you will get from this book. When P/E ratios are rising, the saying that "a rising tide lifts all boats" has been historically true. When P/Es are dropping, stock market investing is tricky; index investing is an experiment in futility. As we will see in later chapters, in these secular bear market periods, successful stock market investing requires a far different (and sometimes opposite) set of skills and techniques than what is required in bull markets.

Figure 5.2 presents a plot of each annual 20-year return and the corresponding starting P/E ratio. This chart emphasizes the very high propensity for 20-year periods that start with high P/E ratios to experience dismal returns and for periods that start with relatively low P/Es to generate the higher returns.

As we look further into the conditions affecting the return profile, we note a strong relationship between the change in the P/E ratio over the 20-year period and the total return for the period. *None—not one—of the periods of strong gains occurred without rising P/E ratios.*

Given the current and recent level of P/Es, the prospects are not encouraging for general market gains (the emphasis is on general or index

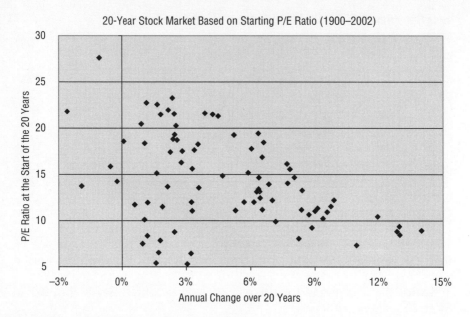

Figure 5.2   Twenty-Year Return and P/E Ratio
Copyright 2003, Crestmont Research (www.CrestmontResearch.com).

funds) over the next two decades. This dismal outlook is not from some congenital bear perspective; it corresponds to the series of factors driving the current secular bear market.

As in the past, after another extended period of a nonproductive market the future should hold solid returns. Unfortunately for those of investing age today and during the next decade, returns from the stock market are likely to be quite disappointing. Fortunately, no one is forcing you to limit your investments to index funds or mutual funds.

(Well, that may not be true. If your 401(k) has only broad index fund options, you do have very limited choices. As time wears on, and as index funds languish, investors will clamor for alternatives. It is for that reason we think certain types of absolute return hedge funds will be available to the average investor by at least the end of the decade, if not sooner.)

The Volatility Gremlins

The average returns trumpeted by the market cheerleaders selling you funds don't deliver the dollars to your account that you might expect. The actual stack of money that you receive is impacted by two dynamics.

The first factor is the disproportionate impact of losses, and the second is the benefit of consistency.

For an example of the impact of losses, consider that the statistical average of +24 percent and –20 percent is +2 percent. However, if your investment delivers those two back-to-back years, the stock market gremlins will leave your account a bit short of breaking even! It doesn't matter which year occurs first, whether the first or the second is the positive year; the result is the same: Your account will be down almost 1 percent.

The greater the variability between the positives and the negatives, the more significant the impact on your account balance. Keep in mind that it takes a 100 percent gain to offset a 50 percent loss—yet the average calculates to a 25 percent gain! Why is this so important? Almost three-quarters of the years of the past century are double-digit deliveries, and half exceed +/– 16 percent. Though there have been more positive years than negative years in the past century, we need more positive years to offset the disproportionate impact of losses. This also gives added emphasis to the importance of avoiding losses.

The second factor is a bit more technical and mathematical. Please be patient with this explanation. When the numbers in a series are farther from the average, the compounded return *decreases*. (Compounded return is the final result in your investment account following years of investing.)

As an example, if the average annual return over several years is +10 percent, the highest compounded return occurs when all three years deliver exactly +10 percent gains. A sequence of three 10s is superior to 5–10–15, 15–10–5, 30–0–0, and any other set that averages to 10. This is true regardless of the previously discussed impact of negative numbers. As the dispersion increases, the compounded return decreases. This can be a significant dynamic affecting the ability of annual returns from the stock market to add cash to your stack. See Table 5.4.

Earlier we mentioned that the simple average stand-alone return for the stock market was 7.2 percent annually, excluding dividends and a

Table 5.4   Compounded Returns

	A	B	C	D
	10%	5%	15%	30%
	10%	10%	10%	0%
	10%	15%	5%	0%
Compounded average	10.00%	9.92%	9.92%	9.14%
Simple average	10.00%	10.00%	10.00%	10.00%

number of other cost factors that affect the actual profits that you receive. However, had you invested $1,000 in the first year, your account would have grown by only a compounded 4.8 percent over the subsequent 103 years. The gremlins of volatility and negative numbers would have consumed one-third of your return. The notion of average return is irrelevant since an investor's actual returns can only be measured as compounded returns. This concept is so powerful that banking regulations require interest rates on loans and certificates of deposit to be quoted also as an annual percentage rate (APR) in addition to the stated rate to truly reflect the impact of compounding. This impact is detailed in Table 5.5.

None of these factors should be construed to dispel the opportunities available through investing in the stock market. The stock market has historically provided a solid long-term rate of return and has built a house of wealth in many investors' accounts. However, stock market returns are quite volatile and cyclical as well. *When* you invest makes a huge difference as to your long-term returns.

Stock market cycles are relatively long, have individual characteristics, and are somewhat predictable. Nonetheless, the upcoming text will provide practical insights and useful perspectives about secular stock market cycles.

The Investment Matrix: The Real Truth about Stock Market Returns

The past 103 years have provided over 5,000 investment period scenarios—that is, the combination of investment periods from any start year to every year since that time. This provides an extensive history across which to assess the potential and likely outcomes. That vast amount of data has been organized into a single visual chart to assist the reader in evaluating all of the scenarios. That chart is included as a foldout page.

Like the movie *The Matrix*, this Investment Matrix slows down the fast-paced motion of the markets, letting us see the ebb and flow of the financial tides over long periods of time.

The chart called "Taxpayer Nominal" is the S&P 500 index including dividends and transaction costs adjusted to reflect the net return after taxes. You will not see this one in a mutual fund sales presentation. It is what happens in the real world to your index fund investments.

If we had wanted to make a more dramatic and bearish case, we could use a chart that is "Taxpayer Real," which reflects the ravages of both taxes and inflation. There are those who would argue that the latter chart is the one we should have inserted in the book. It may more realistically reflect the buying power of the dollars you are currently investing. I would encourage

Table 5.5 What's Average: The Average of the Years versus the Compounded Average (Compounded Returns Are Adversely Affected by Negative Years and Volatility)

Simple Annual Returns

	'00	'01	'02	'03	'04	'05	'06	'07	'08	'09	Average
1900	7%	-9%	0%	-24%	42%	38%	-2%	-38%	47%	15%	
1910	-18%	0%	8%	-10%	-31%	82%	-4%	-22%	11%	30%	
1920	-33%	13%	22%	-3%	26%	30%	0%	29%	48%	-17%	
1930	-34%	-53%	-23%	67%	4%	39%	25%	-33%	28%	-3%	
1940	-13%	-15%	8%	14%	12%	27%	-8%	2%	-2%	13%	
1950	18%	14%	8%	-4%	44%	21%	2%	-13%	34%	16%	Average = 7.2%
1960	-9%	19%	-11%	17%	15%	11%	-19%	15%	4%	-15%	
1970	5%	6%	15%	-17%	-28%	38%	18%	-17%	-3%	4%	
1980	15%	-9%	20%	20%	-4%	28%	23%	2%	12%	27%	
1990	-4%	20%	4%	14%	2%	33%	26%	23%	16%	25%	
2000	-6%	-7%	-17%								

Compounded Annual Returns

	01/01/1900	12/31/2002	Average
Start	66.08		
End		8,341.63	→ Average = 4.8%
Years		103	

Copyright 2003, Crestmont Research (www.CrestmontResearch.com).

you to go to the Internet and look at it at the appropriate websites. (You can view other versions of the chart that show "Taxpayer Real," "Tax-Exempt Nominal," and "Tax-Exempt Real" by going to www.CrestmontResearch .com or John Mauldin's web site at www.2000wave.com under Stock Market Return Graphs.)

These charts are very useful visual aids for understanding the historical flow of investment returns. You might even want to consider getting them color-printed and enlarged to allow for easier study.

Let's take a moment to explain the layout of the chart. There are three columns of numbers on the left-hand side of the page and three rows of numbers on the top of the page. The column and row closest to the main chart reflect every year from 1900 through 2002. The column on the left side will serve as our start year and the row at the top represents the ending year. The top row has been abbreviated to the last two numbers of the year due to space constraints. Therefore, if you wanted to know the annual compounded return from 1950 to 1973, look for the row represented by the year "1950" on the left and look for the intersecting column designated by "73" (for 1973). The result on the version titled "Taxpayer Nominal" is 8, reflecting an annual compounded return of 8 percent over that 23-year period. Looking out another nine years, the return for the 32 years drops to 6 percent after tax. (If we were to use the "Taxpayer Real" for the same period, returns would drop to 2 percent.) There is a thin black diagonal line going from the top right to the lower left. This line shows you what the returns are 20 years after an initial investment. This will help you see what returns have been over the "long run" of 20 years.

Also note: The return number resides in a cell that has been shaded light green. The color of the cell represents the level of the return. If the annual return is less than 0 percent, the cell is shaded red. When the return is between 0 percent and 3 percent, the shading is pink. Blue is used for the range 3 percent to 7 percent, light green when the returns are between 7 percent and 10 percent, and dark green when annual returns are in excess of 10 percent. This enables us to look at the big picture. Whereas long-term returns tend to be shaded blue, shorter-term periods use all of the colors.

As well, note that some of the numbers are presented in white, while the others are black. If the P/E ratio for the ending year is higher than the P/E for the starting year—representing rising P/E ratios—the number is black. For lower P/E ratios, the color is white. In general, red and pink most often have white numbers and the greens and blues share space with black numbers. The P/E ratio for each year is presented along the left side of the page and along the top of the chart.

This theme of rising and falling P/E ratios and the corresponding rise and fall of the stock market is one we are going to return to again and again in these chapters. If you can understand this dynamic, you will be far ahead of most investors in the race to a comfortable retirement.

Lastly, there's additional data included on the chart. On the left side of the page, note the middle column. As well, on the top of the page, note the middle row. Both series represent the index values for each year. This is used to calculate the compounded return from the start period to the end period. Along the bottom of the page, Crestmont included the index value, dividend yield, inflation (consumer price index), real GDP, nominal GDP, and the 10-year annual compounded average for both GDP measures. For the index value, keep in mind that the S&P 500 index value for each year represents the average across all trading days of the year.

Along the right, there's an arbitrary list of developments for each of the past 103 years. In compiling the list of historical milestones, it's quite interesting to reflect on the past century and recall that the gurus of the 1990s actually believed that we were in a "new economy" era. Looking at the historical events, it could be argued that almost every period had a reason to be called a "new economy." But that's an argument for another chapter.

The Investment Matrix Revelations

As we consider the story that the matrix begins to tell, several observations are initially apparent. There are clear patterns of returns relating to the secular bull and secular bear cycles. The periods of red and pink alternate with periods of blue and green. Once the new period starts, it tends to persist for long periods of time. Though the very long-term returns have been positive and near average, investment horizons of 10 years, 20 years, and even longer aren't long enough to ensure positive or acceptable returns.

Note also that we've recently completed the longest run of green years in the past century. Though we've had a couple of down (red) years lately, it has hardly helped to restore the long-term average to "average." We have quite a distance to go to complete what the mathematicians refer to as "regressing to the mean." As you look back over the past 100 years, there has never been a period where the "red bear" stopped after a few short years and morphed into a "green bull."

Secondly, when you look at the "Taxpayer Nominal" chart, you will notice that the returns tend to be in the 5 to 7 percent range after long periods of time. *Often nominal returns are 5 percent or less over multiple decades.* Again, the charts clearly show the most important thing you can do to positively affect your long-term returns is to begin investing in times of low P/E ratios.

The Matrix assumes 20 percent taxes as an average over this period. We are aware that the income tax did not exist in 1901. This was a tricky number to assume, as taxes on stocks are comprised of both long-term and short-term gains, and are taxed at different rates for different times. Also, some investors pay additional state taxes.

Why not just assume all long-term gains? If you buy your stocks through mutual funds, as most individuals do, then you are probably seeing a lot of turnover in your portfolio. Remember Peter Lynch of Magellan fame? His reported average holding period was about seven months during the 1970s. Some of you will pay higher taxes, and some of you will pay lower, depending on your investment styles. Twenty percent is probably fair. You can adjust your expectations accordingly.

Now, what can we learn from this chart?

First, there are very clear periods when returns are better than others. These relate to secular bull and bear markets. No big insight there. But what you should notice is the correlation with P/E ratios. In general, when P/E ratios begin to rise, you want to be in the stock market. When they are falling, total returns over the next decade will be below par. When periods of falling P/E ratios start, they just keep going until P/E ratios bottom out. (More on that phenomenon later.)

Can you use the P/E ratios to signal a precise turn from a secular bull to a secular bear? No, but you can use them to assist you in confirming other signals. And once that turn has begun, the historical evidence is that the trend continues. Investors are advised to change their stock-buying habits. As noted earlier, there will be bear market rallies that will momentarily halt the decline of the P/E ratios. These always end. Reversion to the mean (trend) is simply too strong a force.

Second, the Investment Matrix shows the high probability that a secular bear is currently in progress. High and falling P/E ratios, along with negative returns, are always associated with the beginning of such markets. When you let your eyes follow along the tables, you can see those red periods when annual gains were negative. Look at the corresponding P/E ratio. If it is high, it historically has correlated with the beginning of a secular bear, which always takes years to work itself out. Fighting this trend is frustrating at best.

When Can We Make Long-Term Money in Stocks Again?

When can you profitably begin to be a long-term investor, even in a secular bear market? Look at the chart. You have reasonable to excellent chances of getting above-average returns if you buy when P/E ratios are below 10 to 12. You might have to suffer in the short term, but over the long term you will probably be okay. (Stock market investment strategies will be dealt with at length in Chapters 16 to 18.)

For index investors, a good strategy would be to start averaging in (dollar cost averaging—investing a steady amount each week or month over a long period of time) when the market values drop below a P/E of 10 to 12. Even in the worst of the Depression, you would have done well over the next 20 years using this criterion and strategy. Investors who want to own individual stocks should focus on stocks with deep value and rising dividends, although the evidence indicates you will have periods when you will most decidedly not be happy.

Death and Taxes

If you look at just the nominal returns without thinking about taxes, some would make the case that trying to time the market is pointless. Over enough time, the returns tend to be the same. And we agree, if you have 50 years, time can heal a lot of mistakes. Historically, investing through full cycles would give you a 10 percent compounded return after many decades, and 6 to 7 percent in inflation-adjusted terms.

However, if you take into account inflation, transaction costs, and taxes, real in-your-account returns tend to be in the 3 percent annual average range. And if you begin to invest at the beginning of a secular bear, real returns over the next 20 years are likely to be negative! You actually lose buying power.

Let's look at some other points. First, these tables include dividends. The 6 to 7 percent returns show up over time primarily because of high dividends. Given that dividends are under 2 percent or nonexistent for many NASDAQ stocks, the 3 percent long-term return number becomes far more realistic. Periods of high dividends greatly increase the return potential over using simple S&P 500 index returns.

Second, inflation did a great deal to mask the seriousness of the 1970 bear markets. It took 16 years for the stock market to make new highs from 1966, but it was another 10 years, or 1992, before investors saw a rise in their actual buying power in terms of the S&P 500 index.

On the chart, you see that compounded returns over the 26 years from 1966 to 1992 were 6 percent without inflation and 0 percent taking into account inflation. The actual index in real terms was almost flat. *That means the bulk of earnings on this table over that period came from dividends. The compounding effect of dividends upon returns was huge.*

The 6 percent returns an investor apparently got from 1966 through

1992 depended largely on inflation. The 1 percent real returns are entirely due to dividends. During much of that period, dividends were in the 4 to 5 percent range.

Today, dividends on the S&P are less than 2 percent instead of the 3 to 5 percent of the 1970s. Further, we are not in a period of high inflation, although that may change by the end of the decade.

If you look at the tax-deferred account real returns chart for the period of 1966 through 1992, the after-inflation return numbers for the majority of that period are negative for a long time, until you begin to get to periods of low P/E ratios.

Now, look forward in time from any year in the 1970s when P/E ratios were above 10. Figure out when you want to be able to use your investments for retirement. See if there is enough growth and time to get you to where you want to be.

If you expect to retire in 10 years, you should *not* assume a 5 to 6 percent return on the average stock or index fund from where we are today. The chart suggests it might even be unrealistic to assume a 2 percent real return!

How can we even think that stocks might not compound at 2 percent a year over the next 10 years? It is because there has been only one time when investors have made more than a 2 percent real return (after taxes and other costs) over the next 10 years when P/E ratios are over 21, which is easily where they are today (no matter who is figuring them). That one lone example is from the mid-1990s through today. If our assumptions are correct, and returns become flat, then even that one period will turn out to be closer to 2 percent.

If you are using a standard retirement planning software program, and it asks you to assume how much you are going to get from stocks, you should *not* be using 10 percent or even 5 percent if you are planning on retiring in 10 to 20 years. Yes, that means that when General Motors employees assume they will get 10 percent on their pension portfolios, they are using highly unrealistic assumptions. If 30 percent or so of their portfolio is in bonds, and we know how low those returns are, that means they assume that stocks will be returning 14 percent or more over the next 10 years.

Now, don't jump off that ledge yet. This doesn't mean you can't make 5 to 8 percent on your portfolio. It just means you have to look at alternatives to traditional buy-and-hold mutual funds. Value will rule. Think dividends. Absolute returns from bonds and specialized funds will be critical to the growth of your portfolio.

One last and major point: These numbers are all averages. That means 50 percent of investors will do worse than the numbers suggested on these tables. Of course, all of our readers are above average, but you might want to warn your brother-in-law.

What Are Expected Stock Returns for Next 20 Years?

Over the long term the Ibbotson study, used by stock market cheerleaders everywhere, says we should expect to make real returns of 6 to 7 percent. This statistic is cited by brokers and fund managers who urge investors to buy and hold. Maybe more to the sales point, it is used to urge investors to buy some more stocks or mutual fund shares today and hold them as well. If you just keep buying, the study says you will get your reward, by and by.

This is the sweet buy and buy sales pitch. The Ibbotson study, and numerous other studies, is one of the most misused pieces of market propaganda ever. If we thought for one minute you really could get 7 percent compound annualized real returns over the next 20 years by simply buying and holding, we would agree that it would be a smart thing to do.

[I cannot tell you how many soon-to-be-retired couples I have talked to, after their retirement savings have been hit 30, 40, or 50 percent and their comfortable retirement dreams shattered, who tell me their brokers or advisors told them if they would just hold on the market would come back. Soon, they were promised. These were the investment professionals they trusted and they assumed the pros had done their homework.—John]

Slip-Sliding Away

"The more you near your destination, the more you slip-slide away."

—*Paul Simon*

The long-run profits we read about in the brochures don't seem to match what we see in our accounts. The closer we get to retirement and the need for those funds, the more those profits seem to slip away.

Before we start looking at cycles, let's explore the impact of dividends, transaction costs, slippage, taxes, and other factors on total return.

Ever notice how quickly we're reminded, while looking at the change in the index or basket of stocks, not to forget the added return from the dividends? As we seek to translate the language of benchmark returns into changes in our account balances, let's also not forget a few other components. While annual dividends have averaged 4.4 percent over the course of the past century, transaction costs and taxes have imposed their share of impact on the portfolio as well.

For individual investors, taxes can affect the realized return. To provide a reasonable assessment of the impact of taxes, Crestmont considered several factors and included a number of simplifying assumptions. The objective was to estimate the effect on a typical taxpayer. In general, the average tax rate was approximately 20 percent across the entire period starting in 1913, when the federal income tax was formally introduced.

For each year, Crestmont assumed that 80 percent of gains were long-term capital gains and 20 percent were short-term capital gains. Only 90 percent of gains each year were realized, and the long-term capital gain portion was lagged by one year to simulate the effect of longer holding periods. For a measure of conservatism, 10 percent of gains are never taxed. Most of the capital losses are used to offset gains in future years. It's assumed that dividends are taxed at the short-term rate.

Transaction costs include commissions, asset management fees, bid/ask spreads, execution slippage, and numerous extra costs. Commissions are the transaction costs paid to brokers to buy and sell stocks or mutual funds. The commission cost can be—and certainly was historically—greater for individual investors than for larger institutional investors (i.e., pension plans, mutual funds, etc.). Even with today's low rates, for active and/or small investors they can be very significant.

Asset management fees are charges levied by an advisor, the investment fund, trustees, the pension fund managers, and/or other constituents in the investment process. These can run anywhere from 0.5 percent to 3 percent. Mutual fund fees of 2 percent or more are not uncommon. (As asset managers, we are not against fees, as that is how we make our living. But we do think investors should get a "bang" for their commission "buck.")

The third cost, bid/ask spreads, represents the difference between the price that one pays for a stock and the price at which the stock could be sold at the same time. Index returns are based on the last price traded for each stock, some on the bid (the price at which one can sell) and some on the ask (the price at which one can buy). We can refer to the blend of bid and ask prices as the "mid" price—averaging near the middle. However, investors bear the cost within their account or mutual fund of slightly higher prices for purchases and slightly lower prices for sales.

The cost of the spread is often far more than the commissions. There are reports beginning to surface that show the cost of spreads is actually increasing after the conversion to decimalization of stock prices last year, which was *not* what was expected.

The fourth factor included in this list, slippage, affects larger buyers of stock more than individual investors. While large accounts may pay less in

7	10	9	11	13	16	14	17	16	18	20	21	20	23	26	31	36		42	42	32	26			
77	104	102	119	151	179	156	184	189	209	228	240	240	279	341	428	506		586	599	479	393			
82	83	84	85	86	87	88	89	90	91	92	93	94	95	96	97	98	99	100	101	102				

1900	Rodin Completes 'The Thinker'
1901	First Electric Typewriter
1902	Navy Installs Radio
1903	Wright Bros Fly
1904	Crayola & Jell-O
1905	Pen Gets Pocket Clip
1906	S.F. Earthquake
1907	Photocopier Marketed
1908	Model T Introduced
1909	Chlorine In Drinking Water
1910	Electric Range Invented
1911	Sherman Anti-Trust Act; Airmail Begins
1912	Titanic Sinks; U.S. Radio Act
1913	Income Tax & Federal Reserve
1914	WWI Starts; First Transcon. Phone Call
1915	Americans Avg 40 Phone Calls A Year
1916	Keds & Electric Clock Invented
1917	US Enters WWI; Einstein Theorizes Lasers
1918	WWI Ends
1919	Prohibition; Shortwave Radio; Dial Phones
1920	Women's Right To Vote
1921	World Series On Radio; Quartz Crystals
1922	100,000 Radios Made In U.S.; 3 Frequencies
1923	500,000 Radios Made; Neon Signs
1924	2.5 Million Radios Made; Frozen Food Invented
1925	Commercial Picture Fax By Radio In U.S.
1926	First Publicly Shown 'Talkie'
1927	2-Way Radio Phone: U.S. To London ($15/min)
1928	Teletype Machine; Test TV In 3 Homes
1929	Crash of '29; Car Radio
1930	Photo Flash Bulbs
1931	Radios In 40% Of Homes; Scotch Tape
1932	Radar; 8 mm Cameras; Electric Eye Scanner
1933	End of Prohibition; FM Radio; Wallboard
1934	Radios In 50% Of Homes; AP Wirephoto
1935	Social Security Act Passed
1936	BBC First TV Service, 3 Hours A Day
1937	Hindenburg Airship Crash
1938	National Minimum Wage Enacted
1939	Regular TV Broadcasts In U.S.; Helicopter
1940	World War II Begins; Radar Invented
1941	Pearl Harbor Attack; 2-Way Police Radio
1942	U.S. Office Of Censorship Due To War
1943	Phone Line Repeaters Help Service
1944	D-Day, Normandy
1945	World War II Ends; FCC Sets VHF Channels
1946	ENIAC, 1st Computer; First Copy Machine Sold
1947	Transistor Invented; Microwave Oven
1948	Israel Established; RCA High Speed Fax
1949	NATO Established; Network TV In U.S.
1950	Korean War Begins; Credit Card Created
1951	Color TV; Modern Plastic Invented
1952	Phone Area Codes; EDVAC Computer
1953	Korean War Ends; Magnetic Core Memory
1954	TVs In 54% Of Homes; Transistor Radios
1955	Tests Begin On Digital Fiber Optics
1956	Transatlantic Phone Cable; The Pager
1957	Sputnik, First Satellite; EEC Formed
1958	Stereo LP Records; Data On Phone Lines
1959	COBOL; Microchip; Plain Paper Xerox
1960	90% Homes w/TVs; Laser; Weather Satellite
1961	Berlin Wall Built; IBM Selectric Typewriter
1962	Cuban Missile Crisis; Mariner II At Venus
1963	Kennedy Killed; Income Tax 91% To 70%
1964	Vietnam Begins; Home VCR
1965	First Minicomputer; Car Phones; Hypertext
1966	Dow @ 1,000; 8-Tracks In Cars; Fax Machine
1967	Floppy Disk; Cordless Phones; Dolby
1968	Intelsat Global Satellite Link; Intel 1KB RAM
1969	Neil Armstrong Walks On Moon; ATMs
1970	Barcodes; First Internet Connections
1971	Microchip, Price Controls; Answering Machine
1972	Dow Closes Above 1,000; Pong; HBO
1973	U.S. Leaves Vietnam; International Internet
1974	Nixon Resigns; Wage & Price Controls End
1975	Microsoft; Optical Videodisk Demo
1976	Apple I; Cray-1; Home Satellite Dish
1977	Elvis Dies; TRS-80 PC; Fiber Optic Call
1978	Modems; Cell Phone Tests; Intel 16-bit Chip
1979	CompuServe Online; VisiCalc Spreadsheet
1980	CPI 13.5%; CNN; Sony Camcorder
1981	IBM PC Introduced; 300 bps Modems
1982	Dow Over 1,000; Compact Disk; 5.5 Mil. PCs
1983	AT&T Breakup; 288k Chips; Domain Names
1984	3 1/2" Floppy; Intel 32-bit; 1 MB Chips
1985	Cellphones; 2400k Modems; Windows OS
1986	Laser Printers; TV On 7 Hrs/Day In U.S.
1987	Stock Market Crash; 50% Have Cable TV
1988	Transatlantic Fiberoptic Cable; Internet T1
1989	Poland Solidarity; Nintendo Profits @ $1 Bil.
1990	World Wide Web (www)
1991	Gulf War; USSR Breakup; 75% Have VCRs
1992	65 Mil. PCs; 200k On AOL; CDs > Cassettes
1993	Pentium Chip; HTML; V-Chip
1994	First WTC Attack; Satellite TV; 33% w/PC
1995	NAFTA Enacted; Dot.com; Internet Audio
1996	100k Web Sites; 30 Mil In U.S. On Internet
1997	Internet Video; 43% In U.S. Have PCs
1998	Russia Debt Default; 75 Mil U.S. On Internet
1999	Satellite Can See 3' Objects On Earth
2000	Dow Hits 11,723; NASDAQ Hits 5,048
2001	WTC Attack On 9/11; >50% U.S. On Internet

82	83	84	85	86	87	88	89	90	91	92	93	94	95	96	97	98	99	100	101	102		
77	104	102	119	151	179	156	184	189	209	228	240	240	279	341	428	506	586	599	479	393		
5	4	3	2	3	4	3	3	3	3	3	2	2				1	1	1	1	1.6	4.4%	Avg
6	3	4	4	2	4	5	5	4	3	3	3	3	3	2		2	2	3	3	1.6	3.3%	Avg
4	8	11	7	6	7	8	7	6	3	6	5	5	6	6		6	5.9	2.6	3.6		6.7%	Avg
		+7.9%				|	|			+5.4%												
-2	4	7	4	3	3	4	4	2	0	3	3	4	4			4	4	3.8	0.3	2.4	3.5%	Avg
		+3.0%				|	|			+3.0%												

commissions, some of the advantages of larger-scale asset management require the often underrecognized costs of scale. Slippage is the impact of buying or selling hundreds of thousands of shares—the average cost of completing a large purchase in comparison to the market price for a few shares of a stock. When large buyers of a stock, a mutual fund for example, decide to buy or sell a position, the size of the order can push the market price in one direction or another. Slippage is the difference in the average price when buying or selling a small lot (e.g., 100 shares) compared to buying or selling larger blocks of stock (e.g., 100,000 shares). If you are a large manager trying to beat an index, or a hedge fund getting a piece of the profits, it is likely that slippage is the cause of a great deal of frustration, if not acrimony, on the trading floor.

Finally, you have lots of hidden costs. Account opening fees and loads can add up. Funds of all types have auditing and accounting fees, which are passed directly to the fund and thus to investors. Mutual funds have independent boards whose members must be paid, and most offshore hedge funds are required to have one or more independent directors who generally receive small fees. Add on custodial or administrative fees as well as taxes and fees on trading. (Switzerland and some other European countries charge a small fee for *every* trade. While small, the fees add up over time.)

Is there a consultant in the mix? Does your fund pay higher commissions (so-called soft dollar arrangements) to get access to research or stock quote services? (This happens a lot more than you might think. It is a way to pass operating expenses from the manager to the fund without showing the actual underlying expense. Investors might object to a line item that says "stock quote services" but never see the details if the expense is paid by an extra penny on the commission or the spread.) Attorney fees are often fund-related costs.

If you are a typical individual investor, you have your own accounting costs, investment newsletters, books, planners, consultants, and a host of investment-related expenses. That is not to say that each of them is not necessary to do your job as manager of your portfolio, but the costs do add up. While these are not always directly deducted from your investment accounts, they are still expenses.

The assumptions in the "Taxpayer Nominal" chart included the total cost of commissions, asset management fees, bid/ask spreads, and execution slippage equal to 2 percent per year. Although there are a few (somewhat limited) examples of those investors who can demonstrate a lower overall transaction cost on their stock investments, most professional investors have indicated that we are being too conservative—so the returns in the Matrix could actually be lower for most investors. So a rate of 2 percent is reasonable, with a bias toward being conservative. With current dividend yields averaging less than 2 percent, the net effect of transaction costs may well exceed the benefit of dividends.

Sequences over Time: Cycles

Cycles are defined as events that repeat in a sequence. For there to be a cycle, some condition or situation must recur over a period of time. We are able to observe a wide variety of cycles in our lives: patterns in the weather, the moon, radio waves, and so on. Some of the patterns are the result of fundamental factors, while others are more likely coincidence. The phases of the moon occur due to cycles among the moon, the earth, and the sun. In other situations, apparent patterns are no more than the alignment of random events into an observable sequence.

All cycles have several components in common. Cycles have a start and an end, they have characteristics that repeat from cycle to cycle, and they often have an explainable cause.

Stock market observers have identified what they believe to be scores of cycles, patterns, correlations, and relationships that have become a seemingly endless inventory of predictions and trading schemes. Every trader has his favorite system backed up with back-tested "research" and "facts." These systems all work fine until you begin to use them with real money.

The patterns are so numerous that some market experts discount all theories and acquiesce to a philosophy of randomness. However, just because we don't understand it doesn't mean that there's not useful information contained within the pattern.

In the following pages, we'll attempt to mine one of the major veins that seem to repeat through secular stock market cycles. We'll stop just short of asserting that the factor is causal. Nonetheless, we believe it to be blatantly compelling. Not surprisingly, it suggests we are in a secular bear market. When combined with the research by other analysts in the rest of the book, it becomes extremely compelling. As we go along, we'll also include a few notes that dispel common misperceptions from the pundits.

In Table 5.6, you'll note the general trends just described. As this is not a scientific relationship and many other factors impact the market and the economy, the relationships are not formulaic. Yet the trends and their fundamental relationships are discernible. The cycles are generally long and display many similar characteristics and patterns. Secular bulls are periods of a fairly consistently rising market; secular bears are choppy and consist of flat to declining periods.

We define a secular bull market as a period during which P/E ratios are rising. Similarly, a secular bear market is a period during which

Table 5.6 Secular Bull and Bear Markets Profile

Market Cycle From	To	(#) Total Years	Market	P/E Ratio Beg.	P/E Ratio End	Inflation Beg.	Inflation End	(#) Positive Years	(#) Negative Years	(%) Positive Years	(%) Negative Years	Max Pos. Yrs In Row	Max Neg. Yrs In Row	Avg Gain In Pos. Years	Avg Loss In Neg. Years	Change Begin To End
1901	1920	20	Bear	23	5	-2%	16%	9	11	45%	55%	2	3	30%	-17%	2%
1921	1928	8	Bull	5	19	-11%	-2%	7	1	88%	13%	5	1	24%	-3%	317%
1929	1932	4	Bear	28	8	0%	-10%	0	4	0%	100%	0	4	N/A	-32%	-80%
1933	1936	4	Bull	11	19	-5%	1%	4	0	100%	0%	4	0	34%	N/A	200%
1937	1941	5	Bear	19	12	4%	5%	1	4	20%	80%	4	1	28%	-16%	-38%
1942	1965	24	Bull	9	23	11%	2%	18	6	75%	25%	4	1	16%	-8%	774%
1966	1981	16	Bear	21	9	3%	10%	9	7	56%	44%	3	2	13%	-15%	-10%
1982	1999	18	Bull	74	2	6%	2%	16	2	89%	11%	9	1	18%	-4%	1,214%
2000	????		Bear	42		3%		03		0%	100%	0	3	N/A	-10%	-27%
Weighted Average Bear (excluding 2000)										42%	58%	2.1	2.7	21%	-18%	-14%
Weighted Average Bull										83%	17%	5.8	0.9	19%	-5%	810%

Notes: The index and returns reflect the Dow Jones Industrial Average at year-end from Dow Jones & Company. The P/E ratio is based on the S&P 500 as developed and presented by Robert Shiller (Yale; *Irrational Exuberance*). Bull and Bear Market classifications are based on Crestmont's assessment of cycles using peak and trough P/E ratios, inflation trends, and other analysis. The presentation does not include dividends, taxes, inflation adjustments, or transaction costs.

RETURN PATTERN (dark shading = down year; light shading = up year; #% = annual change in the index; starting and ending DJIA index is presented on the ends of the rows)

1901 – 1920: BEAR — start 71 / end 72
- Annual change: -9% 0% 0% -24% 42% 38% -38% -2% 47% 15% -18% 0% 8% -10% -31% 82% -4% -22% 11% 30% -33%
- P/E Ratio: 23 22 18 16 16 19 19 12 12
- CPI: Inflation: -2% 6% 1% 0% 4% -8% 3% 8% 1% 1%

1921 – 1928: BULL — start 72 / end 300
- Annual change: 13% 22% -3% 26% 0% 30% 48%
- P/E Ratio: 5 30% 29%
- CPI: Inflation: -11% -6% 2% 8% 2% -2%

1929 – 1932: BEAR — start 300 / end 60
- Annual change: -17% -34% -53% -23%
- P/E Ratio: 28 22 15 8
- CPI: Inflation: 0% -2% -9% -10%

1933 – 1936: BULL — start 60 / end 180
- Annual change: 67% 4% 39% 25%
- P/E Ratio: 11 12 13 19
- CPI: Inflation: -5% 3% 2% 1%

1937 – 1941: BEAR — start 180 / end 111
- Annual change: -33% 28% -3% -13% -15%
- P/E Ratio: 19 14 16 15 12
- CPI: Inflation: 4% -2% -1% 5%

1942 – 1965: BULL — start 111 / end 969
- Annual change: 8% 14% 12% 27% -8% 2% 18% 14% 8% -4% 44% 21% 2% -13% 34% 16% -9% 19% 11% 17% 15% 11%
- P/E Ratio: 9 11 11 41 31 81 81 61 51 81 72
- CPI: Inflation: 11% 6% 2% 8% 14% 1% 8% 2% 3% 0% 7% 13% 3% 1% 1% 3% 1% 2%

1966 – 1981: BEAR — start 969 / end 875
- Annual change: 19% 15% 4% -15% 15% 6% -28% 18% 11% 9% -3% 9% -9%
- P/E Ratio: 21 22 17 15 13 17 16 17
- CPI: Inflation: 3% 3% 4% 6% 5% 8% 4% 7% 11% 13% 10%

1982 – 1999: BULL — start 875 / end 11497
- Annual change: 20% 20% -4% 28% 11% 9% 12% 27% -4% 33% 26% 23% 16% 25%
- P/E Ratio: 7 10 9 13 14 17 16 17 42
- CPI: Inflation: 6% 3% 4% 4% 5% 2% 2%

2000 – ????: BEAR — start 11497
- Annual change: -6% -7% -17%
- P/E Ratio: 42 32 26
- CPI: Inflation: 3% 3% 2%

Copyright 2003, Crestmont Research (www.CrestmontResearch.com).

P/E ratios are declining. This is different than most definitions, which focus primarily on price.

In cycle systems that use price, many would define the cycle as beginning with a drop in the market and continuing until the market rises again above that price. While the case can be made for this, it also makes it difficult to decide when it is again safe to reenter the water. The absolute bottom of the broad market often happens many years before a new price high is achieved. By focusing on P/E ratios, one can begin to cautiously enter the market with selective securities that are already favorably priced. As we will note, this allows for a "bull market" in the midst of the Depression, which did indeed happen in a major way. Further, it is difficult to find consistent starts and stops using prices, but cycles in P/E ratios have historically been useful.

(One of the challenges was to determine which specific year represented the start of a cycle and which year should mark its conclusion. In general, it was decided that secular bull cycles start with a positive year following or concurrent with the trough in the P/E ratio and end with the last positive year when the P/E ratio peaks. The secular bear cycles start on a down year after P/Es reach their current cycle pinnacle and secular bear cycles end on a down note as P/Es bottom out.)

There have been eight complete secular cycles (based on valuation, not price) since 1900: four secular bulls and four secular bears. The first cycle of the twentieth century was a bear. It started in 1901 with the market P/E ratio cresting at 23. Twenty years later, with the P/E ratio firmly in single digits at 5, the bear went into hibernation. Over the 20 years of that secular bear, the Dow Jones Industrial Average (DJIA) had managed to tick up from 71 at year-end 1900 to 72 at year-end 1920.

During those two decades, the market moves were not calm. Annual moves from New Year's Eve to New Year's Eve ranged from –38 percent to +82 percent! The best-performing three years were +82 percent, +47 percent, and +42 percent. After each of those years we are sure that pundits proclaimed the death of the bear. Yet the three worst years were –38 percent, –33 percent, and –31 percent. As we'll see with most secular bear cycles, the period was as violent and choppy as the high seas in a monsoon. Across the 20 years in the average bear cycle, 45 percent were positive return years—but never more than two in a row. The 11 down years were generally singles or pairs, with only one three-year streak at the start of the cycle. Although the average gain was +30 percent and the average loss was –17 percent, the change from beginning to end was a paltry +2 percent in total.

Despite the fact that the economy grew and earnings rose during that secular bear cycle, P/E valuations declined and offset virtually all of the economic growth. The market's price was essentially unchanged from start to finish and earnings per share rose sharply. So with the market price virtually unchanged, it is clear that the decline in the P/E ratio offset the gains in earnings. Earnings growth is often strong in bear markets—the benefit of which is eroded by declining P/E ratios.

Let's also look at inflation during this period: The relatively low levels at the start of the cycle eventually gave way to a series of double-digit years toward the end of the bear cycle. It was actually the highest inflation of the entire century. In the early years of the twentieth century, the economy and inflation were much more erratic than in more recent times.

As the 1920s started, so did the century's first secular bull market. As with most secular bull cycles, most years were up years for the market, any down years were modest, and the ride was a rocket ship rather than a trawler in a squall. The 1920s bull lasted eight years, seven of which (i.e., 88 percent) reflected gains; the only declining year gave up 3 percent, and the ending DJIA index marked a gain from 72 to 300.

As for inflation, after a bout of deflation to offset the high inflation, prices stabilized into low single digits by the end of the cycle. And the cycle did end, as the economy entered an economic depression and period of deflation.

The next few cycles were short and dramatic: four devastating years, followed by four phenomenal years, and concluding with a five-year secular bear cycle. Though these three cycles were shorter than the previous and subsequent secular cycles, their characteristics and patterns in the P/E ratio and inflation were fairly consistent.

Many investors normally do not think of the years 1933–1936 as being part of a bull cycle, as the markets did not make a new high from the 1929 high. We think of those times as the heart of the Depression. But P/E ratios rose from single digits to 19, and the market tripled in just a short time. It behooves those who are genetically predisposed to a bearish position to remember that markets have a logic of their own.

The critical factor is to notice that at the start of each bull cycle the markets had single-digit P/E ratios, with no exception. *No* secular bull market has ever begun with high P/E ratios, even though there have often been significant rallies from high P/E ratios. The lesson of history is that all periods of high valuations came to an unhappy end.

On average across the eight cycles, secular bull markets reflect periods of strong stock market appreciation aided by significantly rising P/E ratios. Eighty-three percent of the years during all of the bull market cycles of the last century were positive. Over half of the time, the number of positive years averaged almost five in a row and none of the negative years occurred in succession.

Of the 13 positive series in bull cycles, the top seven average almost five years. The average of such a large range can be distorting (13 sets from one to nine years in a row); it seems that the real message in secular bulls (which we may not see for quite a while) is that a substantial number of the years are positive (83 percent) and that down years are intermittent. The average gain in positive years is +19 percent, while the average loss in down years is only –5 percent. The average total gain from start to finish: 810 percent!

That contrasts with secular bears, where up and down periods come in short spurts. Just under half of the years within a bear cycle are positive years (42 percent). The sequence is also choppy, with positive years averaging two-year streaks and negative years averaging less than three in a row. While the average gain is similar to the bull periods at 21 percent, the average loss is –18 percent. For the typical secular bear cycle, the total return is slightly negative—averaging –14 percent in total from beginning to end.

They Almost Got It Right

Modern financial theories about stock market valuations include an axiom that valuations rise as interest rates decline and vice versa. The logic generally states that (1) the stockholders receive the earnings and dividends from a company in perpetuity; (2) the dividends and retained book value represent the return to stockholders; (3) if interest rates are lower, then investors should be willing to take a lower return from stocks (the risk premium); and (4) if a lower return is acceptable, then investors can pay more for the stock.

We can illustrate this by looking at the inverse of the P/E ratio. Earnings—whether paid in dividends or retained as book value—can be represented by the letter "E." The price paid for the stock can be represented by the letter "P." Simplistically, the return (as compared to the interest rate on a bond) from an investment in a company can be expressed as the E based on the P paid. A percentage can be determined by dividing E by P (i.e., E/P). For example, if E is $1 and P is $15, then the current return is 6.7 percent (i.e., $1/$15). If interest rates fall to 5 percent, then the return an investor might be satisfied with might fall. Since E (the earnings) is likely to remain about the same, if an investor was willing to accept only a 5 percent earnings rate, then he would be willing to pay $20 for the stock (i.e., $1/$20 = 5%).

Most investors are familiar with another version of this relationship: the price-earnings (P/E) ratio. In the first illustration, the P/E is 15 (i.e., $15/$1). When interest rates were said to be lower, the ratio changed to 20 (i.e., $20/$1). So as we've all heard many times from the pundits on television and in print: Lower interest rates drive higher P/E ratios.

This is generally true. But there's an important footnote to that assumption in the fine print that's rarely mentioned: This is true only in periods of positive inflation. When inflation is negative—known as deflation—stock valuations have historically suffered despite lower interest rates. Although we'll explore in much greater detail throughout the following chapter a number of related relationships, the point for now is that stock market valuation as manifested in P/E ratios relates to *inflation* rather than *interest rates*. It might be helpful to think of interest rates as inflation's shadow. Inflation is the substance that gives rise (or fall) to interest rates.

It's Not the (Stupid) Economy

How many times are we told by the financial "experts" that the economy drives the stock market? It's often emphasized that when the economy picks up, the stock market will follow (or even lead).

While this may be true in the short term, the data clearly shows it is not so in the long term. The economy and earnings can be rising even as the market falls or drifts sideways. Over time, the stock market is driven by two major factors: long-term earnings and P/E ratios. We recognize that the economy clearly affects long-term earnings. As a matter of fact, Crestmont's research demonstrates a strong relationship between earnings and nominal economic growth.

However, the most significant driver of stock market returns is the valuation embedded in the P/E ratio. Over the past century, P/E ratios have cycled from higher levels to lower levels. The range from high to low has been substantial.

Let's accept that earnings are generally growing, increasing over time. When P/E ratios are rising, the double impact of rising earnings and rising P/Es produces substantial stock market gains—secular bull markets. When earnings are rising yet P/E ratios are declining, the offsetting impact is a choppy, flat stock market with some rather large downdrafts from time to time—secular bear markets.

Does the economy matter? Yes. Does the stock market necessarily follow the economy? No. The key to knowing the longer-term direction of the market is to know the longer-term direction of the P/E ratio.

Thus, the question of the day becomes: how can we know the direction of P/E ratios?

Crestmont Research's study of secular stock market cycles shows that the wave of the P/E cycle relates to the trend in inflation. Rising inflation (which generally results in higher interest rates) adversely impacts market valuations and results in lower P/E ratios. Declining inflation (which conversely leads to lower interest rates) supports increasing P/E ratios. When deflation has occurred, despite lower interest rates, stock valuations have suffered as P/E ratios declined.

Therefore, P/E ratios improve as inflation or deflation moves toward price stability: periods of stable, low, and positive inflation. This corresponds with the tendency of investors to project the current trends (or expected trends) long into the future. If this (the expectation of the current trend to continue) were not the case, then stock market valuations would be more stable.

The empirical evidence is consistent with modern financial theories of stock market valuation. One such methodology relates to the dividend discount model and its related variations. The model asserts that the value of a stock today is equal to the price that an investor would pay to receive the future earnings and to realize a certain rate of return. As a result, the current earnings and their future growth are discounted at a specified rate of return. As interest rates decline, the discount rate declines, and a higher value results.

However, in periods of deflation, future earnings may be expected to decline. Therefore, even though interest rates and discount rates are low, higher levels of deflation further depress the expected future earnings. The result is a lower valuation and lower P/E ratio. We'll discuss this in greater financial detail in the next chapter.

Of course, a lowering inflation rate that produces lower interest rates promotes stability, which increases optimism about the future. Lowering inflation does many positive things to the valuation of stocks. But there is a limit as to how low inflation can go and still be beneficial to stock market values.

The Opportunity for Current Graduates

When investing, there are always three potential outcomes: win, lose, or tie. The challenge is deciding the expected probability for each outcome and adjusting your investments accordingly. Just as a gambler who bets everything on one roll of the dice will soon go home with empty pockets, an investor who goes against the odds is likely to end up poorer.

Therein lies the definition of risk: What is the probability of a loss? The can of gasoline in the garage or a frayed wire are not risks but are considered hazards. Your insurance company is concerned about the probability of the hazards in your house creating a situation where it has to pay for a loss.

Without the possibility of a loss, arguably there is no risk. If there is no possibility of loss, you would not buy insurance. If a loss is certain, it's no longer a risk but rather a problem. In such situations, insurance cannot be purchased.

What does the current situation tell us about the economic hazards and risk in today's stock market?

Currently, inflation is near levels of price stability. There are three potential scenarios: It can be expected to rise, to fall, or to remain constant over the next decade or two. History suggests that if inflation rises or if it falls into deflation, P/Es will fall and thus stock market returns will be disappointing, perhaps significantly so if you are expecting 9 percent compound growth in order to retire in 10 years.

If inflation remains constant at near 1 to 2 percent levels for a decade, it will make unprecedented history. Look at Table 5.6 again. See if you can find a period of stable, low inflation. (Actually, don't waste your time.)

Even if inflation remained constant at current levels, the expected return from stocks over the next decade given the current P/E valuation levels would be dismal.

If history once again repeats itself, the cycles will lead to a lackluster period of a decade or two, then a period of solid and consistent gains. Oh, to be young again! The graduating classes of today will be matriculating into investment adulthood near the expected start of the next secular bull market. In the meanwhile, many will wrestle and struggle with hopeful periods followed by great disappointment.

During these periods, the traditional sources of investment information will tout the next wave of hope. It will be useful to keep in mind their built-in biases. If the weather reports were being generated by sunglass manufacturers, would you not be wise to be at least a bit skeptical?

Financial Physics: Interconnected Relationships

6

On December 31, 2002, the S&P 500 Index was down 42 percent from its closing high of 1,527.46 on March 24, 2000; the "new economy"–dominated NASDAQ was down 74 percent from its pinnacle close of 5,048.62 on March 10, 2000. For many, the 33 months from the summit seemed to be an eternity. Most investment advisors and investors had only the experience of the past 20-year bull market to influence their perspectives.

In 2003, the market's plunge reversed and by year-end had risen 26 percent for the S&P 500 index and a dramatic 50 percent for the NAS-DAQ Composite. Market pundits are asking if this is the start of the next major bull market.

If you spin around a few times with your eyes closed, your sense of orientation becomes dislocated and disrupted. You quickly seek a point of reference to reset your internal compass. The stock market registered quite an ascent during the 1980s and 1990s, yet retreated significantly for the three years from 2000 through 2002.

Which "bear market bed" have we fallen into—too hard and too far, too soft and not far enough, or just about right?

A + B = C: It's All Connected

One of the reasons that you're reading this book is to gain insight into the expected direction of the stock market. Another is to further understand secular markets and the implications for the next decade or more. In previous chapters, a number of technical factors were described that made the case for a prolonged period of a mundane stock market. Chapter 5 presented a series of analytics and patterns that identified and quantified secular bull and secular bear cycles. In addition to furthering an understanding of the interconnected market and economy-related relationships, we develop a fundamental thesis that this secular bear market will continue for some time. This chapter, like Chapter 5, is co-authored with Ed Easterling, president of Crestmont Holdings, LLC.

What we want to do is explain the connection between the economy and the stock market. You're often told that because the economy is growing, the stock market should be rising. We have seen how that is not always the case but there is still a connection between the fundamentals of the economy and the markets. We first define some statistical concepts, and then show the relationships between them. Now, let's dig into the research that Crestmont has developed and collectively calls "financial physics."

Predicting Earnings

Earnings come from revenues. They are the money left after subtracting all of the costs of doing business. Since earnings result from revenues, and gross domestic product (GDP) reflects a broad measure of overall U.S. revenues, we can use GDP as a surrogate for revenues and then see if we can develop a predicted earnings per share (EPS) based on its historical relationship to GDP.

Real GDP (GDP-R) reflects the growth in the economy excluding the effects of inflation (or deflation during certain periods in the preceding century). As reflected in Table 6.1, GDP-R has grown relatively consistently across the decades of the past century at near 3 percent annually. Though the business cycle will give us periods of above-average growth as well as recession, the historical record across a wide variety of economic, political, and international conditions appears to be relatively consistent over longer periods. Without a reason to doubt the general continuation of the trend, we can reasonably assume that over multiple years economic growth should continue in line with history.

The economy also can be measured in nominal terms, including the effects of inflation. As a matter of fact, the revenues of companies, the wages of employees, and the net profits are all measured in nominal dollars. If there is 2 percent inflation and 3 percent more units are sold, then the nominal growth in the economy will be roughly 5 percent. This is known as nominal GDP (GDP-N). The real growth (GDP-R) was 3 percent, excluding inflation.

Since inflation raises the tide and affects all line items on the income statement (i.e., revenues, costs, and profits), we assess EPS growth in relation to GDP-N. As would be fundamentally expected since profits emanate from revenues, this relationship has been quite consistent over time. As shown in Table 6.2, EPS growth has been slightly less than GDP-N growth.

Table 6.1 Economic Growth Has Been Fairly Constant; Inflation Has Been Variable

By Decade	GDP Nominal	GDP Real	GDP Inflation
1900s	5.4%	4.1%	1.4%
1910s	10.4%	3.0%	7.4%
1920s	3.4%	3.6%	−0.2%
1930s	−0.3%	1.3%	−1.6%
1940s	11.7%	6.0%	5.7%
1950s	6.7%	4.2%	2.5%
1960s	6.9%	4.4%	2.5%
1970s	10.1%	3.3%	6.8%
1980s	7.9%	3.0%	4.9%
1990s	5.4%	3.0%	2.4%
2000s	4.0%	2.1%	1.9%
Average	6.7%	3.5%	3.1%

Note: The average represents the simple annual average from 1900 to 2002. Copyright 2003, Crestmont Research (www.Crestmont Research.com).

Table 6.2 Earnings per Share (S&P 500) Has a Strong Relationship to Economic Growth

By Decade	GDP Nominal	EPS Growth
1900s	5.4%	5.5%
1910s	10.4%	6.2%
1920s	3.4%	7.7%
1930s	−0.3%	−2.1%
1940s	11.7%	13.7%
1950s	6.7%	3.8%
1960s	6.9%	6.1%
1970s	10.1%	9.7%
1980s	7.9%	6.5%
1990s	5.4%	6.7%
2000s	4.0%	−11.2%
Average	6.7%	5.9%

Note: The average represents the simple annual average from 1900 to 2002. Copyright 2003, Crestmont Research (www.Crestmont Research.com).

There are several factors that contribute to this, including the formation of businesses in the economy beyond the largest, publicly traded companies and the generally higher growth rate of the smaller, entrepreneurial companies in the economy.

Therefore, to determine the first of our variables—EPS—we need an estimate for nominal economic growth (GDP-N). If we can somehow know (or guess) GDP-N, we can extrapolate a value for EPS based on the long-term, consistent fundamental relationship between the two variables. Extrapolation is a quantitative technique of predicting a series of numbers based on their relationship to another known series. For example, if children's ages and their heights are closely related, a doctor could estimate future height at various ages based on knowing the age and height history of the child.

To determine economic growth including inflation (GDP-N), we need to know what real growth (GDP-R) will be plus we need to know what inflation will be. Since GDP-R has been so consistent over time at near 3 percent, that's probably a reasonable assumption for real economic growth into the longer-term future. With an estimate for inflation, we'll be able to estimate (extrapolate) a forecast for EPS. We'll return to this shortly.

For the second or last variable in our market valuation equation—the P/E ratio—conventional wisdom asserts that there is a fundamental relationship between interest rates and P/E ratios. Since modern investment theories are based on discounting future earnings at an appropriate rate of return, the valuation multiple increases as interest rates decrease. Just as a bond appreciates when interest rates decline (due to the lower discount rate on the same interest payment stream), stocks should (and tend to) reflect higher values (higher P/E ratios) as interest rates decrease.

In the past 50 years, the financial markets have known only inflation and could hardly conceive of deflation in well-managed economies. For much of that period, the Fed has sought to slay the inflation dragon—ever mindful in its monetary policy that inflation has seemed to be a one-way force. Like gravity or the accelerator of a car, the laws of economic nature seemed only to know acceleration. The Fed's tool kit included techniques of restraint, brakes on inflation.

Deflation is a broad-based decline in general prices over time that results from a decrease in the quantity of money in relation to the available goods. It generally is known to occur when there is a general money supply contraction. Deflation can often occur following a period of excess supply or capacity beyond demand with a pervasive psychology of delayed spending or due to economy-wide debt reduction (or debt destruction). This digression onto deflation is important because the laws of financial gravity pull in an opposite direction once an economy crosses the threshold of zero.

It might be helpful to think of this in terms of the effects on water as the temperature approaches freezing or boiling. Things that were considered normal (water) become something altogether different (ice or steam) as the temperature reaches certain thresholds. Another way might be in terms of the laws of quantum physics as the temperature approaches absolute zero. The laws of physics, which seemed immutable, suddenly change, and atomic particles start to do very strange things.

Inflation, and its "Mr. Hyde" counterpart deflation, generally trend in one direction or another until changed by intervention or natural forces in an economy. Inflation and deflation metaphorically are similar to fire: It either burns stronger or burns out. Without assistance (more fuel), a fire does not burn in a steady state. The tools to control a raging fire are quite different than those needed to stoke a flame. The Fed has a well-developed set of controls to slow down the fire of inflation, yet fewer options to fan the flames.

The Fed's primary tool to reduce the spread of inflation is to reduce the supply of money, generally by making money more expensive. One way that the Fed can discourage money growth is to raise interest rates. To stimulate the economy, the Fed eases off of the brake and allows the money supply to grow. This is often accomplished by lowering interest rates to stimulate the demand for (and supply of) money. However, since investors, consumers, and businesses can step aside when interest rates get to zero by staying in cash, interest rates generally cannot go negative.

As a result, near the point of the inflation/deflation threshold, interest rates stop working to control money growth. Beyond lower interest rates, the impact of deflation on an economy can be debilitating. As demand slows, production declines, unemployment increases, monetary velocity decreases, and a general malaise overtakes the economy. Deflation does not need to cause a depression, though it does create a drag on the economy. As a result, earnings suffer and the future outlook is less certain with little control available to the Fed to restore the economy to a more healthy state.

Furthermore, the market does not receive the benefit of a continuously increasing P/E ratio as interest rates further decline while inflation nears zero. As the prospect of the cliff nears, valuations begin to suffer. Once the day turns to night and the deflation goblins are running amock, P/Es start falling like a boat anchor toward levels generally reached in periods of high inflation and interest rates.

The dynamic that Crestmont Research has named the "Y Curve Effect" is plotted in Figure 6.1. The chart is a scatter plot showing the relationship between P/E ratios and inflation. (It looks like a Y on its side.)

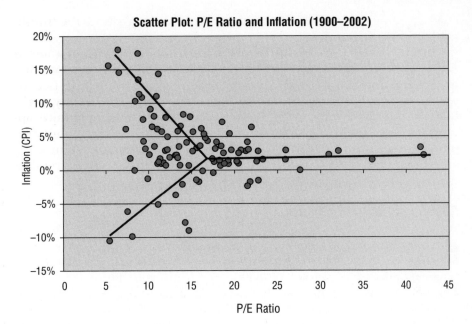

Figure 6.1 The Y Curve Effect
Copyright 2003, Crestmont Research (www.CrestmontResearch.com).

As inflation moves toward high positive or significant negative levels, P/E ratios are predominantly depressed. In other words, as prices move away from price stability (the fork in the Y), P/E ratios decline. As inflation or deflation trends back toward a condition of relative price stability, near 1 percent inflation, P/E ratios expand.

Again bear in mind: An environment of deflation will present very low interest rates—yet the low interest rates will not produce high P/E ratios. There will be a point as the economy is sliding into deflation that interest rates will continue falling, yet P/E ratios, as if they sense the inevitable, will begin to fall as well.

The Y Curve Effect is consistent with modern financial principles relating to stock market valuation, specifically the dividend discount model and its variations. The model asserts that the value of a stock today is equal to the price that an investor would pay to receive the future earnings and to realize a certain rate of return. As a result, the current earnings and future growth are discounted at a specified rate of return. As interest rates decline, the discount rate declines, and a higher value results.

That being said, however, in periods of deflation, future earnings may be expected to decline. Therefore, even though interest rates and discount rates are low, higher levels of deflation depress the expected future earnings. This gets discounted into the price and the result is a lower valuation and lower P/E ratio. As depicted by the scatter plot diagram in Figure 6.1, the Y Curve Effect does not indicate a specific level at which the impact of deflation overtakes the impact of lower interest rates on the P/E ratio. Nonetheless, this is a powerful, counterintuitive force to consider in low interest rate and potential deflationary environments.

Applying Financial Physics

Financial physics, as depicted in Figure 6.2, is Crestmont's term to explain the longer-term and interconnected relationship between the economy and stock market returns. Let's begin with the end in mind. The objective is to determine the fair value of the stock market. The two components that we've discussed—EPS and P/E ratio—are the two variables that we'll need to calculate the value of the market.

The graphic presents a starting point with GDP-R. Real economic growth is considered to be relatively consistent over time since the economic history across many decades has delivered fairly stable real growth. GDP-N is driven by the addition of inflation to GDP-R. As we have discussed earlier, GDP-N drives EPS.

For now, to determine the appropriate (and approximate) fair value P/E ratio, let's adopt the conventional position that interest rates drive P/Es. Likewise, the graphic shows interest rates being driven by inflation. As a result, we can graphically depict the interconnected relationship among the variables.

Though most believe that interest rates play an important role in the relationship, we have discussed previously that interest rates are a simplifying explanation to a more accurate depiction of inflation as the critical variable. This distinction has largely been irrelevant over the past 50 years or more since the economy has only known inflation.

With the prospects of deflation potentially on the horizon, this distinction is now more relevant. Regardless of whether deflation actually occurs, a student of the markets would nonetheless be better served to understand the true culprit (inflation) rather than to focus on the related by-product (interest rates). This is especially true given the disconnected relationship between interest rates and inflation prior to the mid-1960s. As depicted in Table 6.3, the relationship of inflation and interest rates becomes consistent during the 1960s. Prior to that time, inter-

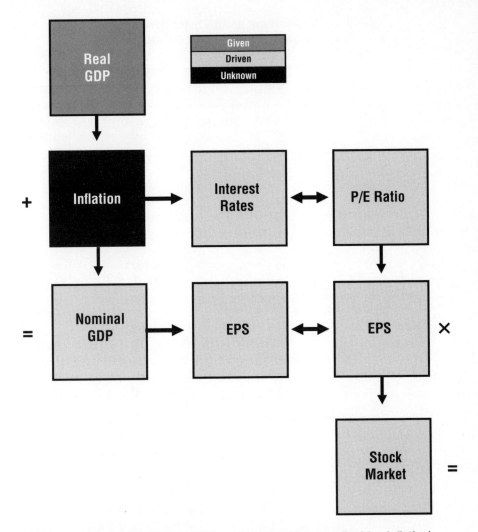

Figure 6.2   Financial Physics: Traditional Thinking (Assumes Positive Inflation)
Copyright 2003, Crestmont Research (www.CrestmontResearch.com).

est rates were relatively stable during periods of wide fluctuations across inflation and deflation. Since that disconnect is unlikely (in our opinion) in the future due to modern financial markets, interest rates could be an acceptable surrogate—except for conditions of deflation. Though inflation can fall below zero and become deflation, interest rates will remain above the surface (or at a minimum fall to zero).

Table 6.3   P/E Ratios and Interest Rates Have a Mixed Relationship before the 1960s . . . As Do Interest Rates and Inflation

By Decade	E/P Ratio	20-Year Bonds	Spread
1900s	5.8%	3.2%	2.6%
1910s	9.8%	3.8%	6.0%
1920s	10.8%	4.2%	6.6%
1930s	7.3%	3.1%	4.2%
1940s	8.7%	2.2%	6.5%
1950s	7.1%	3.0%	4.1%
1960s	4.9%	4.6%	0.2%
1970s	8.3%	7.5%	0.8%
1980s	9.4%	10.5%	−1.1%
1990s	4.3%	6.9%	−2.6%
2000s	3.1%	5.8%	−2.6%
Average	7.5%	4.9%	2.2%

Note: The average represents the simple annual average from 1900 to 2002.

By Decade	20-Year Bonds	GDP Inflation	Spread
1900s	3.2%	1.4%	1.8%
1910s	3.8%	7.4%	−3.6%
1920s	4.2%	−0.2%	4.4%
1930s	3.1%	−1.6%	4.7%
1940s	2.2%	5.7%	−3.6%
1950s	3.0%	2.5%	0.5%
1960s	4.6%	2.5%	2.2%
1970s	7.5%	6.8%	0.7%
1980s	10.5%	4.9%	5.6%
1990s	6.9%	2.4%	4.5%
2000s	5.8%	1.9%	3.9%
Average	4.9%	3.1%	1.9%

Note: The average represents the simple annual average from 1900 to 2002. Copyright 2003, Crestmont Research (www.Crestmont Research.com).

Once the economy has fallen through Alice's "looking glass" into deflation, the laws of financial nature will be in Wonderland. As we have previously discussed, in periods of deflation, future earnings may be expected to decline. Therefore, even though interest rates and discount rates are low, higher levels of deflation further depress the expected future earnings.

As a result, we can eliminate the link to interest rates, and the result is depicted in Figure 6.3. Since GDP-R has been so consistent over time, we consider it the relatively stable factor in the equation. When the interconnected relationships are considered, inflation is clearly our pivot factor in projecting fair value P/E ratios for stocks.

What Does It Mean?

For the past two chapters, we've considered statistical, cyclical, and fundamental reasons that stock market returns are likely to be less than av-

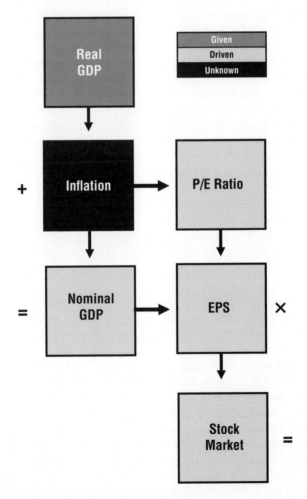

Figure 6.3   Financial Physics: Model for All Environments
Copyright 2003, Crestmont Research (www.CrestmontResearch.com).

erage over the next decade or more. However, a sharper near-term retreat could hasten the next cycle. The confluence of factors that produced the historic secular bull market of the 1980s and 1990s is now
positioned to leave few options for consistent near-term returns.

**What we are saying is that P/E ratios are going lower—potentially
much lower than current ratios.** This can happen by either the market
moving sideways for a long period of time as earnings growth catches up
or a drop in prices to where P/E ratios are consistent with a secular bear
market cycle bottom.

If inflation returns and interest rates rise, P/E ratios will trend downward. If deflation takes hold and economic malaise results, P/E ratios will
also tend downward. Even if inflation and interest rates remain low and
stable, the growth rate in the economy and earnings is likely to be below
average, as we remain in the Muddle Through Economy for an extended
period of time. This would mean that the market could move sideways for
a considerable period of time waiting for earnings to catch up.

In each of these instances, especially given the existing high P/E ratio
of the stock market, returns from equities can be expected to be below average or negative for many years. This is consistent with the bull and bear
secular market analysis detailed in the previous chapter. As well, the environment will be volatile and choppy, consistent with the profile of secular
bear markets.

The economic forces of nature in the market will lead to the reversion
of price from the currently overvalued level to levels that are representative of the longer-term potential of the economy. However, recognition of
the cycles and identification of the causes could lead to minimizing the
market's travels into undervalued territory and may prevent future excessive valuations.

*Crestmont has established a web site to be an interactive resource of research on
the stock market, interest rates, and other financial market topics. Any feedback or
suggested research may be provided at www.CrestmontResearch.com.*

These chapters are not intended to be a comprehensive reference on the
many subject areas discussed. But they should have provided you with an
introduction to the fundamental issues and relationships within markets
and economies, along with a series of observations that can be used by investors in their decision-making process. While some will either support
or refute the analyses with sophisticated analytical techniques, we'll only
know the historical validity of these theses in 20 to 40 years.[1]

Risky Expectations

7

The following analysis of how reasonable investor expectations are is based on a noteworthy article[1] in the *Financial Analysts Journal,* a leading journal for financial professionals, which is published by the prestigious Association for Investment Management and Research (AIMR). AIMR is a very mainstream organization of analysts and economists and is *not* prone to bearish sentiment. My friend Robert Arnott co-authored the piece with Peter Bernstein, one of the more profound financial thinkers of our times.* Arnott, in addition to being one of my favorite fund managers, has since been named the editor of the *Financial Analysts Journal.*

Many individual investors, based on the experience of the two decades of the 1980s and 1990s, assume they can achieve gains of 15 percent per year in the future. Any day now, they reason, the bull market will resume and they can once again look forward to luxurious retirement. Most major corporations assume their pension portfolios will grow 9 to 10 percent or more in the coming years. By the way, these assumptions add to their projected corporate earnings. If their pension portfolios grow at less that those rates, they will have to restate earnings downward and lower future estimates.

A drop of only a few percent in stock market growth expectations can lower future earnings estimates at many companies by as much as 10 per-

---

*Peter Bernstein also wrote an extremely readable book on the history of risk called *Against the Gods* (John Wiley & Sons, 1996) that makes the topic of risk very understandable.

cent. To me, the AIMR article says you can bank on earnings estimates to be dropped as a result of exuberant projections. (You should check to see if any of the stocks you own are in companies that are making aggressive assumptions about their pension plans.)

I once again ask a familiar question to set up the discussion in this chapter: How many times have you had a stockbroker quote the Ibbotson survey or something similar that shows the stock market growing 6.7 percent or 9 percent or more per year over long periods of time? All you have to do is just keep the faith and buy and hold. You should especially never sell their funds.

Arnott and Bernstein show that this number is *very* misleading. If you break it down, it shows you something entirely different. (See Figure 7.1.)

First, the major components of stock market return have been inflation and dividends. From 1801 to 2001, $100 would have grown to $700 million if you assumed all dividends reinvested. If you take out inflation, you are left with a still impressive $37 million. If you take out dividends, however, you find that your $100 is worth only $2,099!

Here's the kicker: In 1982, the stock portfolio would have been worth only $400. The bulk of the growth, over 80 percent of current value, came in the past 20 years.

This data simply shows that conventional wisdom, which says equities

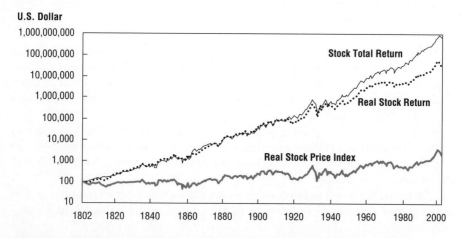

Figure 7.1   Return from Inflation and Dividends: Growth of $100, 1801–2001
Source: Robert D. Arnott and Peter L. Bernstein, "What Risk Premium Is 'Normal'?," *Financial Analysts Journal* (March/April 2002), p. 68. Copyright 2002, Association for Investment Management and Research. Reproduced and republished from *Financial Analysts Journal* with permission from the Association for Investment Management and Research. All rights reserved.

get most of their value from capital appreciation, is false; it is based on recent experience and a bubble mentality.

Risk Premiums

Bonds offer steady returns. Stocks do not. Conventional wisdom therefore says stocks should give investors a better return over time because of the extra risk associated with stocks. This difference is called a risk premium. As we have seen, the majority of stock returns have been dividends, which in the first part of the twentieth century were higher than the returns from bonds. Only in the past few decades have investors been willing to substitute growth expectations for actual dividends when they place a value on a stock.

By this I mean that today average dividends are significantly lower than the yield on a 10-year government bond. Investors today think that stocks will consistently rise in price enough to give them significantly better returns than bonds, and thus they put little premium on dividends. They believe earnings will compound in their favorite companies at 15 to 20 percent forever, thus justifying higher stock prices.

Certain very exuberant authors have stated that:

- History has shown that stocks are not riskier than bonds over the (very) long term.
- Stocks clearly give better performance than bonds.

Therefore, they say, it follows that investors will not demand a risk premium in the future, and that therefore the Dow Jones Industrial Average should rise to the point at which the return on stocks is exactly the same as that for bonds. For some authors this level is Dow 36,000, and others happily see the Dow at 100,000.

Historically, by some measures stocks have been seemingly priced to yield a risk premium of 5 percent over bonds. You can look at the returns of the past 75 years and seemingly demonstrate that fact.

But in 1926, *when you looked at actual expectations,* based on then current yields, the risk premium (that amount by which stocks were expected to outperform bonds) was only 1.4 percent. This was based on dividend yields and expected price growth. Investors in 1926 did not expect to get 5 percent over bonds over the next 75 years. They expected far less than they actually got, even considering the intervening Depression and a few serious bear markets.

But they did receive those returns. Brokers and fund managers give this as a reason for you to always stay invested in the stock market. **The**

questions one should ask are: Why (and how) did this happen? Is the out-performance by stocks over bonds likely to repeat?

Arnott and Bernstein make the case that the higher returns for stocks were due to a series of historical accidents that cannot be repeated. They argue that stocks are unlikely to outperform bonds in the future.

The first reason for the growth in stock values was a "decoupling" of yields from real yields. By that Arnott and Bernstein mean that the coming of inflation changed the way in which bonds were valued. In essence, in 1926, and for many years after that, bondholders assumed no inflation. In fact, real returns on bonds were often negative after World War II. That means inflation was higher than the yields on the bonds. Bondholders eventually began to demand more in order to compensate for the risk of inflation. This change in the way bonds were valued accounted for almost 10 percent of the increase in the risk premium from 1926 to the present.

Second, valuation multiples rose dramatically. From a level of 18 times dividends in 1926, we now see dividend multiples of over 70. This means that a dollar of dividends is valued at over four times what it was 75 years ago. However, the entire increase has happened in just the last 17 years. Not coincidentally, this was when we had a bubble. This accounts for more than one-third of the increase in the risk premium.

Third, investors in 1926 did not believe there was zero risk in living and investing in the United States. There were many citizens still living who vividly remembered the Civil War. Four of the 15 largest stock markets in the world had completely collapsed within recent memory, with many others coming close to collapsing.

The United States was not the preeminent world power it has become in the last two decades. Historical accident number three is that investors have become increasingly confident in America. This is a good thing, I think, but how likely is it that we are going to grow even more confident from where we are today? Using a rough analogy, let us say that we have grown four times more confident in the country's future over the past 75 years in terms of being confident in bonds and stocks. Is it likely we will grow another four times? Thinking back from what the world looked like in 1926, seeing where we have come, and trying to extrapolate that sense of growth in security into the future, I think it is very unlikely we will feel significantly better, and certainly not four times better, in the future than we do today.

Finally, regulatory reform has done much to increase returns in the stock market. In the early part of this century, management would routinely vote themselves more stock if a company did well, diluting current investors and keeping rates of return low. That practice changed as securities laws were introduced. This has been a very good thing, but future regulatory reform having such an effect on stock price is not likely to be repeated.

In short, the events that led to the significant increase in the value of stocks over bonds were basically one-time events and not likely to be repeated. It is very unlikely that this trend will continue. Yet that is what would have to happen if the Dow were to get to 25,000 or 36,000 or more.

If the risk premium reverts to more normal measures, then either the stock market, the bond market, or both are in for some turmoil. By that I mean that if investors start to be unsure about the future growth of stocks and start to demand actual dividends as a reason to hold a stock or to require consistent earnings growth (which studies mentioned throughout this book show is very hard to do) then it is likely the stock market has a lot more pain in its future.

Arnott and Bernstein then show that earnings and dividend growth for the past two centuries is far less than the forward earnings expectations most analysts have today. Interestingly, this study uses a different way to analyze earnings than the National Bureau of Economic Research that I cite later in Chapter 8, but both conclude that total market earnings will not grow faster than the economy.

Let's look at some of their direct conclusions. If you grasp what they are saying, you could save yourself a lot of investment grief over the coming decade.

> The historical average equity risk premium, measured relative to 10-year government bonds as the risk premium investors might objectively have expected on their equity investments, is about 2.4 percent, half what most investors believe. The "normal" risk premium might well be a notch lower than 2.4 percent because the 2.4 percent objective expectation preceded *actual* excess returns for stocks relative to bonds that were nearly 100 bps [basis points] higher, at 3.3 percent a year.
>
> The current risk premium is approximately zero, and a sensible expectation for the future real return for both stocks and bonds is 2 to 4 percent, far lower than the actuarial assumptions on which most investors are basing their planning and spending.[2]

Predicting a 50 Percent Drop

Then we come to the meat of the matter:

> On the hopeful side, because the "normal" level of the risk premium is modest (2.4 percent or quite possibly less), current market valuations need not return to levels that can deliver the 5 percent risk premium (excess return) that the Ibbotson data would suggest. If reversion to the mean occurs, then to restore a 2 percent risk premium, the difference

between 2 percent and zero still requires a near halving of stock valuations or a 2 percent drop in real bond yields (or some combination of the two). Either scenario is a less daunting picture than would be required to facilitate a reversion to a 5 percent risk premium.

Another possibility is that the modest difference between a 2.4 percent normal risk premium and the negative risk premiums that have prevailed in recent quarters permitted the recent bubble. Reversion to the mean might not ever happen, in which case we should see stocks sputter along delivering bondlike returns, but at a higher risk than bonds, for a long time to come.[3]

They then conclude,

The consensus that a normal risk premium is about 5 percent was shaped by deeply rooted naïveté in the investment community, where most participants have a career span reaching no farther back than the monumental 25-year bull market of 1975–1999. This kind of mind-set is a mirror image of the attitudes of the chronically bearish veterans of the 1930s. Today, investors are loath to recall that the real total returns on stocks were negative for most 10-year spans during the two decades from 1963 to 1983 or that the excess return of stocks relative to long bonds was negative as recently as the 10 years ended August 1993.

When reminded of such experiences, today's investors tend to retreat behind the mantra "things will be different this time." No one can kneel before the notion of the long run and at the same time deny that such circumstances will occur in the decades ahead. Indeed, such crises are more likely than most of us would like to believe. Investors greedy enough or naive enough to expect a 5 percent risk premium and to substantially overweight equities accordingly may well be doomed to deep disappointments in the future as the realized risk premium falls far below this inflated expectation.[4]

"Hopeful" Outcomes

I smiled when I read their concept of "the hopeful side." It gives a new meaning to the word "hopeful." Their view of hopeful is only a 50 percent drop in the stock market or a dropping of long-term rates to levels which imply outright and serious deflation. Or we would see a Muddle Through Market, with stocks going sideways for many years.

Plausible Expectations: A Realistic Appraisal of the Prospects for Earnings Growth

8

Following Benjamin Graham's teachings, Charlie [Munger] and I let our marketable equities tell us by their operating results—not by their daily, or even yearly, price quotations—whether our investments are successful. The market may ignore business success for a while, but eventually will confirm it.

As Ben said: "In the short run, the market is a voting machine but in the long run it is a weighing machine."

The speed at which a business's success is recognized, furthermore, is not that important as long as the company's intrinsic value is increasing at a satisfactory rate.

—Warren Buffett[1]

What the market weighs in the long run is earnings: old-fashioned in-your-pocket earnings. Secular bear markets are part of the long run and, as we have seen, can be very frustrating for buy-and-hold investors. Earnings matter more and more as the bear market cycle drags on.

Earlier chapters have made the case that we should look at a secular bear market not just as a decline in stock prices, but as a declining price-to-earnings ratio. The ratio declines as investors increasingly become more conservative in their view of earnings and more skeptical in their optimism about the future. The balancing factor is that earnings will grow over time as well, so that over time (a long time) earnings become "cheap" and a new bull market begins.

The news is not all bad. There are very sound reasons to think that earnings for U.S. business in general will double (or more) over the next

20 years and considerably more so for some sectors. The bad news is that this is nowhere close to what most analysts are now predicting.

The Glass Ceiling

Think of earnings like a glass ceiling. It is hard to see, but it is definitely there. In bull market cycles, these ceilings are shattered as investor concerns about future earnings decrease and optimism increases. In bear market cycles, the market continually bumps up against this barrier to growth, and no amount of cheerleading can remove that barrier.

Thus the key for growth in stock market prices in the future is the quality and quantity of earnings. The higher that both the level of earnings and the growth in earnings are, the less the stock market will fall over time and the sooner the next bull market can begin.

This chapter is critical for your understanding of my belief that the current secular bear market could last for another decade or longer. We are going to look at several very real pressures on companies that will slow the growth in earnings, and then we will look at two major studies that show us how fast we can expect real earnings to grow.

The first step is to decide how we are going to measure earnings. The market would like you to look at "pro forma" earnings. Some call this standard "earnings before bad stuff." I like to call it "earnings before interest and hype." Some suggest you look at EBITDA earnings as a type of pro forma earnings: earnings before interest, taxes, depreciation, and amortization, as if those are somehow not real financial events. Either way, this lets companies report earnings to the public and exclude certain items that actually show up on their tax returns.

The second category is reported earnings, which are earnings as reported to the Internal Revenue Service (IRS) (which deduct employee stock options expense, by the way).

The third category is "core earnings," which Standard & Poor's, among others, is starting to use. S&P announced in 2002 that it intended to start reporting earnings using this new standard, which deals with options expense and pension liabilities, in advance of it being adopted by the accounting industry.

I believe that in the future the new standard for earnings will be the S&P core earnings standard. "Not fair," say the bulls. "To get true historical comparisons, you have to compare apples to apples. The new standards distort the actual profitability of a company and give us no fair historical comparison."

To that, I politely say bunk. Pre-1990, and especially if you go past 1975, pension benefits did not have nearly the impact that they do today, as there was not that much overfunding, and estimates of future earnings on pension fund holdings were far more conservative. Looking at data prior to 1990, there was little difference between pro forma and reported earnings. It is only in the 1990s, the decade of financial engineering, when a CEO could create a 10 percent rise in his company earnings just by changing the assumptions of his company pension fund, that these elusive pension fund earnings started to show up in the profits in a significant way.

Of course, that helped the CEO's personal options, which again the company did not have to expense. Stock options were not a big deal prior to 1980 and not all that significant even until 1990. Prior to those years, after-tax or reported earnings were essentially core earnings.

Accounting standards always tighten up in bear markets. Investors become more conservative. They are not willing to project earnings growth far into the future. That is why the market drops. We will discuss pensions and stock options later in this chapter, but for now, let's look at recent earnings history and see if reality matches expectations.

Earnings Deflation

In the third quarter of 2002, S&P released its study of earnings for the S&P 500 for the four quarters ending in June 2002. Instead of the pro forma $44.93 that Thomson First Call reported, S&P said actual reported earnings were $26.74 a share. (Thomson First Call estimates come from Wall Street analysts. Despite investigations and being clearly shown to be wrong so often, most are still clueless and still shameless cheerleaders.)

Earnings were $26.74, that is, until S&P deducted option expenses and pension liabilities from the companies in their own index, and that dropped earnings to $18.48 a share. Over one year later, subsequent revisions have dropped core earnings to $17.79 per share for that period. Depending on what date you chose in the fourth quarter of 2002, this was a price-to-earnings (P/E) ratio of well over 45 on the S&P 500. That was clearly still stock market bubble territory.

Did things get better in 2003? Yes, undeniably better. Core earnings went up almost 80 percent from the bottom of 2002. Pro forma earnings growth over the same period was up over 18 percent (from $46 to $54), and reported earnings (after tax) were up 63 percent to $45.12.

Whichever earnings standard you prefer to use, earnings jumped significantly in the 18 months since the end of the recession. Investors are once again excited about the market, projecting strong earnings growth well into the future. At the end of 1999, the P/E ratio was 36.81 (on a core earnings basis). At the beginning of 2004, we find investors once again pricing the market close to 27.

And why not? Earnings growth is clearly back. Given the recent growth, it is not hard for many investors to think earnings can once again grow at 15 percent a year, which will mean they double in under five years. The economy is sailing at full speed. Inflation and interest rates are low. The Fed has clearly told us it intends to keep rates low for some time. What more can an investor want? The bull is back.

However, if you look at the numbers for periods longer than 18 months, you find that earnings growth evaporates. I decided to see what earnings actually grew during the bull market. I must confess that the following facts surprised me when I first pulled them from the spreadsheets. I truly expected earnings to grow by around inflation plus gross domestic product (GDP), which as I show, is slightly higher than the historical average. We have, after all, been through a great period of economic growth. I was wrong.

The reported earnings per share number for the 12 months ending in September 2003 was $37.02. (Final 2003 earnings are still estimates as of this writing, but would change the numbers I present by only small amounts.) For the 12 months of 1996 it was $38.73. For the next almost seven years since 1996, per share earnings have managed to slump almost 4 percent. Inflation was 13.7 percent for that period. In inflation-adjusted terms, per share earnings dropped almost 19 percent. That means the dollar in per share earnings that you received in 1996 has lost significant buying value in just seven years.

At the end of 1996, the S&P 500 index was at a then all-time high of 740.

Pro forma earnings rose over 20 percent, though, which simply means that companies choose to tell investors that most of their earnings difficulties are one-time events and that you should ignore them. Next year, we are promised, we won't have different one-time event problems.

Core earnings did manage to rise 3 percent over those seven years. Not per year, mind you, but total. This is a compound growth rate of less than 0.5 percent per year, which is well south of 15 percent.

I have a small confession. I have a second love, and one that my wife is well aware of. I love numbers. I am one of those guys who count the number of tiles in the ceiling, who looks for relationships between all sorts of various and sundry statistics; and I really, really love to look at tables. Things seem to jump off the page when you look at historical tables.

Some of my favorite tables are the earnings tables for the S&P 500 at www.standardandpoors.com. (*Note:* You will have to navigate a little bit, but you can eventually find them, or you can type in: www2.standardand

poors.com/spf/xls/index/SP500EPSEST.XLS?GXHC_gx_session_id_=5
350992f205e73e4&.)

The data in these tables on the S&P earnings goes back only to 1988.
But it becomes quite instructive. Remember that 1988 was the first year
after the 1987 crash, and the beginning of a rather huge bull run.

Operating earnings for 1988 were $23.75. The S&P ended the year at
277. Thus, in 15 years the earnings grew by 56 percent or very close to 3
percent per year. (See Table 8.1.)

Inflation from 1988 through the end of 2002 was 52 percent. What cost
$100 in 1988 would cost $152.01 in 2002. If earnings only kept up with inflation, they would grow from the $23.75 in 1988 to $36.10 in 2003. That
means that earnings barely kept up with inflation, growing less than $1
($.92) in real, inflation-adjusted terms in 15 years! That is a total growth
of less than 4 percent, and clearly a real compounded growth of less than
0.5 percent.

Thus, over 96 percent of the earnings growth in the S&P 500 for the
past 15 years was simply due to inflation!

Mind you, this period included the economic miracle period of
the 1990s, the scene of the largest boom and financial bubble in history. The U.S. GDP grew from $5.3 billion to over $10.8 billion. Inflation accounted for much of that growth. If the U.S. economy grew only
at the rate of inflation, it would be roughly $8 billion today. So slightly
more than half the growth of the economy over the past 15 years has
been "real."

The earnings on the S&P 500 failed to grow anywhere close to inflation
plus GDP.

The price of the S&P 500 was 277 at the end of 1988. If it had only kept
up with inflation, it would be around 421 or so at the end of 2003. Yet it
has actually risen about 2.5 times that amount, even after the bear market
corrected some of the bubble excesses. The P/E at the end of 1988 was
11.69. As noted earlier, in February 2004 it was 27.

Running the numbers, we find that almost 80 percent of the rise in the
value of the S&P has been due solely to increasing valuations. Investors

Table 8.1   Earnings, Inflation, and the S&P 500

	% Change 1988–2003	Implied Value S&P 500
Earnings	56%	432
Inflation	52%	421
S&P 500	360%	996*

*Actual value September 30, 2003.

are willing to pay a great deal more for a dollar of earnings in 2003 than they did in 1988. Presumably they do so because they expect those earnings to grow faster than they have in the preceding 15 years.

April Fools Investing

If you go to www.decisionpoint.com (one of my favorite services), you can see in one of the many hundreds of charts available that if the P/E ratio for the S&P 500 were 15, about average for the preceding century, the market would have been at 420 on April Fools' Day of 2003. Keeping in mind that markets have always overcorrected, generally to below single-digit P/E ratios, if the P/E went to 10 the S&P 500 would fall to 280, down 68 percent or so from where it was. That is pretty ugly.

Given future earnings estimates, if the S&P were to return to its historical P/E average, the number for April Fools' Day 2004 should be up to the area of 750, as earnings are rebounding off their depressed lows since the last recession in 2001. Remember, history teaches us that stock valuations always and eventually regress significantly back below their averages.

I believe we are going to single-digit P/E ratios. I also believe it will take a decade or more, just as it did in the 1970s and in past secular bear markets. During that time, earnings will grow and probably double or more (without having to be too optimistic). What happens in secular bears is that earnings grow and P/E ratios drop. But it does not happen all at once. It takes time.

We can be thankful for that, because if the markets were to drop 68 percent today, we would be facing a depression as severe as our grandparents faced. It would be ugly, ugly, ugly. Thus, in a kind of perverted logic, we should thank market cheerleaders, as they prop up the economy and stave off a disaster scenario. But as individuals, we don't have to listen to them.

The hope of a return to a bull market and a comfortable retirement is why bear markets take years to finally end, and not months. It will take at least two more recessions before investors finally give in and we see the bottom of this one. And for that we should be grateful. If the Dow went to 4,000 next week, we would be in for a severe recession or even a depression very quickly. Because things will drag out for years, we will "enjoy" milder recessions and a Muddle Through Decade. Because you understand what is happening, you can adjust your portfolio accordingly, and do quite well in the meantime. But I feel sorry for those other guys.

No bull market has ever started from such high valuation levels. It is at the core of why I think the recent rise in the market is a bear market rally—a "sucker rally" as Jeremy Grantham puts it. It will be until we see a rise in real earnings.

Now, if you agree to not shoot the messenger, let's slice and dice the S&P numbers and see if we can get a sense for what is coming in the future. First, this is not a debate about whether we should deduct stock option expenses. It is highly likely that it is going to happen, so as investors we need to deal with reality. It is also likely that the way in which corporations account for their pension fund liabilities will be changed as well, and this is going to increase the downward pressure on profits for a significant number of the companies on the stock market. For investors who invest in index funds, this is going to be a real problem. Index funds, and their weak sister mutual fund associates, especially those that invest in large companies, are going to be seen as dog meat at the end of this decade.

How Hidden Options Expenses Will Actually Affect Earnings

The large indexes like the NASDAQ and the S&P 500 are populated with the largest technology companies in the investing world. These technology companies are going to have to start expensing their stock options or paying their employees more, while fighting a tough competitive environment.

A Bear Stearns 2002 report[2] suggests that the aggregate operating income for the S&P 500 drops by 12 percent for 2001 when adjusted for the fair value of employee stock options. 12 percent doesn't seem like that big a deal. It's not until you slice and dice the numbers a little differently that some rather grim statistics emerge.

(Some will argue that 2001 was ancient history—that things are different now. As we will see, they are not so different at all. The more things change, the more they stay the same.)

I was curious as to what effect the expensing of options would have on the NASDAQ in particular. The NASDAQ is heavily weighted with companies that liberally use stock options. The S&P 500 is mainly populated by far more conservative companies. In fact, the bulk of the options expenses in the Bear, Stearns study come from a small percentage of the companies in the S&P 500, so the effect on those firms will be far more pronounced. By and large, these are also the largest NASDAQ companies.

We did a simple spreadsheet. We analyzed the 15 largest NASDAQ companies, which represent about 37 percent, give or take, of the $2 trillion NASDAQ index (in the summer of 2002). We input their 2001 pro forma profits, their real profits, and the fair value of the options expense, and then let the computer tell us what effect this would have on their price to earnings ratio.[3]

(Please note that my results are approximations and not exact, as different firms use different calendar years, may expense items differently, or may have had a particularly bad 2001. Further, we are comparing August 2002 share prices to 2001 earnings. However, the principle is still the same, and the problems are ongoing and not diminished, as the market is up substantially as I write this.)

As an example, Microsoft had pro forma (operating) earnings of $11 billion, and real bottom-line earnings of $7.3 billion. The company also had $3.3 billion of options expenses. At today's price, it has a P/E of 34. Options expenses reduced its income by 46 percent. This would increase the P/E to 63, based on 2001 earnings.

For the group of 15 firms, total 2001 pro forma earnings added up to $25 billion. Real earnings were about half, or $13 billion. But total options expenses for the 15 firms were $12.5 billion. That means pro forma income was cut in half, and real, honest-to-Pete profits were a mere $423 million, give or take a few million.

Earnings before Interest and Hype

These 15 firms have a total market capitalization of roughly $750 billion (the total value of their stock). That means the combined P/E ratio, based on 2001 earnings (which deduct options expenses) and using the stock prices in August 2002, is a little north of 1,789!

I should note the effect of Comcast Corporation and Cisco Systems. If you take away their $4.8 billion losses (after options expenses), the P/E after options expenses is a far more "reasonable" 142.

I should also note that if you take away only Microsoft, the combined earnings of the remaining 14 are a *negative* $3.5 billion. That means 14 of the largest NASDAQ firms could not combine to make a profit, if you deduct the expenses of their options. Seven of these firms had negative earnings once options were deducted.

Now, let's think through a few implications of these numbers.

First, there are clearly many large companies selling product at a loss if you consider stock options as an expense. Since it is likely that the accounting industry will soon require firms to deduct options expenses, this is going to seriously impact corporate strategy. It also calls into question their entire operational premise.

As a CEO, you cannot realistically expect your stock price to rise if you cannot show profits. That means you are going to have to cut costs, raise product prices, or stop giving options. If you have been using stock options as a substantial part of employee compensation, you are in a bind. You are not going to have happy employees if their total compensation goes down.

How much more can firms cut costs than they already have done? In a market with too much production capacity and heavy competition, how much can a firm raise prices?

For some firms, it will simply mean that profits are going to drop to a new level. It certainly means earnings are going to be under severe pressure for firms that have been liberal with stock options, unless they stop the practice.

Second, much of the misery in the above numbers is past history, and these companies are returning to profitability. But in the era of new accounting and a Muddle Through Economy, profit growth is going to be much slower. That means over time that investors will assign these former market darlings much lower earnings multiples, and that means lower share prices. (The current rally notwithstanding!)

Third, these are large companies. Large companies cannot compound earnings at 15 to 20 percent for any length of time. As we will see in a few pages, it is just not possible. At 15 percent, that means a company's earnings would have to double every five years. It is difficult to keep creating billion-dollar revenue streams. Growth in large companies follows a natural evolution and simply slows down. Slower growth eventually means lower multiples.

Finally, at the end of the day, why is a large high-tech company valued more than a company that makes TVs or refrigerators? They both have lots of competition. They both make boxes, and they both will experience normal growth. As industries mature, profit margins fall. Ultimately, investors will lose patience and begin to assign the NASDAQ tech companies earnings multiples similar to those of the old economy companies. They will be based on actual earnings and potential for growth.

If you want to find a growth stock, look for a smaller company in an immature industry. That is not Cisco, Intel, Qualcomm, or Maxim, just to name a few.

How Far Away Is the Bottom?

One of my consistent themes for the past few years is that NASDAQ stocks are greatly overvalued compared to old economy stocks. The earlier back of the napkin study illustrates this point.

Let's say that high-tech CEOs wake up and smell the coffee. They dramatically cut back employee stock options. They get their ships in order. They make an honest $25 billion, instead of merely pro forma. That would put their stock prices today at a P/E of about 30. Is that possible? Yes, but in a slowly growing economy it is not likely.

The NASDAQ is more vulnerable than any other index. This group of 15 stocks is subject to at least a 50 percent drop from today's levels, if historical standards are applied. You do not even want to know the number if you apply bear market standards. I won't print it, as it is all conjecture anyway. Besides, if the potential for another 50 percent drop doesn't cause you to sell now, then telling you it could be worse won't make any difference.

NASDAQ Prediction

There were 5,556 companies listed on the NASDAQ in December 1996. Today there are approximately 3,600 and the number is dropping. The index is a list of survivors. When a company is delisted, it no longer is able to drag the index down. This tends to make the index appear better than what investors actually experienced. It is called survivor bias.

Over $4 trillion of market value has disappeared from the NASDAQ alone since March 2000.

Investors are going to start asking about dividends and dependability. That is going to make a lot of boring old companies look good again. A lot of those companies are in the S&P 500. Even though that index will suffer as we progress into this secular bear market, it will not drop as much as the NASDAQ.

I think the day could come when the NASDAQ index is lower than the S&P 500.

Pension Fund Woes

So much for the tech side. But what about the old-line companies of America? What about General Motors, Delta Airlines, and John Deere? They have been beaten down so much, aren't they full of value yet?

Well, not exactly. We now come to unfunded pension liability. Is this old news, already discounted by the market, or is there more than meets the eye? I think it is the latter, as new data comes to light. Let's look at the implications behind the numbers.

First, there are 360 companies in the S&P 500 that have defined benefit pension plans. That means they have guaranteed their retired employees a defined income for their retirement years, *for as long as they live.* (Remember that last little tag; it will become important in a few paragraphs.)

Credit Suisse First Boston (CSFB) estimates unfunded pension liability as of 2002 for this group was $243 billion. Morgan Stanley estimates $300 billion. In 2001, companies reported a gain of $104 billion from their pension funds, when they actually saw their pension fund assets go down by $90 billion. The CSFB estimate is that companies may report pension losses of $15 billion in 2003 even though their actual losses over time will again be many times that amount. Corporations are not required to report losses under current generally accepted accounting principles (GAAP). In fact, preliminary estimates suggest unfunded pension liabilities may have grown by $100 billion, even after the 2003 rally.

But forget reporting losses. These companies are reporting gains. How do you turn a loss into a gain? You simply go to a pension fund consultant, ask the consultant to make estimates of what the earnings will be in coming years, and if the estimated earnings in the future years are more than enough to cover estimated liabilities in the future, you get to put the positive difference on your company balance sheet. If you need more earnings, you get a higher estimate. It was so easy in the 1990s.

Eric Frye of Apogee tells us of a study done on the 100 largest companies with defined benefit plans. Even though 95 of them lost money in 2001 (and again in 2002), 88 of them still estimate they are going to earn 9 percent or more on their pension fund investments in the future. Hope springs eternal.

Compound interest is the eighth wonder of the world. If you assume 9 percent returns, that means your portfolio is doubling every eight years. If you assume 9 percent returns, you can also pad your corporate earnings. You also don't have to use cash to fund a pension. It does wonders for your stock options.

Let's look at what this assumption actually does. I am going to simplify things a little for illustration purposes, but you will get the general idea.

Let's assume Company ABC is going to need $2 billion in its pension fund portfolio in eight years to meet its obligations to its retirees. At the beginning of this year it had $1 billion in its pension fund. In eight years, if the fund grows at 9 percent, it will have $2 billion. But this has been a tough year and the fund has lost $100 million, so now it has only $900 million. The pension plan is underfunded by $100 million. If the company contributes $100 million to its fund, *plus* makes up the $90 million the fund didn't make, and if from now on the fund grows at 9 percent, then things will be fine.

But what if the fund started with $1.2 billion? It is still down $100 million, but since it assumes 9 percent growth, Company ABC can actually report a profit on its books because the fund still has more than it needs, again as long as it grows by 9 percent. If the company increases the return assumptions, it can book even more phantom profits.

The key is that the company still assumes that 9 percent return for 2004 and for every year in the future. More realistic estimates are in the 6 percent range. However, if you assumed 6 percent returns, the underfunding for Company ABC would be in the $300 million range if it started with $1 billion. If it started with $1.2 billion, instead of a profit it now would have a loss of around $100 million. Under current GAAP rules, it would need to take a charge to earnings this year and start putting cash into the fund. Do you think the CEO of Company ABC is going to let his consultants tell him that 6 percent is more likely? Not on your stock options, he won't.

(I know it is far more complicated. You have to take into account how long you think your retirees are going to live, the liability may last over many decades and not eight years, and so on. The principle is the same; the actual mechanics are just far more complex.)

General Motors reported earnings of $601 million in 2001. But its pension fund lost $7 billion. What would have happened to the stock price of GM if it reported a $6.4 billion loss?

It is not just GM. AMR Corp. (American Airlines), for example, had a pension plan that was underfunded by more than $3.3 billion by the end of 2002, according to CSFB estimates, which was more than seven times the company's market capitalization in May 2003.

AMR has already paid $246 million into its fund this year, said spokeswoman Andrea Rader, who added that the underfunding should not be cause for alarm. "Like everyone, the performance of the market has hurt us, but it's a long-term issue," Rader said. "A lot of this is just temporary market fluctuations that could recover."[4]

I love American Airlines. I am a Lifetime Platinum member (2,000,000 miles), which means I have spent more than a few hours in its planes. I want American Airlines to prosper and do well, as I depend on it. But I think I might be alarmed if the company owed $3.3 billion and the stock market thought it was worth only one-seventh of that. I would be even more alarmed if the company continues to bleed red ink.

The quote by Rader is typical of quotes I have read from companies all over the country. They are all hoping the market will come back and save their bacon. They still make return assumptions that are unrealistic in a secular bear market environment. They still keep talking about the long run, but GAAP rules say the long run may come in the next few years, and then the weeping will begin.

S&P 500 companies are underfunded by a mere $246 billion, if you agree with their future return assumptions. If you take the return assumptions back to 6 percent, the problem is magnified dramatically.

Bulls will argue, "We've earned double-digit returns over the past 5, 10, 15, 20, and 25 years. It's preposterous to expect 7 percent or less, no?"

My answer is, "Not really." Quoting from a private paper by Robert Arnott:

Assuming an asset allocation mix of 70 percent equities and 30 percent bonds (yielding 6 percent), stocks would have to earn 10.7 percent to attain a 9 percent composite return. Stock returns have only four constituent parts:

1.5%   dividend yield
+2.5%   consensus for future inflation
+0.0%   P/E expansion (dare we assume more??)
+ ??   real growth in dividends and earnings

This arithmetic suggests that, to get to a 7 percent return estimate, we need a mere 3 percent real growth in dividends and earnings. We can do far better than that, no? No. Historical real growth in dividends and earnings has been 1 percent to 2 percent. To get to the 3 percent real growth in the economy, we have turned to entrepreneurial capitalism, the creation of new companies. Shareholders in today's companies don't participate in this part of GDP growth. So, even a 7 percent return for equities may be too aggressive. To get 10.7 percent from stocks, we need nearly 7 percent real growth in earnings, far faster than any economist would dare project for the economy at large, let alone for the economy net of entrepreneurial capitalism.[5]

What if pensions start getting less return in their bond portfolios? It is tough to get 5 percent today without taking some real risk. To get to a 9 percent assumption in a 5 percent bond environment, and if you have 70 percent in stocks/30 percent in bonds, that 9 percent overall return assumes you are getting almost 12 percent returns on your stock portfolio. But what if the Dow drops to 6,000 as it might during the next recession and the NASDAQ goes to 600? What if your returns are negative for the next few years?

How much are you underfunded then, as your portfolio drops another 20 percent? The number becomes mind-boggling. If each of the S&P 500 companies lowered its expected rate of return from the current average of 9.2 percent to 6.5 percent, the total cost to earnings would be $30 billion, according to CSFB. But if the Dow drops to 6,000 the number goes off the chart. Remember, the average drop in the markets is 43 percent during recessions. In later chapters, we will look at why a recession may be only a few years away.

Under federal law, if a corporate pension plan is at least 90 percent funded, the extra payments required to bring it up to 100 percent can be spread over a period of up to 30 years. But if the funding level drops below 90 percent of what the actuaries say is needed, companies may be required to refill the fund within three to five years, meaning larger annual cash payments.

Now do you see the problem? In the brave new world of increasing scrutiny of accounting firms, you are going to find them less and less willing to go along with 9 percent earning assumptions. If they use even 7 percent, companies are going to have to start lowering projections, and this is going to send them over the 10 percent underfunded threshold. That means they will have to come up with large capital infusions to their pension funds over the next five years, which come directly out of earnings. If the stock market drops more, the contributions will be larger. Accounting games will not be able to hide the true liabilities.

Earnings from 82 companies would have been cut in half if they did not use phantom pension fund profits in 2001. They were hoping for a new bull market to come to their rescue. What would happen if instead of phantom profits they have to start reporting real losses? At some point, they are going to have to eat those so-called earnings. This is going to come out in future earnings reports, as underfunding becomes more of an issue.

Does this mean those firms are going to go bankrupt, or go away? No. Most of these companies have the ability to fund their obligations out of cash flow. Many of them can do it quite easily. But it means their earnings are going to be less. In some cases, it will mean much less. The airline industry has unfunded pension liabilities of more than $12 billion. The airlines can't even make a profit, let alone fund that type of liability. And that means their stock prices, and those of firms that are in similar situations, are going to go lower. Since the 360 companies with defined benefit pension plans in the S&P 500 make up such a large part of the stock market, the indexes will suffer. It is a cap on any potential bull market for the next few years.

Let's summarize: Many corporations are in a bind. They have overstated earnings because they assume that the stock market will grow faster than is realistic in the current environment. That means instead of earnings from their pension funds, they have pension liabilities for which they have not yet accounted.

Companies are going to have to deal with this issue within a few years. I will make you a side bet right now. When these companies take the accounting hit, it will not be to current or future earnings. They will go back and restate prior-year earnings. They will blame the economy, the stock market, and sun spots. They will fire their consultants and hire new ones with more conservative projections. But future earnings will still be pro forma positive. All the loss will be relegated to the past because of mistaken assumptions by consultants, so pulleeze do not even think about selling our stock.

Call me cynical, but if the bulk of your income is based on stock options, as is the case with most large company CEOs, what else would
you do? This is going to cause a lot of musical chairs in the corporate
boardrooms.

However, if you restate earnings of this magnitude today, it is quite
likely you will get hammered in the stock market. You will be setting yourself up for class action shareholder lawsuits. Of course, management will
trot out the "independent" earnings estimates that they use to support
their assumptions. These "rent-an-assumption" estimates are going to be
seen as a very flimsy excuse in the Enron era.

But these assumptions are going to be changed, even if management is
forced to do it kicking and screaming.

Before we leave this area, I should also mention that this year, the
Boston Globe tells us, pensions are going to have to refigure their actuarial
tables on life expectancy.[6] Since we are living longer, they are going to
need to set aside even more money than they currently plan. And let's
not forget medical costs, which many plans cover. These are increasing
every year and, as we live longer, are just going to become even bigger
drags on income.

The reality is that for some companies the beneficial owners are going
to be the retirees. Shareholders will be asked to take a backseat. Most of
them will simply get out.

The Wendy Gramm Factor

And that brings us to the second reason P/E ratios are going to get
worse even as the economy improves. It's what I sadly call the Wendy
Gramm factor.

Wendy Gramm had the unfortunate position of heading the auditing
committee for Enron. She was head of the Commodity and Futures Trading Commission and Senator Phil Gramm's wife. Those of us who are ac-
quainted with her know she is smart, honest, and as genuinely committed
to integrity as anyone with whom you could hope to be associated. There
are some in Texas who think the wrong Gramm was running for the U.S.
presidency a few years ago.

How could she have let Enron get away with such outrageous accounting practices? Shouldn't she be held responsible for the problems at Enron? It happened on her watch, after all.

And that illustrates the problem. When a Wendy Gramm can be misled
and fooled by management, accountants, and lawyers, what hope does the
average audit committee head have? I can tell you that corporate audit

committees all over the United States, especially if Arthur Andersen was the auditor, are doing some serious soul-searching.

Corporate boards of directors are like mushrooms: They are kept in the dark and fed horse manure. (My less-than-sainted Dad had more colorful terms, but you get the picture.)

The purpose of most corporate boards is not so much to oversee management as to provide access assistance to management. Do you need to talk with the head of another corporation? You call your director who sits on another board with someone who sits on the board of the firm with which you need to talk. That is why so many corporate directors are on multiple boards. It is not their wisdom so much as their Rolodexes that they bring to the table. The boards become a sounding board for management, but only rarely become a true check in a major way. Management usually gets its way—unless managers screw up, and then they get replaced.

But now that will change. The men and women who sit on these boards are not dummies. Many are and were serious businesspeople in their own right. Being on a major corporate board will no longer be seen as a perk. It now can easily become a liability. Why risk your reputation and fortune to lawsuits for relatively poor pay (when compared to your net worth)? There is no amount of money that being on the board auditing committee of Enron, WorldCom, or Global Crossing was worth. The Wendy Gramm factor is now a reality, and every board member in the country wants to make sure he/she avoids it.

In the future, you are going to see boards of directors start to require true independence from their accountants. Many will require the accountants to actually report to the board prior to reporting to management. I think many will start to seek second opinions from outside legal counsel on what could be a controversial position. You will see boards hire outside accountants to ferret out potential problems in accounting. They will start to err on the side of caution and conservatism.

A recent article noted that auditing committees for major boards are meeting 50 percent more than in the past. I bet the meetings are a lot more intense.

Each new shareholder lawsuit is going to reinforce the drive to be conservative. Having a board of directors breathing down your neck is going to make earnings management much more difficult. Boards will instruct management to paint earnings in the most realistic manner possible.

But it is not just boards of directors. It is also going to be the accounting and legal profession. There is a Securities and Exchange Commission (SEC) rule called 102.e. Basically, if you give an opinion or audit that is found to be misleading or wrong, you can be barred from practicing before the SEC or auditing public companies.

My world is full of accountants and lawyers who work to make sure everything I do is correct. I depend on them to help guide me through a maze of regulations. In the past, if they made a mistake, however, it was only my derriere on the line. I am the one who gets thrown out of the pool. They can go back to their practices.

You can already see this climate changing. We will see laws enforced that make lawyers and accountants more responsible for their opinions. Frankly, I will enjoy the company.

This is a good thing, and not just because it will make the numbers we see more believable. I rely on conservative attorneys and lawyers. They have explicit instructions to keep me three feet from the edge. I don't want to get close enough to look over.

But I see other competitive firms doing things my attorneys wouldn't let me get close to. A more conservative world will level the playing field for the vast majority of firms that do their best to be honest and fair. While this will be a good development, it will be negative for so-called earnings. Conservative accounting will mean less room to cook the books.

Plausible Expectations and Irrational Exuberance

Now let's look briefly at two important studies on the prospect for future earnings. The first is an analysis of the long-term trends on earnings in a study for the National Bureau of Economic Research (NBER) by three economics professors (Louis K.C. Chan, Jason Karceski, and Josef Lakonishok).[7]

First these professors looked at a large number of public companies over 50 years. They were interested in two things: "How plausible are investors' and analysts' expectations that many stocks will be able to sustain high growth rates over prolonged periods? Are firms that can consistently achieve such high growth rates identifiable in advance?"

The answer to the first question is not very. Let me run through a number of their conclusions (mostly quotes with some editing for clarity and my emphasis) with a few comments. These are very important if you are going to understand the nature of the markets in coming years. Stay with me here, team.

Our median estimate of the growth rate of operating performance corresponds closely to the growth rate of gross domestic product over the sample period. . . . The growth in real income before extraordinary items is roughly 3.5 percent per year [after inflation and dividends; before them it is about 10 percent]. This is consistent with the historical growth rate in real gross domestic product, which has averaged about 3.4 percent per year over 1950–1998. *It is difficult to see how over the long term profitability of the business sector can grow much faster than overall gross domestic product.*

Although there are instances where firms achieve spectacular growth, they are fairly rare. For instance, only about 10 percent of firms grow at a rate in excess of 18 percent per year over 10 years. . . . An average of only four firms a year (or 0.3 percent) are able to simply show above average (the top 50 percent) growth for 10 years in a row. . . . The patterns in the more recent years do not deviate markedly from the averages across the entire sample period. *The number of firms that grow faster than the median for several years in a row is not different from what is expected by chance.*

Comment: This is why large institutions diversify into different classes of stocks such as large-, mid-, and small-cap growth; large-, mid-, and small-cap value; numerous sectors; and so on. Morningstar has dozens of categories. If you are an institutional manager, your job is to decide how much to allocate to each category and then find a manager who can hopefully beat the market in that category by sifting out the real dogs.

Individuals read the above and get depressed. The average stock does only about as well as the economy? I have to do better than 3 percent growth to retire. The institutional manager, however, hopes that if he is steady, he will get real returns of 3 percent plus dividends plus whatever bonus returns his managers can give him. Over the long term, this compounds quite nicely. Throw in inflation and you can show some nice numbers to your investors.

If you are not prepared to live with institutional returns, then perhaps you should consider an investing methodology somewhat different from Modern Portfolio Theory. Unless you use the methods of a Warren Buffett or a John Templeton, you are not likely to beat the market. Eighty percent of mutual funds do not beat their benchmarks. Yet investors optimistically think they can do better than the pros. While some can, there are not many, in my experience. Chapters 16 to 18 will show you how you can by using the right set of stock-picking principles.

Back to the report:

Security analysts' long-term estimates . . . are overoptimistic and do poorly in predicting realized growth over longer horizons. To sum up, analysts and investors seem to believe that many firms' earnings can consistently grow at high rates for several years. . . . *The evidence suggests instead that the number of [firms growing at high rates] is not much different from what might be expected from sheer luck.*

The lack of consistency in earnings growth agrees with the notion that in competitive markets abnormal profits tend to be dissipated over time. . . . Investors may think that there is more consistency in growth than actually exists, so they extrapolate glamour stocks' past good fortunes (and value stocks' past disappointments) too far into the future.

. . . In summary, analysts' forecasts as well as investors' valuations reflect a widespread belief in the investment community that many firms can achieve streaks of high growth in earnings. Perhaps this belief is akin to the notion that there are "hot hands" in basketball or mutual funds.

. . . *There is no evidence of persistence [consistent repeatability] in terms of growth in the bottom line. Instead, the number of firms delivering sustained high growth in profits is not much different from what is expected by chance.*

Read the above paragraph several times. Memorize it. The report continues:

The results for subsets of firms [like technology or pharmaceuticals], and under a variety of definitions of what constitutes consistently superior growth, deliver the same verdict. *Put more bluntly, the chances of being able to identify the next Microsoft are about the same as the odds of winning the lottery.*

Comment: What the researchers mean by this is that simply investing randomly is not likely to give you the 100 to 1 return, and even with a lot of effort and research there is still a great deal of luck involved. There are thousands of small companies with great stories that all think they will be big someday.

More report:

This finding is what would be expected from economic theory: competitive pressures ultimately dissipate excess earnings, so profitability growth reverts to a normal rate. Analysts predicted a five-year growth for the top 20 percent of companies to be 22.4 percent, which turned out to be only 9.5 percent.

(The researchers also pointed out the actual return rate should be lower because many of these top 20 percent companies actually failed over that period.)

The researchers created sample portfolios based on analysts' forecasts. Predictably, the top portion of the portfolios actually returned only about half of what the analysts predicted: 11 percent actual versus 22 percent predicted. "These results suggest that in general caution should be exercised before relying too heavily on long-term forecasts as estimates of expected growth in valuation studies."

Finally, this very sobering conclusion:

On a broader note, our results suggest that investors should be wary of stocks that trade at very high multiples. Very few firms are able to live up to the high hopes for consistent growth that are built into such stellar valuations. Historically, some firms have achieved such dazzling growth. These instances are quite rare, however. Going by the historical record, only about 5 percent of surviving firms do better than a growth rate of 29 percent per year over 10 years. In the case of large firms, less than 1 percent would meet this cutoff.

On this basis, historical patterns raise strong doubts about the sustainability of such valuations. For example, on average 3 percent of firms manage to have streaks in growth above the median for five years in a row. This matches what is expected by chance.[8]

Conclusions, class? Yes, I see that hand.

First, evidently the brightest minds on Wall Street are verifiably (as a group) really, really, really bad at estimating the future potential earnings and growth of stocks.

Over the next few years, we are going to see a new type of competition among investment firms and analysts. Investors are going to start ignoring overly optimistic analysts and begin looking for some accuracy. This won't happen all at once, as there is still a demand for analysts who will tell investors what they want to hear. But as the secular bear market wears on and the patience of investors begins to wear thin, you will see projections become more in line with reality. It will take four or five years at least for this to become standard, but the S&P announcement of a core earnings standard is the beginning of what will become a trend.

Just as you tell your friends you have a conservative attorney, investors will start to look for conservative analysts. Optimists will come to be seen for what they are: dangerous to the health of your portfolio. Realistic and on target forecasts will become the style to which we all aspire.

Second, broad stock market indexes over long periods of time do not grow faster than the economy. Therefore, if they have grown substantially in the recent past, either they will fall in value until they revert to the average growth trend or they will go sideways for long periods until growth catches up with them. Either way, investors will be frustrated.

The 2 Percent Dilution Factor

Finally, we are going to look at a study from two of the country's premier investment research minds, which shows that it is not even true that earnings for all of corporate America grow as much as GDP. When you actually slice and dice the numbers you come up with a few rather interesting observations about where that growth we saw in the NBER study actually comes from. Jumping to a conclusion, it does not come from large corporations. This will be an important insight for those of you looking for growth in your stock portfolios.

Rob Arnott I introduced earlier in Chapter 7. Bill Bernstein is a principal with Efficient Frontier Advisors, LLC, and the author of numerous important studies. (He is also a practicing neurologist in Coos Bay, Oregon, and a money manager. His new book, *The Birth of Plenty*, will be on my must-read list the day it is out.)

In a study Bernstein and Arnott tell us that investors think that earnings of existing companies can grow faster than the economy.[9] There are two reasons investors are wrong. The first is that much of the growth in the economy is actually due to the creation of new companies. Their growth does nothing for the earnings of existing companies. During the twentieth century, the study shows that stock price and dividend growth were 2 percent less than the actual macroeconomic growth of the country.

> [Investors were told] . . . with a technology revolution and a "new paradigm" of low payout ratios and internal reinvestment, earnings will grow faster than ever before. Real growth of 5 percent will be easy to achieve. Like the myth of Santa Claus, this story is highly agreeable but is supported by neither observable current evidence nor history.[10]

The second false belief is that somehow stock buybacks will allow per share earnings to grow. While this may be true for an individual company, when looking at the entire universe of companies you find that new share issuance almost always exceeds stock buybacks, by around 2 percent per year. We will look at some actual numbers and then go into the very real investment implications.

Since 1800, the U.S. economy has grown about 1,000 times. The record is remarkably consistent, averaging around 3.7 percent per year over that time. The good news is that economic growth over time is consistent. The bad news is that there is no reason to think a "new paradigm" could make it grow appreciably faster. We have had numerous "new paradigms" in U.S. history: railroads, automobiles, electricity, the cotton gin, the reaper, telephones, and so on. They all provided major boosts to the economy. But none allowed it to grow above that trend line for very long. (More on this thought later.)

When measured over decades, the so-called growth reverts to the mean. Yet investors were told to project the recent trend into the future. We are in a new paradigm, we were told. Now we are seeing how that concept is bogus. There have been several periods in the past few centuries when technological changes have been made that had far larger impact on lifestyles than the ones of today. In each of those cases, people were told that this time "things are different." They never are. Investors seem to always project the current trend into the forever, and it does not last into the forever.

Yet it should be intuitively obvious that earnings for U.S. corporations cannot grow faster than the economy for any length of time. Consider the hypothetical economy of the country of Fantasia.

Assume the economy of Fantasia grows by 5 percent a year and earnings of Fantasian corporations grow by 10 percent a year. Earnings are 10 percent of the total GDP or economy. After 14 years, the economy will double. But earnings will have risen by four times! Earnings will now be 20 percent of the economy. If this process were to continue for a few decades, earnings would soon be 100 percent of the economy. The parts cannot grow larger than the whole.

What their research shows is that earnings not only do not grow faster than the economy, they grow more slowly than the economy does. While specific companies can do well for periods of time, other research clearly shows that sustained compounded high growth over decades is very, very rare. And when applied to broad segments of the market, it just does not happen.

How can S&P 500 earnings grow faster than the economy, as they do? Because each year, slow-moving dogs are dropped and fast-growing companies are added. I believe I recently read that 370 new companies have been added to the elite list of 500 as others have been dropped in just the past 30 years or so. So much for buy and hold.

I remember an analyst in early 2000 who breathlessly wrote that the stocks of Microsoft and Intel would do as well in the coming decade as they had done in the prior decade. I pointed out that if this was true, in just 12 years the market value of the two stocks would be more than the entire GDP of the country.

Tokyo real estate in 1989 was not really worth more than all of California, although that is what the prices at the time indicated, and Microsoft and Intel, no matter how wonderful they are, cannot be worth more than the entire economy. There is a balance.

But things are different now, are they not? Bernstein and Arnott give us three reasons why they are not. First, we started the decade with a very low base due to the recession. Measuring growth from trough to peak and then projecting the growth as far as the eye can see is what causes bubbles, and is almost always wrong. (Actually, I cannot think of a time when it wasn't.)

Second, write-offs were frequently ignored, and more and more emphasis was placed on pro forma earnings. While this may be useful when looking at one company, when looking at the economy as a whole there are no extraordinary items. Everything counts.

Third, the peak earnings of the latter part of the decade included three very suspicious parts: not expensing stock options, pension expense, and "earnings management." Bernstein and Arnott present evidence that these three combined could have inflated earnings as much as 30 to 35 percent.

In discussing rapid earnings growth, Bernstein and Arnott point out that the period from 1820 to 1855 actually saw a far greater technological explosion and resulting economic growth than the recent "tech explosion." In 1820, information and trade moved at the speed of a horse. In 1855, speed had grown tenfold and communication was almost instantaneous. While someone from 1967 could recognize the world of 2002, someone from 1820 could not even imagine the world of 1855. The growth of the first period was over sixfold, and was four times greater than the tech revolution we have just experienced. Looking back on a chart of 200 years of growth, the recent years hardly even show an acceleration in the trend of growth!

Since 1871, real stock prices (after inflation) have grown at 2.48 percent while the economy grew at 3.45 percent. There is almost 1 percent of "slippage." Bears could paint a bleaker picture by pointing out that much of the growth was from increases in valuations. By that I mean P/E ratios increased substantially. Investors were paying more for a dollar's worth of earnings. The market was valued at an average P/E of 12 (or 20 times dividends) prior to the last bull market. The current high valuation levels are approaching 30. Almost 1 percent of the growth of the stock market over the past 130 years has been due to the recent bubble in prices.

Wait a minute, what about the studies that show the S&P 500 grew at 10 percent a year? Part of the answer is that indexes such as the S&P include dividends that averaged almost 5 percent. As we saw earlier in this chapter, inflation accounts for a great portion. And part of the answer is that the indexes do not reflect the actual results of the companies. If you measured the Dow or S&P by the companies that were in them in 1950, as an example, the growth would not have been as much. That is not to say the Dow should be fixed and the companies in the index never should change. The changes are made to reflect the broad economy, which is what the Dow and other indexes are supposed to do.

That is what makes index investing so attractive in bull markets, and why it is so hard for a mutual fund to beat an index. Indexes keep adding fast-growing companies and getting rid of the dogs. As valuations increase, the funds become self-fulfilling prophecies.

Nash-Kelvinator, Studebaker, and Other U.S. Giants

For instance, IBM and Coca-Cola were added to the Dow in 1932. Coca-Cola was dropped for National Steel three years later, and IBM was booted for United Aircraft in 1939. IBM was once again put in the Dow in 1979. Coca-Cola returned in 1987. National Steel has long since departed, as has Nash-Kelvinator, Studebaker (I learned to drive in a Studebaker), something called International Shoe, and that staple of U.S. industry, the American Beet Sugar company. Let's hear it for progress.

For those with no lives, or the insatiably curious (I will leave it to you to decide in which category I am placed), you can go to www.dj indexes.com/downloads/DJIA_Hist_Comp.pdf and see the entire history of the Dow.

Clearly, buying the component stocks of the Dow and holding them for long periods would not have produced the same returns as the managed index.

I would invite readers to think about the implications of this for one moment. While today we might smirk at Nash-Kelvinator or Studebaker or American Beet Sugar—or any of the scores of firms that have been added and dropped from the Dow—at one time they were considered worthy of inclusion in the most prestigious roll call of companies.

Proponents of buy and hold use indexes to support their claims of its effectiveness. Indexes, however, are not instruments of a strict buy-and-hold philosophy. They clearly buy and trade. For every General Electric that was added to the Dow in 1896 and then dropped in 1898 for U.S. Rubber, added again in 1899, dropped in 1901, and added yet again in 1907, there are scores of other firms that were once a part of the mighty Dow and have now faded into oblivion. None of the other earlier companies from 1900 are names that are familiar to me, except as historical curiosities.

Thus, when Bernstein and Arnott show actual earnings growth is much less than index growth, it should come as no surprise. The various indexes are comprised of growing companies. The overall economy does not perform as well.

For non-U.S. readers, let me briefly discuss Bernstein and Arnott's study of 16 world markets. Using data from the tour de force book by Elroy Dimson, Paul Marsh, and Mike Staunton called *Triumph of the Optimists* (Princeton University Press, 2002), he shows that among countries that did not experience significant wartime damage, the experience of the United States was not unique.

Dividend growth and per capita GDP growth are always materially below GDP, with the odd exception of Sweden, and there the difference was only minimal. The actual real growth of dividends for most countries was actually negative!

There is an interesting implication that Bernstein and Arnott address. Many suggest the next new waves of wealth will be built on biotechnology or nanotechnology, or the Internet. But what happens is that new firms increasingly make the capital and investment of previous firms obsolete. Bernstein and Arnott ask, "How many of the new paradigm crowd truly *believe* that their beloved tech revolution will benefit the shareholders of existing enterprises remotely as much as it can benefit the entrepreneurs creating the new enterprises that comprise the vanguard of their revolution?"

Our intrepid researchers then turn their attention to the myth of stock buybacks:

> Many investors believed that stock buybacks would permit earnings to grow faster than GDP. The important metric is not the volume of buybacks, however, but net buybacks—stock buybacks less new share issuance, whether in existing enterprises or through IPOs. We demonstrate, using two methodologies, that during the twentieth century, new share issuance in many nations almost always exceeded stock buybacks by an average of 2 percent or more a year. The bull market of the 1990s was largely built on a foundation of two immense misconceptions. Whether their originators were knaves or fools is immaterial; the errors themselves were, and still are, important.
>
> Investors were told the following:
>
> 1. With a technology revolution and a "new paradigm" of low payout ratios and internal reinvestment, earnings will grow faster than ever before. Real growth of 5 percent will be easy to achieve. Like the myth of Santa Claus, this story is highly agreeable but is supported by neither observable current evidence nor history.
> 2. When earnings are not distributed as dividends and not reinvested into stellar growth opportunities, they are distributed back to shareholders in the form of stock buybacks, which are a vastly preferable way of distributing company resources to the shareholders from a tax perspective. True, except that over the long term, net buybacks (that is, buybacks minus new issuance and options) have been reliably negative.
>
> The vast majority of the institutional investing community has believed these untruths and has acted accordingly. Whether these tales are lies or merely errors, our implied indictment of these misconceptions is a serious one.[11]

Bernstein and Arnott then conclude their research with these sobering remarks:

The markets are probably in the eye of a storm and can expect further turmoil as the rest of the storm passes over. If normalized S&P 500 earnings are $30–$36 per share, if payout ratios on those normalized earnings are at the low end of the historical range (implying lower-than-normal future earnings growth), if normal earnings growth is really only about 1 percent a year above inflation, if stock buybacks have been little more than an appealing fairy tale, if the credibility of earnings is at an all-time low, and if demographics suggest baby boomer dissaving in the next 20 years, then we have a problem.[12]

Yes, most investors do indeed have a problem.

The implication of the study is that investors who are looking for growth in stocks based on the belief that earnings can grow faster than the economy are going to be disappointed. And if, as I believe, we are in a Muddle Through Decade of lower than historical average economic growth, then it is possible investors will be disappointed more than they normally would.

Summing Up Our Learning about Earnings

Let's look at the list:

- There has been a dearth of earnings growth in the recent 15 years during the most powerful economic market in history.
- Much of earnings "growth" has been due to inflation.
- Pension assumptions must be made reasonable.
- Accounting standards will become more conservative.
- Options will likely be treated as an expense.
- Boards of directors will demand more open and conservative accounting.
- Accountants and lawyers will be under serious pressure to justify any and all aggressive accounting and financing positions, with real consequences for being wrong.
- CEOs and CFOs are now criminally liable for accounting misstatements.
- Investors will increasingly be interested in true pictures of income and start ignoring EBITDA and other misleading "earnings" numbers.
- Analysts will be under pressure to start making more accurate predictions.

- Stock buybacks increasing earnings are a myth (with some few exceptions).

Little of this will happen overnight. But as time goes on, a more realistic view of earnings will begin to take effect. And what it means is that P/E ratios are going to suffer. And that is not the climate in which a bull market starts to take shape.

The Earnings Road Just Got Steeper

The accounting changes will set a new bar for earnings. The earnings bar that Standard & Poor's suggests is now appropriate is around $40 to $45 for the S&P 500. If you can assume even 10 percent earnings growth, which would be historically very high, it will take four years to get back to $60, which is what analysts were projecting for 2003 only a few years ago. If you take the historical average P/E ratio of 15 you get an S&P of $900 in 2008, which is a negative return as I write this chapter. Forget about what single-digit P/E ratios would do.

This is the glass ceiling I referred to at the beginning of the chapter. It is earnings, pure and simple. Investors are not going to create a new and true bull market until they think earnings are going to grow to levels that justify current stock prices. As more and more investors see these new and lower earnings estimates, they are going to exit until things improve. When new accounting standards are actually adopted, it is my bet that investors will take them seriously. And the standards will seriously lower reported earnings. And this is going to cause problems for index funds. Get out of them. Use any rally as an exit ramp.

When we experience the next recession, the market will simply drop as it did prior to and after the most recent recession.

Optimists will write and say that investors will ignore the new rules. They will continue to look at pro forma earnings. They will continue to listen to Wall Street analysts. Who cares about employee stock options? Pension funding will be a nonissue when the market comes roaring back.

My response is that they have a point in the short term. Many investors will grab onto any life preserver that lets them think their portfolios are going to come back. They want to have the retirement they once thought they would have. But over time, as earnings do not grow rapidly, as analysts continue to be wrong, and as the new standards become accepted in the marketplace, more and more investors will lose the faith.

The age-old pattern of high valuations giving way to low valuations will once again emerge. Market cheerleaders will fight it all the way to the bitter end. But if the past is any indication, it will be a losing battle.

Finally, the problems described in this chapter are those of mostly large companies (and a few penny stocks like Lucent). There are small companies that will do very well in this decade. Just because I am sour on large tech companies does not mean I think all technology is suspect. There are some small firms just starting today that will be giants in the next decade.

Instead of hoping Cisco or JDS Uniphase will come back, I would be looking through the 100 latest companies to go public on NASDAQ. Any company that is too big I would throw out. Find a company with a built-in barrier to entry in its market, solid management, and a reasonable business plan. Or conversely, look for old economy companies with solid track records of growing dividends and low value ratios, and be patient.

In Chapters 16 to 18 we look at the criteria for Bulls' Eye Investing in the stock market during a secular bear market. It is an approach that will take advantage of the problem of weak earnings for large-cap stocks. But first, let's look at some reasons why I think that we may be in for a Muddle Through Economy for the rest of this decade.

Pension Fund Problems in Your Backyard

9

The preceding chapter examines the pension fund problems of public companies. Most of us are not directly impacted because we can simply sell the stocks of companies that have pension fund problems, and we don't have to buy S&P 500 index funds.

But there is a pension funding problem that dwarfs the public company problem, and which will directly affect your pocketbook. Let's look at government pension plans, which your tax dollars must fund. The potential funding problem is more than enough to offset the future Bush tax cuts. This will be a drag on the entire economy over the next decade, and is one of the reasons why I think we are headed for a Muddle Through Economy.

Of the 123 state retirement systems covered in the "2003 Wilshire Report on State Retirement Systems: Funding Levels and Asset Allocation" by Wilshire Associates, 79 percent are now underfunded. In 2000 only 31 percent were underfunded. At least nine states have pension fund liabilities that exceed their annual budgets. Nevada would have to devote 267 percent of its annual state budget to make up its current shortfall. Illinois would need 144 percent of its current annual budget.

Some might think the market has recovered so the problem has gone away. Unfortunately, that is not the case. The study was performed on reports from the retirement systems that were mostly done in June or July of 2002. The S&P 500 was at 989 at the end of June 2002. Since the average state pension fund has 63 percent of its investments in equities (both domestic and international) and the markets have simply retraced their losses, the situation is not all that different today. (This study is the most recent available. The trend suggests it will get worse.)

As of the report date, state retirement systems had only 91 percent of the assets needed to fund liabilities. This is down from 115 percent only two years ago.

And, of course, I have to go on to note that the report gets uglier. Wilshire Associates assumes that these state pension funds will get a 7.5 percent return per year on total assets, which is only 0.5 percent less than the 8 percent the average state plan assumes it will get.

How realistic is that? As noted above, the average state pension fund has 63 percent of its assets dedicated to equities, down from 64 percent last year. Since the stock market had a large drop in 2001–2002, that means funds were selling bonds and putting any new revenue into stocks to maintain their stock/bond ratios. The consultants tell the boards of directors this is a smart thing to do, because you don't want to miss the next bull market. The boards buy into the logic, because the alternative is too hard to contemplate: lowering assumptions of future returns and thus requiring the states to ante up more money.

If you assume you can get 6 percent on your bond portfolio (which is aggressive, as most retirement funds are required to invest in high-quality bonds, which do not pay more than 4 to 5 percent at this time), this means the average fund is assuming it is going to get returns of 10 percent per year on its stock market investments.

This basically would mean that the market will double in the next seven years: Dow 20,000, here we come! An S&P 500 of 2,200 is right around the corner.

As Chapters 1 to 8 argue, an assumption of less than half that number is far more realistic, if not optimistic. But assuming 10 percent is just not appropriate for a conservatively run pension fund.

Simply look at the discussion of the Investment Matrix in Chapters 5 and 6. I can find no period in the history of the U.S. markets in which seven years after such a nosebleed level of valuation the stock market has averaged even 1 percent, let alone 10 percent. You can make an argument that from periods where P/E ratios hit their highs (generally in the area of 22 to 23), there were some periods where the markets averaged 3 percent the next seven years, but you can also find periods where the next seven years showed actual losses.

But there are no examples of 10 percent from the P/E levels we are at today. None.

Nightmare on Pension Fund Street

Let me start with a worst-case scenario, and then see if we can find a way to paint a better picture.

Today, there is more than $1 trillion in equity assets in the 123 state pension funds covered in the Wilshire Associates study. My back-of-the-napkin analysis shows that pension fund estimates assume that the equity portion of the pension fund assets will grow by 10 percent or around $100 billion per year.

That means in seven years and at 10 percent compounding, the pension funds are assuming there will be approximately $1 trillion in growth from the equity portion of their assets.

If the stock market is flat, they will be short $1 trillion in only seven years, from a "mere" $180 billion shortfall today. If the market grows at 3 percent, the states will be down $750 billion from their estimates.

This scenario covers just the 123 largest funds. The United States has about 2,200 state, city, and county pension plans that cover 17 million public workers and 6 million retirees. These pensions have about $2 trillion in assets, mostly stocks and bonds. If we have a typical secular bear market described in previous chapters, it could mean that the underfunding could be in excess of $2 trillion in a decade or so.

Courts have consistently upheld the obligations of municipalities to fund the promised retirement programs. That means taxes will have to be raised or services cut to fund increased contributions.

Can It Get Worse?

Here in Texas, we regard large groups of politicians in one place as dangerous, so we let the state legislature meet for only five months every two years. I called one of the most knowledgeable longtime veterans in the legislature today and asked him how we are dealing with our Texas-sized $19 billion, public pension shortfall.

Bottom line: We aren't. It is not on the leadership radar screen. For the first time, Republicans finally control both houses of the legislature and statewide offices. They ran on a "no new taxes" platform. They are scrambling, as is almost every other state, to balance a huge budget deficit without raising taxes. If they had to kick in another $3 billion a year, or close to 5 percent of the state budget, just to balance the pension fund within 10 years, there would be panic in Austin. There is no way they could find another $2 billion to $3 billion a year without substantial new taxes or cuts in services. The only other alternatives are to raise contributions from the teachers and state employees or reduce benefits. None of those options will be politically popular.

This refusal to act is typical of states throughout the union. It is much easier to assume 10 percent equity growth, increase funding a little, and hope the problem goes away. It is my guess that is why Nevada and Illinois have avoided making the hard decisions. Illinois solved the immediate problem by borrowing $5 billion. The taxpayers still owe the money. All that changed was the person to whom it was owed.

If there are no politically acceptable options, unless there is a crisis facing them today, politicians keep hoping that the market will come roaring back and save the day. They simply refuse to deal with the issue until the wolf is at the door.

My Texas experience is shared by many throughout the United States. Our neighbor to the north, Oklahoma, has even more severe pension problems.

"We can't invest our way out of this hole," says Tommy Beavers, executive secretary of the Oklahoma Teachers Retirement System, which has only $5 billion of the $12 billion in assets needed today to generate enough income to pay retirement obligations. "We've had 40 years of not putting enough money into our system.[1]

Dennis Gartman (in his *Gartman Letter*) brings us this rather chilling story:

> Now the "war" on pensions is brought home as states everywhere seem to be doing rather idiotic financial things as they float debt instruments to put money to work in the equity markets in order to fund shortfalls in pension that they owe to their pensioners. The worst, apparently, is poor li'l W. Virginia that according to Wilshire Associates, as reported by *The NY Times*, "has only $1 [of pension fund assets] for every $5 it owes." The state finds itself in such dire fiscal and actuarial straits that it is now in a court battle over its desire to issue $3.9 billion in new bonds without holding a statewide referendum. It would appear that the state would lose the referendum, but it has to raise the funds somewhere, and the debt markets seems like the best possible [read politically doable] source.
>
> Several states, counties, and cities around the country have done exactly as W. Virginia wishes to do, and most of them, sadly, have regretted having done so. New Jersey has done it; Illinois has done it; the statewide Oregon school system has done it; Kansas, Oregon, and Wisconsin are set to do it before the year end. New Orleans did it and regrets it; so too Pittsburgh. Somehow, we can only see this circumstance as a signal of a market that is toppy . . . too filled with the wrong sort of investors . . . too reminiscent of the euphoria that gripped the markets back in late '99 and early '00. Cities, counties, and states don't buy stocks when they are cheap; they buy them, sadly, when they are expensive.
>
> An anonymous official of Illinois said a rather frightening thing when asked why it was that his state had floated debt to pay for pensions. He said that the state was informed that it could earn 8.0–8.5% annually and was paying only 5.07% on the bonds it sold, and thus "as

long as the actuaries are right, we should be safe." Somehow, we are not nearly as content about the future as this official was . . . and the citizens of Illinois are without even a notion of the problem that may lie ahead unless the equity market continues to return 8.0–8.5% ad infinitum.[2]

The state officials were shown the famous graphs that predict 10 percent returns for the stock market, and because it was what they wanted to hear, they bought it. The naïveté is sad. So very sad.

An article in USAToday.com by Dennis Cauchon quotes Stephen D'Arcy, an accounting professor at the University of Illinois who has studied public pensions. He asserts that tax increases to fund pension shortfalls could be so substantial in some states that they would depress the local economy for a generation. "Aging industrial states—including Illinois, Ohio, and Indiana—are especially vulnerable because the number of workers paying taxes is growing more slowly than the number of retirees. A state with slow population growth runs the risk of being put into a tax death spiral to pay pension obligations," D'Arcy says.[3]

This entire process will put pressure on the ability of local governments to raise debt. Standard & Poor's rates local governments, and points to the potential for municipal credit downgrades due to the increasing pension pressures and how these implications are analyzed. "The magnitude of the current challenge for some could contribute to rating downgrades," S&P analyst Parry Young said recently.[4] A downgrade in a city, county, or state rating means that future borrowing will cost the taxpayers more.

If we see a sustained secular bear market, there is no way that many state and local governments can meet the kind of pension shortfalls I am suggesting without serious consequences to either taxpayers, those who are scheduled to receive benefits, or both.

What will happen? Will the public pension fund world come to an end? No, politicians will eventually step in when things start to get grim. There will be declarations of crisis and emergency, and to "save the system," future benefits are going to be cut or frozen. Future retirees will not be happy. It is probable in many states that defined benefit plans will be changed to defined contribution plans. States will be forced by the courts to honor current retirees, but younger employees will not be able to retire under today's system.

The longer this secular bear market goes on, the worse things will get and the more money states will have to come up with in the future.

The unintended consequences of the current policy of benign neglect will mean either future tax increases, cuts in services, or both. As medical costs rise, the state-funded portion of those costs will rise as well. The pension benefits for younger workers will be cut, and they will be forced to either save more or face a less robust retirement.

Unless steps are taken soon, it is possible we could see shortfalls approaching $1 trillion to $2 trillion in state-sponsored pension funds within 10 years. A deficit of this size on state levels can truly be called a crisis. A tax increase or other adjustments to fund this will be a large drag on the economy.

The problem, in reality, is much larger than the 123 state-funded plans discussed. It involves plans right down to the smallest municipality. The potential tax increases required could more than offset any tax relief from the Bush tax cuts.

I speak at public pension fund conferences that representatives of a number of these smaller pension funds attend. Talking with them after the sessions and during the breaks, especially after they hear my session, I hear how they are clearly worried about their future benefits. For those of you involved with your local political issues, I would suggest you begin to look into your pension fund situation. Specifically ask what future earnings assumptions have been made. See what type of funding needs there will be in the future, and determine what will happen to your taxes if the market stays flat for the next 10 years.

You might find the situation is like the one described in a letter from a reader of my weekly letter after I wrote about pension fund problems.

This article is so right on! I have served on a local retirement board for the past five years, and we were just informed that the County has negotiated increased pension benefits that will cost the taxpayers a significant amount over the next several decades. The pay increases also "spiked" retirement benefits for several outgoing County officials who were in charge of the negotiations. We had to extend our amortization from 9 to 20 years and continued to use a discount rate of 8.25 percent, which must come down next year. We also hit the top of our 120 percent market stabilization account, so now we can no longer smooth actuarial losses and they will drop straight to the bottom line. The overall result was the potential to increase the County's pension cost from about $30 million per annum to about $50 million—even with the lack of reduction in interest rate and also the extended amortization schedule. I am afraid this is going to cost taxpayers dearly in the future and the taxpayers really do not understand that the politicians are basically appeasing the unions (and possibly buying future votes) at our expense and at a time when the economy is in shambles. Some journalists are starting to get the idea, but I heard that whenever local papers try to write a story on this topic, they get pressure from local government leaders! Who knows, but run with this idea because you are onto something big!

The Issue of Retirement in an Aging World: Is It Something in the Water?

10

There are numerous forces that impact the economy, our investments, and our lives, but none is more fundamental than demography: the study of the characteristics of human populations, such as size, growth, density, distribution, and vital statistics.

The popular concept of demographics is wrapped up in our ideas about the baby boom generation. A huge cohort of children born after World War II caused all sorts of changes, positive and negative, in our society. As this group gets older, there will be even more changes that must inevitably occur. And it is not just the United States, but nations throughout the world that have their own aging problems. As we will see, our problems are mild compared to those of Europe and Japan, a situation that has serious implications for the world economy. But there are also nations where the median population is getting younger, and this presents a different set of problems and opportunities.

The aging of America and the world will affect us as almost no other issue. Most other factors have a great deal of volatile possible futures associated with them. How the nation ages is already in the cards. Demographically speaking, we know what the future holds. Now let's look at how that will affect our economy, investments, and possible retirement.

Is Retirement in Your Future?

First, we turn our attention to the question of retirement: Will the boomer generation be able to retire on time? Will Social Security go bankrupt? Is Harry Dent, author of *The Roaring 2000*s, right when he asserts that we will have a boom until approximately 2008 to 2009 because

135

boomers are saving and spending? And then watch as things go bust (an actual depression) because boomers start selling stocks and retiring?[1]

(There are two caveats to which all must agree prior to reading this: First, you cannot shoot the messenger—meaning Robert Arnott, Anne Casscells, and especially me. Second, I am distilling a lengthy paper with a great deal of backup data into a few pages.[2] Do not hold Arnott and Casscells responsible for my efforts.)

We will look at the conclusions first, explain why they came to be, and then explore the implications.

First, the good news: The boomer generation is going to live longer and be healthier than any previous generation. Each succeeding generation, as did our fathers, has lived longer than their parents and will continue to do so.

The bad news is that boomers, *on average*, who are expecting to retire at 65 will not be able to do so. Your individual situation is up to you, but the average boomer will work until at least age 70, and probably 72 or 73. The good news, again, is that we are all healthier. I, for one, do not intend to retire at 70 or even 75. Again, this is an average, and with proper planning many will be able to retire earlier, should they so desire.

(Richard Russell has been writing the *Dow Theory Letters* for 45 years, and now writes daily! He is my hero, going strong and writing more brilliantly than ever at 79. I shall not imitate him by getting up at 3 A.M., however, even in my dotage. I consider him one of the most insightful and savvy financial writers of our times. You can subscribe at www.dowtheoryletters.com.)

Second, this delayed retirement is not a financial problem, but a demographic problem. Thus the solutions are not simply financial, such as save more money or raise Social Security taxes.

Third, Social Security is not the primary problem. Long before we get to the predicted funding crisis of 2017 or 2029 or 2040 (depending on which politician you listen to), we have a market driven-demographic crisis.

Finally, I am going to suggest this is not a crisis at all, in the true sense of the word. It is merely an adjustment in expectations. It may even be a blessing.

Fantasy Island

Arnott and Casscells contend that the markets will force this increase in the retirement age. (See Figure 10.1.) This will happen whether or not politicians adjust the age for Social Security benefits. To explain what they mean by the market forcing the boomer generation to retire later, I

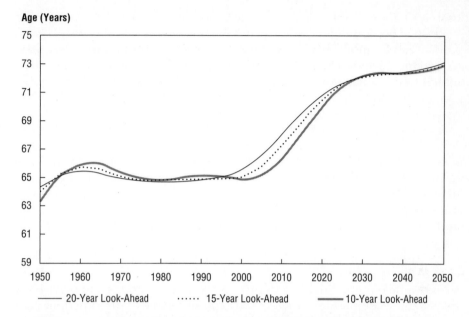

Age (Years)

Figure 10.1   Retirement Age with Look-Ahead, 1950–2050 (If Average of Retiree-Only Dependency Ratio and Adjusted Dependency Ratio Is Held Constant)
Source: Robert D. Arnott and Anne Casscells, "Demographics and Capital Market Returns," *Financial Analysts Journal* (March/April 2003), p. 27. Copyright 2002, Association for Investment Management and Research. Reproduced and republished from *Financial Analysts Journal* with permission from the Association for Investment Management and Research. All rights reserved.

am going to resort to a simplistic analogy. We will examine the merits and weaknesses of the analogy afterward. As you read, please know I am aware of many weaknesses in the story, but am trying to get over a major point that is critical to this argument. (The numbers I use are for illustration purpose only, to help you understand the concepts. They are not meant to be literal.)

Economists like to use an island economy to illustrate a point, and I will do so as well. Let's assume an island where 15 percent of the people are retired, 65 percent of the people are working, and 20 percent of the population are children. The elderly and the children depend on the workers to produce the goods and services they need, in addition to the goods and services the workers need. That means there is a ratio of about two workers for each dependent. The retired swap assets they have saved for the services they need.

Now, let's add something to the water that makes workers want to have more children. Slowly, over time, the number of dependents per worker goes up. The population now needs even more goods and services. Each worker can be more productive, and that helps, as they create more ways to produce goods cheaper and faster. Fortunately, whatever has been added to the water also makes people stay healthy longer, so that people can work a little longer. It is not much longer, just a few years, but it makes enough of a difference to keep things progressing.

The reason working a little longer makes such a difference is that the retired population consumes about three times as much in goods and services as the children do. So even though the percentage of the children in the population rises, it does not require nearly as much community effort to produce the needed goods and services for the young as it does to support the retirees. The combination of increased productivity and the older workers working a little longer makes for generally increasing prosperity.

Notice that it is not the amount of money the retired population has saved. The critical factor is that someone has to do the work so that things and services can be bought. Society produces X amounts of goods and services. If there is more demand for these goods and services by retired people than actual goods and services produced, then:

- The prices of these goods and services go up, or
- The value of the assets the retiring generation wants to trade for services and goods goes down. If every retired person tries to sell the same general assets in order to purchase goods and services, there are fewer buyers of the assets and the prices of the assets go down.

If supply of overall goods and services drops, then prices will rise. Retirees require goods and services. If there are not enough goods and services to meet demand, prices will rise. This will make it difficult for people to afford to retire on their savings, and thus they continue to work.

The earlier adult generation on our island has to work just a little longer to have enough assets to retire on and produce the goods that society needs. Because they work longer, they produce more goods and services, which has the effect of holding down prices and allows them to save more for retirement.

Now, an interesting thing begins to happen 18 years or so after the miracle drug is added to the water. Their kids begin to enter the workforce, and the number of dependents actually falls, as more kids enter the workforce than the number of people who decide to retire. The retirement age actually rises slightly even as those retiring live longer. Thus there are more workers producing goods and services.

Then another funny thing happens. Someone changes the water again, and the boomer generation stops having as many kids per family as their parents did. Because there were so many in the boomer generation, there were still lots of kids, just not as many per family. Even as more and more of their parents retire, the ratio of dependents to workers does not change.

The boomer generation continues the tradition of their parents and becomes increasingly more productive. The amount of goods and services needed to maintain the population does not get out of proportion to the number of workers. Things become stable.

The parents of the boomers, as they retire, exchange their savings for goods and services produced by the boomers and their children. The workers are willing to take these assets at ever-increasing prices for their products, because there is plenty to go around. This is partially because there is not a lot of demand from young dependents.

Then it becomes time for the boomers to retire. Most of them have been saving for retirement. Knowing they are going to need their savings for retirement, they slowly begin to get out of riskier investments long before the time comes for them to actually retire. But they still expect to retire at the age their parents did, or around 65, even though they expect to live at least five years longer, and 15 years longer than their grandparents.

But the boomers have made one big miscalculation. They forgot to have enough kids to support their retirement. So as time goes on, the working population has to produce more goods and services just to keep everybody supplied. The number of dependents per worker rises by 50 percent, until there are only 1.5 workers for every retiree/dependent.

The workers see the time they have to work rise each year, just to produce everything that is needed. This gets old very quickly (pardon the pun). The remaining workers get tired of working 60-hour weeks, instead of the 40-hour weeks their parents worked, just to produce the same amount of needed goods and services.

The workers go to the boomer generation and say, "We want more for our work. Either give us 50 percent more money for what we produce or we are going to give you 33 percent less goods and services for what you give us. But we will not work 60 hours a week any longer for the same amount of your assets as we once took for only 40 hours. If you don't like this, you are quite healthy and can work a little longer before you retire. Take it or leave it."

The boomer generation is quite upset. This isn't the deal they thought they had. They had been promised by their leaders they could retire at 65. Now they find they do not have enough assets to pay for the goods and services they need. It does not matter how much they have saved.

There are only so many goods to go around, and the workers set the price of the goods, plus they have control over the prices they are willing to pay for the assets the boomer generation has spent a lifetime saving.

There is only one solution, as the boomers need the goods and services to live. They have to go back to work.

Supply and Demand Is the Main Culprit

Before we can examine the implications of the story and data, you must get in your mind one main point: This problem is one of supply and demand. It has nothing to do with how much a generation saves or how much a generation gets on Social Security.

Crudely, if there are more rabbits than wolves, you will see an increase in wolves. If there are not enough rabbits, you will see a decrease in wolves. There is a balance in nature, and there is also a balance in economics.

Arnott and Casscells show that when you look at the dependency ratio (the number of workers for each dependent) and adjust for the fact that it takes more to support a retired person than a child, there is a strong correlation and in fact a causation between the average age of retirement and the number of workers still in the workforce.

As the parents of the boomer generation have retired, there have been fewer children demanding resources so that the dependency ratio of workers to children and retirees has been stable. That trend stops in a few years, and they predict the average age of retirement will begin to increase, starting in just a few years and rising to 69 by 2015 and over 70 by 2020, and, if the ratio holds, to 73 by 2050.

Literally, if every one of the boomer generation retired at age 65, there would not be enough people left in the workforce to deliver the pizzas, provide health care, supply police services, and so on. Ironically, one of the bright spots of this report is that it means unemployment for the next generation will probably go down over time as more and more people retire and others must take their places.

In places or countries with shortages of workers, labor costs go up. That means the labor component of goods and services goes up, which raises prices and/or lowers profits.

This process will play out over the next four decades. It will be slow and inexorable. Even dramatically increased productivity, beyond even today's explosive growth, will only mitigate the force of this trend.

The boomer generation will demand goods and services, and because there are not enough workers, the economy will not be able to supply enough goods and services, and workers will demand more of the saved assets of retirees for what they produce. *This can come as increased prices for the production, as a drop in the value of the saved assets, or both. That means either an inflation in prices or a deflation in wealth or a combination of the two.*

If today one share of Cisco will buy you a meal at Denny's, will it buy you a meal in 2020? People investing in Cisco today hope that the price of those shares will rise to where it will buy several meals. They expect stocks to rise 7 percent a year. However, in 2020 when there are not enough workers to produce everything retirees want, the law of supply and demand means that it will take more Cisco shares to buy a dinner than we currently plan on. Unless, of course, we can find more workers.

Health Care Pressures

While we are dealing with demographics and the baby boom generation, a good example of how demographics affect an economy is health care. It is no secret that health care expenses are on the rise. But the changes in how we spend our incomes that are in our future are massive. Let's look at some projections.

In the United States in 2002, we spent $5,427 per person on health care, almost exactly double what we spent in 1990. Centers for Medicare and Medicaid Services (CMS) projections estimate that we will spend $9,972 in 2012. Within another year or so after that, our medical bills will have doubled from what they are today.[3] Keep in mind, the baby boom did not really get started until 1947, so these costs do not begin to reflect the potentially accelerating rise in costs after 2012 as my generation gets older and begins to need ever more medical care.

In 1990, we spent 12 percent of our gross domestic product on health care. Today, that figure has risen to 14.8 percent, and it is projected to rise to 17.8 percent in 2012. It is still categorized as consumer spending, but put another way, that is 3 percent of our economy or $500 billion in 2012 that will not be spent on imported goods, cars, and so on. Yes, that will pay the salaries of a number of people who will produce those products and services, but this still represents a huge shift in buying "preferences."

It will not happen all at once, but the decade-long shift in buying patterns will present significant challenges for many consumer sales products. The percentage of GDP may be understated, as the CMS uses a higher estimate of U.S. economic growth than I would, and assumes we will have no recessions in the next 10 years, which is highly unlikely. However, a recession would do little to slow down the rise in health care costs.

Health care costs rose 8.7 percent in 2001, as an example. Also, the CMS assumes that health care expenditures will rise more slowly in the coming decade than they have the past three years, something CMS attributes to slower rates of growth in disposable personal income, medical price inflation, and Medicare spending.

In 2001 and in 2002, health insurance costs were listed as the biggest barrier to adding workers in a poll of 120 chief executives of very large companies by the Conference Board. Almost 82 percent of 1,017 members surveyed by the Connecticut Business and Industry Association in 2002 said rising health insurance costs were "an important factor" in decisions about whether to hire new workers. Poll after survey shows that small businesses, which typically provide the bulk of new employment in the aftermath of a recession, are increasingly seeing health care as a reason to not hire, or are laying off workers as a result of higher health care costs.

Take an Aspirin and Call Me in the Morning

Think about what this means to the proverbial middle-class family of four making $50,000 today. The total company cost of their insurance is roughly $6,000 or about 12 percent of their income (using my firm's cost as a rough guideline). Let's say their salary is going to grow by about 2 to 3 percent per year over the next 10 years, to about $65,000. Their insurance costs are going to double to about 18 percent of their income or they are going to have significantly less insurance. Can business absorb $500 billion a year in increased costs? Not without serious impact on their profits.

Hewitt Associates projects that the average cost for employee health insurance will be $5,134, up 70 percent just since 1998. Costs rose 14 percent in 2002, and again rose by double digits in 2003. Projections are that employee out-of-pocket expenses will rise by almost 25 percent, as employers shift part of the rising expenses to employees.

Who Really Owns GM and Ford?

Let's look at how health care costs affect one particular industry. Today, the Big Three automakers spend roughly $1,200 per vehicle on health care, according to *Fortune*.[4] Goldman Sachs estimates that the health care liabilities are $92 billion for just the three Detroit automakers, roughly 50 percent greater than their combined market capitalizations. This is three times their unfunded pension liabilities, if you allow them to project 9 percent stock market returns on their portfolios. A real-world analysis would paint a much darker picture.

There are several scenarios for the carmakers, none of them appealing. They could let the health care costs double as a portion of the prices of their cars. This puts them at significant disadvantage to foreign firms that have established U.S. plants and do not yet have huge numbers of retirees. That means they will have difficulty raising prices to cover the increase in costs, which of course hurts their profits and will result in lower stock prices.

They could pass on more of the costs to employees. That means big fights with their unions, strikes, and lost profits (lower stock prices). If they honor their commitments, it means less profit and a reduced stock price. It is my belief that the effective owners of GM, Ford, and other firms with large pension and health care obligations may be their workers and retirees and not their shareholders. The only alternative is a massive restructuring of liabilities. Think about the steel industry as an example.

U.S. automobile manufacturing is an industry I do not want to have in my investment portfolio, and ironically the reason has nothing to do with the quality of their products or service. It is the real uncertainty surrounding their health care and pension liabilities.

What about federal and state expenditures? Of course, their costs are expected to double from 2002 to 2012, rising from $700 billion to $1.4 trillion! Federal government costs will rise by almost $500 billion *annually*. That is without any increase in Medicare coverage, a prescription drug program, and so on. With 41,000,000 Americans not covered by health insurance and a growing cohort of retirees who want (and will get) a federally subsidized prescription health care plan, the probability is high that health care costs will rise even more than these projections.

Could things be improved? Of course. Simply passing tort reform would reduce health care costs by about 4 percent a year. Could we hammer out some increased efficiencies in the system? Sure.

But the main driver behind rising costs is simply the availability of new and better processes, drugs, and equipment. In January 2003, I was operated on using equipment and procedures that did not exist 10 years earlier. Did it cost more than the old-fashioned system? You bet, but the cure rate is significantly higher, the procedure was less painful, and the results were far more certain. I was offered the choice of the old procedure, which I had gone through once before. I opted for new, better, and more expensive. It was worth every penny.

The point is that costs are going to rise dramatically, no matter how we end up paying for them. This is going to shift consumer spending habits in ways we do not yet understand, and is just one of many influences arising from the aging of the boomer generation.

What Happens If You Don't Compound at 10 Percent over the Next 10 Years?

Let's look at it another way. If I am right and we are in a long-term secular bear market, and the average stock does not rise over the next 8 to 10 years, let alone at 7 to 9 percent per year, then how many people will be able to retire on schedule? Especially if they are faced with fixed incomes and rising medical costs that could last for 20 to 30 years or more as we live longer?

How many people go to their financial planners and assume a 7 to 8 percent or more growth in their stocks so that they can afford to retire? What happens to the forecast if the growth rate is only 2 to 3 percent? We will find people coming to 65 and finding they need to work and save a few more years.

In the same way that our grandparents had to work a few more years (on average) than our parents, our boomer generation will have to do the same.

You see, the part of the original island story where our kids come to us and want 50 percent more for their work doesn't happen. We never get there, because slowly my boomer generation, on average, is forced to work longer. Supply and demand balance the scales slowly. There is no crash into the wall, no strike by the younger workers forcing an abrupt change. The market adjusts things slowly.

The data Arnott and Casscells show is that this adjustment is in the retirement age. Will it be forced by a rise in costs or inflation? Or will it be forced by a fall in the price of assets? Or some combination of both?

I can make a cogent argument for all three, although I would choose the combination scenario, which fits into my Muddle Through scenario.

What Could Make a Difference?

One factor that could change this scenario is a dramatic increase in immigration. A selective and aggressive immigration policy could make a big difference. But it would have to be at a level much larger than today's one million or so immigrants. Arnott and Casscells' paper suggests that at the height of boomer retirement, we would need four million immigrants per year.

Right now, that is politically impossible. But in 15 to 20 years I can imagine a set of circumstances that would favor more open immigration.

Another factor that could change would be emigration, or an exodus of retirees from the United States. If you are living on a fixed income and can double your lifestyle by moving to sunnier climes, then I think more and more of the adventurous will choose to do so. There will be plenty of people who will be able to retire long before age 70, when they are capable of active lives, and will choose to do so in Costa Rica, Mexico, New Zealand, or any of a score of countries that offer good services and low costs. With modern communications and cheap travel, there is no reason not to put that possibility into your personal equation.

I do not understand how anyone can retire on a Social Security income alone. It is simply not enough to live on anywhere in the United States. But that same income goes a long way north of Puerto Vallarta in communities filled with retirees. Right now, Social Security income will buy you a lot in Argentina or Brazil.

Social Security Solutions?

I assume you know by now there is no Social Security lockbox, except in the rhetoric of politicians. Social Security is a transfer program. It transfers income from workers to retirees. When you pay into Social Security, you get nothing but a government promise. You do not own any assets, as opposed to what you own in your 401(k).

Do I believe that politicians will honor that "guarantee"? Of course. They wouldn't be politicians otherwise. But I think the terms of the deal will change on the margins. The government will slowly raise the age of retirement and probably do some sort of means testing. Further, the dependency ratio tells us that current Social Security payments won't be enough (surprise, surprise!).

We all know that there is a Social Security "crisis" coming in 2030 or thereabouts. As the dependency ratio rises, costs of services, especially those in demand by retirees, will rise faster than Social Security increases.

If they raised Social Security taxes enough to allow retirees to afford to retire, the percentage deducted from the incomes of those who remain in the workforce would be huge. It is not politically possible. The solution is that retirement ages will rise over time, pure and simple.

Or politicians may punt and let the market do it for them. Let's say Social Security is privatized. If Arnott and Casscells are right, then the market returns on the money saved would not be enough to retire on, so people would need to work longer. The fact that retirement costs more makes the retirement age rise, without politicians having to do anything. The more cynical part of me suggests that this may happen, so that the current generation of politicians, who will "fix" the system, will already be retired when the problem becomes apparent.

Be Honest with Yourself

The most important implication of this study is that the average retirement age will rise because it will cost more to retire. When you are planning for your retirement, you need to factor in a reduced return on your stocks and investments and an increased cost in terms of your assets for what you want to buy.

Let's take a real-world example of what not to do. I recently received the following letter from a reader, which so upset me I decided to make it the lead of my newsletter that week.

> My wife and I just heard another presentation by an investment firm recommending that retired people needing income from their sheltered funds place enough assets in fixed instruments for five years' living expenses and the rest in stock mutual funds. The hope is that within five years there will be an upturn such that stock funds can be sold at a gain, from which to draw income.
>
> Ibbotson data was, of course, used to show how unlikely it was for there to be many consecutive years of down markets. The firm had a CPA and several financial advisors who had been working in the field for 20 to 30 years.
>
> It drove me nuts, especially at this meeting where heads were nodding around the room as these advisors (looking for people to give them their money to manage) explained how scientific their approach was. The CPA member of the firm said (in comparison to 1966–1982) that the market could be that bad or even worse, but that this was very unlikely, and went on to recommend the strategy described above.

Let's review this for a moment. I will leave aside the question of making a one-size-fits-all recommendation for retirees, as I assume such stupidity is self-evident. That alone should be enough to make you run, not walk, to the exits.

In 1976, a young Roger Ibbotson co-authored a research paper[5] predicting that during the following two decades the stock market would produce a return of about 10 percent a year, and that the Dow Jones Industrial Average would hit 10,000 in 1999. Ibbotson, now a professor at Yale, currently forecasts a compounded return on stocks during the next two decades of 9.4 percent—about 1 percentage point a year lower than his earlier projections.

"I'm neither an optimist nor a pessimist," Ibbotson said in a 2002 interview. "I'm a scientist, and I am not telling people to buy or sell stocks now. I'm saying that over the long run stocks will outperform bonds by about four percentage points a year."[6]

It turned out Ibbotson was right about 1999, and with the imprimatur of a Yale professor, investment managers everywhere use this "scientific" study to show investors why they should put money in the stock market and leave it. (I am not sure how economists get to be scientists, or how investment predictions can be scientific, but that is a debate for another time.)

If the S&P were to grow at 9.4 percent for the next two decades, it would be in the range of 4,500, and the Dow would be at 42,000 or so in 2023 (give or take a few thousand). Of course, that's starting at today's market values. If we start out with the market tops in 2000, we get around 8,200 and 63,000 respectively in 2020. Thus, investors shouldn't worry about the short term. Ibbotson assures us, as a scientist, that things will get better by and by.

If you have read this far, you now know why you should leave the room whenever an investment advisor brings out this study to sell you on an investment strategy. If your advisor actually believes this nonsense, then this will help you understand why you should fire him.

There may be reasons to think the markets might go up, but the Ibbotson study is not one of them, in my opinion. Furthermore, over the next 70 years, the market may in fact rise 9.4 percent a year. But to suggest to retirees it will do so over the next few years based on "scientific" analysis is irresponsible and misleading.

Let's start our analysis in 1976, the year Ibbotson did the study. (I could make a much better case starting with another year, but 1976 works just fine.) From 1976 through 2002, the S&P 500 returned an average of 12 percent a year (including dividends), even better than Ibbotson predicted and even after a rather significant drop over the final few years. However, 5 percent of that annual return is due simply to inflation. In real, inflation-adjusted terms the S&P was up 7 percent a year.

The price-earnings (P/E) ratio was a rather low 12 in 1976. It ended up around 27 in 2003, using core earnings numbers. Thus more than half the return from the past 26 years has been because investors value a dollar of earnings more than twice as much in 2003 as they did in 1976.

At a similar P/E ratio to 1976, the S&P would be around 500 today (504 or so as I glance at the screen, again using core earnings numbers). Thus, without increased investor optimism, the compounded growth would be around 6.3 to 7 percent over the past 26 years, or only a few points over inflation during that time. The point is not the exact number but that a significant part of the growth in the stock market is due to increased P/E valuations.

In fact, if you back out dividends, the growth is almost entirely due to inflation and increased P/E valuations. The stock market has been a good investment since 1976 primarily because of these two factors. The question that investors must ask today is, "To what extent will these two factors, plus dividends, contribute to the return from the stock market over the next 5, 10, or 20 years?"

How to Lose 20 Percent in Five Years—Guaranteed

Let's look at the advice the investment managers were suggesting to retirees at the seminar my reader attended. Assume that you can make 5 percent (today) on your investment portfolio. You can take that 5 percent and live on it in retirement (plus Social Security and any pensions) and not touch your original principal. It doesn't make any difference in this example what the amount is. I simply assume you live on a budget of what you actually get.

If that 5 percent is what you need for the next five years, then according to the analysis given at the seminar, you will need to put about 22 percent or so of your savings in bonds, which will be consumed over the next five years (remember the 22 percent will grow because of interest). The other 78 percent or so will be put in stocks. Since the Ibbotson study shows stocks grow around an average of 9.4 percent per year, your total portfolio will have grown to 122 percent of where it is today. For this advice, they want you to pay them 2 percent a year.

You are gambling on that growth. If it does not materialize, you are in a big hole.

If you are not retired but saving for retirement, the principle is the same. If you are expecting investment returns like those of the 1990s to get you to your desired retirement income level at a specific age, you are probably dreaming. You are going to be disappointed. You are going to get to that hoped-for retirement age and still need to save some more and work longer.

But that is not all that bad. Average life expectancy was rising three months for every year over the last part of the twentieth century. That means in the past 28 years, life expectancy has grown 7 years, and more than 14 years since World War II. The quality of that life has increased dramatically as well. If our generation gets to live a lot longer, and if one of the conditions for that increased life span and quality of life is working a little longer than our parents did, then that is a trade I make every day.

In fact, studies show working a little longer is good for you. Retirement is bad for your health.

If you have not done so, you need to begin to adjust your portfolio to the absolute return type strategies we will discuss in later chapters. The returns from these may be less spectacular than what you want, but they will be steady. Making risky investments or hoping that the stock market will come back so you can reach your retirement goals is not healthy. "Reaching for yield" is often a ticket to disappointment.

It is better to put a realistic plan together, and either save more or plan to work longer. If you already have enough retirement savings, then don't let some stockbroker tell you that you must be in the stock market. Secular bear markets are times to be conservative. As Richard Russell says, "He who loses least in a bear market wins."

I am going to end this chapter with some details from Plansponsor.com on a survey on retirement. Read this in light of the previous chapters and see if it fits you or someone you know. If it does, consider changing your plans.

Most have also overlooked what might be a major retirement expense—health care. The vast majority (79 percent) have given little or no thought to the need for long-term care in a nursing home or long-term home health care. More than half (56 percent) have not considered the need for general health insurance coverage.

This survey is particularly unnerving in light of the studies cited at the beginning of this chapter. The average American is simply not prepared financially for retirement, assumes he will be healthy until he dies peacefully at a ripe old age in his sleep, and does not realize the funds he will get from Social Security will not come close to meeting his needs.

April 11, 2003 (Plansponsor.com)—Workers' confidence in their ability to live comfortably in retirement appears unshaken by slumping markets and a soft economy—but that confidence may not be based on good assumptions.

Actually, it may not be based on assumptions of any kind. Sixty-one percent of workers have made no attempt to determine how much they need to save for retirement. Among those who have done a calculation, 36 percent say they do not know, or do not remember, the results of that calculation. Two-thirds did that calculation more than a year ago and, according to the 13th annual Retirement Confidence Survey, many of those who have done the calculation used "less-than-reliable" methods such as guessing or estimating a figure based on inflation or the state of the economy.

The Employee Benefits Research Institute (EBRI), a public policy research group in Washington, [D.C.,] in conjunction with the American Savings Education Council (ASEC) and Matthew Greenwald and Associates, conducted the survey and report.[7]

Despite those shortcomings, the number of survey respondents who felt "very" confident about having enough money to live on comfortably in retirement has remained relatively consistent over the past several years; 21 percent in 2003, 23 percent a year ago, 22 percent in 2001—and 20 percent in 1994.

Some of this confidence might be explained by the fact that nearly half (48 percent) of workers surveyed say they have no stocks or stock mutual funds either inside or outside a retirement savings plan, and may have been spared some of the impact of the slumping investment markets. Still, EBRI CEO and president Dallas Salisbury cautions in a press release "the percentage of those not at all confident is 16 percent in 2003 versus 6 percent in 1993." That figure was just 10 percent as recently as last year [2002].

There are other assumptions apparently in place that could serve to distort these worker perceptions. Seventy percent plan to work after retirement, for one thing, although only 26 percent of current retirees have actually done so, according to Matthew Greenwald, president of Matthew Greenwald and Associates. Nearly 24 percent of those age 45 and older now say they plan to postpone retirement, compared with 15 percent a year ago—yet 4 in 10 current retirees have retired earlier than they had planned, half due to an unexpected health problem or disability and 23 percent as a result of unexpected changes at their companies, such as downsizings or closures.

Additionally, half of the respondents say they will be able to live comfortably on 70 percent or less of their current income in retirement (39 percent say they could live comfortably on less than 60 percent). Most financial experts predict that workers will need at least 70 percent to 80 percent.[8]

Demography Is Destiny

There is no free lunch.

—Milton Friedman

N ow, let's look away from the United States, and focus on the rest of the world. If we think the retirement problems facing the United States are severe, then the facts suggest the rest of the developed world is facing a major crisis. Over the next few decades, we are going to see a shift in economic and political power that is simply staggering in its implications. Let's look at facts first, and then draw conclusions.

I am going to quote at length from a study[1] by the respected *Bank Credit Analyst.* Martin Barnes and his crew at BCA Research have a stellar reputation for having been as accurate as any letter in the world for decades. They give us some sobering thoughts (you can see their work and subscribe at www.bcaresearch.com).

The populations of the developed countries will drop rapidly over the next 50 years, while those of undeveloped countries, especially Islamic countries, will rise dramatically. (See Figure 11.1, Figure 11.2, and Table 11.1.) Germany will experience no population growth and will remain at 80 million people, while Yemen will grow from 18 million to over 84 million.

Russia will drop from 145 million to slightly over 100 million. Iran will grow from 66 million to 105 million. Japan will drop to 109 million, while Iraq and Saudi Arabia will grow to 110 million each. Italy will decline

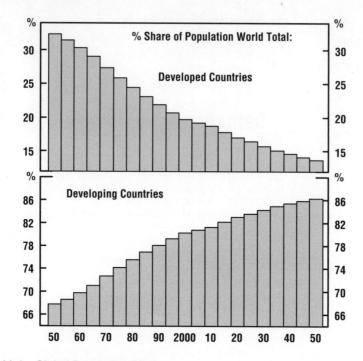

Figure 11.1   Global Population Shares
Source: United Nations, 2002 population report; © BCA Research 2003.

from 57 million to 45 million, while Afghanistan will grow from 21 million to 70 million.

This underscores the 100-page CIA report released in July 2001, entitled *Long-Term Global Demographic Trends: Reshaping the Geopolitical Landscape.* To quote from that report:

> Dramatic population declines have created power vacuums that new ethnic groups exploit. Differential population growth rates between neighbors have historically altered conventional balances of power. . . . Our allies in the industrialized world will face an unprecedented challenge of aging. Both Europe and Japan stand to lose global power and influence. . . . The failure to adequately integrate large youth populations in the Middle East and sub-Saharan Africa is likely to perpetuate the cycle of political instability, ethnic wars, revolutions, and anti-regime activities that already affect many of these countries. Unemployed youth provide exceptional fodder for radical movements and terrorist organizations, particularly in the Middle East.

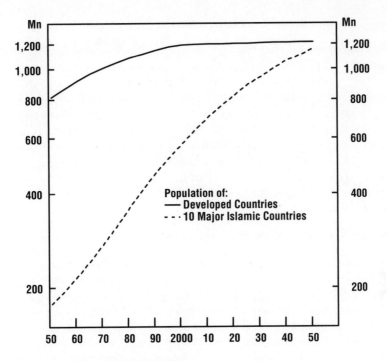

Figure 11.2   A Dramatic Population Shift
Source: United Nations, 2002 population report; © BCA Research 2003.

Table 11.1   UN Population Projections (Medium Variant)

Millions	2000	2025	2050	Change 2000–2050
Germany	82.3	82.0	79.1	–3.2
Italy	57.5	52.9	44.9	–12.6
Japan	127.0	123.4	109.7	–17.3
Russia	145.6	124.4	101.5	–44.1
United States	285.0	358.0	408.7	123.7
Afghanistan	21.4	44.9	69.5	48.1
Iran	66.4	90.9	105.5	39.1
Iraq	23.2	41.7	57.9	34.7
Saudi Arabia	22.1	39.8	54.7	32.6
Yemen	18.0	43.2	84.4	66.4

Source: United Nations, 2002 population report; © BCA Research 2003.

The Canadian-based BCA concludes:

The cynical view is that the U.S. desire to attack Iraq is mainly about oil. That may be part of the agenda, but other long-term strategic considerations are probably at work. The growing number of young people in a number of unstable or troubled countries could work both ways. For example, there are signs that many young people in Iran want the country to move away from fundamentalism toward a more relaxed regime. The rising power of youth can be a force for positive change as opposed to instability. However, there will be a huge challenge in bringing democracy to countries that have no history of it. *This will be especially true if the global economy is struggling because poor demographics are undermining demand in the industrialized world.* (Emphasis mine)

Let's look at some of BCA's other conclusions:

Declining aggregate demand in the developed world. Sharp declines in working-age populations in Europe and Japan will lead to large falls in the demand for consumer goods and real estate. Demand for aging-related services will rise, but not by enough to offset the growth-sapping impact of falling demand in the prime income-earning age group.

Full employment and labor shortages in the industrialized economies. There will not be any problem finding jobs, and a negligible unemployment rate implies that real wages should tend to rise. This will be good for per capita incomes, but not for profit margins.

Steady demand growth in emerging countries. Rising populations hold out the hope that demand growth in many parts of the developing world will offset the weakness in industrialized countries. However, there will be huge regional differences within the emerging markets, with Asia likely to be the star performer, and Africa remaining mired in crisis.

Continued transfer of manufacturing production to Asia. The shift in manufacturing capacity to Asia will continue, not least because of weak demand and labor shortages in the developed world. Even the auto industry may eventually move away from Europe and the United States. The developed economies will thus continue to become increasingly service oriented.

The welfare state will be under threat. It will be difficult to maintain the current level of public sector services and transfer payments as fiscal strains rise. It is almost inevitable that the retirement age will rise in most advanced economies and real benefits may be cut. Meanwhile, aging populations will put immense pressure on state-funded health care facilities. New medical technologies could even exacerbate the problems by creating expensive new treatments and boosting life expectancy rates.

It may be difficult to keep the euro area intact. Europe's grim fiscal outlook raises a big question mark about the sustainability of the euro zone. The Stability and Growth pact will eventually have to be scrapped, and different fiscal positions across countries will create enormous strains, given a common monetary policy and currency. Meanwhile, expanding the European Union eastward will not alleviate Europe's demographic problems as all the new prospective members (Turkey excepted) have even weaker population dynamics than existing EU members.

China will face many of the same problems as the West. The Chinese economy currently is booming, but it too faces demographic challenges down the road. The fertility rate is below replacement level and the working-age population is projected to peak in around 2025. This will make it easier to employ those workers flowing from rural areas to cities, but, as in other countries, the aging population will create a large fiscal problem, albeit later than in the West. Other important issues discussed in the CIA report include the implications of increased urbanization in a number of unstable countries, the global spread of infectious diseases, and the adverse environmental consequence of rapid population growth in the developing world.

The long-run picture for Europe and Japan looks bleak in that a deteriorating fiscal picture will be bearish for bonds while weak aggregate demand is bearish for stocks. *Those two trends would be consistent if the eventual outcome is a stagflationary environment, which could occur in the context of labor shortages and attempts to inflate out of a government debt trap.* (Emphasis mine)

Age Vulnerability: Your Pension or Your Life

Let's next look at a lengthy report entitled "The 2003 Aging Vulnerability Index[2] by Neil Howe and Richard Jackson. (Howe was co-author of the Seminal books on generational behavior trends, *Generations* and *The Fourth Turning.*)

The report analyzes the cost of public pension funds (like Social Security, the state retirement funds mentioned earlier, etc.) for 12 different developed countries. It then analyzes how the various countries will fare in the future, factoring in their economies, taxes, costs, and the actual circumstances surrounding retirement. (For instance, it makes a difference whether you are likely to be supported by your kids or out on your own.)

In short, it clearly shows us that there will be staggering budget problems for these countries, and some more than others. The report categorizes Australia, the United Kingdom, and the United States as low vulnerability countries. (See Table 11.2.) Given what we know of potential U.S. problems from an aging population, this means the report posits grim news for certain countries, especially the mainstay countries in Europe (France, Germany,

Table 11.2   Aging Vulnerability Index 2003 Edition

Rankings from Lease to Most Vulnerable

Low Vulnerability
1. Australia
2. United Kingdom
3. United States

Medium Vulnerability
4. Canada
5. Sweden
6. Japan
7. Germany
8. Netherlands
9. Belgium

High Vulnerability
10. France
11. Italy
12. Spain

© The Center for Strategic and International Studies and Watson Wyatt Worldwide.

Italy, Spain, and the Netherlands). Jackson and Howe give a whole new meaning to the concept of "Old Europe."

Let's look at a few salient items:

Today, there are 30 pension-eligible elders in the developed world for every 100 working age adults. By the year 2040, there will be 70. In Italy, Japan, and Spain, the fastest-aging countries, there will be 100. In other words, there will be as many retirees as workers. This rising old-age dependency ratio will translate into sharply rising costs for pay-as-you-go retirement programs—and a heavy burden on the budget, on the economy, and on working age adults in any country that does not take serious steps to prepare. . . . Public benefits to the elderly will reach an average of 25 percent of GDP in the developed countries by 2040, double today's level.

. . . In Japan, they will reach 27 percent of GDP; in France, they will reach 29 percent; and in Italy and Spain, they will exceed 30 percent. *This growth will throw into question the sustainability of today's retirement systems—and indeed, society's very ability to provide a decent standard of living for the old without overburdening the young. . . . It is unclear whether they can change course without economic and social turmoil.* (Emphasis mine)

For most of history, the elderly—here defined as adults aged 60 and over—comprised only a tiny fraction of the population, never more than 5 percent in any country. Today in the developed countries, they comprise 20 percent. [See Figure 11.3.] Forty years from now, the share will reach roughly 35 percent. And that's just the average. In Japan and some of the fast-aging countries of continental Europe, where the median age is expected to exceed 50, the share will be approaching 50 percent.[3]

Today, looking at the data, the five main economies of the European Union spend about 15 percent of their GDP on public benefits to the elderly. This will rise rapidly to almost 30 percent by 2040. Japanese benefits will rise 250 percent to 27 percent in 2040 from today's "mere" 11.8 percent.

How do you pay for such increases? If the increase were paid for entirely by tax hikes, not one European country would pay less than 50 percent of

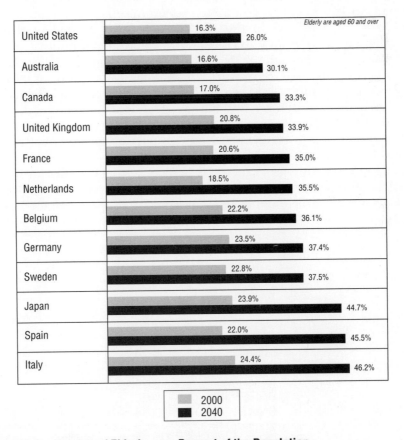

Figure 11.3 Number of Elderly, as a Percent of the Population
© The Center for Strategic and International Studies and Watson Wyatt Worldwide.

its GDP in taxes, and France would be at 62 percent. By comparison, the U.S. tax share of GDP would rise from 33 percent to 44 percent (according to the report; I assume this includes all level of taxes). Japan's taxes would be 46 percent of GDP.

It should be clear to everyone that such an outcome would be an utter economic disaster. Taxes for the working population would be consuming 80 to 90 percent of their income. It would be an economic death spiral. Whatever economic growth might be possible in an aging United States, Europe, or Japan would be completely squelched by such high taxes. The "giant whooshing sound" would be that of young workers leaving for more favorable working and tax conditions.

If the increase in benefit costs were paid for entirely in cuts to other spending projects, Japan would see its public benefits rise to 66 percent of total public spending, France and the United States to 53 percent, and Germany to 49 percent. Today, these expenditures are all around 31 percent. What do you cut? In the United States, you might cut defense spending, but there is little to cut in Europe and Japan. Education? Welfare? Parks? Transportation? Medical or health programs for the working? It gets so very ugly. Since such an outcome (50 percent of GDP for pensions) is impossible, long before that type of debacle is reached, other solutions, painful as they are, will have been chosen.

Table 11.3 shows when government debt will reach 150 percent of GDP if the various governments decide to pay for the costs by running deficits (borrowing).

Some other gleanings: A mere 10 percent cut in benefits pushes approximately 5 percent of the elderly population into poverty in Europe—think what a 20 percent cut in benefits would do. Japan is ranked in the middle of the vulnerability pack, despite its poor economic outlook, be-

Table 11.3   Projected Date for Debt to Reach 150 Percent of GDP

Country	Year
Japan	2020
Canada	2024
France	2024
United States	2026
Germany	2033

© The Center for Strategic and International Studies and Watson Wyatt Worldwide.

cause more than 50 percent of the elderly live with their children. The three most vulnerable countries are France, Italy, and Spain. Australians are expected to live longer (86.7 years) than any group except the Japanese, who are expected to live to an average of 91.9 years.

In France 67 percent of the income of the elderly population comes from public funding and in Germany it is 61 percent, compared with 35 percent in the United States and Japan. (See Figure 11.4.) These percentages are projected to rise only slightly over the coming decades, but because the elderly population is growing so rapidly, actual outlays will soar.

Not surprisingly, if you add in medical costs the percentage of public spending increases significantly, even assuming no new benefits.

Demography Is Destiny

The world economy is currently dominated by the United States, Europe, and Japan. These studies suggest that there will be little or no help from Europe and Japan in regard to world growth. The world is already far too U.S.-centric. Everyone wants to sell to the U.S. consumer. Our international trade deficit for 2003 was over $500 billion, which simply cannot be sustained.

BCA suggests that the Japanese government debt will grow to 300 percent of GDP over the coming decades. To put this into perspective, that would be the equivalent of $36 trillion U.S. debt. Even with zero interest rates, that is a staggering sum. The Japanese economy cannot handle such a deficit without turning on the printing presses in a manner unprecedented for major countries. It is hard to imagine the dollar, as weak

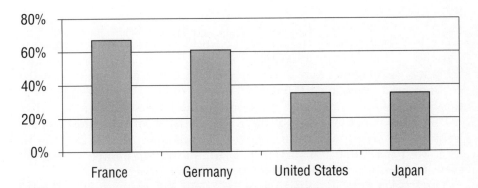

Figure 11.4   Percent of Income of the Elderly Population from Public Funding
© The Center for Strategic and International Studies and Watson Wyatt Worldwide.

as some think it is, to drop long-term (think decades here) against such massive and mounting deficits, which will have to be financed by attempts at inflation.

Europe is already spending a very small percentage of its budget on defense. As one wag puts it, they will be faced with the choice of "guns or rocking chairs." With a declining population, they will be hard-pressed to find enough bodies to man their military as it currently exists.

Unless they unwind their pension promises, European countries will play a smaller role in the world of the future, notwithstanding the view from France. The role of Asia, especially China and India, will be far more significant in the future world of our children.

The problems outlined in the two studies suggest that turmoil is coming to the developed countries of Europe and Japan. They cannot pay for their promises to retirees and still grow their economies. They will have to choose one or the other. If they choose higher taxes and fewer opportunities, the best of young Europe will vote with their feet, as did their ancestors in the eighteenth and nineteenth centuries. That will only make the situation worse. But can a majority retiring population vote to cut their benefits?

In short, for the world economy to grow, developing countries are going to have to look to themselves for growth. The aging developed countries will simply not provide the growth engine that they provided for the latter half of the twentieth century.

For forward-looking investors, that means there will be real business growth opportunities in the emerging markets and those countries that can sell to them.

As strange as it may seem today, in a few decades China will be complaining about cheap labor in the Middle East and western Asia. If that sounds too far-fetched, think Japan only a few decades ago. The next stock market bubbles will be to the west of our shores.

As BCA noted, it is critical that the Iraqi experiment in democracy be successful for the future stability of the world. In 1945, there were many who thought it would be impossible for the regimented Japanese to establish a successful democracy. Today we watch as China moves to a capitalist economy and democracy. What stock market did the best in 2002? It was Russia, which not coincidentally has some of the lowest tax rates.

Call me naive, but I do not think the primary consideration for the Iraqi war was/is oil, American hegemony, or establishing a democracy in Iraq. But I think that the current U.S. administration intends to use the event to do its best to bring about a thriving Islamic democracy.

The Iraqi people are educated and are quite entrepreneurial and business oriented. I expect (or at least fervently hope) that given the chance they may surprise many in the world with how fast they rebound. Given their explosive population growth rate, they could become an engine for growth in the region. If President Bush is serious about helping Iraq, he should get rid of any and all trade barriers with the new regime and stand back and let the free market work.

Only a few years ago, we were fearful of the Chinese hordes and their army. They were the enemy. Today, our economies are so inextricably interwoven that it is in our best interest to work any problems out peacefully. We now depend on each other. If we want to find peace with the Arab world, we need to find ways to establish economic ties with Arab countries as well. If we do not, the demographic issues I outlined earlier will have very negative consequences for us, our children, and our grandchildren.

Finally, if I were young and aggressive or starting out (or starting over) I would seriously consider learning a second and third language, moving overseas, and looking for opportunity. I would learn a business here and go and reproduce it offshore. Or you could consider backing a younger person who has the time and energy to start a business in a foreign country. But be prepared to travel, and even if you are only the investor, learn the local language and customs and be ready to change course quickly.

King Dollar and the Guillotine

Whoever you are—I have always depended on the kindness of strangers.

—Blanche DuBois, from Tennessee Williams' *A Streetcar Named Desire*

The global economy is in the midst of a major transformation. This realignment will mean that a number of trends that have been in place for many years are going to be reversed. These changes have the potential to be quite painful for people and businesses in the United States and overseas as well. On the other hand, they will present opportunities to thoughtful investors and businesses that position themselves to take advantage of these major shifts.

First, we'll examine several individual pieces of the global economic puzzle and then see if we can put them together to get a true picture of what we face as the decade evolves.

The Kindness of Strangers

The United States is "borrowing" roughly $500 billion per year from foreign nations. Much of our economic growth has been predicated on this borrowing. Of course, the growth of the world economy has been based on the U.S. expansion. It has been a virtuous circle that is about to reverse into a vicious cycle.

"A saving-short U.S. economy has had to import surplus saving from abroad, mainly from Asia but also from Europe, in order to support economic growth. And the United States has had to run a massive balance-of-payments deficit in order to attract that capital. As America's federal budget now goes deeper into deficit, the country's net national saving rate—for consumers, businesses, and the government sector combined—could easily plunge from a record low of 1.3 percent in late 2002 toward 'zero' [in subsequent years]. In that case, the U.S. current-account deficit could approach 7 percent of GDP, requiring about $3 billion of foreign financing every business day. The world has never before faced an external financing burden of that magnitude," observes Stephen Roach, Chief Economist of Morgan Stanley.

After hitting record lows in the spring of 1995, the broad trade-weighted dollar surged some 47 percent through early 2002. The broad dollar then began to drop, losing about 8 percent through April. Against the euro (and certain related currencies), the dollar has dropped 50 percent from its high. The euro started at $1.14 in January 1999 and then fell to only $.82 before rising back to $1.15 in early May of 2003. It has since risen to $1.28 in early 2004. Will the dollar drop further? Let's explore what led to the rise of the dollar, and then see how vulnerable it is to further decline.

The Artificial Dollar

The dollar is artificially high because the rest of the world, and especially Asia, is hooked on selling products to the American consumer. If their prices were to rise 30 percent, we would buy less of their products and more of our own. Of course, our cost of living would go up and our standard of living would go down. If they sell less, their unemployment rises and profits drop. Thus they have to take dollars, which may be worth less in the future, for maintaining sales today. There are always trade-offs.

For now, the foreign manufacturers are willing to take dollars to keep their factories going. The dollars are converted into local currency or other currencies, or put into their central banks to hold as reserves. This process has the effect of keeping the dollar higher than it might normally be, as we will see.

In addition, some people hold dollars because the dollar is better than their local currency. Physical dollars are desired in many Latin American and African countries, and other parts of the developing world. The clear pattern is that the dollar is a better value than the local currencies.

(Could the euro become as popular a currency as the dollar? Sure, but then there would be two choices, not an abandonment of the dollar. Will it be more popular than the dollar? In some countries the answer would be yes, especially those closer to the euro zone. But the primary driver for such holdings is not to get the best-performing currency, the euro or the dollar, but to have a currency that is not their local currency, which their local governments continually inflate and debase.)

Furthermore, it should be obvious that if we were not the reserve currency for the world, the dollar would not be as high. The dollar would have less buying power. Foreigners look at that buying power and are often jealous, seeing it is part of American hegemony. But it cuts both ways. An artificially strong dollar has meant that our manufacturing base has slowly been eroding as more and more jobs leave the United States for cheaper production climates. There is no free lunch.

If the dollar is artificially high, is there reason to believe it can drop? A Federal Reserve study on what happens when the trade deficit gets too big in developed countries[1] shows the following:

On average, when the trade deficit widens to more than 5 percent, the currency starts to drop. It typically drops 20 percent over three years, as the trade balance recovers. (The study also shows GDP growth slows down by about 3 percent from the year prior to the trade deficit peaking, and short-term rates rise. We will deal with those inconvenient elements in later chapters.)

Thus, at 6 percent and approaching 7 percent of GDP trade deficits, we are in no-man's-land. There is real precedent for the dollar to continue to fall, *if* the artificial props are removed. Again, those props are the desire to sell to the American consumer, the need for a store of value in developing countries as opposed to the local currency, and the fact that the dollar is the reserve currency for the world. Let's see how likely it is that these could change.

Why the Dollar Rose

At the same time as the dollar was rising, the United States and particularly U.S. consumers were increasingly becoming the engine of growth for the world. The United States accounted for fully 96 percent of the cumulative increase in world GDP (at market exchange rates) over the 1995 to 2001 interval—double its share in the world economy. By way of comparison, over the eight-year period 1995 to 2002, Euroland real GDP growth has averaged just 2.2 percent. Such anemic growth accounted for only a small portion of the average growth in world GDP over that interval, far short of the region's 15.7 percent share of world output (as measured on a purchasing-power parity basis).[2]

There was a massive drive, particularly from Asia, to sell anything and everything to the United States. Indeed, much of the "Asian miracle" was the result of increased sales to the United States. The appetite for dollars was huge. The central banks of the world took those dollars and placed them in their electronic vaults as reserves.

In 2003 and on into 2004, the world continued to buy our goods, stocks, bonds, businesses, and real estate to finance our own buying binge. On balance, the United States owes $2 trillion to foreigners, net of our investments overseas. That number has been growing dramatically for the past few years.

(As an aside, as the dollar drops, it makes our foreign assets worth more in terms of dollars and those dollar assets held by foreigners worth less in terms of their local currencies. Thus the drop of the dollar actually improves our statistical national balance sheet, in a perverse sort of way.)

The noted and celebrated Austrian economist Hans Sennholz notes the following conflicting desires:

> No central bank on earth, not even the Federal Reserve System, can continually inflate its currency and defy market rates of interest without harming both its currency and the economy. Inflation tends to accelerate and ultimately destroy the currency and cripple the economy. And no government whatsoever can suffer budget deficits of half a trillion dollars annually without impairing its standing with its creditors. Piling debt on debt undermines their trust and raises the crucial question of debt resolution.
>
> Important foreign creditors nevertheless may choose to stay the course in the hope that their debtor will bring his house into order. They may continue to peg their currencies to the U.S. dollar, as the government of China has been doing with persistence, and to enjoy the influx of dollars. It not only has given employment to millions of Chinese workers producing goods and services for the American market but also attracted much American capital and technology, enabling them to leap from nineteenth century economic conditions to contemporary high-tech capability and productivity. They obviously will not make haste to increase the value of their currencies, which would depress their sales and curb the flow of American capital. They may even be prepared to bear the costs of a sudden devaluation of their large dollar holdings, if the U.S. dollar should finally fall under the growing weight of foreign indebtedness.[3]

The economists at Morgan Stanley estimate that the trade deficit could be more than 6 percent of GDP in 2004, which would be 50 percent higher than ever seen before. We would need over $2 billion per day from foreign sources. This is unsustainable. Just as Amazon.com could not grow its stock to the sky by borrowing and spending far more than it makes, the United States will one day have to pay the piper.

If the projected 2004 rate were to continue for an extended period of time, foreigners would own everything not nailed down in the United States in a few decades, which clearly cannot happen. Something will have to give, and that something is either the value of the dollar or a massive reversion in U.S. dollar outflows, or a combination of both. We will need to export more and buy less on a huge scale for this adjustment to happen. One of the natural market-driven ways this happens is for the value of the dollar to drop. It makes it more expensive to buy foreign goods (therefore we buy less), and it makes our goods cheaper for foreigners to buy (therefore they buy more).

If something is unsustainable, then at some point it stops. The trend reverses. The hope of the central banks and businesses of the world, all of whom recognize the trend must change, is that it is done slowly with as little pain as possible, rather than in a rapid drop that could precipitate a severe and simultaneous worldwide recession.

Those who are not worried about the trade deficit and the dollar point out that foreign nations have a seemingly bottomless appetite for dollars, and that as long as the dollar and the United States remain as the safe haven of choice, there is little reason for alarm. But when you look into the recent trends of the actual sources of those foreign investors buying dollars, it is easier to be concerned.

When we buy foreign goods, we convert dollars into the currency of the country where the product (or service) is made. When a foreigner wants to buy something in the United States, he must get dollars. An imbalance in the flow of currencies is what makes the value of currencies go up or down. It is supply and demand in its rawest form. If more people want dollars, then the dollar goes up.

But how can the dollar be going up when we are spending so much more than we are selling? It is because foreigners are taking those dollars and buying U.S. companies, U.S. property, and U.S. stocks and bonds. Also, foreign central banks, especially Asian central banks, use the dollar as a reserve currency.

One of the largest sources of dollars during the rise was from foreign companies buying U.S. companies or setting up production facilities in the United States. In the period 1990–1995 average annual European dollar flows from mergers and acquisitions was only $10 billion. In 2000, Europeans bought over $600 billion of goods, services, and investments in the United States. Direct investment was a whopping $237 billion, and purchase of securities other than U.S. bonds was $327 billion. Taking away U.S. investments in Europe it was a net $194 billion to the advantage of the United States. That process alone financed half of the trade deficit.*

---

*You can see the source for these statistics and a mountain of other data at the U.S. Department of Commerce's Bureau of Economic Analysis web site at www.bea.doc.gov.

In 2001 the positive balance from Europe was $184 billion. That process began to dramatically slow down in 2002, as the positive balance was only $3.5 billion. In 2003, the direction is clearly the other way.

But Europe was not the only source for a rising dollar. Asia has been a significant source for dollar power. As an example, Asia increased its dollar holdings substantially in 2001. According to the economists at Morgan Stanley, "Net U.S. inflows from Asia (excluding Japan) totaled $17.3 billion in November and another $19.8 billion in December, the strongest two-month surge on record. In December alone, the region accounted for 42 percent of total U.S. inflows, with China and Hong Kong the primary sources of capital. *The late-year surge in inflows from Asia ex-Japan pushed the regional total to a record $111 billion for the year, more than double the level of the prior year.*"

Unlike Europe, Asian buying of dollars has continued through 2002 and 2003 and into early 2004. There is a considerable time lag in the data on foreign purchases, but in just the month of February 2003 there was large net Treasury buying from Japan ($5.58 billion) and China ($1.80 billion). Preliminary data from 2003 shows still massive buying by Asia, particularly China and Japan. Japan spent $65 billion in January of 2004 to keep the yen from rising against the dollar. Such massive purchases are unprecedented in history.

However, the euro area took out $3.4 billion, the United Kingdom $2.9 billion, and Canada $1.9 billion.[4] Not surprisingly, the countries that are selling are seeing a significant loss on their dollar investments in terms of their currencies.

Now, let's look at one of the reasons why Asia is buying dollars.

The Competitive Devaluation Raceway

Greg Weldon, one of my favorite analysts and the author of the *Daily Money Monitor*, often discusses "The Asian Competitive Devaluation Raceway." By that, he means that Asian countries keep lowering the value of their currency against each other vis-à-vis the dollar, so as to be more attractive to the U.S. consumer. Each country is worried that if its currency gets too strong, the other Asian currencies will have an advantage.

How do you lower your currency? You create more currency than is demanded or is needed. You buy dollars with that currency for your central bank reserves, and invest them in U.S. government bonds.

This race has been going on for years, with one country after another pulling into the lead. It seems no country has been willing to let its currency get significantly stronger than its competitor countries.

That is not good for the consumers of those countries, of course. It means U.S. products and services cost them a lot more, and hurts our exporting businesses. It is not good for their lifestyles or savings.

Then why do they work so hard to keep their currencies low against the dollar? To keep their exports up, which is what they believe will eventually bring prosperity. Each nation feels that if its currency goes too high, the other nations will gain an advantage over them in selling products to the United States.

As just one example of many possibilities, the head of the Thailand central bank gave a short speech last year about his country's problems. Weldon noted he used the word "export" five times in only a few sentences, or 12 percent of his whole speech. He was clearly worried, as Thai exports were down 8 percent at the time of the speech. The head of the bank was focused on exchange rates, and especially the way that the Japanese yen has dropped much lower than the Thai baht.

Of course, the Japanese have publicly argued for several years the yen is too high, and they work aggressively to lower the value of the yen, even as it rises. Some Japanese leaders have publicly stated the yen should be at 160, not the 108 it is at today (in early 2004). Japanese leaders would clearly prefer the yen to be at 130.

Now, here is the heart of the matter: If each of those Asian countries thought they could all simultaneously get a stronger currency against the dollar, they would be for it in a heartbeat. It is not that they want a strong dollar; they just don't want their currency to be stronger than the other Asian currencies. If the dollar were to show weakness against all the Asian currencies at the same time, they would not object. They would be thrilled.

The 900-pound gorilla in this process is China. The Chinese currency is pegged at a fixed rate to the dollar, so there has been no movement. Since China has a very pronounced advantage over other Asian countries in regard to labor costs, these other countries feel forced to keep their currencies low in order to compete. The Japanese have been particularly vocal in their complaints about the value of the Chinese currency.

When does the pain of taking overvalued dollars become more than the pain of selling less to the United States? I think it is when China allows its currency to float. Asian countries do not necessarily want an overpriced dollar; they simply want the price of their currency to be favorable in relation to their neighbors, and when the Chinese allow the renminbi to rise, that will be the real end of the dollar being overvalued, as the rest of Asia will feel comfortable in letting their currencies rise as well.

There is an increasing call from many corners of the world for the Chinese to allow the renminbi to float. They have not responded to the pressure, but they're doing what all countries do—they're not acting until they feel it is in their own best interests. That will probably be when they think their own consumer demand is growing and solid, and thus can sustain a possible slowing of sales to the United States. When that will be is anyone's guess, so the dollar could be somewhat strong for a period of time even when by other measures it should drop.

China will be the surprise move that sets this set of dominoes in motion. This is one area that investors must watch closely, as it will be a surprise and will be the transition to a much lower dollar fairly quickly.

Addressing another point, you will remember I noted earlier that the dollar is down about 8 percent on a trade-weighted basis, but is down 50 percent against the euro. What is holding the value of the dollar up?

Quite simply, Canada, Mexico, China, and Japan account for 47 percent of the trade-weighted currencies. The Canadian dollars and yen are only slightly up, the peso is down, and the Chinese currency is pegged to the dollar, so there has been very little movement from a major part of our trading partners. This will change, of course, but it is one thing holding up the dollar. Thus the drop in the euro (and euro-related currencies) is the single major reason the dollar has dropped slightly on a trade-weighted basis, when seen on multidecade chart.[5]

By the way, the dollar dropping 20 to 30 percent is not the end of the world, as some would have you think. The dollar fell by more then one-third against all currencies in the 1980s and early 1990s, and the United States seemed to move along just fine. Inflation dropped during that time and the economy grew. A falling dollar will help our exports, of course. I expect the Bush administration to continue to tacitly approve a weak dollar policy while continuing to say the market should determine prices.

The Law of One Price

Adrian Van Eck, editor of the *Money-Forecast Letter*, reveals the Bush administrative strategy to address the worldwide problem of an overpriced dollar:

The annual edition of the St. Louis Federal Reserve Bank's *International Economic Trends* opened with an interesting analysis of money and prices. This 2003 report included the following:

"THE LAW OF ONE PRICE states that identical goods sold in different countries should sell for the same price when prices are expressed in a common currency. If, for example, pencils were cheaper in Canada than in the United States, individuals could purchase them in Canada and sell them in the United States at a profit. Such action would raise the price in Canada and lower the price in the United States."

Unfortunately (and this is the true essence of G. W. Bush's problems), THE LAW OF ONE PRICE often does not apply today in America's trade relations with the world. Our number one trading partner is Canada. It has pushed its money down against the dollar to give Canadians a decided advantage in trade. Years ago—and for some time—the Canadian dollar and the U.S. dollar were more or less equal. Then came Bill Clinton and Bob Rubin and the "strong dollar" policy. Even while pretending that we still have a strong dollar policy, the United States has closed half the gap that had opened up between the monies of these two nations. The difference is still enough to allow Canada to sell us $4.9 billion more than they bought from us in the last month and $30.7 billion more than they bought from us in the past year. Given Canada's relatively small population compared to America's, that is a huge gap!

Europe has allowed its money to rise sharply against the dollar. Japan has also been adjusting its money much closer to THE LAW OF ONE PRICE LEVEL. Other nations are now working quietly with our Treasury department to bring their own monies closer into line with the dollar. That will allow for a thriving international free trade based on fair trade.

This has been the message coming out of the entire Bush Administration and both Republican and Democratic members of the House and Senate of late, as voters back home have flooded Washington with angry complaints that one nation—China—does not play fair. Here is one thing that encourages me: All of our major trading partners seem to be moving toward currencies at a fair relative level.

This adjustment of currencies is due to the recent Group of Seven meeting in Dubai when the G-7 threw its weight behind trading under THE LAW OF ONE PRICE. That is the way things used to be back in the administration of President Theodore Roosevelt. In those days of the gold standard, every major currency was in balance with every other currency. You could spend a dollar in Germany and get one dollar's worth of goods.

Conversely, a German tourist could spend one mark in America and get exactly the same value as that mark would buy in Germany. The same held true for French, Italian, and Spanish money. All currencies were linked to gold. Looking back, that was so simple and so very fair.

No country was allowed to monkey around with its money, pushing it down in value against everyone else in order to gain an edge in trade. True competition lifted the standard of living for everyone! Ever since Nixon cut the American dollar loose from gold more than 30 years ago, the world has resembled a jungle. It is like the "kill or be killed" lifestyle of such wild beasts as lions and tigers. The G-7 in Dubai said this kind of monetary conduct in money "must stop now!"

However, after the U.S. economy—and eventually the global economy—has moved into a [hopefully!] strong economic boom and stock prices are at record levels, the Bush Administration and the G-7 will move to shake China's boat. Keep in mind that China has destroyed the manufacturing sector of every country in the world. The Chinese yuan will rise to fair value in an orderly manner. There is no way to put a time frame on it, but it will happen.

THE LAW OF ONE PRICE will be global trade law eventually. There is no other way.[6]

An Uncomfortable Adjustment

While Van Eck's assessment is hopeful over the longer term, such a readjustment is not without its difficulties in the here and now.

In 2002, Morgan Stanley projected that a 20 percent drop in the dollar against the euro would knock 1 percent off of the GDP of Europe, and it looks like it did just that. Such a drop hurts Europeans' sales to us and makes their goods and services more expensive to the rest of the world. If the dollar were to drop another 10 to 20 percent or the euro go to $1.40 to $1.50 (as seems quite possible) you will hear screams and moans throughout Europe, as businesses would have to compete against much cheaper production not only from Asia but from the United States. Germany in particular is vulnerable.

A rise of the euro to $1.40 to $1.50 would mean the prices of products made in Europe would have risen 60 to 80 percent in terms of dollars over a period of just a few years. This would be even more painful for Europe if the euro rises to $1.50 as the respected analysts at BCA Research think. This will give the United States (and Asia until China revalues its currency and the rest go along) a huge advantage in selling products and services to Europe and a major competitive advantage in the rest of the world. If European businesses are already having problems (and the statistics suggest they are) then this would be even more devastating.

What could European nations do? They could ask for an increase in tariffs, but this would start a trade war that they would lose, and could possibly trigger a worldwide recession. It would also contravene a lot of treaties they have worked very hard to get signed, and also cause a major split within the European Union. This is not a likely scenario.

The more likely effort will be intense lobbying to get the Chinese to allow their currency to float against the dollar.

But it does mean Europe will face significant economic difficulty. It could also lead to the very real problem of deflation.

The Artificial Dollar and Deflation

There is a global wave of deflation washing over the countries of the world. One of the not so subtle hints from members of the Federal Reserve, who are concerned about deflation in the United States, is that allowing the dollar to fall will provide significant help in the United States fight against deflation. For the rest of the world, it has the opposite effect.

One of the side effects of the competitive currency devaluation was that Japan and China in effect directly exported their deflation to us. Now Europe is in the same situation. It is quite possible it could see deflation within the next year or so. One of the disadvantages the European Monetary Union has is that its response to economic problems is limited by agreement, so that in extraordinary circumstances the European central bank simply does not have solutions available to it.

As noted earlier, one of the potential outcomes is that China revalues its currency and the rest of Asia goes along. That would be good for Europe. The world moves to balance its books. The countries that can best cope with change will be the winners.

Unfortunately, though, the Japanese get hurt in the process. They are clearly fighting serious deflation, and a rise in the value of their currency would be deflationary. They are starting to paint themselves into a corner.

The Japanese have debt problems that quite simply dwarf those of the United States. To quote *Forbes*:

> Consider the notion that, with perhaps $11 trillion in savings, the Japanese have enough wealth to cope. It sounds as if they do—until you realize that the total on- and off-balance-sheet claims on the household, corporate, and government sectors in Japan are about $30 trillion, according to estimates by Goldman Sachs. That sum is six times Japan's $5 trillion GDP. (The total of U.S. public and private debt is $19 trillion, two times GDP.) Their banks are bleeding and are in a true crisis. The four largest banks are reporting losses approaching 3 trillion yen, or over 20 billion dollars. Analysis of Japanese business is bleak, and consumer demand there is decreasing as the population ages rapidly.[7]

The level of bad debts at Japanese banks is staggering. Many outside analysts believe Japanese banks are essentially bankrupt. Their accounting rules would make Enron executives blush. As an example, they do not mark to market the stocks on their books.

Japan is the third largest economy in the world. It has been a major source of lending in the world, and a weak Japan is good for no one. Can Japan afford to let its currency rise 20 to 30 percent? Can it keep it from happening without massive printing? As of January, 2004 they seem desperately committed to keeping the yen from rising, printing $65 billion in yen to purchase dollars in January alone.

If Japan will not let its currency rise, can the other Asian countries? For instance, if the Korean won rose 20 percent against the yen, that would make a Hyundai cost the same as a Toyota. The price advantage goes away, and Korea suffers. The variations to the currency dance are wide.

Can You Focus the Picture, Please?

Let's look at the puzzle pieces:

- The dollar went to bubble-like artificial heights because the world wanted to sell products to America.
- American consumption was abetted by ever lower interest rates that allowed consumers to borrow money, especially on their homes, and by a stock market bubble that made people feel wealthy. Both of these trends are over.
- There has never been a case in the history of the world that when trade deficits rose to the heights we are at a serious currency correction did not follow.
- Such corrections typically slow down the economies of all concerned.
- The world, and especially Asia, is focused on selling products to the American consumer. The United States was responsible for 96 percent of the growth in world GDP.
- This can't continue forever, so at some point the rest of the world must find additional consumers to sell products to. But the major sources of potential customers are in weak positions. Many of the developing countries have little real internal consumer spending.
- Many world economies are already weak. Japan since 1989 has always been on the brink of or in a recession, and Europe may be in recession by the end of 2004. Bright spot economies like China depend on ever-increasing world trade for their growth.

This means that the developing nations, which have focused on selling to the United States, will have to develop their own internal markets. We will have to make a transition from a U.S.-centric world where all roads lead to the U.S. consumer to a more balanced world.

By "have to" I am not referring to some moral imperative whereby the United States gladly allows the value of the U.S. dollar to drop, thus making the costs of the products we buy more expensive. I mean "have to" in the free market sense. The world simply does not have the choice. There is a limit to everything, even the kindness of strangers.

Until the rest of the world and especially Asia can wean themselves from dependence on the American consumer, the dollar will remain artificially high. That is not to say it will not continue its decline. It will. It is just that it will take longer than it would without the artificial factors cited earlier.

The adjustments among world currency and trade patterns will take years, and will be painful in some circles. It will not happen all at once.

The United States will not go from a huge trade deficit to a positive balance within a year. It will take many years. Foreign sellers will sell wherever they can make a profit and will continue to sell to the United States, just at higher prices. While the United States will not be the only engine for world growth in the future, it will still be a major trading partner. It is not that the United States goes away. It is just that we buy less "stuff" relative to what we sell.

But the adjustments will act as a drag on many of the world markets, perhaps putting the world into a synchronous recession. Such a recession will have the effect of helping the world rebalance its trade priorities, which will mean a much more stable period of growth following this period of transition.

How will it all play out ? What will be the value of the dollar? How will world trade be affected? There is no one answer because there are too many variables to make any realistic prediction.

What we can say is that there is a high degree of likelihood that the dollar will be lower by at least 20 to 30 percent (across the board, with some currencies much higher and some much lower), that the world will find customers in addition to the United States, and that this will cause a major shift in buying patterns within the United States.

We will close this chapter on the dollar with some profound comments from a fascinating paper entitled "Saving the Dollar from Destruction" by the renowned economist Hans Sennholz.[8]

Both U.S. Treasury and Federal Reserve officials seem to underrate the growing international dangers to both the dollar and the economy. But even if they were cognizant of the true situation, their choices of action would be rather limited.

A few academic advisors favor instant removal of the prime causes of the predicament; they would halt the Federal Reserve credit expansion forthwith and balance the Federal government budget with due haste. They would allow interest to find its market rate and capital and labor markets to readjust freely to the preference and choices of the people. In short, they would stabilize the U.S. dollar and release economic life from its most harmful constraints. But they are fully aware that such a solution would be rejected summarily not only by the policymakers but also by the American people.

Under the sway of the policymakers and their spokesmen, most people are unaware of the cause-and-effect relationships of monetary policies and their portentous effects. And even if they were more knowledgeable in monetary matters, they probably would reject a sudden, resolute stabilization of the dollar which would painfully reveal the full extent of the damage inflicted by the fiscal and monetary stimuli. After many years of maladjustment, the withdrawal would usher in a painful recession which probably would be long and severe due to numerous institutional barriers impeding or even thwarting the necessary readjustment. Few Americans are likely to place their trust in these advisors and opt for such a scenario. . . .

This economist cannot envision the total destruction of the American dollar, the primary world currency. Surely, it will continue to depreciate at various rates and the American economy will remain sluggish and unstable. The dollar may even have to share its eminent position as the world reserve currency with the euro which itself suffers from massive deficit spending by the three largest member countries: Germany, France, and Italy. . . .[9]

Sennholz notes at length the growing rise of protectionist sentiment and the pessimistic predictions of many economists. He then comments:

Unfortunately, an American slide into protectionism would have grave consequences not only in the United States but also throughout the world. It would not alleviate the very causes of the present imbalance: the Federal Reserve stimuli and Treasury deficits. In fact, it would aggravate the situation as new import restrictions would cause goods prices to rise, consumption to be curtailed, and standards of living to fall. It would slash various sources of government revenue, which in turn would boost budget deficits and make matters worse. Moreover, the government of China and other countries hurt by American tariffs undoubtedly would retaliate with similar restrictions on American goods. In American footsteps, they would not hesitate to hurt their American trade partner and, in interventionist fashion, impose even more restrictions on their own people.

A more optimistic scenario would be a gradual abandonment of the monetary policies and an orderly readjustment to unhampered market conditions. The Federal government would balance its budget in the next few years by holding the line on both transfer spending and military outlays. The Federal Reserve System would allow the market rate of interest to resume its basic function, the efficient allocation of economic resources in the course of time.

A painful readjustment process would commence immediately; interest rates would rise, calling a halt to misguided spending patterns and encouraging saving and capital formation. Boom industries soon would suffer withdrawal symptoms while others would revive from several years of stagnation. At the same time, China and other creditor countries hopefully would allow their currencies to rise and the U.S. dollar to decline gradually, which would trim America's trade deficits, raise goods prices, and depreciate all dollar debt at home and abroad. With the

Federal budget in balance and interest rates at market levels, the dollar would continue to function smoothly as the primary world currency.

Such a scenario would tell the truth about the international state of affairs. In world money markets a dollar depreciation of 30 percent would reduce the financial as well as nonfinancial American debt of $32 trillion by that percentage of purchasing power. It would diminish the three-trillion-dollar international debt burden of the U.S. government by one trillion dollars. American goods prices would rise at lesser rates, which undoubtedly would bring relief to all debtors while it would diminish the wealth of creditors. There are many ways of cheating a creditor. The United States government would use an old political ruse, the depreciation of its currency.

It is unlikely that present policymakers will soon see the urgent need for basic changes; they like the present system. In contrast, the political opposition, ever eager to take the place of the present team, may recognize the need some day and advocate the return to solvency and integrity. When the electorate finally recognizes the urgent necessity and elects and empowers the opposition to correct the course, the dollar may stabilize. It will need much courage and leadership to endure the pains of readjustment and hold the course.

Our favorite scenario builds on a gradualist adjustment which, in democratic societies, is the only realistic outline of change. When the electorate finally realizes that the U.S. dollar moves from crisis to crisis at ever shrinking value and purchasing power it may want to retrieve the old anchor of all currencies, the gold standard. The world abandoned it in 1971 when President Nixon defaulted in international gold payment obligations and made the fiat dollar the only available medium of exchange. Since then the world has moved from crisis to crisis, suffering from ever increasing maladjustments.[10]

As we will see in Chapter 23, gold, that barbarous relic, will be the beneficiary of a depreciating dollar. Gold functions as a neutral currency that cannot be inflated away by a central bank. While investors can protect themselves from a drop in the dollar by simply rotating into nondollar currencies, stocks, bonds, and other investments, they are still subject to the whims of whatever central bank that prints the currency they choose.

Of all the trends discussed in this book, the drop in the dollar is the one that is the most set in stone. There are simply no realistic scenarios in which the dollar can maintain its current value as long as the trade deficit remains at 4 to 6 percent of GDP. The good news is that such adjustments typically take years, and Bulls' Eye Investors will have time to adjust and benefit from the trend.

The Muddle Through Economy

13

It's tough to make predictions, especially about the future.

—Yogi Berra

I first wrote about the Muddle Through Economy in January 2002. Even while the first quarter grew at a strong pace of 5 percent, I doubted both those who thought we would see a double-dip recession and those on the other extreme who predicted a V-shaped second half recovery. The year seesawed back and forth, ending up with a soft 2.4 percent growth and a jobless recovery.

Since that time I have come to believe that Muddle Through is an apt description for the economic cycle for this decade. We're in a period with overall economic growth, albeit not at the sustained rate of the late 1990s. It will be a period in which we will be forced to work through some of the economic headwinds described in previous chapters.

As I write this chapter, the most recent data tells us that the economy grew in the third quarter of 2003 by 8.2 percent, and the fourth-quarter data show another 4 percent plus! That is hardly Muddle Through. That is Red Hot. Furthermore, it is highly likely that the quarter in which this book comes out will see a very solid growth number, and that 2004 will turn out to be a very good year, barring some shock.

How, then, can I talk about Muddle Through? Why won't things simply continue to improve? First, let me stress that I am talking about a much longer period than just 2004. Second, as I will soon explain, even in

177

lengthy Muddle Through periods there are always (thankfully!) some powerful interludes of growth.

By Muddle Through I do not mean some continual below-trend state of growth. I mean that we must still do the difficult work of rebalancing the economic scales that were decidedly tilted in the last boom. I believe that until we have adjusted these imbalances, we will be fighting an uphill battle for growth. This difficult process will likely take the rest of this decade.

I believe the annual GDP growth of this decade will be somewhat below average, less than 3 percent at the end of the period. There will be some very good periods when the bulls will proclaim the return of the high-growth economy of the 1990s, and some years we would like to avoid, in which the bears will declare the day of reckoning is at hand. Neither will be right, as least during this decade.

This chapter first examines the reasons the economy will grow and then looks at the problems we face. Then I make the classic forecaster's mistake of actually putting in print my thoughts as to how a Muddle Through scenario will play out.

Déjà Vu All Over Again

Let's first look at Table 13.1. This is the growth in GDP for the years 1970 through 1982. The average GDP growth was 2.5 percent, and for the period GDP totaled 37.5 percent.

Yet there were years when the GDP was very high. The years 1976–1979 saw back-to-back growth in real GDP of 5.6 percent, 4.6 percent, 5.5 percent, and 3.2 percent. The average is almost 5 percent. (Of course, inflation for that period was over 7 percent annually.)

Table 13.1   U.S. GDP 1970–1982

1970	0.2	1977	4.6
1971	3.3	1978	5.5
1972	5.4	1979	3.2
1973	5.8	1980	−0.2
1974	−0.6	1981	2.5
1975	−0.4	1982	−2.0
1976	5.6		

Data compiled from the U.S. Department of Commerce: Bureau of Economic Analysis (www.bea.doc.gov).

Not many remember the period of the 1970s as good economic times. Muddle Through is an apt description of the period.

Let's move to more recent times. Stay with me while we go through some numbers. Table 13.2 shows the annual GDP numbers for 1983 through 2002. The average for the 18 years of 1983 through 2000 was 3.54 percent. The average for 1996 through 2000 was 4.0 percent. Not as good as the 1950s and 1960s, where overall real GDP growth was 4.3 percent, but above historical trend and very respectable.

In my opinion, the secular bear market really started in the third quarter of 2000. The collapse in March of 2000 really was the collapse of NASDAQ-related stocks. In a true sense, the resulting tumble was far more than a bear market. That was a bubble bursting.

It did not have that much of an effect on other stocks until a few months later. The broader-based New York Stock Exchange almost reached new highs in the third quarter of that year before starting into its own bear market. The non-NASDAQ component of the S&P 500 was not in bad shape until then, and value stocks were on a run. Then came the beginning of the economic slowdown and the true beginning of the secular bear cycle.

The third quarter of 2000 was the slowest-growth quarter since 1993, and the 2001 recession followed hard on its heels. Since that third quarter the economy has grown at an annual rate of only 2.19 percent, even given the explosive growth of the second half of 2003.

Even if the economy were to grow in 2004 and 2005 at the blistering pace of 4 percent as it did in the late 1990s, the average growth since 2000 would still be less than the long-term trend of 3 percent. If the economy were to grow at 4 percent for the next three years before a historically mild recession (repeat—mild) the economic growth for almost seven years would be back down to 2.5 percent.

Table 13.2   U.S. GDP 1983–2002

1983	4.3	1993	2.7
1984	7.3	1994	4.0
1985	3.8	1995	2.7
1986	3.4	1996	3.6
1987	3.4	1997	4.4
1988	4.2	1998	4.3
1989	3.5	1999	4.1
1990	1.8	2000	3.8
1991	−0.5	2001	0.3
1992	3.0	2002	2.4

Data compiled from the U.S. Department of Commerce: Bureau of Economic Analysis (www.bea.doc.gov).

A decade in which there are two recessions is almost by definition going to grow less than 3 percent on average. And the chances (as we will see) of the U.S. economy getting through the rest of this decade without a recession are not good. Congress and the Federal Reserve can create all the stimulus they like. They cannot repeal the business cycle.

But before we address the problems we face, let's look at the good things that will help offset them. If it were not for these positive aspects, we would not see Muddle Through. We would see the Soft Depression that Bill Bonner writes about in *Financial Reckoning Day*.

The Good News

There is a lot to like about the economy. Let's look at the primary reasons to be optimistic about the future growth of the economy.

- *The American free enterprise system.* Betting against the free market to positively respond to problems has always been a losing bet over time. Notwithstanding the past few years, it is not unusual for the economy to surprise on the upside. The environment for American entrepreneurs to innovate and create is still the best in the world.
- *Tax cuts do make a difference.* The Bush tax cuts were a major factor in softening the recent recession and will be a major stimulus in the future. The U.S. economy got through a stock market bubble and a major drop in capacity utilization and business spending in large part because the consumer had the resources to keep going.
- *Low unemployment.* Unemployment of 5.8 percent and dropping is not all that bad. Historically, during recessions unemployment gets far worse than the 6.4 percent peak we saw. This is a testimony to the power of the U.S. economy. We have lost jobs to globalization, but in turn we get cheaper goods that give U.S. consumers more disposable income. This increased spending power results in more growth potential for sales in other areas and thus creates other jobs at home.
- *Inflation? What inflation?* The Fed has seemingly wrested the last vestiges of serious inflation from the system. We seem to have avoided deflation and can expect some reasonable price stability for some time.
- *Low interest rates.* The Fed has indicated it will keep interest rates low for "some considerable period of time," which may last

through 2004. Even when the Fed starts to raise rates, it will be some time before rates are anything close to high. Such low rates are good for business.

- *Low mortgage rates.* Many consumers were able to lower their mortgage payments by refinancing. This frees up income for other items. These low payments are a permanent fixture and act like a tax cut.
- *Productivity is off the charts.* The technology investments of the 1990s are finally beginning to pay dividends. We are producing more and more with less labor, thus holding down costs and increasing profits.
- *Falling dollar.* The falling dollar makes the farm products and the goods manufactured by U.S. companies more competitive in a world market increasingly dominated by international trade. And it seems that so far, at least, a falling dollar has not brought with it any inflation or interest rate pressures.

Now let's look at the major trends and forces that will offset these positive forces and will slow economic growth, thus bringing about the Muddle Through Decade. Let me repeat, this does not mean every quarter and every year will see below-trend growth. But I think the following points strongly suggest the average for the decade will be less than 3 percent annual GDP.

The Unsustainable Trend—The Trade Deficit

In November 2003, Fed governor Ben Bernanke spoke at the Global Economic and Investment Outlook Conference at Carnegie Mellon University. Quoting from the Bernanke speech (emphasis mine):

> As is widely recognized, the U.S. current account deficit cannot be sustained indefinitely at its current high level and will eventually have to be brought down to a more manageable size. However, eliminating the U.S. current account deficit too quickly is neither desirable nor feasible. Any attempt to do so would probably involve sharp reductions in domestic spending, which would have far worse effects on U.S. employment than the current account deficit does. [To attempt to do so] . . . is simply not a feasible alternative right now. For now, our best strategy is to encourage pro-growth policies among our trading partners, in the expectation that more rapid growth abroad will raise the demand for U.S. exports.[1]

The trade deficit is $500 billion a year and growing. This is an unsustainable trend. When does it stop? Federal Reserve studies suggest it should have stopped $100 billion ago. Practical analysis suggests it could go on for some time. But the longer it goes, the more difficult the adjustment. It will continue as long as foreigners continue to take our electronic dollars for their goods and services. Japan and China alone financed 45 percent of our trade deficit in the first half of 2003 (almost $120 billion) by buying U.S. Treasuries, helping hold down rates.

Bernanke very clearly shows us the consensus thinking among the international central banking community. Slow and steady progress to a "manageable size" (whatever that is) so as not to damage the main engine of the world economy, the U.S. consumer. If foreign nations wanted to pull the plug on the U.S. economy, they could do so in a Shanghai minute. Simply selling our bonds and forcing rates up would tank the economy, as we will note later. That foreign nations do not do so, and are willing to take paper they clearly know will be worth less (*not* worthless, I might add) in the future, is clear testimony to that current consensus.

A dramatic adjustment, such as Bernanke alludes to, would cause a dramatic recession. A slow adjustment, which is the hoped-for outcome, will also be a drag on the U.S. economy.

It will be a drag on the world economy as well. Stephen Roach of Morgan Stanley says that the United States accounted for fully 96 percent of the cumulative increase in world GDP growth (at market exchange rates) over the years 1995 to 2002. This was achieved only through ever-increasing and ultimately massive trade deficits, which, as Bernanke points out, cannot be sustained.

If we are to achieve a more balanced trade deficit, that means the United States must either buy fewer foreign goods or increase exports or a combination of both. But, like a drug addict, the world is hooked on the American consumer.

Where is the engine for world growth if the United States actively works to lower the dollar and balance its trade deficit? If we buy less of other countries' goods that means their economies will not grow as fast, and in some cases will not grow at all. The transition to the point where the rest of the world can create the non-U.S. demand that develops into sustainable growth will be difficult.

There are those who are beginning to argue a "new paradigm"—trade deficits don't matter. This time, we are told, it is really different. Those essays read a lot like the ones that suggested that Japan was different in the 1980s or that the NASDAQ really wasn't a bubble. One should always be suspicious of the "this time it's different" thesis. It hardly ever is.

The world is increasingly interdependent. Slow growth in the rest of the world affects us more than at any time in our history. Slow growth in the world as the imbalances are corrected will act as a drag on the U.S. economy.

The U.S. Government Deficit

Let's be clear. Without the Bush tax cuts, the previous recession would have been much longer and deeper. Many more would have been on the unemployment rolls. But the tax cuts, when coupled with increased spending for the military and the War on Terrorism and a Congress spending like a drunken sailor, has opened up a federal budget deficit that has grown to over $500 billion.

Milton Friedman, Nobel Prize winner and one of the most highly thought of economists of this era, says this rampant growth in spending "is the single greatest deterrent to faster economic growth in the United States today."[2]

Another Nobel Prize economist, James Buchanan, worries that by allowing government to grow so rapidly ahead of the pace of the private sector, we are "killing the goose of free enterprise that lays the golden eggs."[3]

Government debt crowds out private-sector debt and ultimately raises the cost of borrowing if not held in check. A Republican-controlled Washington has shown good skills at cutting taxes but has demonstrated little taste for the fiscal discipline that should come with those cuts. Is it a crisis today? No, as budget deficits as a percentage of GDP are below historical levels. But soaking up $300 to $400 billion from the private sector in order to fund the deficits clearly does not help keep interest rates low, and this recovery needs low interest rates.

The Demographic Conundrum

The baby boom generation will start to spend less and save more as they get increasingly close to retirement and find their 401(k)s have not rebounded to the levels they once expected. Ten percent compounded growth of the stock market will not happen, for reasons listed in numerous other chapters in this book, bear market rallies notwithstanding.

Whatever happens in the next six months or year, the long-term historical trend is clear. It is bearish for boomers who are counting on wealth reflation for their retirement. Pretty soon (in the next few years) you will see savings levels increase and boomers' outstanding debt will be reduced. This will slowly let the air out of the growth in consumer spending, which is a huge part of the U.S. and world economy. Again, this is not some fall-off-the-cliff moment in time, but it will mean gradual slower growth and a Muddle Through Economy.

The Jobless Recovery, Productivity, and the International Labor Arbitrage

What Stephen Roach of Morgan Stanley calls the international labor arbitrage will hold down job growth in the United States for much of this decade. Simply put, there is a good deal of job growth because of American demand and business. It is just that the job growth is in China and India. Until job growth in the United States can maintain itself consistently above trend, it is my position that slower economic growth is in the cards. The adjustment to the increasing international portability of jobs is going to be a drag on job growth. It will not be the end of growth, but it will certainly slow things down. Slow job growth means slow economic growth. Increased foreign competition for service jobs means lower pay levels in the United States, which also reduces growth.

I would also note that productivity rose by more than 8 percent in the third quarter of 2003, and is setting all-time records year over year. This is quite a positive for profits and for the overall economy. However, it means we're producing more goods or services for less per unit cost and therefore it doesn't contribute to a demand for new employees to meet rising demand.

This is illustrated by an essay by the contrarian Bruce Bartlett of the National Center for Policy Analysis.

First, the bad numbers: "According to the Bureau of Labor Statistics, there were 14.6 million Americans employed in manufacturing in July [2003], down from 15.3 million a year earlier, 16.4 million the year before that (2001), and 17.3 million the year before that (2000)—a decline of 16 percent in three years. The recent peak for manufacturing employment occurred in March 1998 at 17.6 million—about the same as it had been for the previous 15 years."[4]

The stories are all over the press about how manufacturing jobs are being shifted to China, Mexico (think NAFTA), and (pick your favorite third world country). They are the same stories, with different countries substituted, that I read in the 1970s. We read in those tough economic times that the United States was then at its zenith and moving into an era of low employment. Eventually we would see Japan eclipse us as the preeminent economic power.

"It is also important," Bartlett tells us, "to note that virtually every other major country has seen declines in manufacturing employment. Between 1992 and 2002, U.S. manufacturing employment fell by 3.7 percent. In Britain, it fell 4.7 percent, in Japan it fell 5.2 percent, and in Germany it fell 6.1 percent."[5]

"How can we," asked my good friend Bill Bonner of the *Daily Reckoning*, as we sat basking at his chateau in the pastoral French evening last summer, "continue to buy goods if all we sell is services? Can we be a nation that just produces services and still maintain our way of life? How can we survive if our largest exports are jobs and the U.S. dollar?" (I note it is easy to ask such pessimistic questions while you bask in pastoral splendor at your chateau enjoying the second bottle of wine.)

A reasonable question by Bill, with a reasonable answer by Bruce:

Industrial production [in the United States] has remained relatively strong. The Federal Reserve Board's industrial production index is up 5 percent since manufacturing employment peaked in 1998, and down just 5 percent from the index's peak in July 2000, despite a rather severe recession in the meantime.

Looking at gross domestic product, real goods production as a share of real (inflation-adjusted) GDP is close to its all-time high. In the first quarter of 2003—the latest data available—real goods production was 39.2 percent of real GDP. The highest annual figure ever recorded was 40 percent in 2000. By contrast, in the "good old days" of the 1940s, 1950s, and 1960s, the U.S. actually produced far fewer goods as a share of total output. The highest figure recorded in the 1940s was 35.5 percent in 1943; the highest in the 1950s was 34.9 percent in 1953; and the highest in the 1960s was 33.6 percent in 1966.

In short, manufacturing output is very healthy. There is absolutely no evidence whatsoever that we are becoming a nation of "hamburger flippers." We are producing more "things" than we have in almost every year of our history for which we have data. The decline in employment is, in effect, a good thing, because it means that manufacturing productivity is very high. That is also a good thing, because it means that employers can afford to pay high wages to manufacturing workers while still competing with low-wage workers in places like Mexico and China.

Remember, what really matters for employers is not absolute wages, but unit labor costs—how much the labor costs to manufacture a given product. If a U.S. worker is five times as productive as a Mexican worker making one-fifth as much [in pay], they are exactly equal from the point of view of a producer.[6]

But what this miracle of productivity also means is the 3,000,000 manufacturing jobs that we have seen evaporate are not coming back. Frankly, it is a testimony to the resilience of the American economy that the high in unemployment in this most recent cycle was only 6.4 percent.

Sustainable long-term above-trend growth needs to see substantial creation of jobs, which is precisely what we have not seen to date (in early 2004). Most economists believe that because of the growth in the population the U.S. economy must generate job growth by 150,000 per month to materially decrease unemployment.

The employment data from the third quarter of 2003 demonstrates some of the problems. In the fastest-growing quarter since 1983, nonfarm payroll employment rose by only 265,000 jobs. The number of unemployed persons, 8.8 million, was essentially flat. Unemployment remained essentially unchanged at 6.0 percent.

Further, the Bureau of Labor Statistics of the Commerce Department tells us, "In October, 1.6 million persons were only marginally attached to the labor force, which is 170,000 more than last year. These individuals wanted and were available to work and had looked for a job sometime in the prior 12 months. They were not counted as unemployed, however, because they did not actively search for work in the 4 weeks preceding the survey. 462,000 of those were "discouraged workers," or people who were not looking for jobs because they believed there were no jobs available to them. This number is up 103,000 in the last 12 months."

If GDP must grow by 1 percent just to create enough jobs to absorb the net new workers (youth and immigrant workers less those retiring) and productivity is rising at very high rates—north of 3 percent—then a 3 percent economy is not enough to create the jobs that are necessary to significantly bring down unemployment.

If unemployment does not fall significantly, then that is a drag on consumer spending and thus a drag on the economy. Over time, new industries and technologies will develop that would be expected to provide the new jobs (on this see Chapter 24), but in the immediate two-to-three-year future, no such powerful job creation industry is making an appearance.

Unemployment should come down in 2004 as the economy could grow fast enough to create new jobs, but this recovery has clearly demonstrated it is different than past recoveries as far as job creation is concerned—it has more to do with stimulus than with business spending (see more later). The combination of increased productivity and the international labor arbitrage will hold down robust job creation for most of this decade, which is a drag on growth. Again, this is not to suggest a falling off the cliff or chronic high unemployment, just more Muddle Through headwinds that the economy has to fight in order to grow.

The Steroid Economy

From a macroeconomic perspective, it's a simple problem. All you have to do is run the economy hotter. We've just got to gun the economy so that demand is great enough to spur job creation.

Dallas Federal Reserve Governor Robert McTeer (October 9, 2003)

Let's start this section with an analogy. In the early 1970s, a young blond demigod became Mr. America on his way to becoming Mr. World. Dave Draper built his massive frame the hard way: He pumped iron. Today he is 62. He is still one of the most muscular, powerful bodybuilders you will have the pleasure to meet. He does it the old-fashioned way. He pumps iron. No steroids, no drugs, no stimulants. Just good nutrition and hard work.

I take a small steroid shot every 12 months, to control my fall allergies. For me, it is a lifesaver. I need that extra something to keep me productive in September and October.

But many athletes take large amounts of daily steroids to make them bigger, faster, and more powerful. Daily steroid use can work wonders. It can make some athletes into superstars. I remember watching Jose Canseco when he was a Texas Ranger. He put up Hall of Fame numbers and was absolutely a physical presence. After he retired, he admitted to using steroids, and was eventually jailed for violating the terms of his probation by using steroids. Did steroids make him a better player? Sure, but there is a price.

We all know what happens over time. The effects are well documented. The hair falls out. Even with the little blue pill, the equipment does not work. Joints begin to fail. There can be liver damage, high blood pressure, acne, irrational behavior, anger, and a host of other side effects.

If you stop taking the steroids, the immediate muscular effect goes away, and pretty quickly. Even pumping more iron will not get you back to where the steroids had you. It is a sad cycle. How many athletes do we look at and wonder, "Is it natural or is it steroids?"

I look at the economy and wonder the same thing. Is it sustainable or is it stimulus?

The Bush tax cuts and lower mortgage payments are a kind of good steroid or stimulus. They offer sustainable benefits over time. Even one-time tax refunds like the child credit payments of the third quarter in 2003 are like my annual steroid shot. It helped stimulate an economy that was ailing. Some economists suggest that almost 50 percent of the powerhouse growth in GDP in the third quarter came from this single source.

But excess debt is more like the debilitating steroid use. There is a limit to the benefits of what it can do.

In 1980, with interest rates at 15 to 18 percent, household debt payments were 11 percent of disposable income. With the lowest rates in 40 years, debt service is now close to an all-time high of 13.3 percent, down slightly in the last year. Total financial obligations are more than 18 percent of disposable income. Again, this is close to an all-time high. We are approaching the limits of significant credit-financed growth.

This is underscored by the fact (see Figure 13.1) that consumer debt grew 140 percent from 1993 through the third quarter of 2003. But nominal GDP only grew by 70 percent. Debt cannot grow faster than

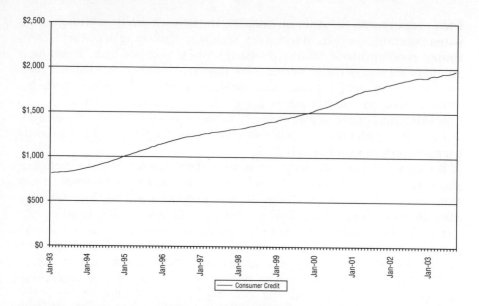

Figure 13.1 Consumer Credit 1993–2003 ($ Billions)
Data compiled from the U.S. Department of Commerce: Bureau of Economic Analysis
(www.bea.doc.gov).

GDP indefinitely. Like any household budget, you can borrow only so much before the debt service and interest payments begin to put limits on your future borrowing.

Where is the current growth coming from? A large part of it is debt financing. Consumer credit grew by almost $10 billion over expectations in October 2003. Estimates were $5.9 billion and actual growth was $15.1 billion. Does anyone think debt did not play a big role in the third-quarter GDP? (Of course, I suppose you could also say that means consumers are more confident.)

The third quarter also clearly benefited from the massive mortgage refinancing boom that occurred in the second quarter. Such refinancing has not stopped, nor will it, but rising rates will slowly cut off that flow of economic stimulus.

Thus, consumer spending grew at a 6.6 percent pace during the quarter, while income barely budged. I note that average hourly earnings rose by one thin penny during September and October of 2003, to $15.46. That is a 0.4 percent annual pace, which is much less than inflation. There was only a 2.4 percent rise in earnings over the past year, or only slightly more than inflation. If one cent was all that earnings could rise in the hottest two months in 19 years (since 1984, if one looks at GDP), then what are we to think of future individual earnings growth? Without consistent earnings growth you cannot have continued and consistent consumer credit growth. There is only so much a family can borrow and adequately service.

The Unsustainable Trend, Part Two

Wait, can't we borrow against the values of our ever-rising home prices? (Note I did not say home values.) Since 2000, mortgage debt has risen $2.65 trillion (with a t) to almost $9 trillion. That is a growth of 42 percent. Nominal GDP (we must include the effects of inflation to be accurate in the assessment) has grown only 14.4 percent over the same period.

Can someone say "unsustainable trend?" Is anyone remotely suggesting that the rate of mortgage debt growth will rise by $2.65 trillion in the next three and a half years, which would be "only" a 30 percent growth rate against a probable nominal GDP of 15 percent? How much stimulus did mortgage refinancing and increased home loans contribute to the growth of the U.S. economy in the past few years?

Interest rates are going to rise over time. It is a matter of when, not if. The carrying cost (interest rate expense) for consumers is going to rise along with the interest rates. Much (but certainly not all) of the growth of the U.S. economy stems from consumer borrowing. While I do not currently think consumer debt levels are in a crisis status, they are approaching a ceiling.

There are limits to the ability of U.S. consumers to increase their exposure to debt. Debt and the cost of interest cannot long continue to rise faster than income, as it has been doing for several decades. Rising rates will mean increased costs for that debt, much of which is not fixed. Increased costs mean less debt growth, which means less consumer spending. That means a slower-growing economy.

Predicting the demise of the American consumer has been a standard line for bearish economists for decades and has been wrong. *Fortune* magazine wrote about the crisis in consumer debt in 1956. Spending is part of our national DNA, and to the extent possible we can count on the American consumer to do his part. Growth in consumer debt in line with growth in GDP plus inflation is reasonable to expect, with the exceptions of periods of very high interest rates and recessions.

I am suggesting, however, that there are limits to the excess growth in debt and thus there are limits to debt-induced growth. You cannot grow debt at twice the pace of income for very long. For a below-trend Muddle Through Economy to once again be manifest, growth in credit and the rate of mortgage growth simply have to slow down.

There are limits to such abnormally high credit growth, and we are near them. Again, please do not take that to mean the world ends. Credit and mortgage growth will simply fall back in line with GDP, earnings, and inflation. But "in-line" growth is not the substance of roaring above-trend economies.

Bulls to the Left of Me, Bears to the Right of Me, Here I Am Stuck in the Muddle Through Middle with You

As we will explore in a few chapters, investors tend to do something called "anchoring." They take the most recent trends, especially the ones that confirm their biases, and project them into the future. Such projections almost always ultimately fail, as trends change. A trend is a trend until it isn't.

Bull's Eye Investors should drop back and focus on the bigger picture rather than the recent past. From time to time you can wander through the piney woods of East Texas and find a large growth of oak trees. But to declare the existence of an oak forest in a sea of pines is misleading. We need to look at the forest rather than a few specific trees.

I believe the facts I have presented suggest a slower-growth economy. That means corporate earnings during this period will grow more slowly than projections. Note that I said "grow." Suggesting slow growth is not gloom and doom. It helps us be realists rather than Pollyannas. It also means there will be lots of opportunities as long as you target your investments to where the market and the economy will really be and not where it was or where you hope it will go.

Now let's look at the central economic fight in the coming years and see how it may affect our investment future.

Chairman Greenspan and the Shoot-Out at the OK Corral

14

One of the key aspects of understanding the future direction of the economy is to recognize the debate over inflation and deflation. To understand this debate, you have to understand Federal Reserve policy. To understand Federal Reserve policy, you have to understand how Alan Greenspan views the debate.

Fortunately, there are several informative speeches that give us more than a few clues as to the Fed's (and thus Greenspan's) policy and help us make some reasonable speculation about the near-term future of the economy.

Let's start with a summary of current Fed policy. Inflation as of 2004 has fallen about as low as it can go without being too close to deflation. Recessions are by definition deflationary, and having one in the current low-inflation environment would probably lead to outright deflation and bring up thoughts of Japan. The Fed repeatedly refers to "an unwelcome fall in inflation" in the meeting summaries as a possible risk to the economy.

Low interest rates have clearly been a major stimulus to the economic recovery. The recession of 2001 would have been much deeper without aggressive Fed action. The lowest mortgage rates in 40 years have led to a booming housing market as more people can afford to buy first-time homes, and more people can afford to move up to larger and newer homes. In addition, mortgage refinancing has allowed consumers to lower their mortgage payments as well as take money out of their home equity for other purchases.

If interest rates (and especially mortgage rates) were to rise significantly in a fragile recovery that is largely stimulus driven, the recovery could be aborted before it has time to develop a firm foundation in business spending. Thus Fed policy has been to keep rates low.

But what happens next? What happens when it is time to raise rates (and/or the market does it for you) or if business spending (the third leg of the economy) is not prepared to pick up the slack from slowing housing and consumer sectors? What does the Fed do then and what are the likely results of its actions?

These are critical questions. To get a handle on the answers we are going to look at two very important speeches by Alan Greenspan and Ben Bernanke. Bernanke tells us the Fed is aware of the problem of deflation and has the tools at its disposal to deal with it, and the Fed is hard at work to make sure it never has to use them by preventing deflation in the first place. Then Greenspan says those tools are not precise but that deflation is such a problem that erring on the side of creating a little excess inflation is preferable to the actual appearance of deflation.

If you're wondering why I'm spending so much time focusing on deflation—which seems unlikely at the present—rest assured that Fed policymakers are focused on preventing deflation. To understand how the U.S. central bank thinks, you must understand the issue. This is quite important.

The Famous Fed Printing Press Speech

Ben Bernanke gave the famous "Fed printing press speech" in November 2002. Prior to his 2002 appointment as a Federal Reserve governor, Bernanke was the chairman of the department of economics at Princeton University. He was the director of the monetary economics program of the National Bureau of Economic Research (NBER) and the editor of the *American Economic Review*. He co-authored a widely used textbook on macroeconomics and is becoming one of the more influential governors.

This was his first major speech as a Fed governor. It was made to the National Economists Club in Washington, D.C., which is not a small venue. Dennis Gartman referred to this speech as "in our opinion the most important speech on Federal Reserve and monetary policy since the explanation emanating from the Plaza Accord a decade and a half ago."[1]

We will look at the particulars in a few paragraphs, but we need to keep in mind this is not a random speech. While Bernanke states that the views in this speech are his own, for reasons I will go into later I believe this speech is indicative of the thinking of various members of the Fed, and was given to make unambiguous the Fed's views on deflation. The title of the speech is very straightforward: "Deflation: Making Sure 'It' Doesn't Happen Here."[2]

First and foremost, as Gartman wrote, "Dr. Bernanke has made it clear that the Federal Reserve governors are painfully aware of the very severe problem that a pervasive deflation would manifest upon the U.S. economy and the U.S. society, and they are not prepared to allow that to happen. They will do what they must in order to alleviate deflation, including erring openly upon the side of inflation."[3]

On one level, this speech breaks no new ground from that of a previous Federal Reserve white paper on the causes of deflation in Japan, and what the U.S. Fed and other central banks could do to avoid deflation. The paper made it clear that the Fed understood the nature of the problem and was telling us it did not intend to see the United States slip into deflation. This is one more reason I believe the speech is reflective of Fed thinking, and not simply Bernanke's thoughts.

A Very Clear Fed Speech

The difference between that white paper and Bernanke's speech is twofold. The paper was presented in the framework of an academic exercise, and had no official stamp of Fed governor approval. It could be viewed as theoretical.

Second, this speech was delivered in very clear, well-written English. The average layman could read and follow it. Bernanke thus disqualifies himself for the role of Fed chairman when Greenspan finally steps down, since it appears that a requirement for the job of chairman is the ability to talk at length and say very little that can be clearly understood.

First, let's go to the more controversial parts of the speech. What is the Fed willing to do to avoid deflation? This is the part that has raised the hackles of more than a few writers. I quote (emphasis mine):

As I have mentioned, some observers have concluded that when the central bank's policy rate falls to zero—its practical minimum—monetary policy loses its ability to further stimulate aggregate demand and the economy. At a broad conceptual level, and in my view in practice as well, this conclusion is clearly mistaken. Indeed, under a fiat (that is, paper) money system, *a government (in practice, the central bank in cooperation with other agencies) should always be able to generate increased nominal spending and inflation,* even when the short-term nominal interest rate is at zero.

The conclusion that deflation is always reversible under a fiat money system follows from basic economic reasoning. A little parable may prove useful: Today an ounce of gold sells for $300, more or less. Now suppose that a modern alchemist solves his subject's oldest problem by finding a way to produce unlimited amounts of new gold at essentially no cost. Moreover, his invention is widely publicized and scientifically verified, and he announces his intention to begin massive production of gold within days. What would happen to the price of gold? Presumably, the potentially unlimited supply of cheap gold would cause the market price of gold to plummet. Indeed, if the market for gold is to any degree efficient, the price of gold would collapse immediately after the announcement of the invention, before the alchemist had produced and marketed a single ounce of yellow metal.

What has this got to do with monetary policy? Like gold, U.S. dollars have value only to the extent that they are strictly limited in supply. **But the U.S. government has a technology, called a printing press (or, today, its electronic equivalent), that allows it to produce as many U.S. dollars as it wishes at essentially no cost.** By increasing the number of U.S. dollars in circulation, or *even by credibly threatening to do so*, the U.S. government can also reduce the value of a dollar in terms of goods and services, which is equivalent to raising the prices in dollars of those goods and services. We conclude that, under a paper-money system, a determined government can always generate higher spending and hence positive inflation. . . . If we do fall into deflation, however, we can take comfort that the logic of the printing press example must assert itself, and sufficient injections of money will ultimately always reverse a deflation.[4]

Bernanke goes on to point out that the Fed could also supply interest-free loans to banks, monetize foreign assets, buy government agency bonds, purchase private corporate assets, or do any number of things that could induce inflation.

Those words, taken out of context, could be seen as rather extreme, confirming the worst fears about central banks among certain groups and providing yet another reason to buy gold. There may be reasons in this speech to want to add a little gold to your portfolio, but these sentences are not among them.

Let's look at what Bernanke really said. First, he begins by telling us that he believes the likelihood of deflation is remote. But, since it did happen in Japan and seems to be the cause of the current Japanese problems, we cannot dismiss the possibility outright. Therefore, we need to see what policies can be brought to bear upon the problem.

He then goes on to say that the most important thing is to prevent deflation before it happens. He says that a central bank should allow for some cushion and should not target zero inflation, and speculates that this cushion is more than 1 percent. Typically, central banks target inflation of 1 to 3 percent, although this means that in normal times inflation is more likely to rise above the acceptable target than fall below zero in poor times.

Central banks can usually influence this by raising and lowering interest rates. But what if the federal funds rate falls to zero? Not to worry, there are still policy levers that can be pulled. Quoting Bernanke:

> So what then might the Fed do if its target interest rate, the overnight federal funds rate, fell to zero? One relatively straightforward extension of current procedures would be to try to stimulate spending by lowering rates further out along the Treasury term structure—that is, rates on government bonds of longer maturities. . . .
>
> A more direct method, which I personally prefer, *would be for the Fed to begin announcing explicit ceilings for yields on longer-maturity Treasury debt (say, bonds maturing within the next two years).* The Fed could enforce these interest-rate ceilings by committing to make unlimited purchases of securities up to two years from maturity at prices consistent with the targeted yields. If this program were successful, not only would yields on medium-term Treasury securities fall, but (because of links operating through expectations of future interest rates) yields on longer-term public and private debt (such as mortgages) would likely fall as well.
>
> Lower rates over the maturity spectrum of public and private securities should strengthen aggregate demand in the usual ways and thus help to end deflation. Of course, *if operating in relatively short-dated Treasury debt proved insufficient, the Fed could also attempt to cap yields of Treasury securities at still longer maturities, say three to six years.*[5]

He then proceeds to outline what could be done if the economy falls into outright deflation and uses various examples. It seems clear to me from the context that he is making an academic list of potential policies the Fed could pursue if outright deflation became a reality. He was not suggesting they be used, nor do I believe he thinks we will ever get to the place where they would be contemplated. He was simply pointing out the Fed can fight deflation if it wants to.

With the above as background, now we can begin to look at what I believe is the true import of the speech. Read these sentences, noting my emphasized words:

". . . a central bank, either alone or in cooperation with other parts of the government, **retains considerable power to expand aggregate demand** and economic activity even when its accustomed policy rate is at zero."

"The basic prescription for preventing deflation is therefore straightforward, at least in principle: **Use monetary and fiscal policy as needed to support aggregate spending**. . . ."

Again: ". . . some observers have concluded that when the central bank's policy rate falls to zero—its practical minimum—monetary policy loses its ability to further **stimulate aggregate demand and the economy.**"

"To **stimulate aggregate spending** when short-term interest rates have reached zero, the Fed must expand the scale of its asset purchases or, possibly, expand the menu of assets that it buys."

Now let us go to Bernanke's conclusion:

Sustained deflation can be highly destructive to a modern economy and should be strongly resisted. Fortunately, for the foreseeable future, the chances of a serious deflation in the United States appear remote indeed, in large part because of our economy's underlying strengths *but also because of the determination of the Federal Reserve and other U.S. policymakers to act preemptively against deflationary pressures.*

Moreover, as I have discussed today, a variety of policy responses are available should deflation appear to be taking hold. Because some of these alternative policy tools are relatively less familiar, they may raise practical problems of implementation and of calibration of their likely economic effects. For this reason, as I have emphasized, prevention of deflation is preferable to cure. Nevertheless, I hope to have persuaded you that the Federal Reserve and other economic policymakers would be far from helpless in the face of deflation, even should the federal funds rate hit its zero bound.[6]

Stimulating Demand

Let's forget for the moment the debate about whether Fed policy can actually stimulate demand at all times and places. The quotes demonstrate that Bernanke and the Federal Reserve Board believes that it does. Beliefs will translate themselves into action. The Fed, if faced with slowing demand and deflation, will act in very predictable ways based on their beliefs. *They will work to stimulate demand.*

Former Fed vice-chairman Wayne Angell is a Greenspan confidant. Angell spoke to the National Public Pension Fund Forum in November 2002. In summary, he said, "Deflation is bad. The Fed gets it. There are still things the Fed can do to prevent deflation, and they will do what it takes."

Bernanke is a Keynesian. Angell is basically a monetarist. (These are schools of economic thought with differing views of how Fed policy works.)

Even with their differences, they both viscerally believe in the ability of the Fed to stimulate demand and prevent deflation. This belief is a part of the Articles of Faith of central banking. That is the lesson you need to take away from the Bernanke speech. We will deal with the implications after we look at an essay by Alan Greenspan.

The Greenspan Uncertainty Principle

For better or worse, Alan Greenspan is one of the most important men in the world. This is one of Greenspan's more significant speeches (it may come to be seen as his most important) and a departure from his usual opaque (or in Texan: clear as mud) style.

This speech puts the nail in the coffin of econometrics and its promise of exactitude in economics. What Greenspan is asserting is that the Fed models are simply not powerful or robust enough to be able to predict anything with a real degree of certainty, no matter how much economists would assure us they do. He opens up a brave new world of uncertainty, and for that candid admission, I say bravo!

I have often been a critic of Greenspan, especially for his lack of clarity. However, I applaud his candor and clarity in this speech. While I quibble with him over some points, overall this is a speech I find refreshing in its acknowledgment of a reality that most observers, including myself, believe to be the case: that fallible humans run the Fed using their best judgment.

(For the rest of this section, quotes in sans serif will be directly from Greenspan's speech. Bold emphasis is mine.

Monetary Policy under Uncertainty

For those who want to believe there is a man behind the curtains who can pull the levers and make the economy move as he wants, this will be a most unsettling speech. The speech is entitled "Monetary Policy under Uncertainty"[7] and starts with the sentence:

"Uncertainty is not just an important feature of the monetary policy landscape; it is the defining characteristic of that landscape."

It then goes on to tell us just how uncertain monetary policy is:

"Despite the extensive efforts to capture and quantify these key macroeconomic relationships, our knowledge about many of the important linkages is far from complete and **in all likelihood will always remain so. Every model, no matter how detailed or how well designed conceptually and empirically, is a vastly simplified representation of the world**

that we experience with all its intricacies on a day-to-day basis. Consequently, even with large advances in computational capabilities and greater comprehension of economic linkages, **our knowledge base is barely able to keep pace with the ever-increasing complexity of our global economy.**"

Greenspan emphatically points out that models give us at best only a reference point for policy. They cannot be prescriptive with any real degree of certainty. Nor does he offer any hope that such models can be developed in the future. Economic models are far from perfect and "in all likelihood will always remain so."

"Given this state of flux, it is apparent that a prominent shortcoming of our structural models is that, for ease in parameter estimation, not only are economic responses presumed fixed through time, but they are generally assumed to be linear. An assumption of linearity may be adequate for estimating *average* relationships, but few expect that an economy will respond linearly to every aberration."

While he says "our structural models" I think he is in fact referencing models in general. By linearity he means straight-line assumptions or connections. It is as if we see that Trend A and Trend D seem to move in lockstep and draw a conclusion about the connection. But hidden, and not in the model, are Trends B and C, which are the real connection between A and D. He is not saying that the Fed knows what B and C are and the rest of the world doesn't.

"Look, guys," he tells us (my paraphrasing), "stop looking at three different trends, running them out ad infinitum and then drawing a conclusion about the wisdom or stupidity of our decisions. The factors affecting your trends are so complex that any number of significant events could change the relationships between your trends and the desired policy."

Further, he points out that the traditional measures of money stock are becoming increasingly meaningless. The obsession with M-2 or M-3 makes for good newsletter copy, but what do such broad aggregates mean in a world where new forms of money (swaps, derivatives, mortgages, bonds, etc.) appear every day? The implication is that the old linear relationships between money supply (as measured by some arbitrary and outdated statistic like M-2) and inflation may no longer be valid.

"Recent history has also reinforced the perception that the relationships underlying the economy's structure change over time in ways that are difficult to anticipate. This has been most apparent in the changing role of our standard measure of the money stock. . . . In the past two decades, what constitutes money has been obscured by the introduction of technologies that have facilitated the proliferation of financial products and have altered the empirical relationship between economic activity and what we define as money, and in doing so has inhibited the keying of monetary policy to the control of the measured money stock."

Not only are past relationships not always linear, but past relationships may change over time. This is the old principle of "past performance is not indicative of future results." Just because things worked in the past does not mean they will in the future, as the world is changing rapidly. A simple example of this is all the analysts who told investors to buy stocks in January 2001 when the Fed started cutting interest rates because the "models" showed that stocks always went up after the Fed started cutting rates. Now we know that such a linear relationship is not always true.

Real-World Central Banking

"What then are the implications of this largely irreducible uncertainty for the conduct of monetary policy? A well-known proposition is that, under a very restrictive set of assumptions, uncertainty has no bearing on the actions that policymakers might choose, and so they should proceed as if they know the precise structure of the economy. These assumptions—linearity in the structure of the economy, perfect knowledge of the interest-sensitivity of aggregate spending and other so-called slope parameters, and a very specific attitude of policymakers toward risk—**are never met in the real world**."

Paraphrase: "How," he asks, "can we base monetary policy on assumptions that we know do not necessarily work in the real world? Clearly we cannot. Therefore, we must find another basis for actions than total reliance on some model. There is no simple answer."

"These considerations have inclined Federal Reserve policymakers toward policies that limit the risk of deflation even though the baseline forecasts from most conventional models would not project such an event."

I have been writing about the potential for deflation for close to six years. I wrote in 1999 or so that Greenspan was also worried about deflation, even though he did not talk about it, as the Fed actions of that time suggested that concern. Few models used by economists at that time suggested deflation, although empirical analysis of the problem was screaming deflation, at least to me. In this speech Greenspan is clearly telling us they *are* worried about deflation, even if the models do not show it.

Then he gives us the rationale for this policy in the next few paragraphs, which are among the most important of the whole speech.

"In implementing a risk-management approach to policy, we must confront the fact that only a limited number of risks can be quantified with any confidence. And even these risks are generally quantifiable only if we accept the assumption that the future will replicate the past. **Other risks are essentially unquantifiable . . . because we may not fully appreciate even the full range of possibilities, let alone each possibility's likelihood.** As a result, risk management often involves significant judgment on the part of policymakers, as we evaluate the risks of different events and the probability that our actions will alter those risks.

"For such judgment, we policymakers, rather than relying solely on the specific linkages expressed in our formal models, have tended to draw from broader, though less mathematically precise, hypotheses of how the world works. For example, inference of how market participants might respond to a monetary policy initiative may need to reference past behavior during a period only roughly comparable to the current situation."

Econometric models, no matter how elaborate and thoughtful, are not enough to establish policy. Welcome to the world of behavioral economics.

When analyzing the risk of investment portfolios, an analyst will use something called a Monte Carlo simulation to develop all the possible combinations of funds and their histories to try to understand what the probabilities of certain outcomes might be. Then the analyst begins to work to mitigate or hedge against the more negative potential outcomes.

Greenspan is saying that in essence the Fed does the same, only not just with computers as do analysts, but through the filters of their judgment. The world is far too complex to be understood totally in some linear, static computer model. There are too many variables, and as soon as one starts changing, the interrelationships in and of themselves begin to change, thus making the model less useful.

Thus he asserts not only that without human judgment, the Fed simply could not do its job, but also that it would do far worse if it were relying on rules or econometric models.

"**Rules by their nature are simple, and when significant and shifting uncertainties exist in the economic environment, they cannot substitute for risk-management paradigms, which are far better suited to policymaking.**"

In this and other paragraphs following, he answers critics who want the Fed to set precise rules for its policies. Such rules, he avers, not only are simplistic, they can lead to major policy errors. Any such rules are subject to interpretation and thus only serve to compound a policy problem by seemingly imposing hard interpretations when such actions might create the opposite of the desired result. Judgment, or at least

Greenspan's judgment, when it comes to central banking, is better than hard and fixed rules.

For instance, France and Germany are ignoring the European Union rule that says they cannot have a deficit of more than 3 percent of their GDP. They both believe they need to stimulate their economies and that an austere budget would throw their respective countries into deepening recessions or worse. The other nations are demanding they adhere to the rules, because not to do so adversely affects the other countries. Who is right? The answer depends on who is experiencing the recession.

Here we have the refreshing acknowledgment of a reality we should all know exists: there is no Fed chairman pulling levers behind the curtain, à la the Wizard of Oz, who can control the economy. They cannot manage all the risks. All they can do is manage some risks, so it comes down to a decision as to which risks to try to mitigate or work against.

Repeating the first sentence of the speech:

"Uncertainty is not just an important feature of the monetary policy landscape; it is the defining characteristic of that landscape."

I think it is no small thing to recognize that Greenspan is taking on a goodly portion of his economic peers. The econometric model king has no clothes, nor is it likely that it will ever be able to weave any. It is an illusion some economists foster among themselves.

Greenspan Says, "Trust Me"

Now let me give you a few more of my first thoughts on the speech before getting reaction from others. Let's start with a story from Dennis Gartman. He was once playing in a four-man group for a state golf team championship. They were in the hunt, and on the 17th hole one of the team members (interestingly, his last name was Duffer) missed a seven-foot putt by half an inch. Hearing the groans of his teammates, he turned around and said quietly, "Gentlemen, that is the best I could do at the time."

First, Greenspan is saying that human beings run the Fed, and they have to make judgments. The best way to do that is to try to avoid the big risks. In essence, the Fed is like a giant economic insurance company, trying to avoid the big risks that could wreck the economy (like deflation, in their view) and thus being willing to take smaller risks (like inflation, again in their view).

He tells his critics who look at static models that they are being too simplistic, and with some justification in most cases, I might add. That is not to say I would agree with a certain policy, but in this Greenspan is right: You cannot focus on just a few trends and extrapolate to a correct policy.

Second, Greenspan is saying, "Trust me." Not explicitly, but implicitly it is all over this document. As he answers critics about specific actions (like 1998 monetary easing), he confidently asserts, "Gentlemen, that is the best I could do at the time."

Third, he acknowledges what everyone knows: The world is vastly complex and cannot be understood in any one way. Further, every action will have unintended consequences, and the best you can strive for is not trying to "fix" the economy, but assessing risk and trying to avoid the worst-case scenarios based on that risk assessment.

Fourth, I hope this means we can do away with all the silly economic models that are bandied about showing how the Fed actually thinks and upon which supposedly "they base their decisions." The models may be interesting, even useful and instructive, but Greenspan makes clear they have not been, nor will they be, the final basis for any decisions.

Fifth, as we look at future Fed policy actions, we now need to start looking at future risks rather than current statistics. As an example, when the Fed tells us that it is more concerned about unwelcome disinflation, this may mean the Fed is not going to raise rates until we face a bout of unwelcome inflation, no matter what some historical models state about the economic recovery and the Fed raising rates.

The preceding is my analysis of these two speeches. I am not advocating the speakers' positions, and have distinct problems with the lack of transparency that Greenspan is advocating. Personally, I would like to see a significant restructuring of the system along more free market lines. But that is not going to happen. The important thing for this discussion is not what my views are on the issues, but rather what the opinions of Greenspan and his fellow Reserve Board members are. They will be the ones making decisions, and these speeches give us the basis for how they will approach the decision-making process.

(For those interested, you can read my analysis of the thoughts of several different authors on this debate about Fed policy in my September 19, 2003, weekly letter in the archives at www.2000wave.com.)

The End Game

How will all this work out? When will the Fed allow short-term rates to start to rise? The Fed is in a difficult predicament.

At a a private reception late in 2003 in Dallas for Jim Rogers (former partner of George Soros and author of *Investment Biker* and *Adventure Cap-*

italist) given by David Tice, who runs the Prudent Bear Fund, there were a few genetically predetermined bearish souls in attendance. One complained to me that recent Fed actions are only going to make things worse—that we need to go through the economic rebalancing, deal with the recession that would occur, and move on, or words to that effect. He was from the "take your medicine now" school of thought.

Typically, short-term rates are 1 percent or more above the rate of inflation. A rise in interest rates to normal levels would give us federal funds rate of 3 percent to 4 percent instead of current Fed policy of 1 percent less than the consumer price index (CPI). This would put the 10-year Treasury at 6 percent and the 30-year mortgage rate at 7.5 percent. If this were to happen too quickly, it would abort the recovery and risk a deflationary recession. It would increase housing costs, increase the payments of the 20 percent of homeowners with adjustable rate mortgages, increase borrowing costs, and create a significant drag on consumer spending. Many analysts feel that too rapidly rising rates would also be a considerable negative for the stock market.

The Fed hope is that if it can keep the economy moving along, even slowly, excess capacity will eventually go away and U.S. businesses will regain their ability to raise prices. The longer the Fed can postpone the next recession, even by excess stimulation, the more likely it is that businesses will be in better shape. Hopefully, personal debt will start to decrease as well, and we can slowly over the next few years grow ourselves out of the current problems.

But rapidly rising rates in 2004 will not happen. The members of the Federal Reserve are programmed, deep within their economic DNA, to fight recessions with all the tools available, and especially a deflationary recession that might develop. They do not believe that it will make things worse. The two speeches make that very clear. They will risk a little inflation in order to drive a stake through the heart of the deflationary vampire.

The belief (or hope) at the Fed is that with enough stimulus we can work through the hangover of the 1990s (debt, deflation, excess capacity, dollar bubbles, trade deficits, etc.). Rather than one very big recession that hits the reset button on the economic imbalances created during the 1990s, the Fed hopes to slowly deal with them one by one by growing our way out of the problems, stimulating demand every time we slip nearer to deflation and/or recession.

The Fed will not raise rates until either one of two conditions appear:

1. The Fed believes the recovery is sustainable and it can raise rates in a historically normal fashion. Rising interest rates as a result of solid economic activity is a good sign.
2. Rising inflation forces the Fed to raise rates.

One can speculate about all types of plausible economic outcomes, and I do in my weekly letter, looking at current events. But at the end of every scenario the outcome is that interest rates are going to rise.

Even if a worst-case scenario develops in which the recovery fails before the Fed can begin to raise rates, the two speeches make it clear the Fed will do what it takes to bring about inflation. Longer-term interest rates would drop temporarily in such a situation, but the end result would be inflation and thus ultimately higher and rising rates.

Rising rates are not a stimulus. They are a headwind. They are one more reason to believe this decade will be one of an overall Muddle Through nature. They also have serious implications for Bull's Eye Investing in bonds, which is discussed in Chapter 19.

Why Investors Fail: Analyzing Risk

L ike all the children from Lake Wobegon, my readers, I am sure, are above average investors. But I am also sure you have friends who are not, so in this chapter we look at the reasons why they fail at investing, and how they should analyze funds and determine risk. Hopefully this will give you some ways to help them. *I will show you a simple way to put yourself in the top 20 percent of investors.* This should make it easier to go to family reunions and listen to your brother-in-law's stories.

A key part of successful Bull's Eye Investing is simply avoiding the mistakes that the majority of investors make. I can give you all the techniques, trading tips, fund recommendations, forecasts, and so on, but you must still keep away from the patterns that are typical of failed investors.

What I want to do in this chapter is give you an "aha!" moment: that insight which helps you understand a part of the mysteries of the marketplace. We look at a number of seemingly random ideas and concepts, and then see what conclusions we can draw. Let's jump in.

Investors Behaving Badly

T he Financial Research Corporation (FRC) released a study[1] in 1999 prior to the bear market, which showed that the average mutual fund's three-year return was 10.92 percent, while the average investor in those same periods gained only 8.7 percent. The reason was simple: Investors were chasing the hot sectors and funds.

If you study just the past three years, my guess is those numbers will be worse. According to Jeffrey A. Dunham,

The study found that the current average holding period was around 2.9 years for a typical investor, which is significantly shorter than the 5.5-year holding period of just five years ago.

Many investors are purchasing funds based on past performance, usually when the fund is at or near its peak. For example, $91 billion of new cash flowed into funds just after they experienced their "best performing" quarter. In contrast, only $6.5 billion in new money flowed into funds after their worst performing quarter."[2]

I have seen numerous studies similar to the one cited. They all show the same thing: that the average investor does not get average performance. Many studies show statistics that are much worse.

The study also showed something I had observed anecdotally, for which there was no evidence. Past performance was a good predictor of future *relative* performance in the fixed income markets and international equity (stock) funds, but there was no statistically significant way to rely on past performance in the domestic (U.S.) stock equity mutual funds. (I will comment on why I believe this is so later on.)

The oft-repeated legal disclosure that past performance is no guarantee of future results is true at two levels:

1. **Absolute returns** cannot be guaranteed with any confidence. There is too much variability for each broad asset class over multiple time periods. Stocks in general may provide 5 to 10 percent returns during one decade, 10 to 20 percent during the next decade, and then slip to the 0 to 5 percent range.

2. **Absolute rankings** also cannot be predicted with any certainty. This is caused by too much relative variability within specific investment objectives. Number 1 funds can regress to the average or fall far below the average over subsequent periods, replaced by funds that may have had very low rankings at the start. The higher the ranking and the more narrowly you define that ranking (i.e., #1 vs. top decile [top 10%] vs. top quartile [top 25%] vs. top half), the more unlikely it is that a fund can repeat at that level. It is extremely unlikely to repeat as #1 in an objective with more than a few funds. It is very difficult to repeat in the top decile, challenging to repeat in the top quartile, and roughly a coin toss to repeat in the top half.[3]

This is in line with the study cited earlier in Chapter 8 from the National Bureau of Economic Research. Only a very small percentage of companies can show merely above-average earnings growth for 10 years in a row. The percentage is not more than you would expect from simply random circumstances.

The chance of you picking a stock today that will be in the top 25 percent of all companies every year for the next 10 years is 50 to 1 or worse. In fact, the longer a company shows positive earnings growth and outstanding performance, the more likely it is to have an off year. Being on top for extended periods of time is an extremely difficult feat.

Yet what is the basis for most stock analysts' predictions? Past performance and the optimistic projections of a management that gets compensated with stock options. What CEO will tell you his stock is overpriced? His staff and board will kill him, as their options will be worthless. Analysts make the fatally flawed assumption that because a company has grown 25 percent a year for five years that it will do so for the next five. The actual results for the past 50 years show the likelihood of that happening to be small.

Analyze This: Analysts Are Useless

David Dreman points out in a study[4] that he conducted from 1982 through 1997 that analysts were on average wrong by 200 percent. Dreman tells us,

> Earnings performance for 2002's first half was a sorry one. Company after company was forced to lower expectations or restate past results downward. How can the consensus justify such a healthy-looking multiple for the year as a whole? By forecasting a second-half profit boom that gushes up from nowhere: a 48 percent gain (from a year earlier) in the third quarter and a 45.7 percent one in the fourth, according to S&P analysts' forecasts. Included in the forthcoming profit explosion, as reported in First Call, are a 127 percent income increase in technology stocks in the third quarter and a 73 percent jump in the fourth and a hardly modest 19-fold rise in transportation earnings in the third quarter (mainly airlines), with an even larger gain forecast for the fourth.[5]

Another longer-term study (cited previously in Chapter 8) published by the National Bureau of Economic Research shows that analysts typically overstate earnings by at least a factor of 2. From the report: "Analysts predicted a five-year growth for the top 20 percent of companies to be 22.4 percent which turned out to be only 9.5 percent." The researchers also pointed out the actual return rate should be lower because many companies failed over that period.

The researchers created sample portfolios based on analysts' forecasts. *Predictably, the top portion of the portfolios actually returned only about half of what the analysts predicted:* 11 percent actual versus 22 percent predicted. "These results suggest that in general caution should be exercised before relying too heavily on long-term forecasts as estimates of expected growth in valuation studies."[6]

Here's a business opportunity for some enterprising new analyst. Start your own analysis firm. Go to First Call (a division of Thomson Financial that compiles estimates from numerous sources) and look at the consensus estimate for earnings on any given company. Cut it in half and publish your estimate. Hire a few MBA financial types to write reports that reflect your "analysis." Then go to work on your golf handicap for the rest of the month.

Results: You will be closer than 90 percent of all analysts. After a year or two, you will look like a genius. You will be able to sell your analysis to firms all over the world for big bucks. You will be rich and you will have a single-digit handicap. The irony is that your analysis has a better basis in historical fact than the estimates of the guys who are actually trying. If you can deal with the conscience thing (which does not seem to be a problem for some analysts), it would not a bad life.

Tails You Lose, Heads I Win

*F*ooled by Randomness: The Hidden Role of Chance in the Markets and in Life by Nassim Nicholas Taleb[7] is an excellent examination of the role of chance in the marketplace.

Assume you have 10,000 people who flip a coin once a year. After five years, you will have 313 people who have come up with heads five times in a row. If you put suits on them, sit them in glass offices, and call them a mutual or a hedge fund, they will soon be managing a billion dollars. They will absolutely believe they have figured out the secret to investing that all the other losers haven't discerned. Their seven-figure salaries prove it.

The next year, 157 of them will blow up. With my power of analysis, I can predict at least one of those that will blow up. It will be the one in which you invest!

Ergodicity

In the mutual fund and hedge fund world, one of the continual issues of reporting returns is something called "survivorship bias." Let's say you start with a universe of 1,000 funds. After five years, only 800 of those funds are still in business. The other 200 had dismal results, were unable to attract money, and simply folded.

If you look at the annual returns of the 800 funds, you get one average number. But if you add in the returns of the 200 failures, the average return is much lower. The databases most statistics are based on look only at the survivors. This sets up false expectations for investors, as it raises the average.

One of Taleb's insights is especially useful. He points out that because of chance and survivorship bias, investors are likely to find out about only the winners. Indeed, who goes around trying to sell you the losers? The likelihood of being shown an investment or a stock that has flipped heads five times in a row is very high. But the chances are that hot investment you are shown is a result of randomness. You are much more likely to have success hunting on your own. The exception, of course, would be my clients. (Note to regulators: That last sentence is a literary device called a weak attempt at humor. It is not meant to be taken literally.)

That brings us to the principle of ergodicity, "namely, that time will eliminate the annoying effects of randomness. Looking forward, in spite of the fact that these managers were profitable in the past five years, we expect them to break even in any future time period. They will fare no better than those of the initial cohort who failed earlier in the exercise. Ah, the long term."[8]

Why Investors Fail

While the professionals typically explain their problems in very creative ways, the mistakes that most of us make are much more mundane. First and foremost is chasing performance. Study after study shows the average investor does much worse than the average mutual fund, as he switches from his poorly performing fund to the latest hot fund just as it turns down.

Mark Finn of Vantage Consulting has spent years analyzing trading systems. He is a consultant to large pension funds and Fortune 500 companies. He is one of the more astute analysts of trading systems, managers, and funds that I know. He has put more start-up managers into business than perhaps anyone in the fund management world. He has a gift for finding new talent and deciding if their ideas have investment merit.

He has a team of certifiable mathematical geniuses working for him. They have access to the best pattern recognition software available. They have run price data through every conceivable program and come away with this conclusion:

Past performance is not indicative of future results.

Actually, Mark says it more bluntly: Past performance is pretty much worthless when it comes to trying to figure out the future. The best use of past performance is to determine how a manager behaved in a particular set of prior circumstances.

Yet investors read that past performance is not indicative of future results, and then promptly ignore it. It is like reading statements at McDonald's that coffee is hot. We don't pay attention.

Chasing the latest hot fund usually means you get into a fund that is close to reaching its peak, and will soon top out. Generally that is shortly after you invest.

What do Finn and his team tell us does work? Fundamentals, fundamentals, fundamentals. As they look at scores of managers each year, the common thread for success is how they incorporate some set of fundamental analysis into their systems.

This is consistent with work done by Dr. Gary Hirst, one of my favorite analysts and fund managers. In 1991, he began to look at technical analysis. He spent huge sums on computers and programming, analyzing a variety of technical analysis systems. Let me quote him as to the results of his research:

> I had heard about technical analysis and chart patterns, and looking at this stuff I would say, what kind of voodoo is this? I was very, very skeptical that technical analysis had value. So I used the computers to check it out, and what I learned was that there was, in fact, no useful reality there. Statistically and mathematically all these tools—stochastics, RSI, chart patterns, Elliott Wave, and so on—just don't work. If you code any of these rigorously into a computer and test them they produce no statistical basis for making money; they're just wishful thinking. But I did find one thing that worked. In fact, almost all technical analysis can be reduced to this one thing, though most people don't realize it: The distributions of returns are not normal; they are skewed and have "fat tails." In other words, markets do produce profitable trends. Sure, I found things that work over the short term, systems that work for five or ten years but then fail miserably. Everything you made, you gave back. Over the long term, trends are where the money is.[9]

I've Got a Secret System

If you go to an investment conference or read a magazine, you are bombarded with opportunities to buy software packages that will show you how to day trade and make 1,000 percent a year. For $5,000 you can buy an "exclusive" letter (just you and a thousand other readers, and their friends and clients) that will give you a hot options or stock tip. You will be shown winning trades that make 100 percent or more in a short time. You, too, can use this simple tested method to enrich yourself. Act now. (Add $6.95 for shipping and handling.)

Full disclosure here: I am a manager of investment managers. I look for investment managers and funds for clients. Most of the funds I look at are in the private fund or hedge fund world. I get to see the track records and talk with some of the crème de la crème of the investment universe—the true Masters of the Universe. These are the managers available only to accredited investors ($1,000,000 or more net worth). This world is growing by leaps and bounds as more and more sophisticated investors and institutions are looking at these managers now that mutual funds and stock managers are having bad years.

None—not one—nada—zippo—zero of the best managers in the world can deliver the consistent results that you read about in these ads. The best offshore fund in the world for the five years ending in 2000 did about 30 percent a year. You can't get into it. But in 2001 and 2002 it was flat.

Steve Cohen can deliver some spectacular returns and has for almost 20 years. His fund been closed to new money for years. But even this legend can't put up numbers like I see in the ads.

Here's the reality. If you could make 20 percent a year steady, in five years—ten at the most—you would be managing all the money you could run. Trust me, the money will find you. You will charge a 2 percent management fee and keep 20 percent of the profits. On $1 billion, that amounts to $60 million in fees. That's every year, of course. Why would you sell a system that could do 20 percent a year?

Once everyone knows about a system, it won't work like it has in the past. One of the problems I wrestle with every day is trying to figure out which investment styles may be at the end of their runs. Every dog has its day in the sun. The trick is to figure out when the sun is setting.

Now, saying that, there are exceptions. I used to get an e-mail every day from a reader. In it were his trades for the next day. (Now I get weekly summaries.) He is uncanny. He is compounding at something like 200 to 300 percent year, with around 75 percent of his trades working. I called him to discuss his system. I was interested in starting a fund. The problem is that his style would top out at about $1,000,000 under management (he thinks). After that, he would not be able to get enough trades. But he does nicely for himself. Most managers are too optimistic about how much a particular system can handle. That means you could only have a fund for about $250,000 and let it grow, and of course there would be a thousand other problems.

Could he sell his system to a wide audience? You bet. But the minute he did, it would stop working.

Every style has its limits, whether it is $1 million or $250 million or $1 billion. Just because you have a successful operation with 25 stores doesn't mean you can expand to 500.

There are physical limits to everything and every system. Knowing your limits, and the limits of your investment managers, is critical. Many of the spectacular blow-ups have been from managers who did not understand the limits of their styles.

Take the Janus 20 fund. This is a fund that focuses on the 20 "best" companies, mostly technology. It had an incredible record, and grew to manage tens of billions of dollars. This was good for the managers, as annual bonuses grew each year as well. They told their investors that the secret to their success was doing their homework and being expert on analyzing companies. They were bottom-up value investors looking for growth potential, and boy were you lucky to have found them.

The reality is they were a busload of investors on their way to a train wreck. No one seemed to think the party would end. But when it did, they had no exit strategy or even the ability to exit. If you own $5 billion in Cisco, you are not a shareholder. You are a partner. You are stuck. If you try to get out, the market will soon get the word that Janus is bailing, and the shorts will eat your lunch.

In hindsight, their incredible track record was less brilliant investing and more simply participation in the largest investment bubble in history, with no exit strategy. They flipped heads eight times in a row.

Smaller investors and funds could have taken the exact same approach, but because they were smaller would have had the ability to exit.

When Will the Next Bull (or Bear) Market Run Begin?

First, let me make this very clear: There is no technical indicator, or even fundamental system, that can tell us when the next bear market rally will begin or end, or when the bear market will be over and a new bull will begin. All of this talk on TV or in newsletters about this indicator or that system telling us we are at the exact top or bottom is just voodoo investing. It is an exercise in wishful thinking.

The Nobel Prize in economics in 2002 went to a psychologist, Dr. Daniel Kahneman, who helped pioneer the field of behavioral finance. If I can crudely summarize his brilliant work, he basically shows that investors are irrational. But what gets him a Nobel is he shows that we are predictably irrational. We continue to make the same mistakes over and over. One of the biggest is our common inability to take a loss. He goes into long and magnificent explanations of why this is, but the bottom line is that taking a loss is so painful, we simply avoid it.

While technical indicators cannot be rigorously programmed to yield an automatic, always winning or low loss, don't-think-about-it trading system, they do provide some useful insight. Volume, direction, momentum, stochastics, and so on are reflective of market psychology. With a great deal of time and effort, astute traders can use this data to determine what Mark Finn calls the "gist" of the market.

The great traders become adept at using this data to help them determine market psychology and thus market movement. They also employ excellent money management and risk control skills. My contention is they have the "feel." Just like some people can hit 95 mph fastballs, they can look at amazing amounts of data and feel the market. They use solid money management techniques to control the risk, and they make money for themselves and their clients. Like Alex Rodriguez at the plate, they make it look easy.

And thus many ordinary people think they can do it. And most fail.

For some reason, we take this failure personally. It seems so easy, we should be able to do it. But after years of interviewing hundreds of managers and looking at thousands of funds and mounds of data, I have come to believe it is a gift, just like hitting baseballs or golf balls.

If it were easy, everybody could do it. But it's not, so don't beat yourself up if you are not the one with the gift. It would be like me getting angry at myself for not being a scratch golfer. It is not going to happen in my lifetime. It does not matter how much I practice. I simply don't have the talent to be a scratch golfer. If I wanted to bet on golf, I would bet on a pro, not on me.

Analyzing a Fund

Okay, here is a confession. There are thousands of funds and managers for me to investigate. When I go to my databases, I do a sort for high Sharpe ratios, low standard deviations, low betas, and, yes, good returns. Returns do matter. Then I begin to do the real work of investment analysis. There is a lot more in this world than numbers.

There are lots of questions to ask. First, I want to know, "Why do you make money?" Then I ask, "How do you make money?" Then I want to know how much risk they are taking, and the last question is, "How much money do your investors make?"

Janus 20, to pick on that fund again, made money because it was in a bull market. Period. It lost money because it was in a bear market and it was a long-only fund. Some market timers made good money in the last bull market, but lost their touch as we went into more volatile bear market conditions. The irony is that their systems need bull markets to be successful, but it was not until we were in a bear market that we knew that.

Unfortunately, this was at precisely the time you wanted a market timer to work for you. So you have to find out what market managers are trading in and look at their performances in light of that. That simple process will often tell you whether you are dealing with good managers or lucky traders. Or they may even be good managers at the right place at the right time. The question then becomes, how long will the time for that investment strategy be right?

If you understand why they made money in the past, you have to ask yourself whether the conditions are likely to remain in place for them to continue to make money in the future.

If they can give you a good reason for why they make money in their niche, then you start to look at how they do it. What is their system? Do they really have one or are they flying by the seat of their pants? Every manager will tell you he has a proprietary trading system. You start with that as a given. What you want to be able to do is see into the basics of the system. If they refuse to show you—if you cannot get enough information to get comfortable with their system—then simply walk away. Do not give that person your money.

I am consumed with wanting to know how a manager controls risk. I understand that you can't make above-market returns without risk. But not all risk is apparent from past performance. (The blow-up by Long-Term Capital Management comes to mind. Right up until the end, it was as steady as you could find. Then: *ka-boom.*) All styles will lose money from time to time. I want my risk-to-reward ratio to be reasonable and controlled.

After you understand all this, looking at a track record can make sense. Did the manager add value in the markets he is in? Did he give us "alpha," that bit of profit over what we could expect blind dogs to make in his market trading style? (That is not the technical definition for alpha, but it is more understandable.)

There are a lot of managers and funds that do deliver alpha. Mostly, they are managers who have found a niche to work in, and stick to their knitting. They manage their risks well. They have good operational staff and administration. It takes a lot of work (and some luck) to find them.

Becoming a Top 20 Percent Investor

Over very long periods of time, the average stock portfolio will grow at about 7 percent a year, which is GDP growth plus dividends plus inflation. This is logical when you think about it. How could all the companies in the country grow faster than the total economy? Some companies will grow faster than others, of course, but the average will be 7 percent. There are numerous studies that demonstrate this. That means roughly 50 percent of the companies will outperform the average and 50 percent will lag.

The same is true for investors. By definition, 50 percent of you will achieve the average; 10 percent of you will do really well; and 1 percent will get rich through investing. You will be the lucky ones who find Microsoft in 1982. You will tell yourself it was your ability. Most of us assign our good fortune to native skill and our losses to bad luck.

But we all try to be in the top 10 percent. Oh, how we try. The FRC study cited at the beginning of this chapter shows how most of us look for success, and then get in, only to have gotten in at the top. In fact, trying to be in the top 10 percent or 20 percent is statistically one of the ways we find ourselves getting below-average returns over time. We might be successful for a while, but reversion to the mean will catch up.

Here is the very sad truth. The majority of investors in the top 10 to 20 percent in any given period are simply lucky. They have come up with heads five times in a row. Their ship came in. There are some good investors who actually do it with sweat and work, but they are not the majority. Want to make someone angry? Tell a manager that his (or her) fabulous track record appears to be random luck or that they simply caught a wave and rode it. Then duck.

By the way, is it luck or skill when an individual goes to work for a start-up company and is given stock in a 401(k) that grows at 10,000 percent? How many individuals work for companies where that didn't happen, or their stock options blew up (Enron)? I happen to lean toward grace, rather than luck or skill, as an explanation, but this is not a theological treatise.

Most millionaires make their money in business and/or by saving lots of money and living frugally. Very few make it by simply investing skill alone. Odds are that you will not be that person.

But I can tell you how to get in the top 20 percent of investors. Or better, I will let FRC tell you, because they do it so well:

For those who are not satisfied with simply beating the average over any given period, consider this: **If an investor can consistently achieve slightly better than average returns each year over a 10–15-year period, then cumulatively over the full period they are likely to do better than roughly 80 percent or more of their peers.** They may never have discovered a fund that ranked #1 over a subsequent one- or three-year period. That "failure," however, is more than offset by their having avoided options that dramatically underperformed. *Avoiding short-term underperformance is the key to long-term out-performance.*

For those that are looking to find a new method of discerning the top 10 funds for 2002, this study will prove frustrating. There are no magic shortcut solutions, and we urge our readers to abandon the illusive and ultimately counterproductive search for them. For those who are willing to restrain their short-term passions, embrace the virtue of being only slightly better than average, and wait for the benefits of this approach to compound into something much better.[10]

That's it. You simply have to be only slightly better than average each year to be in the top 20 percent at the end of the race. It is a whole lot easier to figure out how to do that than chase the top 10 funds.

Of course, you could get lucky (or blessed) and get one of the top 10 funds. But recognize it for what it is and thank God (or your luck if you are agnostic) for His blessings.

I should point out that it takes a lot of work to be in the top 50 percent consistently. But it can be done. I don't see it as much as I would like, but I do see it.

Investing in a stock or a fund should not be like going to Vegas. When you put money with a manager or a fund, you should think as if you are investing in their management company. Ask yourself, "Is this someone I want to be in business with? Do I want him running my company? Does this company have a reasonable business objective? What is its edge that makes me think it will be above average? What is the reason I would think this manager could discern the difference between randomness and good management?"

When I meet a manager and all he wants to do is talk about his track record, I find a way to quickly close the conversation. When managers tell me they are trying to make the most they can, I head for the door. Maybe they are the real deal, but my experience says the odds are against it.

It is not settling for being mediocre. Statistics and experience tell us that simply being consistently above average is damn hard work. When a fund is the number one fund for the year, that is random. It had a good run or a good idea and it worked. Is it likely to repeat? No.

But being in the top 50 percent every year for 10 years? That is *not* random. That is skill. That type of consistent solid management is what you should be looking for.

By the way, I mentioned at the beginning of this chapter that past performance was statistically useful for ascertaining relative performance of certain types of funds like bond funds and international funds. In the fixed income markets (bonds) everyone is dealing with the same instruments. Funds with lower overhead and skilled traders who aggressively watch their trading costs have an edge. That management skill shows up in consistently above-average relative returns.

Likewise, funds that do well in emerging market investments tend to stay in the top brackets. That is because the skill set and learning cost for international fund management is rare. In that world, local knowledge of the markets clearly adds value.

But in the U.S. stock market, everybody knows everything everybody else does. Past performance is a very bad predictor of future results. If a fund does well in one year, it is possibly because its managers took some extra risks to do so, and eventually those risks will bite them and their investors. Maybe they were lucky and had two of their biggest holdings really go through the roof. Finding those monster winners is a hard thing to do for several years in a row. Plus, the U.S. stock market is cyclical, so that what goes up one year or even longer in a bubble market will not do well the next.

Investors Behaving Badly

Gavin McQuill of the Financial Research Corporation sent me his rather brilliant $5,000 report called "Investors Behaving Badly."[11]

Earlier we looked at a report that showed that over the past decade investors chased the hot mutual funds. The higher the markets went, the less likely it was that they would buy and hold. Investors consistently bought high and sold low. Investors made significantly less than the average mutual funds did.

McQuill focused on six emotions that cause investors to make these mistakes. You should read these and see if some of these emotions are all too familiar.

1. "Fear of regret—an inability to accept that you've made a wrong decision, which leads to holding onto losers too long or selling winners too soon." This is part of a whole cycle of denial, anxiety, and depression. As in any other difficult situation, we first deny there is a problem, and then get anxious as the problem does not go away or gets worse. Then we go into depression because we didn't take action earlier, and hope that something will come along and rescue us from the situation.

2. "Myopic loss aversion (a.k.a. "shortsightedness)—a fear of losing money and the subsequent inability to withstand short-term events and maintain a long-term perspective." Basically, this means we attach too much importance to day-to day events, rather than looking at the big picture. Behavioral psychologists have determined that the fear of loss is the most important emotional factor in investor behavior.

Like investors chasing the latest hot fund, a news story or a bad day in the market becomes enough for the investor to extrapolate the recent event as the new trend that will stretch far into the future. In reality, most events are unimportant and have little effect on the overall economy.

3. "Cognitive dissonance—the inability to change your opinion after new evidence contradicts your baseline assumption." Dissonance, whether musical or emotional, is uncomfortable. It is often easier to ignore the event or fact producing the dissonance than to deal with it. We tell ourselves it is not meaningful, and go on our way. This is especially easy if our view is the accepted view. "Herd mentality" is a big force in the market.

4. "Overconfidence—people's tendency to overestimate their abilities relative to individuals possessing greater expertise." Professionals beat amateurs 99 percent of the time. The other 1 percent is luck. The famous Clint Eastwood line, "Do you feel lucky, punk? Well, do you?" comes to mind.

In sports, most of us know when we are outclassed. But as investors, we somehow think we can beat the pros, will always be in the top 10 percent, and any time we win, it is because of our skills and good judgment. It is bad luck when we lose.

Commodity brokers know that the best customers are those who strike it rich in their first few trades. They are now convinced they possess the gift or the holy grail of trading systems. These are the people who will spend all their money trying to duplicate their initial success in an effort to validate their obvious abilities. They also generate large commissions for their brokers.

5. "Anchoring—people's tendency to give too much credence to their most recent experience and to show reluctance to adjust their current beliefs." If you believe that NASDAQ stocks are the place to be, that becomes your anchor. No matter what new information comes your way, you are anchored in your belief. Your experience in 1999 shows you were right.

As Lord Keynes said so eloquently when forced to acknowledge a shift in a previous position he had taken, "Sir, the facts have changed, and when the facts change, I change. What do you do, sir?"

We expect the current trend to continue forever, and forget that all trends eventually regress to the mean. That is why investors still plunge into index funds, believing that stocks will go up over the long term. They think the long term is two years. They do not understand that it will take several years—maybe a decade—for the process of reversion to the mean to complete its work.

6. "Representativeness—the tendency of people to see patterns within random events." Eric Frye did a great tongue-in-cheek article in *The Daily Reckoning*, a daily investment letter (www.dailyreckoning.com). He documented that each time *Sports Illustrated* featured a model for the cover of its swimsuit issue who came from a new country that had never been represented on the cover before, the stock market of that country always rose

over a four-year period. This year, it is time to buy Argentine stocks. Frye evidently did not do a correlation study on the size of the swimsuit against the eventual rise in the market. However, I am sure some statistician with more time on his hands than I do will brave that analysis.

Investors assume that items with a few similar traits are likely to be associated or identical, and start to see a pattern. McQuill gives us an example. Nancy is an English and environmental studies major. Most people when asked if it was more likely that Nancy would be a librarian or work in the financial services industry will choose librarian. That would be wrong. There are vastly more workers in the financial industry than there are librarians. Statistically, the probability is that she will work in the financial services industry, even though librarians are likely to have been English majors.[12]

The preceding 15 chapters have looked at the trends in the markets, the economy, and the difficulties of investing in today's world. Today's environment is challenging, to say the least.

Now let's turn our thoughts to how to take these ideas and turn them into actual investment strategies. It's time to talk about Bull's Eye Investing.

Taking Stock: The Fundamental Nature of Bull's Eye Investing

16

> *Price is what you pay. Value is what you get.*
>
> —Warren Buffett

Most of the preceding chapters have discussed the long-term secular bear market along with the slow economic growth I predict for the rest of the decade. Now, however, I'm saying you should invest in stocks. How can you dance with a bear without getting claw marks all over your back?

The answer is straightforward, if not exactly simple: When you dance with this bear, you need to be the one leading! You can use this bear cycle to create wealth and opportunity rather than let it destroy your assets. The next few chapters won't provide you any specific stock picks. I will, however, offer you principles for finding stocks that will increase your wealth. I'll also explain how to evaluate when is the right time to make these investments. Contrary to what your broker says, today may not always be a good time.

Later chapters look at some special types of funds that are effective ways in which to invest in the stock market. But for now, let's look at a few rules about how to directly invest in stocks in a secular bear market.

First, when I showed you that we are in a long-term secular bear market cycle, I used broad market averages that are basically comprised of large companies. In this cycle, we will see the price-earnings ratio (the value) of these index averages slowly come down.

The two key words here are *value* and *average*. If the average P/E is 15, then it means that there are many stocks with P/E ratios of 20 and others with P/Es of 10. As the index averages come down over time, there are going to be stocks that begin to have low P/E ratios for one reason or another. When the index average P/E is 12, that means there will be stocks with P/E ratios of 5, 6, and 7! There will be real value in our future!

Many investment advisors and fund managers want you to be invested in the stock market 100 percent of the time. They tell you to buy an index or broad-based mutual fund (preferably mine). You diversify by investing in niche stock funds. If you stay the course long enough you will succeed. Unfortunately, in a secular bear market, as I have clearly demonstrated, that is a losing proposition.

Instead of investing in the stock market (broadly defined), Bull's Eye Investing tells you to invest in particular stocks and strategies. Don't think of equities as a stock market, but rather as a market of stocks. An easy-to-understand analogy is an Italian restaurant in New York City with more than 100 items on its menu. You don't order the entire "Italian menu" and take something of everything. Instead, you order specific items, according to your preferences and diet.

Second, defining a secular bear market in terms of value rather than price allows us to begin to reenter the market as value presents itself. Thus, even as we can believe that the broad stock market has more room to go on the downside, we can still find ways to put money to work in certain stocks that have already fallen to a point where there is now real value.

Third, there are two basic ways to approach value stock investing. You can buy stocks to generate income or buy stocks that have the potential for growth, or you can hunt for stocks that offer both. This isn't a new concept, but the way we will define income and growth potential will be somewhat different.

The Home Field Advantage

During the most recent bear market rally (which we are currently in as I write but may be over or on its last legs as the book is published) my readers kept asking me, "What are investors thinking? How can you be right about being in something called a secular bear market if stocks just keep going up? Isn't it time for you to throw in the towel, admit you were wrong, and declare a new bull has begun?"

Undoubtedly, I will be asked the same question frequently over the next few years. Remember the study in Chapter 6 that showed that 50 percent of the years in a secular bear cycle the market goes up, and often by 20 percent or more? Frequent rallies are typical of bear markets. I answer these questions and more as we ponder the meaning of several important, if somewhat obscure, academic studies.

Butch, an astute businessman and reader, and I were watching the Texas Rangers from my balcony office suites in right field at the Ballpark in Arlington. On this particular Saturday, the team played like world champions, with six home runs, solid pitching, and great fielding. The fact they were in last place and going lower did not diminish our enjoyment of the atypical display in front of us. Alas, one game does not make a trend, nor a season. And as you'll see, our home team bias provides us with an analogy that will give you some insights into the direction of the markets.

"Where," Butch asked, "is the stock market going? Will it go higher before the end of the year?" It was of more than academic interest to Butch, as he had December 2003 LEAPS put options (a bet the market was headed down), which were losing value every day as the market went up.

My quick answer was, "I don't know where the market will be in December." We were approaching stock market valuations that were last seen in the run-up to the bubble. This time, we are (always) told, it is really different. The economy is improving; therefore, it is only right that the stock market should be. Never mind that the economy was improving in 1999 and 2000. Investors have learned their lessons.

The P/E ratio of the S&P 500 on March 31, 2000, was 29.41. In February 2004, the P/E ratio was at 27 and climbing as the market kept rising. The NASDAQ P/E number was back to bubble-type levels.

Butch and I agreed that the market was irrationally high, based on historic trends. But that did not mean it could not go higher. And, in fact, it did.

As the father of seven kids, I have some experience with teenagers. I have learned to never underestimate the potential for a teenager to act irrationally. Just because they acted irrationally yesterday and have seemed to learn the error of their ways does not mean they cannot think of completely new and even more astounding ways to become irrational tomorrow. Even as I write these very thoughts, my wife calls to inform me of the evidence of my words. When my friends ask me, "How are your kids doing?" it is more with prayerful hope than any sense of real certainty about the future that I answer, "They're doing fine."

Of course, many parents wish they had to deal with my set of "irrational" teenage behaviors rather than those of their own lovely offspring. There are many different types of irrationality. As parents, we all have our own definitions. My kids have regularly informed me that my standards are way too conservative, especially when compared to those of "everybody else."

As investors, we seem to have a wide variety of standards as to what is actually an irrational price for a stock as opposed to a screaming value. Yet history shows us that valuations will revert to the mean over time and even move significantly below trend. There has never been a time in history when P/E ratios have been in the range they were in 1999 or the end of 2003 that 10 years later investors in the broad stock market have outperformed a money market fund. None. Yet investors pile into the markets in a belief that the markets will behave in entirely new and different fashions.

Insanity, my wife frequently informs me, is doing the same thing over and over and expecting different results. Yet investors keep running stocks up to nosebleed valuations and somehow expect that this time it will all be different. It never is.

Let's look at some of the reasons for such behavior. They are rooted not in mathematics and economic foresight, but in psychology.

There is a school of economic thought called the Efficient Market Theory that says that security prices correctly (and almost immediately) reflect all information and expectations. It says that you cannot consistently outperform the stock market due to the random nature in which information arrives and the fact that prices react and adjust almost immediately to reflect the latest information. Therefore, it assumes that at any given time, the market correctly prices all securities. The result, or so the theory advocates, is that securities cannot be overpriced or underpriced for a long enough period of time for you to profit from the changes.

The only way to profitably invest is to buy and hold broad market baskets.

The theory holds that since prices reflect all available information, and since information arrives in a random fashion, there is little to be gained from any type of analysis, whether fundamental or technical. It assumes that every piece of information has been collected and processed by thousands of investors, and this information (both old and new) is correctly reflected in the price. Returns cannot be increased by studying historical data, either fundamental or technical, since past data will have no effect on future prices.[1]

Nobel Prizes in economics have been given for developing this theory. Careers have been built upon expanding such knowledge. Whole books have been given over to the math that proves the theory. Sadly, such economists are like a blind javelin thrower. They are not likely to win on accuracy, but they will be sure to keep the crowd's attention.

Some academic economists, though, are beginning to assert that the theory is fundamentally at odds with reality. Some of us less scholarly types simply note that it is a silly way to look at the world, the economic equivalent of asserting it is mathematically impossible for bumblebees to fly. It demonstrates that even though an academic, even a Nobel laureate, presents mathematic "proof" of a proposition, we would be wise to examine the assumptions made in developing his theory. As we will see, the theory does not hold up well under examination.

(Why is this important to you as an investor? Because marketing types will use it to demonstrate that you should invest in certain ways, like buy and hold stocks and mutual funds. How can you disagree with an idea that won a Nobel Prize? "Trust me, or at least trust the Nobel genius," you are told. I should note that the vast majority of Nobel economic laureates deserve your trust for their ideas, but there are a *few* ideas that either get very abused by those who want to sell you investments, or they make nice theories, but bad investments.)

Home Field Bias

There is a growing field of study called behavioral finance. These researchers try to determine why we do what we do when it comes to money. And yes, two psychologists were recently awarded a Nobel Prize for economics for their contribution to this field. We are going to look at some examples and research of why investors do seemingly irrational things.

Arnold Wood, CEO of Martingale Asset Management, recently gave a speech to a group of financial analysts in Dallas. He highlighted two interesting studies.

First, a researcher takes a deck of 52 cards and holds one card up. Watchers pay a dollar for the chance to win $100 if that card is picked out of the deck. Keep in mind the expected payout is $1/52 \times 100 = 1.92$. Las Vegas would quickly go broke with such odds. Then they are asked if they would like to sell their chances: roughly 80 percent would sell if they could, asking for an average price of $1.86. If you could get such a price, it would be a reasonable sell. For someone who could buy all 52 chances, it would be a good purchase or arbitrage. He would make a quick 3.18 percent.

Now it gets interesting. The next time, someone is allowed to pick a card out of the deck and offered the same chance, but now he has a personal attachment to the card because he touched it. Only about 60 percent of those who picked cards were willing to sell their chances, and they wanted an average price of just over $6. And when this same trick was performed at MBA schools the average sale price has been over $9.

"I know this card. I have studied it. I have a personal involvement with the card; therefore it is worth more," thinks the investor. Of course, it is worth no more than in the first case, but the psychology of "owning" the card makes investors value it more. Hold this thought as we explore the next idea.

Familiarity Breeds (Over)Confidence

Think this doesn't play out in the real world? Let's look at a few studies in a recent special edition of the *Journal of Psychology and Financial Markets* (www.psychologyandmarkets.org).

First, Michael Kilka and Martin Weber's study of "Home Bias in International Stock Return Expectations" compares German and U.S. investors. Each group feels more competent about their home markets and stocks. And each group assesses the probable future returns for their "home" stocks to be higher than those of the foreign stocks.

Simply because they are more familiar with a stock they think it is more likely to go up than another stock with which they are less familiar. Rationally, how could you make such a statement if you do not know much about the other stock? What is your basis in fact for making such a comparison? The fact that they know nothing about the other stocks does not deter them from making a judgment.

Think this applies only to the small guy? Think again. The study shows a similar bias seems to apply for professional (institutional) investors. The study reveals that for both test groups the stocks with which they are familiar are judged more optimistically than stocks that are "foreign" or about which they know little.

Kilka and Weber then cite other studies that support this point. Heath and Tversky[2] "demonstrate that people on average prefer to bet on their own judgment over an equally probable chance event when they consider themselves competent about the event being judged. Otherwise, they prefer betting on the chance event."

This is why local horses (at the horse races) generally get better odds from the local bettors than these horses do when they are racing out of town. It is why the bookies know my local fellow citizens will bet more on the Dallas Cowboys than they would on the Seattle Seahawks. We read and study the papers every day, learning more and more about "our" teams. Since we know more about them, we judge them more likely to win. Of course, you don't have to be from Dallas to be sucked into such irrationality. The same phenomenon occurs all over the world.

This is not just a German/U.S. issue. Kilka and Weber mention another study[3] done in 1996 that shows the exact same response from institutional investors with regard to Japan and the United States. Yet another study shows that the more we know about a stock, the more likely we are to be optimistic and the more likely we are to judge ourselves competent and to trust our analysis.

Familiarity in stocks does not breed contempt. It breeds confidence. Worse, what we will find from the next study is that given enough time, it can breed unreasonable confidence. Pride goeth before a fall, we are told by the ancient fount of wisdom. Overconfidence seems to result in market losses. Either can be painful.

Evidence for Investor Overreaction

It typically takes years for valuations to fall in bear markets to levels from where a new bull market can begin. Why does it take so long? Why don't we see an almost immediate return to low valuations once the process has begun?

Investors overreact to good news and underreact to bad news on stocks they like, and do just the opposite to stocks that are out of favor. Past perception seems to dictate future performance. And it takes time to change those perceptions.

This is forcefully borne out by a study produced in 2000 by David Dreman (one of the brightest lights in investment analysis) and Eric Lufkin. The work, entitled "Investor Overreaction: Evidence That Its Basis is Psychological," is a well-written analysis of investor behavior that illustrates that perceptions are more important than the fundamentals. Let's look at that study in detail.

In any given year, there are stocks that are in favor, as evidenced by high valuations and rising prices. There are also stocks that are just the opposite. Dreman and Lufkin look at a database for 4,721 companies from 1973 through 1998. Each year, they divide the database up into five parts, or quintiles, based on the companies' perceived market valuations. They separately study price to book value (P/BV), price to cash flow (P/CF), and the traditional price to earnings (P/E). This creates three separate ways to analyze stocks by value for any given year so as to remove the bias that might occur from using just one measure of valuation.

The top and bottom quintiles become stock investment "portfolios" for all three valuation measures. You might think of them as a mutual fund created to buy just these stocks. The researchers then look 10 years back and five years forward for these portfolios. There is enough data to create 85 such portfolios or funds. They first analyze these portfolios as to how they do relative to the market or the average of all the stocks. They then analyze these portfolios in terms of five basic investment fundamentals: cash flow growth, sales growth, earnings growth, return on equity and profit margin. They do this latter test to see if you can discern a fundamental reason for the price action of the stock.

Here's my review of the most relevant parts of their presentation.

First, both the "outperformance" and "underperformance" of these stocks happens in the 10 years leading up to the formation of the portfolio. Almost immediately upon creating the portfolio, the price performance comparisons change, and change dramatically. The in-favor stocks underperform the market for the next five years, and the out-of-favor (value) stocks outperform the market.

I should point out that other studies, which Dreman and Lufkin do not cite, seem to indicate that the actual experience of many investors is more like these static portfolios than one might at first think. That is because investors tend to chase price performance. In fact, the higher the price and more rapid the movement, the more new investors there are who jump in. The 1995 Dalbar study ("Quantitive Analysis of Investor Behavior," www.dalbarinc.com), among many others, shows us that investors do not actually make what the mutual funds make because they chase the hottest funds, buying high and selling low when the funds do not live up to their expectations. The key word, as we will see later, is "expectations." Other studies document that investors tend to chase the latest hot stock and shun those which are lagging in price performance. Thus, forming portfolios of the highest- and lowest-performing quintiles is an uncanny mirror to what happens in the real world.

Why does this "chasing the hot stock" happen? Dreman and Lufkin tell us it is because investors become overconfident that the trends of the fundamentals in the first 10 years will repeat forever, "thereby carrying the prices of stocks that appear to have the 'best' and 'worst' prospects. Investors are likely to forecast a future not very different from the recent past, i.e., continuing improving fundamentals for favorites and deteriorating fundamentals for out-of-favor issues. Such forecasts result in favorites being overpriced, while out-of-favor issues are priced at a substantial discount to the real worth. The extrapolation of past results well into the future and the high confidence in the precise forecast is one of the most common errors made in finance."[4]

Remember the study first mentioned? The more we learn about a stock, the more we think we are competent to analyze it and the more convinced we are of the correctness of our judgment.

Since you are not looking at the graphs, let me describe them for you. Predictably, the fundamentals improve quite steadily for the first 10 years for the favorite stocks in comparison to the entire universe of stocks. But the price performance rises at very high rates, far faster than the fundamentals, particularly in the latter years. It clearly accelerates. It seems the longer a stock does well, the more confident investors are that it will continue to do well and therefore they award it with higher and higher multiples. The exact opposite is true of the out-of-favor stocks. Even though many of the fundamentals were actually slowly improving, in relation to the market as a whole they were lagging and the market punished them with ever lower relative prices.

At five years prior to the formation of a portfolio, the trends of each group were set in place. The next five years just reinforced these trends. This reinforces the perceptions about these stocks and increases the level of confidence about the future. Again, past (and accumulated and reinforced over time) perception creates future price action.

Never mind that it is impossible for Dell Computer to grow 50 percent a year or General Electric to compound earnings at 15 percent forever. As many times as we say it, investors continue to ignore the old saw "Past performance is not indicative of future results." And that is not to say Dell and GE are not wonderful companies. They are. But their share values, and those of any in-favor stock, eventually rise too high.

How much better did the well-performing stocks do than the poorly performing stocks in the 10 years prior to creating the portfolios? The highest P/BV (price to book value) stocks outperformed the market by 187 percent. The lowest stocks underperformed the market by –79 percent for a differential of 266 percent! If you look at the P/CF (price to cash flow), the differential between the two is 172 percent.

Yet in the next five years, the hot stocks underperformed the market by –26 percent on a P/BV basis and –30 percent on a P/CF basis. The out-of-favor stocks did 33 percent and 22 percent better than the market, respectively. This is a huge reversal of trend.

What happened? Did the trends stop? Did the former outcasts finally get their act together and start to show better fundamentals than the all-stars? The answer is a very curious "no."

Dreman and Lufkin find that "there is no reversal in fundamentals to match the reversal in returns. That is, as favored stocks go from outperforming the market, their fundamentals do not deteriorate significantly; in some case they actually improve. . . . The fundamentals of the 'worst' stocks are weaker than both those of the market and of the 'best' stocks in both periods."

In some cases, the trends of the worst stocks actually got worse. Even as the out-of-favor stocks improved in relative performance in the prior five years, their cash flow growth actually fell from 14.6 percent to 6.6 percent. While cash flow growth for the best-performing stocks did drop by 6 percent, it was still almost 2.5 times that of the lower group. Read the following observations of Dreman and Lufkin carefully:

Thus, while there is a marked transition in the return profiles [share price], with value stocks underperforming growth in the prior period and outperforming growth stocks in the measurement period, this is not true for fundamentals. In nearly every panel [areas in which measurements were made], fundamentals for growth stocks are better than those for value stocks *both before and after portfolio formation.*

Although there is a major reversal in the returns [prices] to the best and worst stocks, there is no corresponding reversal in the fundamentals.

In fact, in many cases the fundamentals continue to improve for the growth stocks and deteriorate for the value stocks. The data and the graphs clearly show the fundamentals for the growth stocks clearly beat those of the value stocks even for the five years after portfolio formation.

And yet, there is a very stark reversal in price. Why, if not based on the fundamentals?

Dremen and Lufkin go to another research paper,[5] which shows "that even a small earnings surprise can initiate a reversal in returns that lasts many years." They demonstrate that negative surprises on favorite stocks result in significant underperformance of this group not only in the year of the surprise but for at least four years following the initial event. They also show that positive surprises on out-of-favor stocks resulted in significant outperformance in the year of the surprise, and again for at least the four years following the initial event. They attribute these results to major changes in investor expectations following the surprise.

So where was the overreaction? Was it in the years leading up to the surprise that resulted in a very high- or low-priced stock (relative to the fundamentals), or was it in the immediate reaction to the surprise?

Other studies show that analysts (as opposed to investors) are too slow to react to earnings surprises by being too slow to adjust earnings forecasts. Even nine months later, analysts' expectations are too high.

Stock Prices Are in Our Heads, Or Maybe Investors Are Just Head Cases

Dreman and Lufkin then come to the meat of their analysis. For them, underreaction and overreaction are part and parcel of the same process. The overreaction begins in the years prior to the stock reaching lofty heights. The more comfortable we get with a given condition or trend, the longer it will persist, and then when the trend fails, the more dramatic the correction.

The cause of the price reversal is not fundamentals. It is not risk, as numerous studies show value stocks to be less risky.

"We conclude," write Dreman and Lufkin, "that the cause of the major price reversals is psychological, or more specifically, investor overreaction."

But they go on to point out that when the correction comes, we tend to underreact. While we do not like the surprise, we tend to think of it as maybe a one-time event. Things, we believe, will soon get back to normal. We do not scale back our expectations sufficiently for our growth stocks (or vice versa), so the stage is set for another surprise and more reaction. It apparently takes years for this to work itself out.

As Dreman and Lufkin note in their conclusion, "The [initial] corrections are sharp and, we suspect, violent. But they do not fully adjust prices to more realistic levels. After this period, we return to a gradual but persistent move to more realistic levels as the underreaction process continues through [the next five years]."

The studies clearly show it takes time for these overvalued portfolios to "come back to earth" or back to trend. Would this not, I muse, apply to overvalued markets as a whole? Might not this explain why bear market cycles take so long? Is it not just an earnings surprise for one stock that moves the whole market, but a series of events and recessions that slowly change the perception of the majority of investors?

Thus my contention that we are in just the beginning stages of the current secular bear market. These cycles take lots of time, anywhere from 8 to 17 years. We are just in year four, and at nosebleed valuation levels. The next surprise or disappointment will surely come from out of nowhere. That is why it is called a surprise. When it is followed by the next recession, stocks will drop one more leg on their path to the low valuations that are the hallmark of the bottom of secular bear markets.

Given the level of investor overconfidence in the marketplace, and given the length of the last secular bull market, it might take more than one recession and a few more years to find a true bottom to this cycle. It will come, of course.

The French/Fama Connection

In 1992, a study by two Nobel Prize-winning economists, Eugene Fama and Kenneth French, was published in the *Journal of Finance*.[6] The two professors studied the prices of all stocks on the New York Stock Exchange, the American Stock Exchange, and the NASDAQ from mid-1963 through 1990. They were looking for the difference in performance between those stocks that were the cheapest in terms of value and those that were the most expensive. The study shows that buying value stocks is an extremely effective way to invest, especially in difficult times.

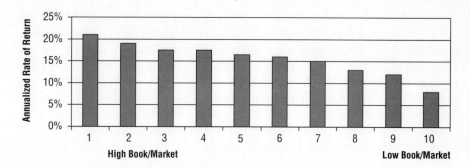

Figure 16.1   Book-to-Market as a Predictor of Return
Source: Robert A. Haugen, *The New Finance: The Case against Efficient Markets*, 2nd ed. (Upper Saddle River, NJ: Prentice Hall, 1999).

As Figure 16.1 illustrates, the 10 percent of stocks that were the cheapest more than doubled the performance of the stocks that were the most expensive. The returns over the period were 2.5 times as great.

Second, the study shows a direct and linear relationship between the price of a stock relative to its assets and the future price performance of the stock.

Even more interesting is Figure 16.2, which shows that the price volatility of the value stocks was far less than that of the most expensive. But that

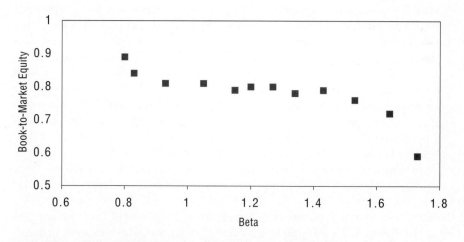

Figure 16.2   Book-to-Market Equity of Portfolios Ranked by Beta
Source: E. Fama and K. French, "The Cross-Section of Expected Stock Returns," *Journal of Finance* (June 1992), Table II.

doesn't mean they weren't volatile. In a few chapters, we will look at a famous warning from Warren Buffett, who recommended buying stocks over bonds in 1978, based on relative values between the stocks and bonds of the same companies. It was clearly a winning position, both logically and over time. But for the next few years, if you took his advice, Buffett writes in 2001, "Oh, how you suffered!" if you bought early. Patience was rewarded, but at the cost of lots of stomach acid.

Returning to the study, William Bernstein wrote in *Efficient Frontier* about the important French/Fama article:

Ten years ago this month, Eugene Fama and Kenneth French fired the shot heard 'round the world. Its echoes still plainly reverberate today in boardrooms and trading floors. And although most investors are unaware, these effects also appear regularly in their mailboxes under the guise of investment-account statements.

The projectile in question was a 39-page piece . . . published in the June 1992 edition of *Journal of Finance*. It was no walk in the park; even among the Journal's rarefied readership, I doubt many grasped the full meaning without multiple readings and hours of peer discussion.

Its import lay on three levels:

The month-to-month performance of a diversified portfolio of U.S. stocks can be explained by only three factors: the portfolio's exposure to the market itself, to small-cap stocks, and to value orientation (the latter defined by price-to-book ratio). In plain English, "Show me the returns series of any U.S. diversified portfolio and, in almost every case, I can explain nearly all its performance based on these three factors; the precise securities are irrelevant." And, "Oh, by the way, without knowing exactly what's in this portfolio, I can tell you the median market cap and price-to-book ratio just by looking at its returns."

. . . Most importantly, the size and value factors, because they were surrogates for risk, had positive returns. Therefore, value stocks should have higher returns than growth stocks, and small stocks, higher returns than large stocks; small value stocks should have the highest returns of all. The one place where the model "didn't work" was with small growth stocks, which empirically had much lower returns than expected, having the worst performance of the four "style corners" (large growth, large value, small value, and small growth).[7]

Bernstein then showed what would have happened had an investor read the French/Fama article and decided to put the concepts to work. For the next six years you would have done okay, but your brother-in-law in Janus 20 was beating the pants off you.

Annualized Returns, January 1993 to December 1999

Small value: 13.90%
Small growth: 16.92%
Large value: 15.72%
Large growth: 21.64%
Wilshire 5000: 20.47%

But what would have happened over the next three years? The bear market happened. I want you to particularly notice that even during this time small value increased, although there was quite a bit more volatility than in the bull market period. Every other style did not do well.

Annualized Returns, January 1993 to April 2002

Small value: 15.23%
Small growth: 8.20%
Large value: 10.43%
Large growth: 11.08%
Wilshire 5000: 11.69%

Value Is Where You Find It

Every value manager and investor has his own formula, but they all have their roots in the classic investing book *Security Analysis* written in 1934 by Benjamin Graham and David Dodd. The book is rather hard to read, so I would recommend Graham's more succinct work, *The Intelligent Investor*.

But for those unfamiliar with some of the terms, let me briefly give you an idea of what I mean when I say value. We will start with a statistic called "Graham's number." It is simply current assets minus all liabilities, including preferred stock. This tells you what the company is really worth at liquidation.

If the total market capitalization of a company (the number of shares times the price per share) is not larger than Graham's number, you have a situation where the company is worth more in breakup or liquidation than the market is willing to pay for the shares. Generally there is some reason, but the research shows that quite often it is simply because a stock is too boring for most investors.

Dan Ferris noted in the November 2002 issue of *Extreme Value*[8] that: "In 1988, a DePaul University professor named Joseph Vu wanted to find out how effective Graham's number was at finding profitable investments. In his research, Professor Vu assumed that a stock would be bought when its price dipped below Graham's number and sold two years later. The results Vu discovered could make you richer than Buffett himself. You'll recall that Buffett has compounded at a rate of 22 percent a year. Professor Vu's research results showed that *buying stocks that sold for less than Graham's number and holding them for two years produced average annual returns of just over 24 percent a year."*

We are going to look at other research in just a few pages that will update the persistence of the superior performance of value-oriented investing over growth stocks. The body of investment research literature is replete with such examples. As we will see, the research is seemingly so self-evident that we collectively scratch our heads and wonder, "Why?" It all but begs the question: "So why do bubbles get created?" Why do we see such large growth in certain periods (secular bull markets) and then the opposite in the periods (secular bear markets) that immediately follow them? Why do people keep investing in stocks that by reasonable historical standards are at worst overvalued or at best way ahead of themselves?

Part of the reason is that is what is sold to them, but that is not an entirely satisfactory answer. No one is forcing millions of investors throughout the world and throughout history to participate in madness. Thus part of the reason may be they do not know any better, but after all the evidence they have been shown and the material that has been written, it seems rather tough to blame ignorance on the poor results that investors achieve. Investors are willing participants in the game. Part of the reason is that stocks simply reflect the boom and bust cycles of the underlying economies, although stocks more often than not help create, or at least amplify, that very effect. But it seems to me there must be more than these surface reasons.

This pattern is persistent throughout the world and throughout history across many cultures. What is there about the human species that makes us do the things we do?

For now, we're going to examine the psychology of investing, why we might possibly make the mistakes we make, and what we can do about it. Then we will once again take up our search for Bull's Eye Investing. By then, we will have prepared ourselves mentally to do the often counterintuitive things that are necessary for successful investing.

Bringing Out Your Inner Spock

17

Insanity, my bride tells me again and again, is doing the same thing over and over and expecting different results.

Extraordinary Popular Delusions and the Madness of Crowds[1] is a popular book on the history of investment bubbles. Delusions and madness seem to repeat. Daniel Kahneman and Amos Tversky received the Nobel Prize in economics for showing us not just that investors are irrational, which is a readily observed fact, but that they are irrational in predictable ways. There is a branch of psychology that seeks to determine whether there is a biological or evolutionary reason for that predictable irrationality.

It is self-evident, at least to me, that many of our most basic social institutions are having difficulties in adapting to a modern and fast-changing world. As an example, the situations and pressures faced by my children are far different than those of my Revolutionary War era ancestors, and are even more remote from those of my forebears (probably peasant, at least on my father's side) who lived in medieval Europe.

Yet I can recognize responses in myself to the problems of my children that were "learned" from my dad, which he "learned" from his dad and so on. They were culturally ingrained—loosely speaking of my family behavior characteristics as cultural. It is why we all tend to notice family traits, not to mention attributing some traits to nationalities or regions.

Trying to raise twenty-first-century children using seventeenth-century models is futile, if not damaging. I know some will fondly recall the superiority of the old ways and days, but a little research shows that not all the family practices of the past were helpful. Do we really want our daughters marrying in their early teens (without their consent to men chosen by their families) or our sons to be basically limited to following in their fathers' occupations? How do we teach them the old values in a modern context? It is only as I consciously adapt those inherited family biases that I can even hope to raise my kids to cope with a world that will change even more for them and their kids.

I suggest it is no different with economics and investments. We have within us a set of survival instincts, values, and biases that were developed for living first in hunter-gather societies and then in small subsistence agrarian communities. As we will see, these do not necessarily translate well into the investment world. (I highly recommend the Pulitzer Prize winning book *Guns, Germs and Steel*[2] by Dr. Jared Diamond for those interested in learning how difficult and long the road to modern civilization has been.) In fact, these hardwired responses may in fact be responsible for most of the common mistakes we make as investors. In this chapter we look at them one by one, as we examine why we do the things we do.

This chapter is based on the rather substantial and very impressive research of James Montier, the Global Equity Strategist for Dresdner, Kleinwort Wasserstein Research based in London, England. He is the author of the well-reviewed and very readable book *Behavioural Finance: Insights into Irrational Minds and Markets*. He has produced a large body of work analyzing numerous books, studies, and research papers on the neurological and psychological reasons for our investment decision-making process. Rather than having me quote his works at length, he has graciously consented to let me use a few of his papers as the basis for this chapter. I have edited and added a few illustrations and examples, but the bulk of the material and conclusions is the fruit of years of his concentrated research.

James is an economist by training. [But don't hold that against me—James] He has worked in financial markets for the past 10 years, including time working in Japan and Hong Kong, a great stomping ground for bear market training. He also suffers delusions of being a partial academic, having spent a fair amount of time teaching behavioral finance at a U.K. university. It is somewhat intimidating to me personally to note that he is only 32 and has already published a significant amount of very high-quality work. [It may amuse readers to know that my colleagues recently threatened to send me out for carbon dating given the discrepancy between the age I claim and my appearance!—James]

(Before we start, let me note that we will be looking into a field called evolutionary psychology. For some readers, the concept of evolution is controversial. For the purposes of this discussion and the conclusions, it matters not if our psychological actions are the results of an evolutionary process or were hardwired by the Creator in the beginning. This is not a theological tome on the teleological nature of the universe. We are looking at not how the watch was made [or Who made it and when] but how the watch works. However we explain the process of how we are the way we are, the important thing to keep in mind is how our thinking contributes to our investment mistakes.)

Let's begin what I believe will be an important part of your investment journey to becoming a Bull's Eye investor. I think you will get more than a few "aha!" moments as you absorb these very important concepts from Montier. I certainly did.

A Litany of Mistakes

Our minds are far more suited for dealing with the basic decisions of survival than for choosing stocks and investments. Jumping to some of the conclusions, we will see that our emotions rule our minds for good reason: If you took time to analyze a situation you could soon be dead. Flight or freeze is a basic response to fear. We all know that when fear rules our minds, the investment decisions we make may not be the best. The problem is, however, that it is not simply a matter of repressing our emotions, for we will find that without our emotions we cannot make decisions. There is a process we all go through to make decisions that needs to be adapted to the investment world. We need to develop our "inner Spock" (the ultralogical character in *Star Trek*) so that we can keep our emotions in balance.

We are going to look at two fields of study to see if we can get some insight into how this all works.

Evolutionary psychologists ask us to understand that "our brains are shaped for fitness, not for truth," to borrow Steve Pinker's turn of phrase. That is to say, our minds are best suited to a past environment where the problems we faced concerned survival rather than the kinds of problems we face today.

Modern industrial society did not begin until about 300 years ago, and then only developed slowly for the first couple of hundred years across the face of the planet. Before that, it took millennia for an agrarian-based society to develop and become the dominant form of social structure.

Neuropsychology looks at the mind and tries to determine how the very structure of our brains (the left brain/right brain process as an example) influences our decisions.

The simple truth is that we make mistakes when we come to decisions. Psychologists have spent years documenting and cataloging the types of errors to which we are prone. The main results are surprisingly universal across cultures and countries.

David Hirschleifer[3] suggests that most of these mistakes can be traced to four common causes: self-deception, heuristic simplification, emotion, and social interaction. Montier suggests that these can be further simplified to just three basic conditions that promote a bias toward or the conditions for making a mistake.

Taxonomy is the practice of classifying plants and animals according to their presumed natural relationships. We are all familiar with the charts that break the world down into mammals, birds, reptiles, and such, with the various subgroups in each column. Montier does this for us for the biases that cause us to make our decisions and our mistakes. Remember the preceding chapter when we discussed the "home field bias"? Simply because a person touched a card it became more valuable to them. That logical error can be caused by several of these biases.

Figure 17.1, called "A Taxonomy of Biases," tries to classify the major biases along these three categories. The chart outlines the most common of the various biases that have been found, and also tries to highlight only those with direct implications for investment. Don't concentrate on the chart right now, but we will refer to it as we go along.

What a Tangled Web We Weave, When First We Practice to Deceive

It starts with self-deception. We feel we need to justify our actions and look for reasons to do so. The brain literally weaves a tissue of lies to justify its behavior. If we don't have the facts, we make them up. A classic example from research done by neuroscientist Michael Gazzaniga shows that we lie to ourselves.

Most functions from the sensory inputs to the brain are "cross-wired." By that we mean the right half of the brain processes the input from the left eye, and vice versa.

Split-brain patients are individuals who have had their cerebral hemispheres surgically disconnected, typically as a treatment for epilepsy (the corpus callosum is severed). Each half of the brain still functions, but there is no longer any communication between the two halves.

In a 1972 study Gazzaniga found that letting split-brain patients see instructions with their left eyes, which were then processed by their right hemispheres, had some rather bizarre results. The patients generally did as instructed on the cards, for example "walk" or "laugh."

However, when the patients were asked why they walked out of the room or started laughing, the left hemisphere, which is the area of the brain that would supply the answer, started to make up motives. Keep in mind that the information on the card was seen only by the right hemisphere. The left hemisphere could look into the right brain for the answer. The "thinking link" had been severed. For instance, when asked why he walked, one of the patients stated he wanted to get a Coke. When

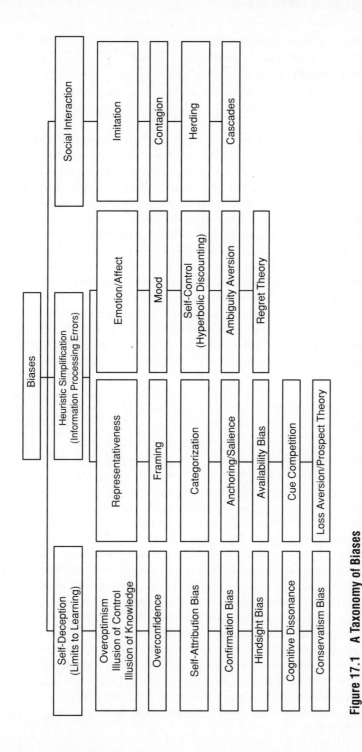

Figure 17.1   A Taxonomy of Biases
Source: David Hirschleifer, "Investor Psychology and Asset Pricing," *Journal of Finance* 56 (2001); Dresdner, Kleinwort Wasserstein Research.

asked why he was laughing, a patient replied, "You guys come here and test us every month. What a way to make a living!"

It should be noted that only the "thinking link" between the hemispheres of the brain was cut; the emotional link (stemming from the anterior commissure—a far older and deeper hidden part of brain) still functioned at a base level.

Nor is it just split-brain patients who make up excuses to justify/rationalize their behavior. In 1977 Nisbett and Wilson[4] laid out many pairs of stockings, and asked ladies to select which pair they liked the most. When the women were questioned as to the reasons for their selection, they volunteered all sorts of wonderful excuses about texture and sheerness. However, all the pairs of stockings were actually identical!

This happens from a very early age. Parents can recall any number of times when asking their children why they did something that they were met with the most unusual and creative of reasons. It certainly extends to our teenage years. Wives know that husbands have become the masters of such rationales. Note this is different from simply lying. The people in question actually believes that their stories and motives are true.

How on earth could self-deception actually prove to be an evolutionary winner? Two avenues can help explain our natural tendency toward self-deception. First, within communal living, the ability to spot cheaters will be a useful function.

Homo sapiens seems to have generally lived in small groups throughout mankind's history. Indeed, even our evolutionary ancestors such as Australopithecus seem to have lived in groups. The logic for group living is obvious within the evolutionary ancestral environment.

The most immediate benefit of communal living is the safety in numbers concept; indeed such behavior is visible with chimpanzees today. Secondly, humans were effectively hunter-gatherer societies. Food was shared out to smooth fluctuations in the food cycle. Freeloaders for protection or food sharing would be a burden on the group; hence the ability to spot cheaters becomes a useful skill.

To demonstrate our skills in cheater spotting Cosmides and Tooby[5] suggested looking at Wason selection tests (a type of testing system). They suggested two forms of the test. First, look at the four cards in Figure 17.2; each is labeled with a letter on one side and a number on the other. If I tell you that if a card has a vowel on one side it must also have an even number on the other side, which card(s) do you need to turn over to see if I am telling the truth?

Before I give the answer, consider the following. You have been employed at a nightclub as a bar manager. However, the club is keen not to allow underage drinking. Anyone under 18 years old must not drink alcohol. In the problem in Figure 17.3 each card is a customer: The cus-

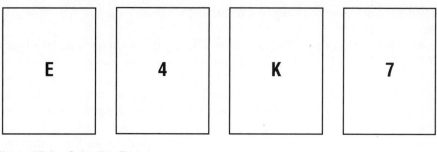

Figure 17.2   Selection Test

Figure 17.3   Selection Test

tomer's age is on one side, and what he/she is drinking is on the other side. Which card(s) do you need to turn over to check that there is no illegal underage drinking going on in the club?

In both cases, the correct answer is the first and last cards only. In the latter problem this should be obvious. You are looking at only those people drinking alcohol and those people under the legal age for drinking. In the first problem, these are the only two cards that can prove I was lying (if you thought E and 4 then you are suffering from confirmation bias, looking for information that agrees with you, another limit to learning!)

Cosmides and Tooby carried out numerous control tests to ensure that the framing of the cheater selection problem was at the heart of their finding, and each test confirmed that it was indeed. Effectively, the human race is a group of walking lie detector machines!

However, note the importance of framing. We find it incredibly hard to see through the way in which information is presented to us. The brain is effectively modular; if a problem is presented in a familiar fashion we can solve it, but in another guise we fall flat on our faces. Hence framing could become the most important bias of all (more on this further on in this chapter).

Now how does this all relate to self-deception? Well, Trivers[6] argues that in a world of walking lie detectors one of the easiest ways to fool them is to fool yourself. In order to avoid detection we effectively lie to ourselves. If we don't consciously know that we are lying then we are likely to be able to fool those who are seeking to assess such motivations.

We are all familiar with the problem of employees who think they are working hard, give the appearance of working hard, but in actuality are producing very little product. When confronted they sincerely believe they are working hard. Maybe more familiar (sadly) to parents are teenagers who really believe they are studying hard and cannot understand why their grades are so poor. It *must* be the teacher!

Of course, knowing the truth could be useful to us, but it is contained in a walled-off area of the brain, hidden from both the conscious part of the brain and other people.

A second evolutionary rationale for self-deception comes from the work of Taylor and Brown.[7] They take issue with psychologists' usual belief that somehow a "well-adjusted" person engages in accurate reality testing. The usual shorthand definition of mental health is a well-adjusted person who sees what is actually there. Taylor and Brown go on to argue that "positive illusions—namely unrealistically positive self-evaluations, exaggerated perceptions of control or mastery, and unrealistic optimism" are actually positive for mental health and well-being.

In another paper, Freedman[8] finds that most people report being happy most of the time. Around 70 to 80 percent of respondents report themselves as moderately to very happy. Whereas most believe that others are only average in happiness, fully 60 percent of people believe they are happier than most people! Freedman goes on to link high self-esteem and high ratings of control as correlates of happiness.

Taylor and various authors[9] have found that certain groups (such as cancer patients and AIDS sufferers) may benefit from positive illusions. The belief that one is healthier or coping better than other similarly afflicted patients is associated with reduced distress.

In general, Taylor finds that a mild degree of self-deception as it applies to self-evaluation and similar processes fits far better with psychologists' working definition of mental health. Indeed, those who are classified as mildly depressed by psychologists seem to lack the positive illusions that dominate the rest of us. Taylor and Brown point out that these individuals tend to recall both the positive and negative self-relevant information with equal ease, show greater evenhandedness in their attributions of performance, and display a high degree of congruence between self-evaluations and external evaluations. They conclude, "In short, it appears to be not the well-adjusted individual but the individual who experiences subjective distress who is more likely to process self-relevant information in a relatively unbiased and balanced fashion."

Since happy, well-adjusted people will more likely have families, and since mental health is an important fitness trait, self-deception once again helps an individual to be a Darwinian winner.

We now examine 11 guidelines for overcoming common investor mistakes that stem from these forces. We first examine the problems and their solutions that come from self-deception.

- **You know less than you think you do.**

Economists frequently assume that people will learn from their past mistakes. Psychologists find that learning itself is a tricky process. Many of the self-deception biases tend to limit our ability to learn. For instance, we are prone to attribute good outcomes to our skill, and bad outcomes to the luck of the draw. This is *self-attribution bias*. When we suffer such a bias, we are not going to learn from our mistakes, simply because we don't see them as our mistakes. Furthermore, we make up reasons to deceive ourselves.

The two most common biases are *overoptimism* and *overconfidence*. For instance, when teachers ask a class who will finish in the top half, on average around 80 percent of the class think they will!

Not only are people overly optimistic, but they are overconfident as well. People are surprised more often than they expect to be. For instance, when you ask people to make a forecast of an event or a situation, and to establish at what point they are 98 percent confident about their predictions, we find that the correctness of their predictions ranges between 60 and 70 percent! What happens when we are only 75 percent sure or are playing that 50–50 hunch?

Overoptimism and overconfidence tend to stem from the *illusion of control* and the *illusion of knowledge*. The illusion of knowledge is the tendency for people to believe that the accuracy of their forecasts increases with more information. So dangerous is this misconception that historian Daniel Boorstin opined, "The greatest obstacle to discovery is not ignorance—it is the illusion of knowledge." The simple truth is that more information is not necessarily better information. It is what you do with it, rather than how much you have, that matters.

This leads to the first guideline: *You know less than you think you do.*

The illusion of control refers to people's belief that they have influence over the outcome of uncontrollable events. For instance, people will pay more for a lottery ticket that contains numbers they choose than for a random draw of numbers. People are more likely to accept a bet on the toss of a coin before it has been tossed than after it has been tossed and the outcome hidden, as if they could influence the spin of the coin in the air! Information once again plays a role. The more information you have, the more in control you tend to feel.

Overoptimism and overconfidence are a potent combination. They lead you to overestimate your knowledge, understate the risk, and exaggerate your ability to control the situation. This leads to bold forecasts (overoptimism and overconfidence) and timid choices (understated risk). In order to redress these biases:

- **Be less certain in your views; aim for timid forecasts and bold choice.**

People also tend to cling tenaciously to a view or a forecast. Once a position has been stated most people find it very hard to move away from that view. When movement does occur it does so only very slowly. Psychologists call this *conservatism bias* (it can lead to anchoring, which will be discussed a little later).

Figure 17.4 shows conservatism in analysts' forecasts. We have taken a linear time trend out of both the operating earnings numbers and the analysts' forecasts. A cursory glance at the chart reveals that analysts are exceptionally good at telling you what has just happened. They have invested too heavily in their view, and hence will change it only when presented with indisputable evidence of its falsehood.

[*Note:* This confirms and somewhat explains the earlier studies in this book that show the rather sad track record of analysts—John]

Investors should note that these analysts are professionals. We tend to think of them as accountants sitting around looking at tables, numbers,

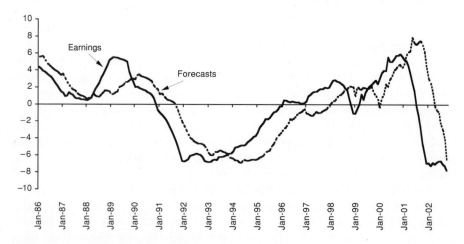

Figure 17.4   Analysts Lag Reality
Source: Dresdner, Kleinwort Wasserstein Research.

and mind-numbing mounds of data and coming to a rationally based conclusion. The real view is that they are all too human and their humanity shows up all too readily in their forecasts.

This leads to our third rule:

• **Don't get hung up on one technique, tool, approach, or view. Flexibility and pragmatism are the order of the day.**

We are inclined to look for information that agrees with us. This thirst for agreement rather than refutation is known as *confirmatory bias*. The classic example is to consider the four-card test mentioned earlier. If you will remember, each card carries one alphanumeric symbol; the set comprises E, 4, K, 7. If someone tells you that if a card has a vowel on one side, then it should have an even number on the other, which card(s) do you need to turn over to see if he is telling the truth?

You now know the answer, but most people go for E and 4. [Confession: I chose E and 4.—John.] The correct answer is E and 7. Only these two cards are capable of proving the person is lying. If you turn the E over and find an odd number, then the person lied, and if you turn the 7 over and find a vowel then you know the person was lying. By turning the 4 over you can prove nothing. If it has a vowel then you have found information that agrees with my statement but doesn't prove it. If you turn the four over and find a consonant, you have proved nothing. At the outset the person stated a vowel must have an even number, not that an even number must have a vowel! How the problem is "framed" affects our answers.

By picking 4, people are deliberately looking for information that agrees with them. Our natural tendency is to listen to people who agree with us. It feels good to hear our own opinions reflected back to us. We get those warm fuzzy feelings of content.

This is all tied up in our human quest for certainty. It is notable that we tend to associate with those who think like we do and confirm the rightness and wisdom of our judgment and views, whether on investments, politics, or religion. This only reinforces the tendency to set in concrete wrong views and notions.

Sadly, this isn't the best way to make optimal decisions. Instead of listening to the people who echo our own view we should:

• **Listen to those who don't agree with us.**

The bulls should listen to the bears, and vice versa. You should pursue such a strategy not so that you change your mind, but rather so you are aware of the opposite position.

Our final bias under those related to self-deception is *hindsight bias*. It is all too easy to look back at the past and think that it was simple, comprehensible, and predictable. This is hindsight bias—a tendency for people knowing the outcome to believe that they would have predicted the outcome ex ante or beforehand. The best example I can think of is the U.S. stock market over the past few years. Now pretty much everyone agrees that the U.S. market witnessed a bubble, but calling it a bubble in 1998, 1999, or 2000 was an awful lot harder than it is now! This faith in our ability to "forecast" the past gives rise to yet more bias toward overconfidence. This leads to our fifth rule:

 • **You didn't know it all along; you just thought you did.**

Before we depart this section on self-deception, let's look at one way in which confidence is actually necessary for investment success. Albert Wang[10] in his article "Overconfidence, Investor Sentiment, and Evolution" in the 2001 Academy of Sciences' *Journal of Financial Intermediation* also finds that modest self-deception may be an evolutionary stable strategy. Wang uses evolutionary game theory to study the population dynamics of a securities market. In his model, the growth rate of wealth accumulation drives the evolutionary process, and is endogenously determined (meaning that only the data and not some outside factors influences the determination of winners and losers). He finds that neither underconfident investors nor bearish sentiment can survive in the market. Massively overconfident or bullish investors are also incapable of long-run survival. However, investors who are only moderately overconfident can actually come to dominate the market!

In the world of our ancestors, overconfidence will get you killed. Lack of confidence will mean you sit around and starve. Cautious optimism is the right approach.

What Wang is showing is that the same is true in the new world of investments. It should be self-evident that it is necessary to play if you are going to win. Further, a willingness to accept some level of volatility and risk is characteristic of successful investors. But taking too much risk will soon get you sent to the sidelines.

The Problem with Assumptions

It is now time to move from the problems caused by self-deception to those under the category of heuristic simplification. Heuristics are a fancy way of saying rules of thumb for dealing with massive amounts of information. In many settings heuristics provide sensible shortcuts to the "correct" answer, but occasionally they can lead us to some very strange decisions.

For instance, a rule of thumb for measuring wood says that a 2 × 4 piece of lumber (at least in the United States) is 2 inches by 4 inches on each side. If you had 10 of them stacked on top of each other, a simple heuristic or rule of thumb would say you have 20 inches of board. But the actual width of the board is 1.875 inches, so the exact measurement is 18.75 inches. This is not a problem if you are only trying to figure out how many boards you can get into the back of your pickup. However, if you are trying to load 30 railroad cars with boards, it could cause a significant error in your freight bill.

This second group of biases effectively represents information processing errors. They cover biases that result from the admission that we aren't supercomputers capable of infinite dynamic optimization.

When faced with uncertainty, people will grasp at almost anything when forming opinions. In the classic 1974 experiment Tversky and Kahneman[11] asked people to answer general knowledge questions, such as, what percentage of the UN is made up of African nations? A wheel of fortune with the numbers 1 to 100 was spun in front of the participants before they answered. Being psychologists, Tversky and Kahneman had rigged the wheel so it gave either 10 or 65 as the result of a spin. The subjects were then asked if the answer was higher or lower than the number on the wheel, and also asked their actual answer. The median response from the group that saw the wheel present 10 was 25, and the median response from the group that saw 65 was 45! Effectively, people were grabbing at irrelevant anchors when forming their opinions. This is known as *anchoring*.

Think about this in the context of valuation. In the absence of any reliable information, past prices are likely to act as anchors to current prices. Does it not strike you as strange that the average analysts' price target is 28 percent above current market price?

Too many discounted cash flows (DCFs) are anchored around current market prices. Montier cites personal stories where some analysts deliberately seek to arrive at a DCF target that is close to market price, apparently in an effort to justify their analysis and the price on which they are fixated.

The best way of beating this problem when it comes to stock valuation is to use reverse-engineered DCFs. That means backing out what is implied by the current market price, and then seeing if it matches your view. For instance, for the U.S. market the current dividend yield is around 1.5 percent, assuming that investors want a 3.5 percent equity risk premium and given a nominal bond yield of 4.4 percent, we can see that the current pricing of equities is consistent only if dividends can grow 6.4 percent per year forever! However, if you change your assumption of the risk premium, you can make the number say anything you want. Sadly, the empirical evidence suggests that such growth is highly unlikely, but some analysts simply ignore the evidence because it does not fit with their biases.

The other element to beware of is relative valuation. All relative valuation measures should be ignored. It is simply far too easy for an analyst to fixate (anchor) on her sector average as the "correct" value. For instance, in the past Montier has been asked by analysts to construct tables of valuations on criteria such as P/E and price-to-book ratios across industries, so that the analyst can compare the stock under investigation with its peer group. This tells us nothing about the true "fair value" of the equity.

The tendency to anchor provides our sixth rule:

• **Forget relative valuation and forget market prices. Work out what a stock is worth (use reverse-engineered DCFs).**

When information is presented to us, we aren't very good at seeing through how it is presented. We tend to take things at face value rather than drilling down to get to the detail. As an analogy consider the lines in Figure 17.5. Which is longer?

Most people will go for the lower line. However, as Figure 17.6 makes clear, both lines are exactly the same length. We fail to see through the way in which the lines are presented. Yet when we make the frame transparent (i.e., we add the vertical lines) it becomes immediately clear that both lines are exactly the same length. This inability to see through the way in which things are presented is called *narrow framing*.

Think of the Ibbotson studies mentioned earlier in the book. It is not that the data is wrong. It is scrupulously accurate. The problem is that it is used to suggest that the immediate decades following today will look like the past—that if investors will simply be confident in the data and stay the course, they will be rewarded. The data is not "framed" by the other numerous studies presented that show that valuation, the direction of interest rates and inflation, international currency flows, and a host of other factors may perhaps influence the market in a less than satisfactory manner.

Let's think about another example from finance. One of the easy illustrations is stock buybacks. Given that we have promoted the importance of dividends in contributing to total returns, a common retort is that surely we have missed the point that buybacks have replaced dividends as a cash distribution mechanism among investors.

When most investors talk of buybacks they are referring to announced buybacks. However, that is of no interest to us. After all, there is nothing to prevent a company from announcing a buyback but not carrying it

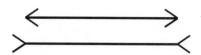

Figure 17.5

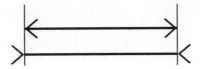

Figure 17.6

through. Hence the very least we should examine is completed buybacks. But even that is not enough. Too many buybacks are related to attempts to offset issuance (via option plans) and prevent dilution. These buybacks don't matter to me as an investor. I should really care only about net buybacks. Figure 17.7 shows the enormous gulf that appears when one starts to look at net rather than announced buybacks.

When is a buyback not a buyback?

This kind of narrow framing generates our seventh rule:

 • **Don't take information at face value; think carefully about how it was presented to you.**

Let us turn our attention to Linda. Linda is 31, single, outspoken, and very bright. She majored in philosophy at college, and as a student was deeply concerned with issues surrounding equality and discrimination. Is it more likely that Linda works in a bank, or is it more likely that Linda works in a bank and is active in the feminist movement?

Strangely, many people go for the latter option. But this can't possibly be more likely. The second option is a subset of the first option, and a subset can never be larger than one of the contributing sets!

So what is happening? Well, people judge events by how they appear,

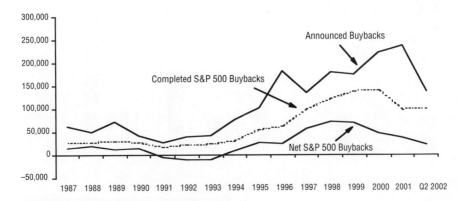

Figure 17.7   Net versus Announced Buybacks
Source: Dresdner, Kleinwort Wasserstein Research.

rather than by how likely they are. This is called *representativeness.* In the example of Linda, people who pick the option that Linda works in a bank and is active in the feminist movement are underweighting the base rate that there are simply more people who work in banks than people who work in banks and are active in the feminist movement!

Representativeness has many applications in investment. For example, do investors think that good companies make good investments? If so, this is a potential case of representativeness. A further example of representativeness is outlined in the Figure 17.8. It shows portfolios based around long-term earnings growth forecasts for consensus analysts. Stock portfolios are broken into five groups of quintiles (thus Q1, Q2, etc.) based on actual earnings growth for five years. The first bar in each group (or quintile) shows the per annum growth rate in the five years immediately prior to expectation formation. The second bar shows what the analysts projected for the next five years. The next three bars show the actual growth in earnings per year in the one, three, and five years following the forecasts.

The results show that analysts suffer representativeness twice over. First, companies that have seen high growth in the previous five years are forecast to continue to see very high earnings growth in the next five years.

Second, analysts fail to understand that earnings growth is a highly mean-reverting process over a five-year time period. The actual (base) rate for mean reversion is very high. The low-growth portfolio generates nearly

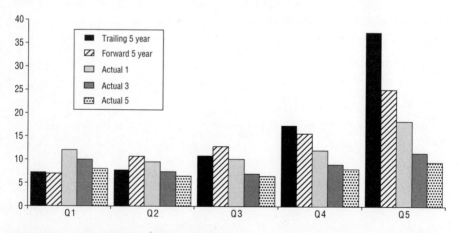

Figure 17.8   Earnings Growth Isn't Persistent
Source: Based on work by Chan et al. (2002), "The Level and Persistence of Growth Rates," *Journal of Finance*, Vol. 58, Issue 2 (April 2003), p. 643, and Montier's and Dresdner, Kleinwort Wasserstein Research's work.

as much long-term earnings growth as the high-growth portfolio. Effectively, analysts judge companies by how they appear, rather than how likely they are to sustain their competitive edge with a growing earnings base.

These mistakes lead us to our eighth rule:

• **Don't confuse good firms with good investments, or good earnings growth with good returns.**

Our minds are not supercomputers, and are not even very good filing cabinets. They bear more resemblance to Post-it Notes that have been thrown into a wastebasket, and covered in coffee, which we then try to unfold and read the blurred ink! In particular, the ease with which we can recall information is likely to be influenced by the impact that information made when it went in. For instance, which is a more likely cause of death in the United States, a shark attack or a lightning strike?

Most people go for shark attacks. Largely this is a result of publicity that shark attacks gain in the media and the fact that we can all remember the film *Jaws*. In actual fact, the chances of dying as a result of a lightning strike are 30 times greater than the chances of dying from a shark attack. (Curious unrelated fact: Orlando, Florida, is the place with the most lightning incidents in the world.)

A less drastic example comes from Kahneman and Tversky.[12] They asked people the following: "In a typical sample of text in the English language, is it more likely that a word starts with the letter k or that k is its third letter?" Of the 152 people in the sample, 105 generally thought that words with the letter k in the first position were more probable. In reality there are approximately twice as many words with k as the third letter as there are words that begin with k. Yet because we index on the first letter, we can recall them more easily.

Think about this in the context of stock selection. How do you decide which stocks you are going to look at when you arrive at work in the morning? Is it because you read about them in the *Wall Street Journal* or *Financial Times*? Or, heaven forbid, that some broker sent you an e-mail mentioning the stock, or some analyst wrote a research report on it? It is worth noting that S. Gadarowski[13] investigated in 2001 the relationship between stock returns and press coverage. He found that stocks with the highest press coverage underperformed in the subsequent two years! Be warned all that glitters is not gold.

• **Vivid, easy-to-recall events are less likely than you think they are; subtle causes are underestimated.**

Our penultimate bias beater is best explained by offering you the following bet on the toss of a fair coin. If you lose you must pay £100 [We will leave it in pounds in honor of Montier's home country, noting that the pound is worth considerably more than the dollar.—John]. What is the minimum amount that you need to have a chance of winning in order to make this bet attractive?

There are, of course, no right or wrong answers. It is purely a matter of personal preference. The most common answer is somewhere between £200 and £250. That is to say, people feel losses around two to two and a half times more than they feel gains. Figure 17.9 shows the outcomes when Montier asked this question of a set of colleagues at a previous employer (still an investment bank).

The mean answer is around the £200 mark. However, a considerable number of individuals required massive compensation in order to accept the bet—perhaps they just didn't trust a strategist!

[It is noteworthy that some players would have accepted the bet for a chance to win *less than* the £100 they were risking. It is giving nothing away when I tell you that a tech analyst was willing to accept £50. This told me everything I needed to know about tech analysts' ability to value companies!—James]

There is a serious point to all of this. People hate losses (*loss aversion*) and find them very uncomfortable to deal with in psychological terms. Because losses are so hard to face, we tend to avoid them whenever possible. For instance, a loss isn't perceived as a loss on some level so long as it is not realized. Losses will therefore be realized infrequently, in the hope that they will become winners (overoptimism again!).

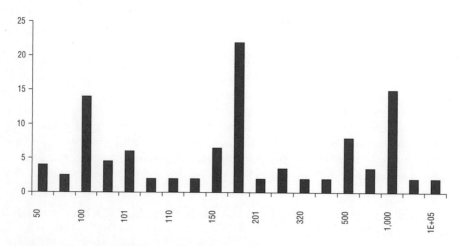

Figure 17.9   Loss Aversion among Stockbrokers
Source: James Montier, *Behavioral Finance: Insights into Irrational Minds and Markets,* Hoboken: John Wiley & Sons, 2002.

This tendency to ride losers and sell winners is known as the *disposition effect*. Even if we are right (and most of the time we aren't) that our losers will become winners, there will be better opportunities to put the trade on lower down, rather than riding the position all the way down. This generates our tenth bias beater:

• **Sell your losers and ride your winners.**

[And now we come to my favorite part of Montier's work, and the one bias to which I am most personally susceptible.—John]

Addicted to Growth

Why is it that investors are repeatedly drawn to growth investment styles when the research and our experience so clearly show that value investing is the long-term winner and even the less risky investment? It doesn't matter whether it is the latest technology innovation, the fascination with the power of all things Chinese, the belief that Internet stocks can grow at incredible rates forever, or the belief that "this time it is really different," investors seem drawn to growth stories like sailors to the sirens.

There is reason to suspect the answer lies in the very way in which our minds are structured. One of the most exciting developments in cognitive psychology over recent years has been the development of dual-process theories of thought. That is the academic way of saying that we tend to have two ways of thinking embedded in our minds. There may be in fact a real reason that you feel schizophrenic on some days.

Psychologists posit two different systems called Experiential and Rational. Experiential is essentially the emotional part of the brain. It is automatic and effortless in the way that it processes information. That is to say, the Experiential prescreens information before we are consciously aware that it even made an impact on our minds. Hence, the Experiential is effectively the default option.

Experiential deals with information in an associative way. Its judgments tend to be based on similarity (of appearance) and closeness in time. Because of the way the Experiential deals with information, it can handle vast amounts of data simultaneously. To computer nerds it is a rapid parallel processing unit. In order for the Experiential to believe something is valid it may simply need to wish that it were so.

Rational is the "Vulcan" part of the brain. For non–science fiction fans, this refers to the character Spock on the early *Star Trek*, who was from the planet Vulcan, where emotion had been banished and all decisions were made based on logic. To use Rational requires deliberate effort. It is logical and deductive in the way in which it handles information. Because it is logical, it can follow only one step at a time, and hence in computing terms it is a slow serial processing unit. In order to convince the Rational that something is true, logical argument and empirical evidence will be required. Table 17.1 provides a summary of the main differences between the two systems.

Do not misunderstand: One system is not better than the other. In fact, neuropsychologists have found that if the emotional decision-making areas of the brain are extremely damaged then decision making becomes impossible. Effectively, the unfortunate individuals afflicted by this problem make endless plans but seem to be incapable of choosing which they wish to follow.

Tasks may also migrate between the systems. We have all had the experience of driving to and from work. When the route is new to us, we need to concentrate. However, after driving exactly the same roads for a year, we find that the task largely appears to have transferred from being a Rational function to being an Experiential function. How many times have we arrived home not realizing how we got there? Or even more to the point, how many times do you find yourself on the way to a meeting and deep in thought and catch yourself actually making the turns to take you to home? When the Rational is busy, the Experiential can take over.

Just in case you think this is all just a pleasant psychological theory, neuropsychologists have started to work out the neural correlates of the

Table 17.1   Two Systems of Reasoning

Experiential	*Rational*
Holistic	Analytic
Affective (what feels good)	Logical
Associative—judgments based on similarity and temporal contiguity	Deductive
Rapid parallel processing	Slow serial processing
Concrete images	Abstract images
Slower to change	Changes with speed of thought
Crudely differentiated—broad generalization	More highly differentiated
Crudely integrated—context-specific processing	More highly integrated— cross context processing
Experienced passively and preconsciously	Experienced actively and consciously
Automatic and effortless	Controlled and effortful
Self-evidently valid: "Experiencing is believing" or perhaps wishing is believing	Justification required via logic and evidence

Source: Modified from S. Epstein (1991), "Cognitive-Experiential Self-Theory: Implications for Developmental Psychology." In M. Gunnar and L. A. Sroufe (Eds.), *Self-Processes and Development*, Minnesota Symposia on Child Psychology, Vol. 23 (Hillsdale, NJ: Erlbaum), pp. 79–123.

Table 17.2 Neural Correlates of Two Reasoning Systems

X-System	C-System
Amygdala	Anterior cingulated cortex
Basal ganglia	Prefrontal cortex
Lateral temporal cortex	Medial temporal lobe

Source: Dresdner, Kleinwort Wasserstein Macro Research.

two systems. (See Table 17.2.) Decisions that are made using X-system seem to use very different parts of the brain from those that are active when C-system decisions are being made. (Researchers use all sorts of brain imaging systems to determine this.)

By now you might just be wondering, not without reason, what on earth any of this has to do with investment. The answer lies in the fact that the X-system has a strong influence over many of the decisions we make, including those relating to investment.

Gary Klein[14] has identified some of the conditions under which we are likely to see decisions be made by the X-system.* The X-system is more likely to dominate when:

- The problem is ill structured and complex.
- Information is incomplete, ambiguous, and changing.
- Goals are ill defined, shifting, or competing.
- Stress is high because of time constraints and/or because high stakes are involved.
- Decisions involve multiple participants.

We would assert that pretty much every decision of any consequence that we make falls into one or more of those categories. It certainly characterizes many of the decisions that we make when faced with an investment proposition.

However, we are not powerless in the face of X-system influence. We can force the C-system into action. And this brings us to our eleventh guideline:

• Focus on the facts, not stories.

We all love a good story. In fact, we are hardwired to focus on stories. However, good stories aren't the best foundation for investment. The best

---

*Klein actually refers to something he calls naturalistic decision making (NDM). I believe that NDM and the X-system are highly related, if not in fact identical concepts.—James

company in the world won't be a good investment if everything is already in the price.

Think about the CEOs of companies. Do we not admire the ones who can tell good stories about their companies? How many times have we invested in a company or fund solely on the basis of the story we were given by the broker or manager? [How many knives or pots and pans have we bought on the Home Shopping Network because of those incredible stories?—John]

As human beings, we learned to communicate by stories even long before the written word. The love of a story is deeply embedded in our brains. Our greatest religious leaders of yore and the current preachers of today use parables and stories to communicate their teachings and principles.

In order to beat the love of the story bias we need to focus on the facts rather than the stories. This is the easiest way of forcing the Rational to handle the problem.

But the Experiential doesn't handle facts. By their nature, facts are *generally* characterized by low valence (emotion/affect) and thus the Experiential doesn't react. Instead the Rational is called up to logically assess the situation.

This can be related to the simple valuation equation. The return (R) you get from an equity investment is the sum of the dividend yield (Dy), dividend growth (G), and any change in valuation of the dividends that occurs over the holding period, or:

$$R = Dy + G + \Delta P/D$$

The Greek letter delta (Δ) is a way of noting change and is used in finance more and more. By $\Delta P/D$ we mean that change in the price-to-dividend ratio. In earlier chapters, we have shown that much of both the long-term and the recent rise in stocks is because of the rise in the price people are willing to put on a dollar of earnings or dividends, and not on the underlying growth of the earnings or dividends themselves. A positive delta means that valuations are rising and a negative delta means they are falling.

Of course, betting on $\Delta P/D$ is pure speculation and hardly advisable in the long run. By that, we mean that to bet on a rising or falling $\Delta P/D$, you are making assumptions (or more probably wild guesses) about how your fellow investors will act in the future.

So long-run returns expectations should really be based on Dy + G— the dividend yield plus growth in the dividend. This allows us to focus on where we are likely to see investors' biases show up. For instance, when we are talking about value stocks we are generally referring to those with high dividend yields. So dividend yield will form a very large chunk of our total return. For instance, since 1977 some 43 percent of the total return to the S&P/Barra value universe has come from dividend yield.

Conversely, within the growth universe the dividend yield should be much less important. In fact, it accounts for 30 percent of the total return achieved, whereas dividend growth has contributed 44 percent in the growth universe, and 30 percent in the value universe. Interestingly, the change in valuation is roughly equal between the two style universes.

Thus the issue with growth stocks comes from speculation over their future growth, since they are already expensive. Look at Figure 17.10. The near equality of return over the time period may well be a function of the way in which the indexes are constructed.

So for value stocks we would expect to see biases relating to errors over the sustainability of the dividend *level*, whereas within the growth universe we would expect to see investors getting carried away with the dividend *growth* story. The empirical evidence would tend to support these conclusions and uphold the usefulness of quantitative screens in the investment process. By that we mean we let a set of facts determine our investment process rather than the story. We screen out all stocks that do not fit into our fact-based system.

For instance, Joseph Piotroski[15] shows that the value premium (the amount that value outperforms growth) is generated by a minority of cheap stocks. That is to say Piotroski finds that less than 44 percent of all companies with low price-to-book valuations earn positive excess returns in the two years following the formation of sample portfolios. He goes on

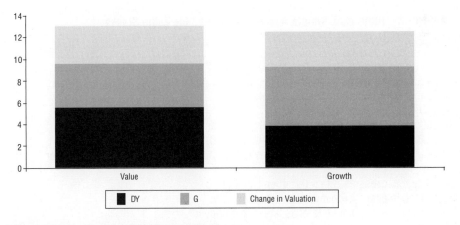

Figure 17.10   Value versus Growth Stocks
Return attribution: U.S. S&P/Barra Style Indexes (since 1977, % per annum)
Source: Dresdner, Kleinwort Wasserstein Macro Research.

to ask if he can identify the minority of value stocks that generate this out-performance using a simple accounting-based screen. The idea of the screen is simply to pick stocks that are cheap but aren't going bust. So he applies the screen outlined in Table 17.3 to the bottom 10 percent of the U.S. market by price-to-book valuation. For each of these categories he assigns a value of either one or zero points.

The results of this simple screen are incredibly impressive. A long/short (zero net investment) strategy buying those firms that have a score of 5 or more and shorting those with scores less than 5 generated an annual average return of nearly 10 percent, and saw only three years of negative returns over Piotroski's sample (U.S. market, 1976–1996). The long side of the portfolio generated an average return of 10.6 percent per year whereas the short side delivered an average return of 0.9 percent per year. (That is, even the short side rose, resulting in a loss to the investor. We should note that this was during a roaring bull market. We might suspect overall results to be similar during a bear market, but the two components to have significantly different results. The short portfolio should outperform the long portfolio in such circumstances.)

Recently, Partha Mohanram[16] has explored the use of a similar screen on growth stocks. (See Table 17.4.) Mohanram selects the top 20 percent by price-to-book ratio as his base universe, and asks if a simple accounting screen can help differentiate good and bad growth stocks. Because of the different nature of growth Mohanram chose to focus on variables that should indicate a true growth stock rather than a glamour stock.

Table 17.3   Piotroski's Simple Accounting Screen for Value Stocks

Criteria

1. Return on assets (ROA) > 0 (either 1 point or 0)
2. Cash flow from operations (CFO) > 0 (either 1 point or 0)
3. Change in ROA > 0 (either 1 point or 0)
4. CFO > ROA (either 1 point or 0)
5. Change in long-term debt < 0 (either 1 point or 0)
6. Change in current ratio > 0 (either 1 point or 0)
7. Equity offering if the firm didn't issue equity in the preceding 12 months (either 1 point or 0)
8. Change in gross margin > 0 (either 1 point or 0)
9. Change in asset turnover > 0 (either 1 point or 0)
All variables are scales by total assets where relevant.

Source: Dresdner, Kleinwort Wasserstein based on the work by Joseph Piotroski, "Value Investing: The Use of Historical Financial Statement Information to Separate Winners from Losers," *Journal of Accounting Research* 38 (2002).

Table 17.4 Mohanram's Growth Stock Criteria

Criteria

1. Variance of return on assets over 5 years < Industry median (either 1 point if true or 0 if not true)
2. Variance of sales growth over 5 years < Industry median (either 1 point if true or 0 if not true)
3. Growth in earnings > Growth in revenues (either 1 point or 0)
4. Firm's R&D > Industry median (either 1 point or 0)
5. Firm's capex > Industry median (either 1 point or 0)
6. Firm's advertising spending > Industry median (either 1 point or 0)

All variables are scales by total assets where appropriate.

Source: Dresdner, Kleinwort Wasserstein Macro Research.

Once again the results were very impressive. Mohanram formed long portfolios with scores of 4, 5, or 6, and short portfolios of firms scoring 0. This zero net investment portfolio generated an annual average return of 18.1 percent! However, an interesting finding is uncovered when the long and short portfolios are examined. The long side generated an average return of only 1.9 percent per year. However, the short side generated an average return of 16.2 percent per year. This means that being short these stocks in the portfolio made far more than did being long. This was over a sample period 1976–1996, which encompasses the bulk of the bull run in the 1980s and 1990s. This confirms something Montier has written about in his book *Behavioural Finance.*[17] *The key skill in growth investing is avoiding the losers rather than picking the winners!*

Regardless of your style predilection, the chances are that a quantitative approach would be a useful check on your thought process. By creating screens and rigid criteria for investments, you will hopefully avoid the major mistakes. However, growth investors need to take special heed because the psychological evidence suggests that they will be particularly prone to the Experiential running amok, buying into stories that will eventually fall far short of expectations.

And thus we come full circle. You can bring out your "inner Spock" by thinking and acting on the 11 guidelines in this chapter, letting the facts be your guide to your investments.

Final thoughts from Montier:

This isn't a comprehensive survey of biases and their impact. We haven't addressed any of the emotional aspects of investment or indeed any of the social aspects (such as herding). However, the rules we have set out should help guide us to better decisions. All too often when we present on behavioral finance, institutional investors think that it applies to private clients and not to them. This is surely a prime example of the illusion of knowledge creating overconfidence. At the end of the day, each and every fund manager is an individual, too. They, too, will be subject to the biases outlined here.

Being aware of the mistakes we make is the first step. To really avoid them takes a great deal of practice. After all, how many of us can remember how to perform long division by hand? Without regular use skills recede in our minds, and we will continue to fall into the regular pitfalls outlined earlier. Perhaps the best defense of all is to design an investment process that deliberately seeks to incorporate best mental practice!

Despite having spent the best part of 10 years learning, studying, and teaching all these biases, I can assure you that it doesn't make them any easier to beat. I still find myself falling into the same mental traps that we've outlined here. When other psychologists give me tests, my knee-jerk reaction is still wrong, only now I've learned to take a deep breath and look for the deliberate flaw in my thinking. However, at least these days I know the proper names to give the mistakes I make!

The Value in Stocks

The experiences undergone by one generation are useless, as a rule, for the generation that follows, which is the reason why historical facts, cited with a view to demonstration, serve no purpose. Their only utility is to prove to what extent experiences need to be repeated from age to age to exert any influence, or to be successful in merely shaking an erroneous opinion when it is solidly implanted in the mind of the masses.

—Gustave Le Bon, *The Crowd—A Study of the Popular Mind* (1895)

As the politician Boss Jim Gettys warned Charles Foster (Citizen) Kane, "Anybody else, I'd say what's gonna happen to you would be a lesson to you. Only you're gonna need more than one lesson. And you're gonna get more than one lesson."

Last chapter we noted that all-important formula for investors, which should rank right up there with $E = MC^2$.

$$R = Dy + G + \Delta P/D$$

The return you get from an equity investment is the sum of the dividend yield (Dy), dividend growth (G), and any change in valuation of the dividends that occurs over the holding period.

The equation implies that there are two reasons to invest in stocks (as opposed to trading or speculation): You can invest in the stock of a company for the dividends or you can invest for growth in the valuation of the company; or you can combine the two reasons.

This chapter first looks at investing in stocks for growth and then turns to investing in stocks for income. Then I look into the crystal ball (always a dangerous thing to do) and talk about timing your entry into the market. Finally, while the first two sections deal with investing, in the concluding section I look at trading.

Value, Value, Value

I want to return briefly to the two papers cited at the end of the preceding chapter. The first, by Piotroski, shows that basic fundamental analysis on value stocks and screening for stocks with low valuations and good fundamentals yield very good results, far better than what the market as a whole does over time, but not, of course, every individual month and year.

The second paper, by Mohanram, does the same type of analysis on growth stocks or stocks with high valuations using a different set of fundamental criteria appropriate for growth stocks. It also is very successful. Interestingly, it is more successful in finding potential failures than in finding winners.

Throughout this book, I show how value wins time and again. We have also seen numerous studies that show that buying deep value for the long term is a strategy that works in all types of markets. It is the *only* thing that works for stocks in a secular bear market cycle.

The essence of Bull's Eye Investing is quite simple. Target your investments to where the market is going, not to where it has been. Steady, stable, sure. Buying something that is undervalued, perhaps grossly undervalued, and waiting for the value to be seen by others is the way to real returns. Buying what everyone else is buying, after it has already risen in value, is why most investors simply do poorly.

However, in a market that has such high valuations, where do we find value? Can we just pick a group of mutual funds that look for value and be finished with our weekend investment allocation?

That's one possible strategy, but not the one I would suggest will be a winner. The only reason you should be investing in the stock market is if you are looking for returns in excess of what you can get with less risk in other investments.

The stock market is not a place to "save" money. It is a place in which you invest in the hope of growth. Let me give you a strategy for finding that growth in a way that the small investor actually has a significant advantage over the large funds and institutions.

Let's look at the problem of the large institutional investor. Let's assume a pension fund manager reads this book and wants to buy true deep value stocks with strong fundamentals. His investment committee says he must be invested 60 percent in stocks, so he takes his billion or so dollars and starts looking for value.

He decides that 100 stocks are about all he and his team can really say grace over, so that means he must invest $10,000,000 in each of 100 stocks. Since he does not really want to own more than, say, 2 percent of any one firm, that means he must not buy a company with a market cap of less than $500,000,000.

"Oh, wait," he sadly learns as he runs through his database, "there are not 100 deep value stocks with a market cap of over $500,000,000."

Depending on what criteria he used, there are likely only a handful. To find "value" he must keep making his criteria less and less stringent, until the stocks in his portfolio look more like a typical mid-cap value mutual fund.

But let's say you are a small investor and don't have to put $10,000,000 in any one stock. You can put in a lot less.

James Boric, editor of *CXS Penny Stock Fortunes* newsletter, spends his days sorting through databases looking for undervalued stocks of small companies. He has 10 criteria that he uses to evaluate a company, giving each of the 10 criteria a numerical rating and then choosing only stocks whose ratings add up to 8 or more.

To find a "CXS pick" Boric uses the following criteria:

1. Must trade on a major exchange (0.25 point).
2. Must have a market cap of at least $100 million (0.25 point).
3. Must have an average trading volume of at least 100,000 shares daily (0.25 point).
4. Price must be $10 or less (0.25 point).
5. P/E (price-to-earnings) less than or equal to 25 (2 points).
6. P/S (price-to-sales) less than or equal to 1.5 (1 point).
7. P/B (price-to-book) less than or equal to 1.5 (1 point).
8. Sales must have increased from the most recent quarter (2 points).
9. Net income must have increased from the most recent quarter (2 points).
10. Insider buying is greater than insider selling (1 point).

As mentioned, in order to get Boric's attention, a stock must score at least 8 points. He assigns a point value for each criterion based on his perception of importance. It's his contention that stocks that meet his requirements give you the biggest bang for your buck.

I asked Boric why he stops at a $100,000,000 market cap. The answer was simple. His subscriber base is too large to suggest stocks any smaller than that. He needs stocks of at least that size, and preferably larger, to get any liquidity for his readers. (You can see his letter at www.psfortunes.com.)

The Small Investor Advantage

As a small investor, you don't have the problem of too much money and too few good investments.

Let's go back to the French/Fama study mentioned in Chapter 16, which showed that the best value stocks outperformed the stocks with the highest P/B (price-to-book) ratios by 13.4 percent per year. The best portfolio did 21.4 percent, and the high-priced portfolio did only 8 percent.

Robert Haugen in his book *The New Finance* (Prentice Hall, 1999) pointed out that if you invested $2,000 per year for 30 years on an 8 percent return, after inflation you would have buying power of about $2,698 per year.

But if you invested in the true value stocks, your portfolio would have grown to $1,839,369 (in real, inflation-adjusted numbers) and your income would be $279,216 per year!

That is a big difference. Why wouldn't anyone simply follow his advice and the advice of so many others we have written about in the preceding chapters?

Because it runs counter to our psychology. We want to bag the big game and bring home dinner. We follow the crowd. We believe trends will continue. And on and on.

But your "inner Spock" should be telling you to forget all that. Buy value. That means you have to be patient. You have to believe in what you are doing and the stocks you buy. And that means they cannot be simply numbers on a computer screen.

If you are going to invest in stocks in a secular bear market, you must buy value. And you must be prepared to do a lot of homework if you are going to undertake it yourself. If you are not prepared to do the basic research, then you must find someone else to do it for you. Using screens like Boric's or Ferris's or Piotroski's or Mohanram's or Haugen's or using Graham's number is just the beginning. All it does is get you a handful of candidates for further research. Great candidates, to be sure—far better than the average large mutual fund can ever hope to deal with. But it is only the beginning of your work.

From there, you must begin to learn everything you can about the company. Get the 10-K and 10-Q reports the companies file with the SEC. Read their other filings as well. One simple thing you can do is go to Google and type in the company name to see what comes up. Visit the firm if you can. Do background checks on the senior management. Are there any potential problems such as lawsuits that keep showing up? Read the past audits.

If the stock is such a good deal, then why are you, an investor sitting in Peoria or outback Saskatchewan, getting a chance to own it? Be brutal. Look at the due diligence questions I use for analyzing hedge funds in Chapter 22.

Talk to your target's competitors and go to industry trade shows to learn more about the industry. Sit in the bars at these shows (drinking Coke, of course) and talk to the people who work for the firm and those who compete against it. Ask the people who really know the industry the following question:

"Let's pretend I am Warren Buffett and I want to buy a company in your industry. I am going to make you president of the company and give you 25 percent just for making it run smoothly. What company would it be? If it's not my target company, then why not?"

Go to the annual meeting. Meet the management. Do you like them? Are they winners? Are they focused and driven? Would you want them to run your company? Would you hire them? If not, why are you investing in a company they run?

In short, act as if you were planning to buy the whole firm lock, stock, and barrel. Act as if you were Warren Buffett. When you find those stocks, you have found a Bull's Eye stock. Put it in your sights and pull the trigger! And then stay on top of the stock. Keep up your research and be patient. Let your "inner Spock" keep you focused.

Of course, that is a lot of work. Buffett buys only a few firms, at most, every year. Over time, he has collected quite a portfolio, though. And you can do the same.

In fact, you have an advantage over Buffett. He can't really focus on small and micro-cap companies. He has gotten so large he has to focus on the bigger deals. Oh, the pressures of wealth.

Look at the example of *The Millionaire Next Door*.[1] So many of these people have made their money not by investing, but through owning their own businesses.

In essence, you are trying to find the right people to partner up with, those hard at work on becoming one of those next-door millionaires, who will take you along for the ride, even if in a small way.

One final thought as you look for value. As you evaluate management, make sure your interests are aligned with theirs. I know of a company whose value is so extremely low it is almost silly because of the valuable land it owns. The stock sells for a fraction of just the value of the land. But the majority owners are not going to sell any land in my lifetime. They are content with clipping their coupons and have no need or reason to sell. While that company has value, there is a reason no one wants the stock.

Get Some Help

If I was serious about wanting to become a value investor, I would do all the above. But I would recognize there is just too much for one person to do. So I would look for nine other people who thought the way I did and form a club for the purpose of finding Bull's Eye stocks.

Get a diverse group of people from a broad work background, with different age and experience levels. You don't want all accountants or lawyers or engineers. You don't have to all be in the same city or even country! You can meet and share ideas online. If things progress, you can consider getting together maybe once a year.

And after you have formed the group, have each member commit to finding three investment ideas that meet your group criteria and research them, bringing the single best idea to the group at the end of the process. You might even want to use several different screens in order to improve your chances for finding companies. Graham's number works, clearly, but it limits you to certain types of stocks. Boric's or Mohanram's ideas might give you more chance to find growth potential and value.

It would be highly desirable to have members look at firms for which they have some understanding. You want a biologist looking at biotech companies and not at a new machine for improving gas mileage.

Share research and ideas as you go along. While one member may be investigating a biotech firm, he might stumble across information on a piece of equipment made by a firm that someone else in the group is looking at.

When one member is convinced he has that one best idea, then two other members should take the time to thoroughly understand that firm, challenging the assumptions and confirming the merits of the idea. Is there substance? Or has the member bought into a good story? Keep in mind, all good stock promoters have good stories. Remember the Internet stocks? What stories they had!

If, at the end of the process, you do not feel confident about your decision, then don't buy. Remember, the clear lesson to successful investing is to avoid major losers!

At the end of this process, you will have 10 investment ideas over which to diversify. Ten Bull's Eye stocks with low values and potential growth, and which are solid businesses. Ten stocks with the potential to double in three, four, or five years! Ten stocks about which you can feel confident. They will probably be under the radar screen of most large fund managers, but if you do your work right, not for long!

I would think 10 stocks comprise the minimum diversification for an investor. The older you are, or the more near retirement, the more diversification you should want, while the less of your total portfolio should be in stocks. Ten stocks provide enough diversification, combined with stop-loss orders, to prevent a major setback for a younger investor.

But do not add companies just for the sake of doing so.

In fact, if you find a new company that is really exciting, you might consider dropping one before adding the new one. It is easier to focus on 10 stocks than 40.

A couple of hints on starting your search:

Consult the SEC Edgar database at www.freeEdgar.com and see who files a 13-G or 13-G/A. This means that someone has bought more than 5 percent of a firm as a passive investment. People are required to do another filing when they get to more than 10 percent of a firm. Why would somebody buy 5 percent or 10 percent of a firm? Presumably because they think it is a good value. That's why! For more information on the rules you can go to www.sec.gov/rules/extra/amnd13dg.htm.

What happens if you find a known value investor like Peter Lynch or Jeff Vinik or Julian Robertson showing up on the 13-G for a small micro-cap? That firm would immediately go to the top of my list for research! Notice if there are funds that show up as buying large chunks of a firm. Sometimes you can find value following hedge funds that specialize in such companies.

A Few Ground Rules for Bull's Eye Investing in Stocks

Okay, you have found your Bull's Eye stocks. What else do you need to remember?

- *Put in a real stop-loss order and stick to it.* Period. The rule is cut your losers and let your winners ride. Every stock should have its own individual stop loss based on its history. Don't set it too tight and do *not* post it with your broker for all the world to see. If market makers see your targets, they might push the stock down if it gets close to get your stock cheap.
- *Be very patient.* Trust your research. Remember, you have found stocks that presumably others have not yet discovered. You must allow time for the rest of the world to acknowledge your research. Of course, if I were you, I would share that research with anyone and everyone I could.
- *Set a target for profits and take them.* Do it when you invest. When a stock rises in value, gradually take some profits. When it gets to be a growth stock, moving with the herd, sell it. Find another value stock.

It takes almost as much emotional energy to sell something that has done well as it does to take a loss. Setting targets at the beginning will help you take your emotions out of the picture.

- *Diversify. Diversify. Diversify.* As my dad would often say to me, "Son, betteth not thy whole wad!" Maybe bad wording, but good advice. Do not invest more in any one situation than you can afford to lose. No matter how much good research you have or how wonderful the story is, there is always the chance that something totally unexpected will happen.

- *This is not trading.* This is investing. Unless you have a firm belief that your stock is getting ready to stumble for some fundamental and long-term reason, don't try to time the stock.

- *Do not fall in love.* I can say it no better than the master, "Adam Smith," who summed it all up in a neat little paragraph in *The Money Game.*

A stock is, for all practical purposes, a piece of paper that sits in a bank vault. Most likely you will never see it. It may or may not have an Intrinsic Value; what it is worth on any given day depends on the confluence of buyers and sellers that day. The most important thing to realize is simplistic: *The stock doesn't know you own it.* All those marvelous things, or those terrible things, that you feel about a stock, or a list of stocks, or an amount of money represented by a list of stocks, all these things are unreciprocated by the stock or the group of stocks. You can be in love if you want to, but that piece of paper doesn't love you, and unreciprocated love can turn into masochism, narcissism, or, even worse, market losses and unreciprocated hate.[2]

And so, even in a bear market, we can look for value, even if we have to work hard to find it. We are swimming upstream. At the end of the cycle, almost everything will look like your portfolio screens. Everywhere you look there will be value, even in the largest stocks. That is when you will once again start buying index funds with both fists.

Too Much Work and Not Enough Time

Many of you are muttering to yourself right now, "John, I just can't do that. I have a day job." Or, "Stock picking is not my skill or anything I want to do." Or, "I am retired and don't want the hassle." That is all fair enough.

Let me make a confession. I don't pick stocks. I research funds and managers. I think about the macroeconomic environment. I write. I travel and speak. I don't pick stocks. Stock picking is serious work and demands time and focus. I am focused on other things, and specifically, I am focused on what my clients pay me to do. They do not pay me to pick stocks.

I am a broker, but I do not have a quote screen on my desk nor have I ever taken an order for a stock. I hope I can finish my career continuing to say that. I let others buy and/or trade stocks for me. And most of you should do the same.

Finding and choosing a manager is hard work. Many of the questions in Chapter 22 will help you understand what you need to know, but for now, let me give you the basics.

I once read a survey that showed the primary reason investors used in choosing an investment advisor was that he (or she) was in their area. I remember thinking that was the worst reason I had ever heard. High on the list, maybe second, was the fact they liked the advisor. Track record and performance were around fifth place.

You are thinking about trusting your hard-earned money to an advisor. You should know just as much about him as you would want to know about a company in which you are going to invest. Ask to see client accounts that have been with him for some length of time. You want to see references—and really, scout's honor, call them.

See how much total money the advisor is managing. Is it so much that he cannot look for smaller value plays? Remember, if an advisor puts $5,000,000 of client money into a small company, he may not be able to get everybody out, even if each individual client has only a small amount invested.

You want to know what kind of investment philosophy he believes in. Is he an active manager or a passive one? If you are looking for a broker or advisor who does the type of investing I have been talking about, let him show you some accounts that have been with him for a while. Ask to see his five best ideas.

Don't be afraid to use someone not in your area. In your search, be specific about what you are looking for. If you want someone to manage your stock portfolio, then say so. That may not be the same person to whom you want to give your bond portfolio.

If there is enough demand, I will establish (or help someone else establish) a web site for investors and professional investment advisors and brokers to meet and form Bull's Eye Investing teams and a forum for them to trade ideas.

Where Are the Funds?

Are there any mutual funds that could be good sources for value investing? The answer is yes. I would narrow my search by looking for funds under $200,000,000 and preferably under $100,000,000 so the managers would not be forced to look only at larger value stocks with a less rigorous screening process. Look at the recent reports and see what type of stocks the manager has chosen and then do some homework on those firms. Are they really value driven or are they playing momentum models while talking a value game? Is their portfolio laden with familiar large-cap stocks?

Compare how the fund has done to how its peers and its benchmark have done. And the benchmark is *not* the S&P 500. Think about how that portfolio will do in a recession. If you like the manager and his style, but are uncomfortable with the timing, keep him in mind for when we are in the middle of the next recession and his portfolio has been beaten down. The time to buy is when a good manager is down, not when he is up.

And now let's turn to thinking about investing in stocks for income.

Suffering Along with Warren

There are some books and essays I keep near me. One of them is an article by Warren Buffett in the December 10, 2001, *Fortune.* I read it probably three or four times a year. (It is available in the archives of www.fortune.com if you search for Buffett and are a subscriber to *Fortune.*)

In 1978, he wrote an article noting that the Dow had dropped 20 percent in the prior six years, book value had risen 40 percent, and these stocks were earning about 13 percent on book value. The Dow was trading at or below book value for parts of 1979. Remember, this was still three years before *BusinessWeek* printed its now-famous cover that proclaimed "The Death of Equities." Writing in 2001, Buffett noted:

> At the time of the [1978] article, long-term corporate bonds were yielding about 9.5 percent. So I asked the seemingly obvious question: "Can better results be obtained, over 20 years, from a group of 9.5 percent bonds of leading American companies maturing in 1999 than from a group of Dow-type equities purchased, in aggregate, around book value and likely to earn, in aggregate, about 13 percent on that book value?" The question answered itself.
>
> Now, if you had read the article in 1979, you would have suffered—oh, how you would have suffered!—for about three years. I was no good then at forecasting the near-term movements of stock prices, and I'm no good now. I never have the faintest idea what the stock market is going to do in the next six months, or the next year, or the next two.
>
> But I think it is very easy to see what is likely to happen over the long term. Ben Graham told us why: "Though the stock market functions as

a voting machine in the short run, it acts as a weighing machine in the long run." Fear and greed play important roles when votes are being cast, but they don't register on the scale.

. . . How could a [13 percent return on book value] not be better than a 9.5 percent bond? From that starting point, stocks had to out-perform bonds over the long term. That, incidentally, has been true most of my business lifetime. But as Keynes would remind us, the supe-riority of stocks isn't inevitable. They own the advantage only when cer-tain conditions prevail.

That is an important point, and one that will become quite clear in the rest of this chapter. "They own the advantage only when certain condi-tions prevail." The key is to figure out what the conditions are that create the advantage.

Investing in Stocks for Income

This section is actually quite straightforward, especially with the new and low dividend tax rate provided by the Bush administration. A stock with a 6 percent dividend rate will roughly double your portfolio every 14 years after taxes, even if there is no growth in the stock or growth in the dividend. While not exciting returns, 5 percent compound returns (which is a 6 percent dividend after the new Bush tax cut) will grow your portfolio or provide needed income in retirement.

Better yet is a stock that has a tendency to increase dividends so that over time the actual stock price is likely to rise. Even better is a stock that pays good dividends and is also undervalued.

When do you buy these value stocks? As they say, timing is everything. As Buffett's article notes, suffering is possible if you buy at the wrong time or too soon.

As we have documented in earlier chapters, during a recession the stock market (broad) typically drops over 40 percent. High-dividend-pay-ing value stocks will drop less than the broad market, but they will likely drop nonetheless.

Thus, if you are buying a dividend-paying stock, you have two choices. You first need to decide if the dividends you get between now and the next recession will be more than the drop in the value of the stock. Or you need to decide whether you are the very patient type and willing to take some fluctuation in price as long as you are getting paid to wait.

As a reminder, I think the lessons from history suggest we do not get to the real bottom of this bear cycle until after the second recession. That being said, there will be some real values created during the next reces-sion, and even now there are opportunities for patient investors.

As I edit this chapter, the P/E ratio on the S&P 500 is well over 25. Dividends are less than a paltry 2 percent. Yet my friend Tom Donaldson, a rather curmudgeonly and successful value-driven investment advisor in Maine, tells me he is putting together very diversified portfolios that are yielding 6 to 8 percent, and there are some places he can go to find 9 percent. By searching far and wide, he finds value even in a market that is overheated by historical standards.

I hesitate to mention a specific stock, as things can and will change over time, and what might be of interest today may not be in 2 or 6 or 12 months. But given that caveat, let's look at some stocks from a portfolio of a client of Tom's.

He has her in Allied Capital paying 9 percent, several trust preferred shares paying 8 percent, Chinese Petroleum paying 4 percent, several energy trusts paying over 9 percent, a health care property REIT paying 13 percent(!), the odd smattering of gold stocks and other special situations, and, of course, a little cash. The total portfolio is paying just south of 6 percent. The portfolio is up almost 25 percent over the past few years, although at one point it was down 10 percent during the serious bear market in 2002.

"Why," Tom continually asks, "do I not put more of my client money with him to manage?" What's not to like about such a portfolio?

My running, and very good-natured, debate with Tom centers on timing. We agree wholeheartedly on value and dividend investing. He has a long career of doing just that. But since I think we may see a recession in 2005 or at the latest in 2006, the potential for his favorite value stocks to drop is real. But he points out they are paying 6 to 7 percent yield today. Will they drop as much as 14 percent in a recession that may be two years away? My thinking is that is quite possible, so I would rather wait and then buy when there is even more value.

First, he asks very correctly, "What if there is not a recession until 2007 or 2008? You have given up some real growth in the meantime." Further, he is not convinced high-dividend-paying stocks will drop all that much, as there might be a rotation from overvalued stocks into high-dividend-paying, solid value stocks that will drive the prices of his favorite stocks up. But if you are getting 6 to 7 percent in the meantime, then time will reward your patience. My answer is that they did drop around 10 percent during the last bear market, and I can see no reason to think they might not again.

At the bottom of the next recession, one of us will be right. If I am right, then his investors will have given up a few points of opportunity, but will not be seriously hurt, as high dividends do limit the loss of share price. They will have suffered somewhat, but will have the substantial comfort of dividends each quarter, which will soon (hopefully) get them back to whole.

If he is right, then those who have stayed on the sidelines with me (waiting for the right moment) will have missed an opportunity. But then, there will be other stocks—in fact I believe there will be far more from which to choose—that will be good values going forward.

The reality is that a stock that pays a steady 7 percent dividend will allow you to double your money in 10 years. That offers a form of portfolio insurance that stocks that do not pay dividends just cannot match.

How do you find good dividend-paying stocks? The Bull's Eye Investing process is the same as for value stocks. You screen for the stocks with the basic characteristics you want, and then you do your homework.

I can hear a few people grumbling at this point. Not you, of course. You are quite reasonable. But I am talking about that guy over there—the one who wants a quick fix. What he wants is for me to give him a web site, a search engine, and five criteria so he can create his portfolio in a few minutes a week and go on about his life. At 20 percent compound returns, of course.

If it was easy, everybody could do it, and there wouldn't be any money in it. Investing in stocks is hard work.

If you are not prepared to pay that price, then the solution is to find a manager to do it for you. By the way, income investing typically does not cost as much in terms of annual management fees as more active management styles, so I would shop fees as well. When you are trying to get a 6 percent return, a fee difference of 1 percent a year can make a real difference.

Trading Away

There are people who use the stock market for trading and speculating. Some are quite good at it. But not many.

Let's have a real-world chat here. I spend my time looking at hedge funds. I have been privileged to meet some of the better managers and traders. They have lots of resources: staff, research teams, software (and they often write much of their own software), experience, tons of contacts and sources of information, and a certain basic instinct.

Do you think you are going to buy some software trading system and beat these guys? I know one firm that buys the packaged software trading systems just to figure out what the rookies are doing so he can trade against them.

Unduly harsh? I hope so. The 1 percent of my readers who are really traders at heart will not be discouraged by my little rant. It is in their blood. They know it, and nothing I can say will keep them from the pits and trading rooms. They will learn their profession and do well. They will come to know the markets in which they move like their own backyards. The rest will serve as cannon fodder for them.

Dr. Gary Hirst, one of the smarter analysts and fund managers I know, tells me I should not discourage you from trading. "We need these guys. Where else are we going to find sources of mispricing and poor trading?"

I have heard that sentiment echoed time and again. Listen up. The pros see you as red meat. They eat you for lunch.

Plus, what do these guys make? Fifteen to 20 percent a year for the better ones, with the odd year when they knock the lights out, and the occasional year that they all wish they could forget. Remember, I am talking about the better ones. But an average of 15 to 20 percent over time is hard to do, and 10 to 15 percent with reasonable volatility is more rare than you would think. The funds that do 20 percent or better over time, and there are some, also do it with a lot more volatility.

And that level of earnings is about what the research tells us value investing will make you over time. In that world, you have the advantage, because you can focus on smaller game. If you want to play in the investment arena, I would encourage you to put your desire and efforts into playing on a field where you have the advantage and not offer yourself as a midday snack to the pros.

Investing in Bonds: Or the Sisyphus Syndrome

19

I n Greek legend, the mortal Sisyphus was doomed to continually push a rock up a hill only to watch it roll back down just as he finished his task. Frustration would set in as he watched the fruits of his labor vanish. Wearily, we imagine, he marched back down the mountain to put his shoulder to the stone once more.

For the past two decades, bond investors have watched as the Fed has fought inflation. At first, they were dismayed as interest rates rose and the values of their bonds plummeted. But then, after rates soared in the early 1980s, the rock rolled back down the mountain for the next 20 years. As interest rates dropped, the value of long-term bonds soared. Investors have been rewarded for holding long-term bonds.

In Chapter 14, we looked at my forecast for interest rates for the Muddle Through Economy. With a possible brief respite during the next recession, I believe rates are headed up. If I am wrong and the economy booms ahead, it is also reasonable to assume rates will rise.

The rock has rolled about as far down the hill as it can. Rates could go lower, but not by much. Amidst this new climate for bonds, a vastly different approach to the usual bond fund is required.

I firmly believe that bond investors must now avoid bond mutual funds and buy the bonds directly for their own accounts.

The basic premise that bond investors must realize is that a bond rises in value as interest rates fall and falls in value as interest rates rise. Sadly, 45 percent of bond investors in a recent survey conducted by Schwab did not realize their bond fund could lose money if interest rates rose. In a rising interest rate environment, boring old bonds are anything but safe.

This can be easily illustrated. Let's say you lend your neighbor $10,000 for 20 years at 6 percent interest. Things go well for the first two years, but then you decide you need the money. You ask him to pay you back, but he declines, noting that you agreed to lend him the money for 20 years.

So you go to your other neighbor and offer to sell him the note. But in the intervening two years, interest rates have risen to 9 percent. Your neighbor, simply by going to the bank, can get 9 percent for a 20-year note, or approximately $300 a year more. Why would he buy your note, which pays only 6 percent and gives him less income? The only way he would is if you discount it to him, or sell it for less than the face value.

In order for him to get the same return over time, he is willing to pay you only $6,500. Your bond value has dropped 35 percent. (The actual calculations are quite a bit more complex, involving an 18-year bond versus a 20-year, but the principles are the same.)

Figure 19.1 shows you how much your bonds can drop in value as interest rates rise. (It doesn't take into account time value and other factors, but still shows you this concept.)

As you can see, a 2 percent rise or fall in interest rates can make a big difference in the value of your bond portfolio.

You may feel that by holding a bond until it matures, you haven't lost any of your principal and you have still earned interest.

That is true, but that is not what happens in a bond fund. In a bond fund, the value of the bond is "marked to market" every day, just as if the bond manager would have to sell the entire portfolio. That means that although the interest payments may be stable, the value of the underlying bonds can change dramatically.

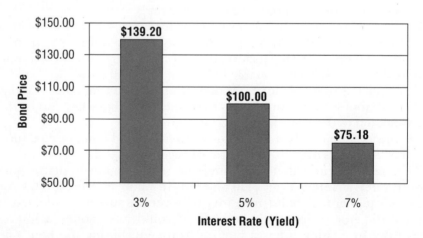

Figure 19.1 Bond Price Change to Change in Interest Rates, 30-Year Bond with a 5 Percent Coupon

Let's consider two examples. The American Century Target 2025 Fund (BTTRX) was a favorite of mine for many years as interest rates were dropping. It invested in long-term (25 to 30 years) zero-coupon government bonds. These are special types of bonds that pay no coupon (interest), are sold at a deep discount to their face value, and mature at their face value. Such bonds tend to be very sensitive to changes in interest rates, since there are no coupon payments (interest payments) to reduce the impact of interest rate changes. In addition, markets for zero-coupon bonds are relatively illiquid.

The second fund is the Vanguard Long Term Treasury Fund (VUSTX). The fund invests in long-term government bonds with an average maturity of 16 years.

Table 19.1 compares the funds' performances to how the underlying interest rates did for the year. Clearly, rising rates are not good for bond funds. While bond investors could be patient in an environment in which rates were generally falling, as the wind was more or less at their back, the winds are shifting. Now the general direction for rates is back up.

This table shows my position on bond strategy for investors. First, let me say that the older you are, the more bonds you should have in your portfolio. The amount varies according to your personal circumstances and income needs. There is no one-size-fits-all advice, and even rules of thumb (our old friend heuristics) can be misleading.

The general advice I have on bonds for the coming years:

- Buy the bond direct and plan to hold it to maturity. Yes, the actual value of the bond may vary within your portfolio, but that matters very little to your actual principal if you hold to maturity.

Table 19.1   Bond Funds versus Interest Rates

Year	30-Year Treasury Yield (January)	Change in Yield $Y_1 - Y$	Rate Direction during Year	American Century (BTTRX)	Vanguard (VUSTX)
1993	7.33	(0.98)	Falling	N/A	16.79
1994	6.35	1.53	Rising	N/A	(7.03)
1995	7.88	(1.93)	Falling	N/A	30.11
1996	5.95	0.68	Rising	N/A	(1.25)
1997	6.63	(0.71)	Falling	30.10	13.90
1998	5.92	(0.85)	Falling	21.80	13.05
1999	5.07	1.47	Rising	(20.70)	(8.66)
2000	6.54	(1.11)	Falling	32.70	19.72
2001	5.43	0.06	Rising	(2.70)	4.31
2002	5.49	(0.66)	Falling	20.50	16.67
2003	4.83	0.24	Rising	2.00	2.68

- I would not have a bond portfolio with longer-term bonds in my portfolio at this time. Since rates are going up, presumably we will be able to get better yields in a few years. While your specific holdings will vary and you should go over this with your personal investment advisor, I would keep my average bond portfolio duration at three to five years at present. As rates rise, you can lengthen the maturities.
- I would "ladder" my portfolios to achieve that average yield. A bond ladder is a portfolio of fixed income securities with maturities staggered at regular intervals. By diversifying the maturities in your portfolio, you will have funds available for reinvestment on a consistent basis. The staggered maturities mean that you will have funds to invest as interest rates increase, and yet avoid the current pain of extremely low rates on short-term funds.
- I would look offshore for a significant portion of your bond portfolio. You can buy high-quality corporate bonds in euros, Canadian dollars, Australian dollars, and so on. I notice as I write a GM $7\frac{3}{4}$ percent 10-year bond denominated in euros. This gives you not only the $7\frac{3}{4}$ percent interest income, but the potential for a little boost as the dollar falls. I would also keep most of these maturities less than five to seven years, as the dollar will eventually reach its bottom.
- Avoid high yield bonds. While a smart timing strategy can benefit from the high volatility in these funds, they can also be disastrous in a rising interest rate environment. These bonds are for the brave (or foolish) and the professionals who can actually rate such things.
- Over time, I believe that we will see more and more bond trusts created by the major investment banks, as investors will demand them. These will be self-liquidating trusts, which means that if you hold them to maturity, you will get your entire amount of principal back. When these are readily available, I think they will be ideal for investors, as they will give you excellent diversity.
- Diversity for the smaller investor will be tough. That means you have to stick with the bonds of highly rated (A or preferably above) companies or governments.
- If you manage your own bond portfolio, pay particular attention to the price and commission you pay. You should buy from firms that will cater to smaller investors and don't impose outrageous markups. However, you shouldn't plan to sell small lots, as you can find the selling price to be at a steep discount.
- Be careful of "reaching for yield." I know that it is tough to live on the paltry returns of bonds and certificates of deposit in the interest

rate environment of today. But do not start taking more and more risks with your bond portfolio. The reason to buy bonds is because you want part of your portfolio to not be subject to large swings in value. You want that part of your portfolio to be safe. Going to higher-yield instruments almost always means higher risk. While an oil partnership that is paying 14 percent certainly seems attractive (won't oil only go up in price?), there are many factors that can harm the payout and thus the value of your investment.

Individual investors can learn to buy bonds themselves by devoting the time to learn the market and the terms. That does not mean a weekend course. It means reading through several books and going online to see how you can buy bonds and follow your bonds.

Appendix B, gives definitions of the basic terms of bonds investing, plus descriptions the various types of bonds and income instruments. I get a selection on bond offerings every day sent to my computer by TD Waterhouse, varying from governments and utilities to high grade corporates. (Other brokerage firms like Schwab or Fidelity will also have the ability to sell you bonds directly.) I take one of these reports and basically describe some of what is available. A large number of bonds in small or odd lots is available to the smaller retail investor.

The ones I describe are issued at par. That means the commission and offering costs are absorbed by the issuer, which is of course reflected in your price, but is an indirect cost. If you ever try to sell your bond, you will *not* get par or face value. Selling odd lot bonds is not a good experience. Do not buy a bond thinking you can sell it when you feel like it.

You can go through a broker like TD Waterhouse or Schwab or a full-service broker to maintain your accounts. Again, the smartest investors do their homework first before buying the bonds.

If you don't want to maintain your own portfolio, there are many experienced investment advisors who specialize in bond portfolios. Just make sure the costs are in line. (You shouldn't be paying a 2 percent wrap fee, for instance, as you might in asset allocation or timing portfolios. There is less value added by advisors in a bond portfolio.)

There are also brokers who will help you find foreign bonds. You'll also have to find out what the commissions are and make sure there aren't any hidden markups. Compare the costs at several brokers before choosing one.

Another source of foreign-denominated fixed income instruments is the online bank Everbank, which offers certificates of deposit of varying maturities in a number of currencies. This bank can handle smaller accounts, which are FDIC insured, although subject to currency fluctuation. This is an excellent way to get interest income and also hold foreign currencies. Foreign currency prices change frequently so I can't make a recommendation today. Check with Everbank at (800) 926-4922 or www.everbank.com. You might want to ask them to send you the daily newsletter from Chuck Butler called *A Pfennig for Your Thoughts.*

(*Note:* My e-letter publisher has an advertising arrangement with Everbank, so there is a potential conflict of interest. That being said, I do not know of another bank in the United States that makes such accounts available.)

Hedge Funds 101: The Basics

W here can you find funds with performances that average 10 percent a year for the past five years and have little correlation to the stock or bond markets or are much less volatile than the stock market?

These funds do exist, but finding them is tough. These are private funds—known as hedge funds—and are not allowed to advertise, according to federal regulations. Even if the managers wish they could crow in public about their results, they cannot.

Hedge funds limit the number of investors who can join them. There are high minimum requirements and the funds are often closed to new investors. Furthermore, there may be risks that are not apparent in the track record. The funds often have lockup periods of one year or more. But savvy investors are finding and flocking to hedge funds in an effort to keep their investment portfolios moving upward.

The investment universe consists of traditional investments like stocks and bonds, which can be broken down into many categories and subcategories. Then there is the nontraditional world of investing, which includes real estate, venture capital, commodities, and absolute return or skill-based strategies typically characterized by hedge funds and some mutual funds. This chapter focuses on hedge funds.

In a presentation to investment industry professionals, Jeff Joseph of Rydex, a mutual fund company, outlined seven reasons why investors are interested in the absolute return strategies that are sought after by hedge fund managers:

1. The focus is on risk and the preservation of capital.
2. Investors' interests are closely aligned with those of managers.

3. Attractive performance-based compensation drives managers toward achieving alpha.
4. There is a low correlation to traditional stocks and bonds.
5. Managers can employ a wider range of skill-based strategies to capture a specific investment idea or to exploit an identifiable source of return.
6. The industry strives to attract high-quality investment managers.
7. There is a mandate to produce consistent positive returns, regardless of market direction.[1]

I believe that the positive values that hedge funds offer to rich investors should also be offered to the middle class, within a proper regulatory structure. The current two-class structure limits the investment choices of average Americans and makes the pursuit of affordable retirement more difficult than it should be. The rich have a considerable advantage in growing assets for retirement because they simply have more assets to begin with. They should not also have the added advantage of better investment choices.

Specifically, why should 95 percent of Americans, simply because they have less than a million dollars, be precluded from the same choices as the rich? Why do we assume that those with less than a million dollars are sophisticated enough to understand the risks in stocks (which have lost trillions of investor dollars), stock options (the vast majority of which expire worthless), futures (where 90 percent of retail investors lose money), mutual funds (80 percent of which underperform the market), and a whole host of very high risk investments, yet they are deemed to be incapable of understanding the risks in hedge funds?

There is no good answer. However, while the rich still have a distinct advantage, there are alternatives beginning to develop.

(When considering alternative investments, including hedge funds, you should take into account various risks, including the fact that some products: often engage in leveraging and other speculative investment practices that may increase the risk of investment loss; can be illiquid; are not required to provide periodic pricing or valuation information to investors; may involve complex tax structures and delays in distributing important tax information; are not subject to the same regulatory requirements as mutual funds; often charge high fees; and in many cases have underlying investments that are not transparent and are known only to the investment manager. Past performance is not indicative of future results.

The Technical Beginning

The current state of the hedge fund industry is the result of regulations dating back to the 1930s and 1940s, long before the creation of this type of fund. Consider the following quote:

Because of the high standards of the people whose work has been described, and many others, the field is rapidly improving in respectability. However, it is still in part a financial half-world frequented by at least a few shabby, chronic bulls (the fundamentalist camp has them, too) who sell their ideas to a constantly changing clientele seeking only easy encouragement on the bull side of the market. It has also its honest, earnest, and fascinated, but impecunious, system seekers and chart bugs.[2]

Surprisingly, this quote is from an article published in 1949 in *Fortune.*

The Jones Model—The Birth of Hedge Funds

Alfred Winslow Jones is credited as the inventor of hedge fund investing—or at least with bringing the long/short hedge fund to light for the investment community. Jones, a sociologist for *Fortune* magazine in the 1940s, discovered his new investment style in 1949. His article, quoted above, looked at some of the technical analysis techniques then being used in the stock market. Jones decided that he could use some of the ideas discovered in his research to invest money in the market. So he and four friends put together an initial investment of $100,000, and a long/short hedge fund was born in 1952.

Jones had the novel idea that by having a fund that could be long stocks he thought would go up in value and short stocks he thought relatively overvalued, he could produce better risk-adjusted returns for his clients. He also decided to keep a percentage of the profits he made for his clients. Due to limitations imposed by federal securities laws, the only available legal vehicle for him at that time was a private limited partnership. Thus he was forced to not advertise or publicly solicit investors. This became the pattern from which future hedge funds were cut.

It was not until 1966 that hedge funds gained wide public exposure, when an article in *Fortune* magazine by Carol J. Loomis titled "The Jones Nobody Can Keep Up With" profiled Jones' strategy. The 1966 article does point out that Jones was not the first to use a long/short investment strategy or its fee structure; however, this article gave him the notoriety. The article detailed how Jones outperformed some of the best mutual funds of his day, and as a consequence long/short equity hedge funds are still sometimes referred to as the Jones model.

Up until this article, there were only a small handful of hedge funds. By 1970, there were roughly 150 hedge funds, but they were not all as successful as the original Jones model. Others who learned about Jones' success started their own hedge funds, but many did not stick to the Jones model to their later chagrin. Many of these new managers got caught up in the bull market of the late 1960s and used leverage to increase their long exposures instead of hedging long against short like Jones did. The results were even worse in 1973–1974, as the bear market resulted in many funds being closed.

Plus Ça Change, Plus C'est le Même Chose

The heading is a famous French saying, for "the more things change, the more things stay the same." A 1970 article in *Fortune*[3] is interesting for a few notable points. The American Stock Exchange changed its rule to make trading far more difficult for hedge funds. Client suitability was a key topic (as it is today), and one hedge fund manager acknowledged turning down potential clients, "mostly women," as not suitable, whether or not they had the net worth. Try telling a woman she is not suitable today because of her gender.

Someone named Warren Buffett made 24 percent a year for his clients the previous nine years. I pass this quote on for its historical interest:

> But now, to the immense regret of his limited partners, Buffett is quitting the game. His reasons for doing so are several, and include a strong feeling that his time and wealth (he is a millionaire many times over) should now be directed toward other goals than simply the making of more money. But he also suspects that some of the juice has gone out of the stock market and that sizable gains are in the future going to be very hard to come by. Consequently, he has suggested to his investors that they may want to take the "passive" way out, investing their partnership money not in the stock market but instead in municipal bonds.[4]

In 2003, the SEC spent considerable time and effort to learn about hedge funds. It seems the SEC was looking into regulating hedge funds in 1970 as well, and even toyed with interpretations of the rules that would outlaw them. The following quote actually was from the 1970 article, but just as easily could have been written in 2003.

The next disastrous happenings [for hedge funds, other than bear markets] may emanate from the SEC, which for years has been fretting about the hedge funds and which lately has been trying strenuously to arrive at some decisions about them. A year ago the SEC sent out an exhaustive questionnaire to some 200 investment partnerships that it had spotted by one means or another. . . . The Commission is now compiling the answers to this questionnaire, and is virtually awash in facts about hedge funds. In the meantime, certain members of the SEC staff have already concluded that the Commission must take steps to regulate these funds. The staff rests its case on legal arguments, maintaining that two laws the SEC has long administered, but has never interpreted as applicable to the hedge funds, do apply to the funds and do require their registration with the Commission. Be that as it may, it also seems clear that the staff thinks the hedge funds should be regulated and that the Commission must find a way to do it. One staff member spoke recently of the "crisis numbers" to which the funds have grown, and there has been much SEC talk about the "impact" of the funds on the market. Some hedge-fund operators ask bitterly whether it is not premature to be forming opinions about impact, since the questionnaires have not yet been analyzed.[5]

The "crisis numbers" that some long-forgotten regulator worried about were 150 some odd funds managing less than $1 billion. In fact, the *Fortune* article listed funds with a total of less than $500 million.

Other than a few larger-than-life names, like George Soros and Julian Robertson, or the occasional problem, after this flurry of concern hedge funds returned to public obscurity until 1998, when Long-Term Capital Management drew a great deal of attention as it took the world to the brink of the abyss. Today, there are some 8,000 funds managing over $700 billion, and the numbers are growing rapidly. Once again, we have been hearing the call for regulations.

The most significant reason for the growth of the hedge fund industry is investment returns. Simply put, if high-net-worth investors and institutions could get the same returns as hedge funds by simply investing in stocks, bonds, or mutual funds, why would they choose hedge funds, which have higher fees and are harder to find and research? The answer is they would not. The demonstrably observable higher potential risk-adjusted returns seem to be the driving force behind the effort.

Legal Structure and Restrictions

Many articles portray hedge funds as secretive, unregulated investments, but let's look at the reasons hedge funds behave this way. Many investment strategies employed by hedge funds are restricted and/or prohibited by the Securities Act of 1933 and the Investment Company Act of 1940 and thus may not be used in conventional mutual funds. Therefore, the manager structures the fund to avoid registration under these acts. While you as an individual can execute these strategies in your private portfolio, they cannot be done within a mutual fund or regulated public fund.

The two key factors that exempt the manager from registration under the acts mentioned are: (1) not advertising to the public and (2) accepting only what are known as accredited investors. The definition of an accredited investor is an individual with $1,000,000 in net worth or $200,000 in personal income ($300,000 in personal income with a spouse) over two consecutive years and no reason to doubt that that income level will continue. In addition to the net worth requirement, the securities laws also limit the number of investors the fund can have to avoid registration. The number of investors is limited to 99 or 499 depending on the net worth of the investors.

(The concept of net worth and suitability is actually far more complicated. If you are worth more than $1,000,000 and have an interest in investing in hedge funds, I suggest you read Appendix D for further information on the various levels of net worth required for different types of hedge funds.)

The trade-off for managers who operate under these limitations is that they have full use of leverage, derivatives, and short selling. These investment tools are greatly restricted if even available to the mutual fund manager.

Oddly, you have the right in your personal accounts to execute any of these strategies no matter your net worth, but the laws passed by Congress forbid you to hire someone to do them for you in a fund unless you are wealthy. In practice, it should be no different than hiring the mutual fund manager to purchase your stocks or bonds.

Business Model

Hedge funds are typically structured as limited partnerships. The manager is the general partner and the investors are the limited partners. Quite often, the manager puts a significant portion of his own net worth into the fund, which helps align his interests with the other investors. (Ask your mutual fund manager what percent of his portfolio is in his fund.) Hedge funds should be thought of as an asset class or a business model rather than as another way to invest in bonds, equities, or derivatives.

There are many different hedge fund strategies, and they cover a broad range of risk and return. These strategies will be explored in more detail later in the chapter, but there is one common denominator for the vast majority of hedge funds, and that is the pursuit of absolute returns, meaning that the manager is trying to produce positive returns no matter what the rest of the markets are doing.

This contrasts with mutual funds, which seek relative returns. Relative returns judge the manager's performance relative to a benchmark, like the S&P 500 or one of the Lehman Brothers bond indexes. The relative returns manager doesn't care if his fund is down 15 percent if the benchmark is down 18 percent, because the manager's directive is to outperform the index whether it is up or down.

In addition to the manager putting a substantial amount of his own money at risk in the hedge fund, there is another characteristic of hedge funds that aligns the managers' and investors' interest in achieving absolute return—the fee structure.

Management Fees

The most typical fee schedule for a hedge fund is a 1 percent management fee and 20 percent of profits, although some funds charge 3 percent and 35 percent (or more!), and others charge only an incentive fee of 20 percent. The range of fees and costs is quite varied.

The measurement of profits typically uses what is referred to as a "high water mark." The fund can collect 20 percent of only the gains above the old high water mark, so if the fund has a negative return it must make that back up before collecting 20 percent of the gains. Other funds also have a hurdle rate, which means they must yield an agreed-upon return before the management gets incentive fees. (Typically the hurdle rate is some type of bond or money market index.)

As an example, if the fund falls from $100 to $90 in the first year, the manager will get only the 1 percent management fee. He will not collect the 20 percent until the fund gets back above $100. If the fund goes back up to $95 the second year, the manager collects the 1 percent management fee and no 20 percent. Let's say the fund gets to $105 at the end of the third year. The manager will collect the 1 percent management fee again and 20 percent of that $5 above the $100 high water mark or $5 × .2 = $1. Now the new high water mark is set at $105, so the manager must get above this value to collect the 20 percent of profits in the future. As you can see, the incentive is for managers to perform consistently with absolute returns so they can collect the 20 percent fee. (Sometimes the incentive fees are calculated quarterly.)

Since many hedge funds start with limited capital, if they don't perform well the first one to two years they shut down—they simply cannot afford to continue. The reason is pure business economics. A 1 percent management fee on $10 million in capital is only $100,000. From that relatively small sum, the manager must cover operating costs such as payroll, rent, data feeds, and equipment costs. For the smaller startup funds the 1 percent and 20 percent are not as lucrative for the manager as some might suggest. Of course, they all hope to manage much larger funds, and thus a new fund is formed somewhere almost every day.

Funds of hedge funds add additional management fees and/or incentive fees, which can vary considerably. The benefit is the ability to diversify into multiple managers at a lower cost, because the one investment gets spread across multiple underlying managers. We will look at funds of hedge funds in depth in Chapter 21.

Let me give you a few thoughts on the higher fees charged by hedge funds. Let's be clear. The fees charged by hedge funds are high and are significant. Twenty to 30 percent of profits is a big chunk, no matter how you look at it. While fees are important, they are not as important a factor as they are in mutual funds in determining fund performance. The differences among the returns on index funds, as an example, are highly correlated with the levels of fees.

With hedge funds, you are hoping to buy a certain level of management expertise within a defined market. Not all long/short Jones model hedge funds are the same. Not all funds of funds are the same. Management, in my opinion and in my experience, is a far more influential factor on returns than fees are.

That being said, investors should do correlation analysis when choosing between funds that have similar investment strategies. When there are high correlations, the lower-fee funds often prove to be the ultimate winners of the beauty contest.

Quality management costs. If they price themselves too high relative to the value they offer, they will lose clients. When you're evaluating hedge funds, you should look at management, performance, risk, and fees. Fees should be considered but your focus should be on your return, not how much the manager earns.

For instance, I can think of several major corporations that I would gladly offer to run for half the compensation of the current CEO. (Note to Citicorp board: Sandy Weill's job and perks are pretty attractive! And I do have some financial services industry experience.) However, shareholders would rightly bail out of the stock were any board to make me such an offer. When it comes to management, you need to focus on the manager and what he really brings to the table.

Investment Minimums

Historically, hedge fund minimum investments have been quite high, running from $250,000 up to $1,000,000 or more. The incentive for the manager is to try to attract as much money from each investor as possible, because the number of investors that can be let into the fund is limited. Some strategies work well only with large amounts of capital, like global macro where the manager might want $500 million under management at a minimum, while others can take only a limited amount, like a micro-cap strategy where the manager might want a maximum of $30 to $50 million in the fund.

The funds of hedge funds tend to have much lower minimums. In general the minimum is in the $25,000 to $250,000 level, but new products are coming that could go as low as $5,000. Keep in mind, however, that even with a low minimum, the investor currently has to meet the appropriate suitability requirements.

That is changing, as we will see later. There are now funds available to the average investor that have low minimums and are legitimate hedge fund strategies.

The Most Important Factor

The manager of the fund is the single most important factor in selecting the hedge fund. His or her expertise and knowledge are what make the fund profitable. Many hedge fund strategies are not extremely difficult to understand, but to be successful investing with these strategies you must have the intimate knowledge that the manager brings to the game.

Many of the hedge fund managers come from trading desks at major investment banks and/or are mutual fund managers who believe the hedge fund world can be more lucrative, such as Jeff Vinik (more on him later) who left Fidelity Magellan to run his own hedge fund. Also, analysts with specialized knowledge, like in corporate mergers, bankruptcies, or corporate financing, could move into hedge fund management.

Choosing the right manager will require a thorough due diligence process, reviewing many aspects of the fund's structure and management. You'll have to review back office operations, amounts of the money flows into or out of the fund, position concentrations, transparency, and the manager's background. The back office or outside firm hired to perform these services must be reputable and efficient.

Almost without exception, hedge funds use outside auditors. This does not imply that the investment strategy is safe, but only that the assets really exist.

Money flows can have an adverse effect if a large percentage of assets under management is from one investor. The departure of that investor could cause the manager, especially in an illiquid strategy, to sell off assets at an inopportune time, thereby hurting the remaining investors. Position concentrations can cause excessive risk as the manager puts too much of the fund into one investment. This may be fine, though, if that is the type of swing-for-the-fences strategy that is wanted, but most hedge funds are more interested in controlling risk than hitting home runs.

Transparency is the ability to look at the portfolio of the manager. This helps monitor problems like position concentration, strategy drift, and risk management by the fund manager. Transparency has become much more open than in the past, but is still not as apparent as in other investments. You'll also want to review a one-time event that may cause the manager to show great returns that are unlikely to be be repeated. The key is to make sure the manager is consistent over time and not just lucky. As an example: If the manager gets a return of 50 percent the first year and negative 5 percent the next two years, his three-year annualized return looks great, but the returns going forward may be more like the last two years than the first one.

Due diligence is not simply a one-time review you undertake before making an investment; it's a a continuous process for as long as the money is invested with the manager. The investor must be able to collect and understand the data, and this can be costly and time-consuming. This is why, for the small investor, using a consultant who can perform these tasks makes lots of sense.

Presumably, the management of a fund of hedge funds where a basket of hedge funds is put together also continues to monitor and replace them as warranted. The fund of hedge funds manager's job is, after all, all about continuous due diligence and risk management. For more discussion of due diligence, read Chapter 22.

Hedge Funds: Strategies and Returns

It would be impossible to cover every nuance of every hedge fund strategy in only one short chapter, but I will try to give you a general overview of the more mainstream tactics, along with a relevant performance index (or maybe two) to give you an idea of the types of returns each strategy has produced.

Before we proceed, we need to have a frank discussion about hedge fund indexes. They are useful when you know what they actually represent. They can also be misleading, just as some Ibbotson studies can be used to suggest returns that may not happen again.

The Index Dilemma

There has been an increased interest in indexes to track hedge funds. This is partly due to the increasingly institutionalization of hedge funds. Hedge funds and marketing groups recognize that there is a large wave of potential money that can flow into funds if the funds can make themselves look more conventional to the average institution. Institutional investors have $42.8 billion in hedge funds worldwide, with the United States making up $34 billion of this amount. However, U.S. institutional investors have only 0.6 percent of their assets invested in hedge funds, according to Greenwich Reports, so there is plenty of room to grow. In order for institutional investors (like pensions, endowments, and charitable organizations) to invest in hedge funds, keep their plan sponsors happy, and meet their fiduciary duties, they need an index against which to monitor their performance.

Some of the best-known U.S. universities have increased their exposure to hedge funds and the results have been satisfying. Harvard, Yale, and the University of Virginia have respectively 12 percent, 25 percent, and 60 percent targeted hedge fund allocations, far above the average of 6 percent for private schools (as of the time of this writing). All three universities recorded roughly flat returns for 2002, while the average large endowment lost 3.8 percent, the average midsize endowment lost 5.3 percent, and the average small endowment lost 6 percent.[6]

The industry has created many indexes and more are sure to follow. Table 20.1 lists of some of the companies offering indexes for hedge funds, funds of hedge funds, and commodity trading advisors.

There is a problem with hedge fund indexes, however. What exactly do they track? Which funds? How are they priced? There is survivorship bias and the problems of funds simply not reporting. There can be too much diversification in the index to make it meaningful. If no one can invest in the fund (it is closed to new investors), should it be included in an index? What about outliers, backfill, mark-to-market issues, liquidity, and transparency? At the end of this chapter I discuss indexing problems in detail for those who are interested. (And you should be, and not just because of hedge funds. Indexes in general are tricky little animals and can be misleading.)

Now, given all these problems, are indexes useful? They are, as a rough benchmark for comparisons, as long as we don't ascribe too much by way of comparison. Furthermore, since past performance is not indicative of future results, I trust by now none of my readers would make the mistake

Table 20.1   Hedge Fund and Commodity Trading Advisor Indexes (Alphabetical)

Alternative Asset Center	www.aa-center.net
The Barclay Group	www.barclaygrp.com
Center for International Securities and Derivatives Markets (CISDM)	www.umass.edu/som/cisdm
Credit Suisse First Boston Tremont	www.hedgeindex.com
EurekaHedge	www.eurekahedge.com
Evaluation Associates Capital Markets	www.eacm.com
Hedge Fund Intelligence	www.hedgefundintelligence.com
Hedge Fund Research	www.hfr.com
Hennessee Group	www.hennesseegroup.com
International Traders Research	www.managedfutures.com
MSCI	www.msci.com
Mt. Lucas	www.mtlucas.com
Rogers Raw Materials	www.rogersrawmaterials.com
Standard & Poor's	www2.standardandpoors.com
Van Hedge Fund Advisors	www.hedgefund.com

of thinking these or any other historical indexes in any way predict future returns. They are simply a tool for comparison.

But that is precisely where they have their usefulness. When I compared the average return of a convertible bond mutual fund with that of a convertible bond arbitrage hedge fund, the differences were clear. Would the worst fund in either index be one to which you would gravitate? Obviously not, and most investors would like to be able to choose a fund whose management has been able to consistently perform in the upper ranks of its respective index. But the indexes allow us to get an idea of the relative performance enhancement that hedging a convertible bond portfolio yields.

Now, let's look at actual hedge fund strategies.

Hedge Fund Strategies

Hedge fund styles can be classified into three basic types with multiple styles possible in each one (starting with the least risky to the most risky):

1. *Market neutral strategies* such as convertible arbitrage, bond (and various fixed income) arbitrage, and long/short equity (which itself has multiple sectors).
2. *Event-driven strategies* such as merger arbitrage and distressed assets.
3. *Directional strategies* such as global macro and managed futures.

Let's look at some of the individual styles.

Convertible Arbitrage

This is one of my personal favorites, and has been the source of steady returns for many hedge fund investors. An important caveat worth mention is there are several significant variations among many of the convertible arbitrage funds, with significantly different levels of risk. Don't assume they are all alike, even if the returns appear similar.

Convertibles can come in the form of bonds, preferred stock, or warrants, but for our discussion we will concentrate on the convertible bond. Convertible bonds allow the holder to convert, at a specific conversion price, the bond for a fixed number of shares of stock in the underlying company. The bond can be viewed as a bond combined with a call option, so the hedge fund manager buys the bond and shorts the stock to create the possibility for hedged interest rate income.

Let's say ABC Company wants to issue a convertible bond with an 8 percent interest rate. Hedge Fund Y will buy the bond and immediately short the stock. The managers don't care if the stock goes up. They simply want the 8 percent. If the stock goes up, they lose on their short position, but the convertible bond is more valuable. If the stock goes down, their short position increases in value even as the bond becomes less valuable.

But look at what happened. Hedge Fund Y invested $1,000,000 in the convertible offering. There is not a one-to-one relationship between the bond and the stock, but typically you might see the hedge fund short 80 percent of the value of the bond. That means they get back $800,000 in cash from selling the stock short. They are getting $80,000 in interest payments from the bond, plus whatever is earned on the $800,000. At 2 percent, the fund would be getting $96,000 in interest or a 9.6 percent return on their original investment. Leverage this up a few times, and you can see where convertible arbitrage can produce some excellent returns.

If only it were that easy. The manager is betting on the stock falling more than the bond in a down market, or the bond rising more than the stock in an up market. Since the bond is convertible into shares, once the conversion price has been passed the bonds should go up in tandem with the shares. The problem is that option and bond prices are nonlinear, meaning that they will not move one-to-one with the underlying stock when the stock price is close to the conversion price. Therein lies the problem and the opportunity for a skilled convertible arbitrage manager. The manager will analyze credit quality, equity valuation, and option pricing models to try to find a bond he feels is priced wrong, or to properly hedge the risk of a convertible bond already in his portfolio.

In periods of high interest rate volatility, these funds will in most likelihood lose money. Those with significant leverage or direct rate exposure can lose a lot of money. Think the summers of 1998 and 2003. However, patient investors (by that I mean those with a multiyear time horizon) in well-managed funds have been amply rewarded. If your concept of a long time is three months, then you will not be happy, as every few years these funds seem to lose money or at best simply go flat.

Morningstar has an index of mutual funds that invest in convertible bonds. This index represents the typical return an average investor would have received from a long-only strategy in a convertible bond mutual fund.

Notice what happens (Figure 20.1) when appropriate hedging techniques are used. Returns are tripled over the last five years and volatility is halved. Why do we assume investors can understand the risks of investing in IBM and cannot understand this rather straightforward process? Why should the average investor be denied access to this investment strategy if he/she wants to invest in convertible bonds?

Please remember my cautions about indexes earlier in this chapter. These are not investable indexes. By that I mean you cannot invest in a

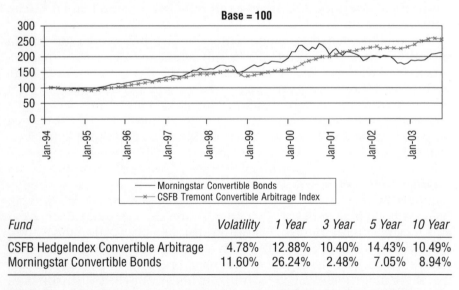

Fund	Volatility	1 Year	3 Year	5 Year	10 Year
CSFB HedgeIndex Convertible Arbitrage	4.78%	12.88%	10.40%	14.43%	10.49%
Morningstar Convertible Bonds	11.60%	26.24%	2.48%	7.05%	8.94%

Figure 20.1 Morningstar Convertible Bonds versus CSFB Tremont Convertible Arbitrage Index
Source: Raw data from Credit Suisse First Boston Tremont Index LLC and Morningstar, Inc.

fund that will give you the performance of the index, as you can with the S&P 500.

Fixed Income Arbitrage Funds

Fixed income arbitrage is similar to convertible arbitrage except instead of buying a bond and selling the stock short, the manager buys a bond and sells a similar bond or interest rate future short. The manager is trying to exploit small pricing inefficiencies in the bond market. Since the inefficiencies are small the manager will employ a large amount of leverage to "juice" the returns of this low volatility and low return strategy. If he did not leverage up the fund the return would not be great enough to justify the investment.

The manager will utilize actual bonds, interest rate futures, and interest rate swaps. The manager uses sophisticated models to determine when a pricing relationship is out of whack. Statistical models will track the historic yield spreads and if the spread is wider than normal the manager will bet on the spread returning to the historical average. The strategies can involve mispriced relationships based on yield spreads, yield curves or embedded options in the bonds. As an example, the manager would take two similar bonds and sell the higher-priced bond, which has a lower yield, and buy the lower-priced bond, which has a higher yield, hoping the spread will converge.

The fixed income arbitrage manager is also playing the volatility game. As volatility goes up the manager decreases leverage, and as volatility falls the manager will increase leverage.

There is a subcategory within this style that concentrates on mortgage bonds. These funds can be among the steadiest of performers and again are one of my favorite styles.

This simply involves buying mortgage bonds (typically from Ginnie Mae or Freddie Mac) with short-term money. If you can borrow at 2 percent and invest at 5.5 percent the spread allows for some nice profit. Leverage this up and you have a nice return. Quick investors will note that there are some real risks here. What if interest rates rise and bond values fall? What if the spread narrows? The manager has to take some of the profit on the trade and invest in futures or other derivatives and financial instruments to hedge out or balance the interest rate directional risk.

What if interest rates fall? The risk then becomes prepayment risk. You actually lose your high-paying asset, and when you go back into the market you have to purchase lower-yielding paper. Again, you can hedge the prepayment risk for a price.

Some fixed income funds buy corporate bonds and use leverage. Some buy orphan bonds (small bonds large institutions don't want to bother with). Some use the "repo" market as a source for very cheap leverage money (costs may be less than 1 percent) and buy U.S. bonds or highly rated corporate bonds.

Here the wide variety of management experience kicks in. Most of these funds are started by individuals who come from major investment banks. They learn their craft by trading for in-house "prop trading" desks, meeting investors, and noticing lucrative niches. At some point, they solicit money from friends and go out on their own; using the ideas they developed to create a stream of alpha or absolute returns.

Note: Some fixed income hedge funds are relatively stable, steady funds. Some are highly risky. It all depends on how they hedge. To see if a manager understands the meaning of the word "hedge," as a quick rule of thumb, I often look to see how a fund performed in the summer of 1998 or 2003, when interest rates were extremely volatile. Remember, however, to ask if they are using the same hedge strategies today. (Past performance is not indicative of future results.)

That being said, fixed income funds can make an excellent addition to an investment portfolio and are among the more popular of funds. In Figure 20.2 we look at one example comparison.

Let's take the most prosaic and basic of investments: the Ginnie Mae bond. Again, hedge funds have outperformed their mutual fund counterparts. But that does not tell the whole story.

Hedge funds have achieved their gains by hedging out the interest rate directional risks and use leverage to increase the returns. Mutual funds have achieved their gains by benefiting from the lowering of rates which causes the value of their bonds to rise.

What will happen when the economy recovers and interest rates start to rise? A rapid rise of 2 percent on a 30-year mortgage bond that sells for 5.3 percent today would cause the value of the bond to drop 24.21 percent. Even a slow change could cause values to drop by 10 to 15%. That will cause the funds to lose money. Investors who thought they had a conservative government-backed bond fund will find themselves with no returns.

Which is the better and more conservative approach to investing in Ginnie Mae bonds? Do you want to take the risk of rising rates or do you want the risk of leverage? (There are other and quite serious risks of investing in Ginnie Mae bonds, mortgage-bond-based mutual funds, and hedge funds. I do not want to suggest these are the only risks. Read a prospectus carefully and consult with your investment professional.)

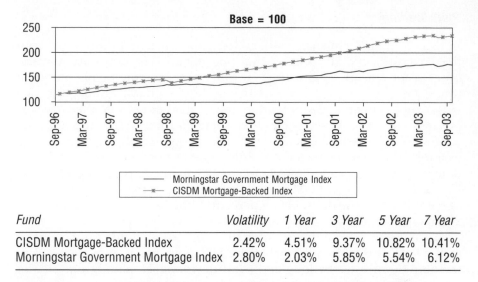

Fund	Volatility	1 Year	3 Year	5 Year	7 Year
CISDM Mortgage-Backed Index	2.42%	4.51%	9.37%	10.82%	10.41%
Morningstar Government Mortgage Index	2.80%	2.03%	5.85%	5.54%	6.12%

Figure 20.2 Morningstar Government Mortgage Index versus CISDM Mortgage-Backed Index

Source: © CISDM 2002. All rights reserved. Reproduced from www.marhedge.com and Morningstar, Inc.

Long/Short Equity Funds

Long/short equity involves going long one stock and shorting a different stock. Long/short offers the manager the potential to produce alpha* (the positive return you get over simply index investing) from positive and negative judgments on stocks or industry groups instead of just being long and fully invested like most mutual funds. Trading costs can vary greatly among these funds, as some funds feature very rapid trading and others have much longer time horizons.

Long/short trading has several very distinct styles, with different risk-reward characteristics. As you might expect, these often yield quite different returns and have different losing periods.

---

*Alpha measures a manager's return that cannot be attributed to the market. It shows the difference between a fund's actual returns and its expected performance given its level of risk.

Pairs Trading

In pairs trading the manager will go long one stock and short another in the same industry. He believes that one stock is too expensive and the other is too cheap relative to each other. An example of pairs trading would be going long Ford and being short General Motors (or vice versa). Stocks in an industry tend to move together because they have exposure to the same business conditions and customers. But since all companies are not created equal, they do not move exactly together. In our example, the fund manager is predicting that Ford will perform better than GM in both up and down markets. The manager is placing a bet that if Ford is up 10 percent GM is up only 8 percent or that if GM is down 10 percent Ford will be down only 8 percent. Either way he makes a profit of 2 percent.

As can be seen from the example that each trade should not be looked at as a lone event, but as a total trade. The alpha generation comes from the convergence of the long and short decisions. Hopefully, one side of the trade will make money while the other loses less money.

Long or Short Biased

Long biased is the traditional Jones model and would involve the manager being more long than short, so that the overall portfolio is net long. Typically the strategy uses modest amounts of leverage. As an example, if there is $100,000 to invest the manager might go $80,000 long and $40,000 short, for a $120,000 portfolio. This would hedge $40,000 of the long with $40,000 of the short and leave another $40,000 unhedged long. The manager is then considered 50 percent hedged. Keep in mind a long-only investor is 100 percent unhedged. Short biased is the opposite of the long biased strategy, and a manager may move from one to another depending on his outlook for the market.

This strategy generally focuses on stock quality: Managers go long the stocks they like and short those they think are overvalued. Managers attempt to make money on both their long and short positions over time, but the "hedged" portfolio will tend to be less volatile than a straight long- or short-only portfolio.

Let's now look at one of the largest and most popular of technology funds, invested in a highly concentrated portfolio of technology stocks. Management for the fund told investors it was their stock analysis that enabled them to give investors very high returns. This fund was up 679 percent from March 1990 until March 2000. Since then, it has dropped as much as 67 percent, cutting its return by two-thirds and costing average investors over $10 billion of net worth. Volatility was almost eight times

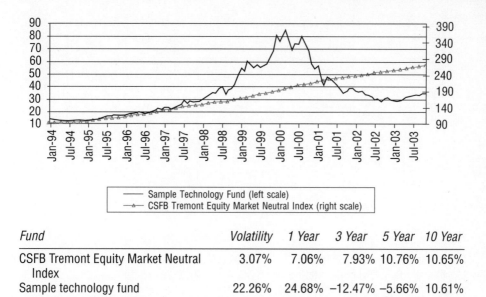

Fund	Volatility	1 Year	3 Year	5 Year	10 Year
CSFB Tremont Equity Market Neutral Index	3.07%	7.06%	7.93%	10.76%	10.65%
Sample technology fund	22.26%	24.68%	−12.47%	−5.66%	10.61%

Figure 20.3 CSFB Tremont Equity Market Neutral Index versus Sample Technology Fund
Source: Raw data from Credit Suisse First Boston Tremont Index LLC.

that of the market neutral index. This fund is by no means the worst-performing technology fund. At its peak, it had over $25 billion, much of it from small investors. (See Figure 20.3.)

Finally, let's look at the entire range of equity mutual funds* versus the entire range of hedge funds. We asked Morningstar to give us an index of all equity mutual funds, and took the Tremont index of all hedge funds. (See Figure 20.4.)

Let me again emphasize that hedge funds are not investment nirvana. Some hedge funds are very volatile and extremely risky, as are some mutual funds, stocks, and futures. Some hedge funds are fairly stable and boring, as are bonds. Lumping all hedge funds styles into the same category can be very misleading. Simply because a person is a member of Congress does not mean he or she is the same as all other members.

---

*This is an average of all U.S. diversified equity funds that fit with in the nine Morningstar style boxes, which include growth, value, blend, small-cap, mid-cap, and large-cap. It excludes any hybrid funds that include bonds and sector funds.

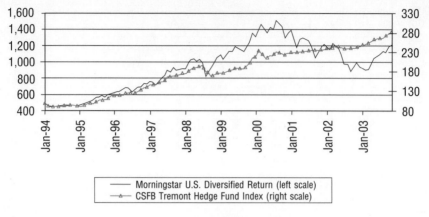

Fund	Volatility	1 Year	3 Year	5 Year	10 Year
CSFB Tremont Hedge Fund Index	8.48%	15.46%	7.50%	9.96%	11.11%
Morningstar U.S. Diversified Return	16.28%	32.79%	−2.49%	3.29%	10.41%

Figure 20.4   CSFB Tremont Hedge Fund Index versus Morningstar U.S. Diversified Return
Source: Raw data from Credit Suisse First Boston Tremont Index LLC and Morningstar, Inc.

But just as voters get to choose the type of congressional representative they want, so too should investors be able to choose the type of funds and risk they or their advisors feel appropriate.

Market Neutral

There is an additional layer of constraint that can be used in long/short and that is to make the strategy market neutral. Market neutral tries to eliminate the exposure to the market and depends purely on the manager's ability to produce alpha. Pairs trading would fit in here if it used one of the two following structures: beta neutral or dollar neutral.

Beta neutral is a long/short strategy that uses complex statistical models to try to be market neutral. The manager will use a calculation of each stock's beta to determine the right ratio of long to short to achieve market neutral. The basic concept is that the market has a beta of 1 and more volatile stocks like growth stocks will have a beta greater than 1, while less volatile stocks like value stocks will have a beta less than 1. The stock with the beta above 1 in theory will go up or down more than the market, and the stock with the low beta will go up or down less than the market. The manager will use a ratio of the two betas to determine how much to invest in each position.

He still decides which stocks he believes are going up or down. He just balances the portfolio in an attempt to take out the market risk. The risk he hopes to be left with is his judgment risk.

Dollar neutral is similar to the beta neutral example, but the manager puts equal dollar amounts on the long and short. So the manager could be long a financial company stock like Citigroup by $100,000 and be short a financial stock like JP Morgan by $100,000. This trade will not be beta neutral if the two stocks have different betas, but it is dollar neutral. The other thing to realize is that depending on where the share price is trading the manager will be going short a different number of shares than he is going long.

For purposes of illustration, if JP Morgan is trading close to 30 and Citigroup is close to 40, for dollar neutral to be achieved the manager would buy 3,333 shares of Citigroup and sell short 2,500 shares of JP Morgan.

Now, let's compare the market neutral index with the S&P 500 (dividends included), as many investors use an S&P 500 index mutual fund as their proxy for the market.

(Volatility here is defined as standard deviation. Standard deviation quantifies the dispersion or scattering of returns around the average return for a given period. The higher the standard deviation, the more volatile the investment. Hedge fund investors typically seek lower standard deviations and steady performance. For this statement we use monthly returns over the entire period to produce an annual volatility.) (See Figure 20.5.)

The typical S&P index fund had volatility as measured by standard deviation of more than five times the market neutral index. High-net-worth investors have watched their returns drop in the past few years, but are still comfortably in the black with this strategy. I am at a loss as to a reason for why the average investors should not be allowed to invest in such a fund strategy.

In Figure 20.6 let's compare hedge funds to one of the largest and most popular of mutual funds.

Investors were well served by this fund during the bull market of 1982–2000. This fund seriously outperformed not only this index, but most hedge fund indexes in the recent bull market, rising 598 percent from March 1990 until March 2000. Since that time, it has seen its assets lose as much as 42 percent, although it has recovered somewhat in 2003. The annual volatility of this fund was over five times that of the average market neutral fund.

The management of this fund is some of the best available anywhere.

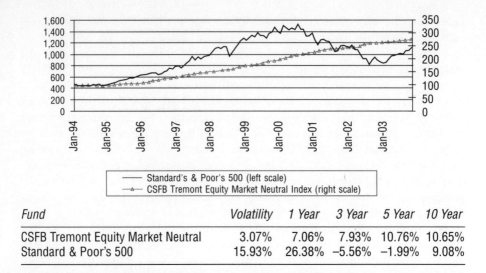

Fund	Volatility	1 Year	3 Year	5 Year	10 Year
CSFB Tremont Equity Market Neutral	3.07%	7.06%	7.93%	10.76%	10.65%
Standard & Poor's 500	15.93%	26.38%	−5.56%	−1.99%	9.08%

Figure 20.5   CSFB Tremont Equity Market Neutral Index versus Standard & Poor's 500

Source: Raw data from Credit Suisse First Boston Tremont Index LLC and Standard & Poor's.

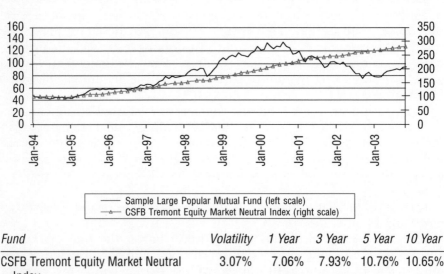

Fund	Volatility	1 Year	3 Year	5 Year	10 Year
CSFB Tremont Equity Market Neutral Index	3.07%	7.06%	7.93%	10.76%	10.65%
Sample large popular mutual fund	16.75%	24.05%	−5.77%	−1.10%	9.13%

Figure 20.6   CSFB Tremont Equity Market Neutral Index versus Sample Large Popular Mutual Fund

Source: Raw data from Credit Suisse First Boston Tremont Index LLC.

However, the managers are limited to a long-only strategy. You live by the bull and die by the bear.

Short-Term Trading

There are any number of funds that simply try to earn profits from trading aggressively. They all use "proprietary" systems, at least in my experience.

Some managers are true day traders. The manager of one of my favorite funds I call a "day and a half" trader. Some hold stocks for days or weeks, and some think 30 minutes is a long holding period.

These funds, more than any others, are truly dependent on the personal skills of the managers. A fixed income manager can train another trader to follow his system. While short-term traders all have systems, much of the skill resides with the "wet" software of the trader's brain.

The edge they have is hard to quantify. You can see it in their returns and in their portfolios. How consistent are they at following their own system guidelines? How hard do they and their teams work at improving their systems?

There is one consistent characteristic of successful traders: They have access to good information and the ability to act quickly on it. Whether you are talking about commodity traders or stock traders, the access to information is critical.

Event-Driven Funds

Event-driven can include such things as mergers and distressed securities.

Merger Arbitrage

Merger arbitrage is where two companies announce a merger, friendly or not. Either way there are risks the deal will fall apart and this is where the hedge fund manager looks to make money. The share prices will trade at a spread to the merger price. That means even if company A is offering $20 per share for Company B, the actual stock price of Company B may be only $19, as the market prices the risk that the merger may not happen. The more sure the merger, the closer the price of the stock to the offering price. The hedge fund manager tries to determine the probability of the merger happening or failing, and then initiates a strategy based on his opinion.

If the manager believes the deal will go through he can buy the acquired company and short the acquiring company's shares. When the deal goes through the manager pockets the spread in price. If the manager believes the deal will not go through he shorts the acquired company and goes long the acquirer. Once the deal busts, the takeover stock should fall and the acquiring company should stay flat or rise slightly. This is called doing a reverse spread on the merger. These funds are often highly leveraged, as the price spread movement in the actual merger may be quite small. (See Figure 20.7.)

Distressed Securities

Companies in financial trouble offer the hedge fund manager profit opportunities in what are called distressed securities. This market is more inefficient because most institutional investors have to avoid distressed companies due to their investment policy and that leads to a market segment with less liquidity. This segment can include companies in severe financial trouble or already in bankruptcy. The manager looks to buy distressed securities that are underpriced by the market, but it can take a longer period of time for the strategy to pay off. These funds often have

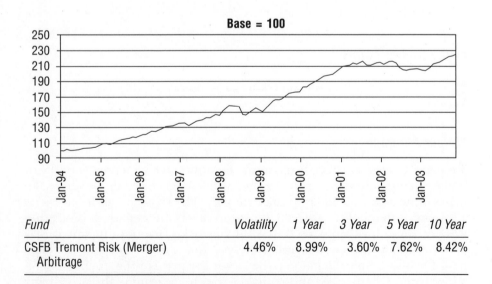

Fund	Volatility	1 Year	3 Year	5 Year	10 Year
CSFB Tremont Risk (Merger) Arbitrage	4.46%	8.99%	3.60%	7.62%	8.42%

Figure 20.7   CSFB Tremont Risk (Merger) Arbitrage Index
Source: Raw data from Credit Suisse First Boston Tremont Index LLC.

long lockup periods and special provisions for redemptions. They are not for short-term investors. (See Figure 20.8.)

There are funds that specialize in "work-outs." They buy debt in distressed companies at a steep discount and then, in tandem with other debt holders, either take over the company and liquidate it at a profit or figure out a way to fix the problem.

For patient investors, these funds can be very rewarding. But they are not without risks. Again, management is everything. You need management with strong stomachs and even stronger contacts. The nature of a distressed fund is that they are dealing with problems. It is not necessarily fun. It takes a certain mind-set.

It is not unusual for these firms to have more lawyers in their ranks than investment analysts. They are often referred to as vulture funds. But it is precisely because nobody wants to mess with a problem that the opportunity is created.

One of my favorite and more extreme examples of distressed debt is that run by a firm now based in Washington, D.C. I first met these managers years ago in Africa where they would buy African government debt and figure out a way to make a profit.

This is an actual deal described to me. They bought Nicaraguan debt owed to Bulgaria from the Bulgarian government at $.07 on the dollar. Bulgaria had long since written it off. Because Nicaragua had pledged assets worth the entire amount, it was possible to go into a European court and get a judgment against the government of Nicaragua. Knowing this,

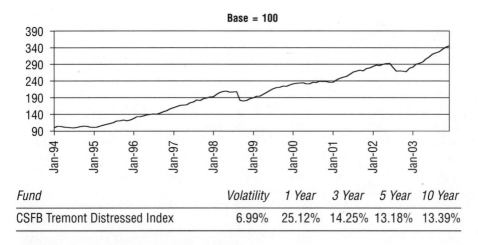

Fund	Volatility	1 Year	3 Year	5 Year	10 Year
CSFB Tremont Distressed Index	6.99%	25.12%	14.25%	13.18%	13.39%

Figure 20.8   CSFB Tremont Distressed Index
Source: Raw data from Credit Suisse First Boston Tremont Index LLC.

the Nicaraguan government gave the fund 50 cents on the dollar for half of the debt in local currency. The fund then sold this at a 25 percent discount to an investor who needed local currency for a construction project. These managers have now made five times on their original investment.

But wait, there's more! They then got a Scandinavian country to fund a deeply discounted buyback of the remaining 50 percent of the debt, doubling their money again! They made almost eight times on their money.

Sound easy? You may not want to know how much "inventory" they still have, how much they have written off already after holding it for years, what their legal bills were, how long it took to actually do the deal, how much time and money they invested in chasing down the players, the long (I mean long) plane trips, trips dealing with bureaucrats, weeks in hotels in less than exotic locations, waiting, waiting, waiting, missed family events, and so on and so forth.

As an investor, your money is locked up for years, while in the meantime it is in assets that are worthless until the deal is done.

This isn't a stupid investment, but it's one that is right only for investors who have the proper risk tolerance and understanding of the markets.

The description of the aforementioned fund is not too different from a venture capital fund. Many, if not most, of the new ventures started by such funds are never profitable. You know going in that some will go completely south and the entire investment will be written off. But you are looking for the one or two that go 10 (or more) to 1.

There are many distressed debt funds that deal in far less exotic fare. As an example, the management of one fund I know is expert in finding what I call "baby and the bathwater" investments. As an example, if a company has its debt downgraded by the rating agencies, or the company files for bankruptcy, the typical response is that all the debt of the company gets sharply revalued. All of the debt is thrown out with the bathwater, as it were, yet there may be some very healthy babies in the tub.

Some of the debt may be tied to specific assets, which makes that debt more valuable. Other debts might be senior to all other debt, so as to make the debt quite secure. Yet you could buy this debt at a discount. For a period of time, the distress on the company creates a buying opportunity for those who care to go through the thousands of pages of loan documents to find the opportunity.

Another fund I know specializes in just the opposite. It looks for debt that is priced for perfection. As often happens with corporate bonds, their value could rise as interest rates fall, or the company is seen as more secure. This fund shorts such "perfect" debt from companies that it thinks might have problems in the future. This is a fairly sophisticated strategy, but illustrates the creativity that hedge fund managers can wield in an effort to find mispriced securities to produce absolute returns.

Please note, these funds do not have steady performance, nor are their returns safe and guaranteed. There can be considerable risk in them. Remember, they are buying things no one else wants, and usually there is a reason for that disfavor.

Global Macro Funds

Global macro involves making directional bets on trends in the global economy. This is the arena of George Soros, Monroe Trout, Louis Bacon, John W. Henry, Bruce Caxton, and scores of other funds and managers. The manager will follow government policy, political unrest, currencies, interest rates, stocks, bonds, options, and metals. This is a high-risk/high-reward strategy that often is highly leveraged and sometimes not hedged. They take a top-down approach to investing by trying to predict where the global trend will go. The returns are generated by going long or short and tend to be in highly liquid investment instruments. (See Figure 20.9.)

These funds tend to do well during global crisis situations and therefore have a low correlation to equity market returns. In fact, their best returns usually come during times when equities are doing their worst. But they are also among the most volatile of funds. Losses of 20 to 25 percent or more are frequent in many of these funds.

I will write more on these funds in Chapter 23, as certain types of them

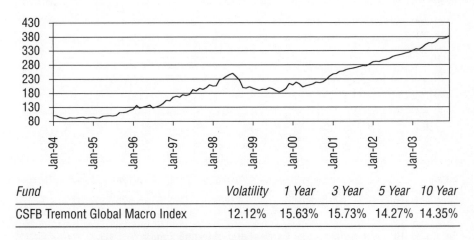

Fund	Volatility	1 Year	3 Year	5 Year	10 Year
CSFB Tremont Global Macro Index	12.12%	15.63%	15.73%	14.27%	14.35%

Figure 20.9   CSFB Tremont Global Macro Index
Source: Raw data from Credit Suisse First Boston Tremont Index LLC.

are available to the average investor and may be appropriate for the aggressive portion of your portfolios.

Fund of Hedge Funds

One other structure that has evolved is a fund of hedge funds. The manager of the fund of funds puts together a basket of hedge funds, anywhere from a minimum of 3 to as many as 100 in some large funds, which may invest in similar or broadly different strategies. (See Figure 20.10.) We will deal with the fund of funds in detail in the next chapter, as this style of hedge fund is beginning to be available to the average investor.

A Modest Proposal

In May 2003, I was invited to testify at a congressional hearing on hedge funds. I advocated a new regulatory approach that would allow smaller investors access to the hedge funds. What follows is the summary of the testimony. The entire testimony is available at www.accreditedinvestor.ws.

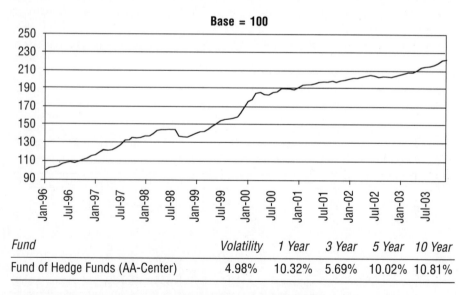

Fund	Volatility	1 Year	3 Year	5 Year	10 Year
Fund of Hedge Funds (AA-Center)	4.98%	10.32%	5.69%	10.02%	10.81%

Figure 20.10   Alternative Asset Center Fund of Hedge Funds
Source: Copyright © Alternative Asset Center. All rights reserved. www.aa-center.net.

The Hedge Fund Investment Company

Let me suggest the following: the creation of a new type of investment company vehicle. Simply modifying the current mutual fund rules might work, but it is not direct enough, in my opinion. Let's call this new vehicle a hedge fund investment company (HFIC). I will describe it first and then outline some of the advantages.

A hedge fund would be allowed to register with the SEC or the Commodity Futures Trading Commission (CFTC) as an HFIC. It would be required to have an annual independent audit and at least quarterly independent valuations of its assets and independent administrators, plus it would be subject to SEC or CFTC advertising rules. There would be few, if any, limits on the strategy the fund could employ, and it could charge a management fee and an incentive fee. It would have to fully disclose not only the relevant risks, but all information on its strategies, personnel, and management experience.

As with mutual funds, there would be no limits on the number of investors. These HFICs would be allowed to advertise within current regulatory guidelines. With certain restrictions outlined later, they would be able to take nonaccredited, or average, investors.

As noted, hedge funds pose a set of different and unfamiliar risks than do stocks, bonds, or mutual funds, not to mention futures, options, and real estate, all of which are available to the average investor today. I would suggest that for a certain period of time, say 7 to 10 years, an HFIC be limited to investors who can demonstrate a required level of investment sophistication or to investors who use an investment advisor or broker who has passed an appropriate exam demonstrating competency in hedge funds (such as the Chartered Alternative Investment Analyst program sponsored by the Alternative Investment Management Association) or has had a sufficient number of years of experience in the industry.

After the end of the period for investors to come to some understanding of what an HFIC is, as well as develop sufficient track records, these funds would then be available on an equal basis with mutual funds, stocks, bonds, futures, real estate, options, and a host of other risky investments currently available to the average investor. This time period would also allow for a support industry and independent analysis firms to develop.

The simple fact is that most institutional funds hire outside analysts to evaluate and recommend hedge funds. They also hire consultants and outside managers to recommend stocks and bonds. The actual individuals sitting on institutional and pension boards do not make the initial investments decisions, although the final authority is in their hands. I would suggest for your consideration that many of the people on these boards are not accredited investors. Yet they are considered capable of evaluating the appropriateness of whether to invest in hedge funds. The evidence is that increasingly large numbers of them are doing so.

They are no different than the individual smaller investor. If you create a situation where they can access appropriate sophisticated advisors, they will do so. Indeed, they do so now. There are tens of thousands of advisors and brokers who offer investment services to the public. They simply do not have hedge funds as a choice.

Would hedge funds willingly register? My belief is that they will. To state that there are thousands of funds that are seeking money is not an exaggeration. The problem today is that they must do so privately and only to high-net-worth investors and institutions.

If they could approach a new class of investor, I believe that many of them would do so. The current rules do not allow them to do so, and so they do not. It is not the desire of the industry to be secretive. It is the requirement of the law. Hedge fund managers certainly have no personal bias against small investors. The reason hedge funds avoid small investors is primarily legal. The large majority of managers simply want an appropriate amount of money to manage. If the rules allowed for appropriate and knowledgeable investing by smaller investors, they would adjust their programs to accept such.

A few comments follow on what might happen in the real world if such an investment vehicle as the suggested HIFC came about.

The likelihood is that a large majority of the initial HIFC funds would be existing funds of hedge funds. Many of these have long-established track records and are well diversified. The process of taking numerous smaller investors would be no more problematic for a fund of funds than for a mutual fund. Certainly those funds of hedge funds that are registering under the currently available system anticipate taking many investors.

Secondly, I think it is likely to drive down fees over time. Just as the outrageously high fees of commodity funds came down in the 1990s as more funds became available, and many mutual funds are available with quite low fees, I think you would see an investor-friendly fee structure develop, especially for funds that are similar in nature.

The advantage of developing a new fund structure is that it does not displace the current status quo. If a fund wishes to remain private, it can do so. If it wishes to go through the hoops of registering, that avenue would be available.

The reality is that the disclosures I suggest are no more than what funds already do today. If I or other professionals cannot get the information we need to evaluate a manager, we simply do not invest. "Black box" investing is an invitation for serious problems. Thus, as time went on, managers with good programs and steady risk-adjusted returns would realize that an HFIC requires no more than their current high-net-worth clients are requiring on a private basis today. The HFIC would simply be seen as another way for raising funds.

Finally, funds should have the choice of whether to be regulated by the CFTC or the SEC. The CFTC currently regulates 55 out of the 100 largest hedge funds since they are registered as commodity pools. Patrick Mc-Carty, general counsel for the CFTC, noted at the 2003 SEC Hedge Fund Roundtable that out of the 2,400 funds registered with the CFTC, there were 10 complaints last year. If an HFIC uses futures, then it should be allowed the choice of which regulatory authority to choose, but not be subject to duplicative processes that force extra expense.

The good news for investors is that over time they would be able to access these funds now only available to the rich. I should point out that even though the rules say an accredited investor is someone with $1,000,000 or more, that does not mean that on a practical or legal basis such an investor can access the large majority of hedge funds. On a practical basis, a net worth of $5,000,000 or more is required before you can begin to avail yourself of many of the better managers, and the top funds, which have high minimums, often have a much higher practical requirement for net worth.

This new industry would grow slowly, as did mutual funds when they were first offered. Over several decades, I would suggest that they would become standard fare for investors. They would not replace mutual funds or other investments. They would simply be one more choice, just as they are now for the rich.

We should evaluate the decision whether to allow smaller investors the same rights as larger investors in the light of three questions:

1. Is it appropriate?
2. Is it the right thing to do?
3. Is it fair and just?

Is It Appropriate?

The premise of Modern Portfolio Theory is that you can increase the returns and decrease the risk of an investment portfolio by adding noncorrelated investment asset classes, even if those individual classes are individually highly volatile. Many hedge funds styles, by any reasonable assessment, are highly uncorrelated with the stock and bond markets. High-net-worth individuals and institutions are taking advantage of this fact by diversifying part of their portfolios into hedge funds. This reasonable diversification should be made available to smaller investors as well.

No one would suggest that all or even a significant proportion of an investor's portfolio should be in hedge funds. But a reasonable diversification is appropriate.

There is no real reason to believe that smaller investors cannot understand hedge fund strategies if properly explained. If investors can be assumed to understand the risks involved with individual U.S. stocks, foreign stocks, commodity futures, currencies, options, mutual funds, and real estate, not to mention a host of Regulation D limited partnerships, then how can anyone suggest that hedge fund strategies are beyond the ken of investors?

I would suggest that investors can understand quite readily the logic and value of hedging the interest rate directional risk from a bond fund, or pairing undervalued and overvalued stocks, or hedging a convertible bond. While management competence is the real issue investors should focus on, how difficult is it to understand the concept behind buying undervalued assets in a distressed debt fund?

A hedge fund is a business, generally with a straightforward premise. It is no more, and often far less, difficult to understand the business risks and plans of the typical U.S.-based company, to say nothing of a biotech or high-tech firm or international company, than the risks and concepts of a typical hedge fund.

Is It the Right Thing to Do?

Most hedge funds have an offshore version with lower minimums. The reality is that investors from Botswana have more and better investment choices than do U.S. citizens from Baton Rouge, Louisiana.

If you ask the brokers and investment advisors on the front lines of serving the public whether they wish they had access to hedge funds on behalf of their clients during these past three years, the answer would be a large yes. If you ask investors whether they should be able to make their own decisions—to have the same choices as the rich—the answer would also be yes.

The only people who benefit from limiting investor choice are those who have a vested interest in not facing the competition from hedge funds. As they seek to protect their turf, they have lost sight of the interests of those whom they should be serving.

Those who oppose allowing average investors to have the same choices as the rich must tell us why smaller-net-worth investors are less intelligent or are deserving of less options than the rich. They should show why average investors should only be allowed funds that are one-way bets on an uncertain future.

I believe that investors would tell you that not allowing them the same choices as the rich is the type of government protection that they do not need.

Is It Fair and Just?

With all the proper regulatory scrutiny being devoted to hedge funds, with the concern of hedge funds that such activities could restrict their investment options and business, it would behoove us to remember the small investor, who is not even allowed a hedge fund crumb from the rich man's table. The focus of future regulation should be to make sure there is an honest game on an even playing field, not to exclude certain classes of citizens.

To put it simply: It is a matter of choice. It is a matter of equal access. It is a matter of equal opportunity.

I believe it is time to change a system where 95 percent of Americans are relegated to second-class status based solely on their income and wealth, and not on their abilities. It is simply wrong to deny a person equal opportunity and access to what many feel are the best managers in the world based on old rules designed for a different time and different purpose. I hope that someday the small investor is invited to sit at the table as equals with the rich.

Finding Hedge Funds

Until Congress changes the rules, finding hedge funds will require some work. Let's look at how you might go about the task.

First, there is now one fund of hedge funds that is available to the average investor. It is called the Rydex SPhinX Fund, and it invests in the S&P Hedge Fund Index. In my opinion, these will be among the first to be made available to the public. Rydex has pushed the fund of fund's camel nose under the mass market tent with its introduction of the SPhinX Fund. This will open a floodgate of similar funds. Within a few years the world of hedge funds may be open to everyone, as it should be. I will write more about the SPhinX Fund in the next chapter. This fund is available to nonaccredited investors ($25,000 minimum) if a registered investment advisor deems them to be suitable for this fund and makes the investment for them. You can buy it directly through Schwab (and others) if you are an accredited investor.

Why the distinction? This is a good place to go into the question of investor suitability. The professional investment firms, advisors, and brokers are charged with determining investor suitability. While an accredited investor is allowed to access the fund directly, it seems with the Rydex fund the regulators want a professional to determine whether the fund is suitable for individual smaller investors.

In fact, if you work with any professional advisor or broker, they are required to go to great lengths to get to know you personally. They should not be making one-size-fits-all recommendations. This includes knowing your net worth, tax status, income, investment objectives, investment experience, what types of investments you currently have, and a great deal more. Typically, they should go through this process for at least 30 days before they make a recommendation or give you any information about a specific fund.

Interestingly, a fund that is unregistered can take your money if you simply check the appropriate boxes that attest to your net worth and suitability. There are databases where you can get information about funds and contact them directly. I think we will see legislation and new policy that more clearly defines this seeming gap in the rules.

There are several databases of hedge funds. The two main lists are the Investorforce and the TASS databases. Access to these databases, with sufficient software and search capabilities, runs in the $6,000 per year range. These databases have about one-third of the universe of hedge funds. They are a good starting place, but they have huge gaps. Although they are growing, there are still large numbers of hedge funds that simply do not participate.

Generally, those funds that are not on these databases are either the better-established funds, which do not need any marketing exposure, or funds whose performance does not look good in comparison with other funds. There are also many funds whose attorneys do not want them on a database. Any serious hedge fund analyst must develop his own sources, and not rely on the databases. There are just too many great funds not in those databases.

To go beyond the standard databases, you have to do a lot of legwork. You can attend hedge fund conferences. (See more hedge fund resources in Appendix C to see how to find out about conferences.) You can attend these and network with the managers and other investors.

A family office is generally the heirs or principals of a substantial sum of money who work together to manage a trust or other assets. Some of these offices are very large. They have considerable resources and typically are very good at networking. I find they are often willing to share information on their favorite funds if they think you can reciprocate. This is also true with a number of endowment funds.

This can be more than a full-time job. I know of several consulting firms that have four to eight employees who do nothing but find, analyze, and do due diligence on hedge funds. They charge their clients considerable sums to build portfolios of hedge funds, and to do the necessary ongoing monitoring.

For all but a few individuals, doing your own research and analysis of hedge funds is just not feasible. That means you need to find third parties who can introduce you to hedge funds. Let's look at the possibilities.

First, if you want to put $10,000,000 or more into hedge funds, it may make sense (on a cost basis) for you to seek out one of these consulting relationships. But for most accredited investors, this is not a realistic choice.

Second, major prime brokers, like Morgan Stanley or Bear, Stearns, have divisions that will introduce you to hedge funds. These are usually limited to funds with which they have a marketing relationship or which do major trading with their firms. Typically, these funds have $1,000,000 minimums and are single strategy funds.

One major prime broker comes to Dallas every few months and brings four hedge funds to do a "dog and pony show" during a dinner. These are generally new funds. I always attend if I can. I am always looking for funds, but what I really find valuable are the other investors who attend who are also are looking and are willing to share ideas.

You can call these major investment banking firms and ask for their prime brokerage desk, and then ask to speak with someone who can refer you to hedge funds. If you indicate you are willing to invest $1,000,000 into single hedge funds, you will find them quite helpful. The downside is that they do *not* do any real due diligence on the funds. You must be prepared to do your own thorough due diligence. Consult Chapter 22 to see what I mean by thorough due diligence.

Third, most of the national broker/dealers have a one or more fund of hedge funds they manage, with minimums in the $200,000 range, and some as low as $25,000. Quite often, they have gone through public registration with the SEC so they can offer the funds to an unlimited number of accredited investors. This is a viable option for many investors. If your personal broker can't get access to these funds, ask to be put in touch with one who can.

Fourth, there are boutique firms that specialize in representing hedge funds and alternative investments. The easiest way to find one of these firms is to go to a major hedge fund conference and simply network. If you ask attendees to direct you to such a firm, you should be able to find several within a short time. You can find some of these firms on the Internet, although it is not easy.

Typically, these firms have a particular area of expertise they understand well, and look for funds to represent in that area. In the hedge fund industry they are called "third-party marketers." I work with a number of such firms. I find some of these firms can be quite useful. The downside is that some firms are indiscriminate in whom they represent, working with any firm that will pay them to represent it. You have to know with whom you are working.

As for fees, most third-party marketers are paid by the funds they represent, so there is no additional charge to the client. Consultants, on the other hand, charge a fee generally based on the assets under management, with large minimums.

Further Resources for Information on Hedge Funds

- HedgeFund.net, at www.hedgefund.net, is a web site that has information on more than 1,000 hedge funds. You have to be an accredited investor to register.
- Hedge Fund Association, at www.thehfa.org, is an industry association.
- HedgeWorld, at www.hedgeworld.com, offers a daily newsletter on hedge funds.
- A good academic site is at www.umass.edu/som/ciasdm; this University of Massachusetts center offers a lot of independent research papers on hedge funds.
- The Alternative Investment Management Association has some good information but is more valuable for its links to other sites: www.aima.org.
- For those who are interested and who qualify, I write a free letter on hedge funds and private offerings called the *Accredited Investor E-letter*. You must be an accredited investor (broadly defined as an investor with a net worth of $1,000,000 or $200,000 annual income—see details at the web site). You can go to www.accreditedinvestor.ws to subscribe to the letter and see complete details, including the risks in hedge funds. (I am a registered representative of and president/owner of Millennium Wave Securities, LLC, a National Association of Securities Dealers (NASD) member firm.)
- For more information about what I do and to subscribe to my weekly letter on economics and investing, you can go to www.john mauldin.com. You will also find information on other products and services.

There are also more resources in Appendix C.

Now, as promised earlier, let's look at some of the issues regarding hedge fund indexes.

Hedge Fund Indexes and the Investment Process

Survivorship Bias and Not Reporting

There are four major reasons that would cause a hedge fund to not report to an index. First, since hedge funds are private partnerships they do not have to report their results to anyone; therefore, any data from a fund must be voluntarily offered by the manager. Firms registered under the SEC must report the returns to the SEC and they are on public record. So, the other three reasons a manager would not want to report his returns all hinge on the fact that it is in his discretion whether to report.

For instance (and the second reason), if a fund has poor performance, then the manager may not report its performance. Hedge funds shut down at a large rate. It is estimated that roughly 1,000 hedge funds will be shut down in 2004. Many of these funds never build up long enough track records to be included in the index, as most indexes require roughly a three-year record unless the managers are an offshoot from another larger, well-established fund. If a fund has a low or negative return record, the manager will not attract additional money and will choose to close down. Plus the fee structure of hedge funds is stacked against the poor-performing manager, as noted earlier. Research has shown that survivorship bias may cause reported returns by indexes to be roughly 2 percent higher per annum[7] or 4 to 6 percent higher per annum when accounting for funds that were never included in the index.[8]

Third, a hedge fund that is closed to new investors has no incentive to report results. There is a difference between a fund that simply stopped reporting and one that closed down due to poor performance, but both will not be reflected in the index data.[9] Why tell others how your fund is doing if you can't accept any new investors anyway? Managers may want to keep their success private in order to not attract more participants to their strategy. Especially since some of the strategies are in less liquid markets and additional participants may arbitrage the profitability away. This is the opposite problem of the previous one, as it means that indexes may not be including the better-performing funds. I know one fund manager in particular who is quite adamant that his track record not be shared outside of a close group of contacts.

Fourth, if a hedge fund does extremely well the manager may close down the fund. The manager may decide to pursue other interests after years of good results. If the manager was key to the investment strategy, no one may be able to continue running the fund and achieve similar results. Another scenario is that the manager makes a lot of money, shuts down the fund, pays out all the proceeds to investors, and manages only his own money going forward. One of the most famous examples of this is an ex-Fidelity Magellan manager some of you may recognize, Jeff Vinik.

In 1994, Jeff Vinik, the high-profile former manager of the Fidelity Magellan fund, and partner Michael Gordon started a fund with $800 million and quickly closed to new investors. They operated the fund for approximately four years and achieved an annualized gross return of 66 percent. The general partners' share of profits would have totaled over $800 million. After four years, they liquidated the fund and turned to managing strictly their own capital.[10]

Transparency

A survey by the Hennessee Group (a hedge fund research group) finds that transparency is one of the most important factors concerning investors in hedge funds, and 56 percent of hedge fund investments come from high-net-worth individuals and family offices, not institutional investors. While individuals seek transparency, it is an even larger issue for institutional investors. The "black box" of the past is not acceptable to them. A black box means the investor gets little or no detail on the manager's strategy or the fund holdings. It is as if the manager keeps them hidden in a black box. That's not to say investors need daily or real-time transparency, but they need some insight to perform their due diligence. Transparency helps investors watch for strategy drift and other signs of trouble.[11]

As one veteran hedge fund investor relates,

> They [managers] come to me with all types of philosophies on transparency, and I have the shortest conversations (i.e., I show them the door) with those who say "My process is so complicated that you couldn't understand it." I have a very low "trust me" coefficient that comes from years of dealing with stock, bond, and commodities traders. I am quite leery of dealing with hedge fund managers who are unwilling to provide sufficient transparency about their process and the attribution of their returns.[12]

Mark to Market—Liquidity

Hedge fund strategies can sometimes involve illiquid investments. The hedge fund may hire a third party to independently price each illiquid investment in the portfolio, but it could get "stale prices." The prices are stale because they are estimated from infrequent trade information, or estimated from other comparable assets. While this is an acceptable way to price the portfolio, it does cause a smoothing effect in the volatility depending on the method and frequency of the pricing. Lois Peltz of Infovest21 found that over the past nine years there have been 10 hedge fund blowups, and the underlying reason was problems of liquidity from illiquid securities.[13] If there is more volatile price movement in between the repricing of the portfolio it will not show up in the numbers.

As an example, imagine looking at the Dow Jones Industrial Average (DJIA) Monday before the market opens and it is at 8,500. At the close Friday the DJIA is at 8,550. A 50-point move does not look very dramatic, but if the average had gone down to 7,800 before rebounding to 8,550 an investor might have a different perspective on the volatility of prices that week. Now it can be seen that the DJIA had a swing of 750 points from low to high rather than just 50 points. By pricing the assets at less frequent intervals, as the DJIA example shows, the hedge fund's volatility may look better due to smoothing.

Backfill

Backfill happens when a new fund is added to an index. Remember that most funds operate for close to three years before being allowed into an index, so once the fund is added all the previous or back performance is incorporated into the index history. This creates what they also call an instant history. The problem is that the fund record is now part of the index, but investors may not have had access to the fund during the earlier years. So if the fund had exceptional performance during those early years, it causes an upward bias in the index results and the appearance of underperformance by hedge fund investors. Conversely, if the fund had poor performance in one year, it can understate the index.

The upshot of this means it is important to know how many funds are in a given index. A small number means one fund can make an exaggerated difference on the index. Larger numbers of component funds help alleviate this issue.

Outliers

Hedge funds tend to have a lot wider dispersion of returns among managers in some strategies. These extreme positive or negative results can skew the average results. The problem comes from the variation and classification of hedge funds. Let's use a long-only strategy as an example. Long only is what mutual funds do, but hedge funds have more flexibility in that they can move to cash or add leverage. As an extreme example, consider two hedge funds classified as long only with one stating that it will employ no leverage while the other will utilize up to 200 percent leverage. These two funds can have significantly different return and risk profiles; however, they will be averaged together in the index. The wide dispersion of returns will make the average less meaningful.

Is the Fund Investable?

In a comparison on hedge fund indexes Bing Liang found that of the 1,162 funds in the Hedge Fund Research database and the 1,627 funds in the TASS database there was an overlap of only 465 funds at the time.[14]

According to a presentation by a representative of CSFB/Tremont at the 2003 Global Alternative Investment Symposium, the CSFB/Tremont index is developed from a universe of 2,800 funds; of those 780 were deemed appropriate for use in the index, 403 were chosen for the index, and roughly 100 to 110 of the ones included are closed to new investors.

What does this mean for you? If the best-performing funds are the ones closed, the returns available to investors may differ from the index and the index becomes a biased benchmark. Furthermore, once a good fund is included in the index, money may flow into the fund and it will close to new investors, so the window of investment opportunity may be short.

Funds can also be "soft closed" in that the official stance is that the fund is closed, but it may have a few slots still open. The manager will selectively add new investors. These investors may have a previous relationship with the manager, be able to invest larger sums of money, be known to leave money locked up for longer periods of time, or be willing to add money when the manager wants the cash flow.[15]

Overdiversification

One last thought on hedge fund indexes and their application to the investment process is that overdiversification can defeat the purpose of investor diversification. The number of funds in the index creates an average that may not be representative of investors' experience if they invest in only a few hedge funds or a fund of hedge funds. Liang found that "Because of this concentration, the hedge fund indexes understate the diversity of hedge fund trading styles in general and overstate the risk of style convergence. When a large number of hedge funds in a portfolio converge into a similar set of bets, portfolio diversification implodes."[16]

Let's look at this subject another way using the S&P 500 index as an example. The index includes 500 of the larger-capitalization stocks, and Barra uses a valuation technique to divide the 500 stocks equally into growth and value based on market capitalization (not the number of companies). Assume an investor bought five stocks from the growth list and five stocks form the value list; the return of this portfolio has a low probability of matching the return of the S&P 500. The return would have more to do with how those 10 stocks behaved than how the index performed. Now if the investor increases the stock purchased to 75 percent of the growth stocks in the index and 75 percent of the value stocks in the index, the return will start to converge to the return of the S&P 500. To take it one step further, if the investor bought the S&P 500/Barra growth and the S&P 500/Barra value the combined portfolio would match the S&P 500.

Investing in a Fund of Hedge Funds

21

> My ventures are not in one bottom trusted,
> Nor to one place; nor is my whole estate
> Upon the fortune of this present year.
>
> —Antonio, from Shakespeare's
> The Merchant of Venice, Act 1, Scene 1

It is my contention that investing in hedge funds should be approached in the same way one considers investing in a public company. We examined this in the preceding chapter so now I want to discuss what I think should be the basic hedge fund investment vehicle for most investors: the fund of hedge funds.

Two of the reasons for investing in a fund of hedge funds are quite similar to those for investing in an equity mutual fund—diversification and professional management. In addition, a good fund of funds will give you access to hedge funds that are difficult to find or invest in, and also should provide smoother risk-adjusted returns.

Since a fund of hedge funds is likely to be where most hedge fund investors will start, it is important to understand these types of funds. Furthermore, while there are some parallels with mutual funds, there are also some distinct differences that you should know about. There are now funds of hedge funds available (more or less) to the general public. Finally, there can, and often are, significant variations among the quality and value-added features of funds of hedge funds.

For the historians among us, the fund of funds concept was originally credited to Georges Coulon Karlweis. Mr. Karlweis started Leveraged

Capital Holdings for Rothschild's (offshore to the United States) in 1969 as a fund of hedge funds vehicle. Over the first 28 years of the fund's existence it had an average total return of over 15 percent, according to *BusinessWeek.* Several years later the first fund of hedge funds was created in the United States by Grosvenor Partners.[1] The Hennessee Group estimates the number of fund of hedge fund assets reached $115 billion in 2002 in more than 1,500 funds of hedge funds. That may be about 25 percent of the total hedge fund universe and about 20 percent of the actual money in hedge funds.

That is certainly explosive growth. Let's look at why investors have flocked into funds of hedge funds, and why these funds should be seen as a starting point for most investors who are looking to invest in hedge funds.

First, let's look at Figure 21.1, a very interesting chart by George Van of

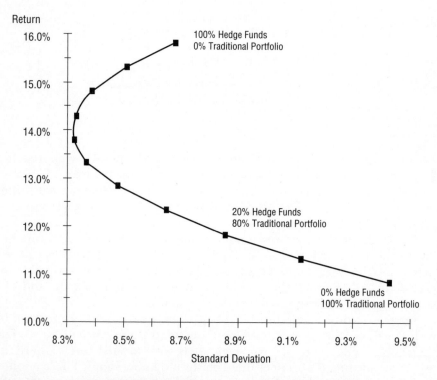

Figure 21.1   The Effect of Adding Hedge Funds to a Traditional Portfolio
Notes: Based on 1Q1988–3Q2003 data. Hedge fund statistics based on the Van Global Hedge Fund Index. Traditional portfolio = 60% S&P 500, 40% Lehman Brothers Aggregate Bond Index. Copyright © 2003 by Van Hedge Fund Advisors International, Inc., and/or its licensors, Nashville, TN, (615) 377-2949.

Van Hedge Fund Advisors. Van looks at returns from 1988 through the third quarter of 2002. This is a traditional efficient frontier chart. He assumes a 60–40 split for a traditional portfolio between the S&P 500 and the Lehman Brothers Aggregate Bond Index. Then he asks what would happen if you added various percentages of hedge funds to diversify the portfolio. He uses his own Van U.S. Hedge Fund Index as the proxy for hedge funds.

The figure shows that as you increase the proportion of hedge funds in your portfolio, you also increase the returns. Until you get about 40 to 50 percent of your portfolio in hedge funds, you also decrease your volatility. You can use varying proxies for stocks, bonds, and hedge funds, and the charts would all generally show the same thing. The addition of hedge funds simply improves a portfolio. Thus, it comes as no surprise that institutions and wealthy individuals are increasing the proportion of hedge funds in their portfolios.

The problem is that not all hedge funds are created equal, as we have shown, and there is even debate on how to measure hedge fund performance.

The primary strategy investors use to solve this problem is through diversification. But given the difficulty in finding and analyzing hedge funds, the high minimums and such, diversification can prove difficult for the individual or even smaller institutions. Increasingly, the answer has been to use a fund of funds approach to investing in hedge funds.

There are four main reasons that explain the popularity of funds of hedge funds even among the most sophisticated investors—access, liquidity, diversification, and research.

Access

Hedge funds have high minimum investment requirements, with some of the top funds being as high as $5 million to $10 million. That makes it difficult to get a diversified portfolio for all but the largest institutions. Yet, many funds of hedge funds have 50 or more funds in their portfolios, with much smaller minimums, ranging from $25,000 and up for publicly registered funds to $250,000 and up for private funds.

Appendix D describes the various levels of net worth required for investing in hedge funds. It is not always a million dollars (often it is more), and later in this chapter I talk about how average investors can now invest in a fund of funds. If you are looking to invest in a fund of funds, you should know what type of funds you'll be able to choose.

In hedge funds, not only are the minimums requirements high, but the fund may be closed even to investors who can meet the minimum. The fund of hedge funds helps to get around some of these obstacles. The most successful and popular funds may be what are referred to as "soft-closed." That is, the fund's official stance is that it is closed to new investors. Management may be getting close to the maximum amount it feels it can manage, or the fund may be running out of slots. However, even with a soft close, the managers may allow some money to come in from previously established or potentially new relationships that may be of strategic importance. Due to the amount that a fund of funds may commit to invest and the fact that the fund of funds is counted as one investor, the hedge fund will let the fund of funds have some allocation to the fund. The sponsoring organization of the fund of hedge funds can therefore give access to funds that would otherwise be closed to even the most affluent investors.

Liquidity

Another obstacle that the fund of hedge funds addresses is liquidity. While hedge funds can have a one-year or longer lockup period for the investor's money, most funds of hedge funds generally offer a shorter initial lockup period. After the initial lockup period, many hedge funds have quarterly, biannual, or annual redemption periods. The fund of hedge funds can reduce the redemption time to as often as monthly on the underlying investment funds. The fund of hedge funds offers the investor more liquidity in terms of moving one's money out of the fund.

(I should note that if every investor, or even most, within a fund of funds attempted to head for the exits at the same time, a fund that normally has monthly liquidity will not be able to meet that redemption standard. That is because the funds in which it invests have longer lockups.)

Diversification, Risk, and Returns

Let's talk about risk and diversification. Does a portfolio of just one stock have more risk than a portfolio of three stocks or 20 stocks? The answer is not necessarily. A portfolio of all Internet or technology stocks probably has more risk than an investment in a single water utility or preferred trust share in a large company in a stable industry.

Are there funds of funds with substantially more volatility than single hedge funds? Yes, there are. Investing in a fund of funds does not necessarily reduce your risk. It all depends on the underlying investments, whether they are stocks or hedge funds.

That being said, if you invest in a single manager hedge fund, you are exposed to single manager and/or single market event risk. No matter what the track record looks like, no matter how stable the history or how large the fund family, there is single manager and single market event risk.

Just as a previously solid company can have an unexpected downturn, so can a fund. You can limit the risk by investing only in funds on which you or your consultants have done thorough due diligence. You may even believe the risk to be quite small that the manager is going to have problems or that the fund strategy could produce large losses. But the risk is there. The fact that we will be surprised will come as small consolation if we lose a significant amount of money. A properly diversified fund of funds limits single manager risk, just as a properly diversified mutual fund limits single company risk.

Diversification also provides one other significant benefit: Properly executed, it should smooth out overall return.

Table 21.1 shows the annual returns for 10 different sectors of the stock market since 1990. Notice that the difference from the best to worst within the groups was never less than 30 percent, and was as high as 95 percent! It averaged over 50 percent, which is a huge differential. While technology did have a great run in the last part of the 1990s, much of those gains have been given up in the past three years. This underscores the argument for diversification within a stock market portfolio.

Table 21.2 shows the differences between the best- and worst-performing of 11 different styles of hedge funds. While the average difference is roughly half that of the stock market, it is a still considerable average difference of approximately 25 percent.

Going back to a chart we used last chapter, let's look at the returns in Figure 21.2, which are for the entire range of equity mutual funds* versus the entire range of hedge funds. We asked Morningstar to give us an index of all equity mutual funds, and took the Tremont index of all hedge funds.

If you refer again to Table 21.2 you can find some hedge funds styles that would have given superior performance to the entire index. But the question you must ask is, "Would I have been lucky enough to have chosen that style 10 years ago and to stick with it when the returns were not as good for two or more years?"

---

*This is an average of all U.S. diversified equity funds that fit with in the nine Morningstar style boxes, which include growth, value, blend, small-cap, mid-cap, and large-cap. It excludes any hybrid funds that include bonds and sector funds.

Table 21.1 Sector Selection Is Difficult with Equities: Wide Disparity of Returns between Best- and Worst-Performing Sectors

	1990	1991	1992	1993	1994	1995	1996	1997	1998	1999	2000	2001	2002	2003
Energy	(1.41)	2.39	(2.34)	11.15	(0.40)	25.97	21.74	22.01	(1.95)	15.96	13.23	(12.28)	(13.33)	22.39
Materials	(13.94)	21.54	7.21	10.55	3.32	17.29	13.38	6.30	(7.98)	22.96	(17.72)	1.00	(7.71)	34.77
Industrials	(10.30)	25.99	6.78	15.84	(4.76)	35.93	22.73	25.01	9.29	19.94	4.53	(7.00)	(27.57)	29.73
Consumer discretionary	(14.94)	38.26	17.46	12.80	(9.88)	18.19	10.55	32.32	39.56	24.06	(20.73)	1.95	(24.44)	36.08
Consumer staples	12.40	38.39	3.03	(6.27)	6.80	36.22	23.18	30.52	13.88	(16.58)	14.47	(8.30)	(6.31)	9.23
Health care	14.14	50.20	(18.08)	(10.98)	10.23	54.50	18.77	41.65	42.29	(11.64)	35.54	(12.94)	(19.97)	13.31
Financials	(24.39)	43.82	19.76	7.76	(6.39)	49.64	31.87	45.39	9.57	2.34	23.43	(10.53)	(16.42)	27.92
Information technology	0.47	6.61	0.58	20.45	19.11	38.77	43.27	28.13	77.64	78.43	(40.97)	(26.00)	(37.57)	46.55
Telecommunication services	(17.67)	7.89	11.01	10.85	(8.41)	37.33	(2.19)	37.14	49.26	17.41	(39.67)	(13.68)	(35.89)	3.28
Utilities	(7.31)	15.99	0.35	7.83	(17.15)	25.19	0.18	18.41	10.02	(12.83)	51.67	(32.47)	(32.99)	21.10
Δ Best to worst	38.53	47.81	37.83	31.43	36.26	37.20	45.45	39.09	85.62	95.02	92.64	34.42	31.27	43.27

Source: Standard & Poor's, "The S&P Hedge Fund Index—Balancing Representativeness and Investability." Data from Standard & Poor's, S&P 500 Sectors.

Table 21.2 Strategy Selection in the Absolute Return Universe: Wide Disparity of Returns between Best- and Worst-Performing Strategies

	1990	1991	1992	1993	1994	1995	1996	1997	1998	1999	2000	2001	2002	2003
Barclays CTA	21.02	3.73	-0.91	10.37	-0.65	13.64	9.12	10.89	7.01	-1.19	7.86	0.84	12.36	5.31
Convert Arb.	2.16	17.6	16.35	15.22	-3.73	19.85	14.56	12.72	7.77	14.41	14.5	13.37	9.05	8.89
Distressed	6.64	35.66	25.24	32.54	3.84	19.73	20.77	15.4	-4.23	16.94	2.78	13.28	5.28	26.77
Equity Hedge	14.43	40.15	21.32	27.94	2.61	31.04	21.75	23.41	15.98	44.22	9.09	0.4	-4.71	18.36
Equity Mkt. Neutral	15.45	15.65	8.73	11.11	2.65	16.33	14.2	13.62	8.3	7.09	14.56	6.71	0.98	2.78
Fix. Inc. Arb.	10.84	12.89	22.11	16.64	11.94	6.08	11.89	7.02	-10.29	7.38	4.78	4.81	8.78	8.00
Fix. Inc. Mortgage	—	—	—	14.55	11.61	16.57	17.08	17.31	-9.18	11.28	-1.37	21.17	8.62	6.43
Macro	12.56	46.66	27.17	53.31	-4.3	29.32	9.32	18.82	6.19	17.62	1.97	6.87	7.44	17.35
Merger Arb.	0.44	17.86	7.9	20.24	8.88	17.86	16.61	16.44	7.23	14.34	18.02	2.76	-0.87	7.20
Event Driven	11.19	17.84	10.77	12.62	4.67	14.25	19.63	19.36	10.14	-0.17	8.89	1.59	-3.17	3.36
Special Situations	-0.47	27.42	19.46	28.22	6	25.11	24.84	21.23	1.7	24.33	6.74	12.18	-4.3	22.86
Δ Best to Worst	21.49	42.93	28.08	42.94	16.24	24.96	15.72	16.39	26.27	25.52	19.39	20.77	17.07	23.99

Source: Standard & Poor's, "The S&P Hedge Fund Index—Balancing Representativeness and Investability." Data from HFR Indexes and Barclays CTA Index.

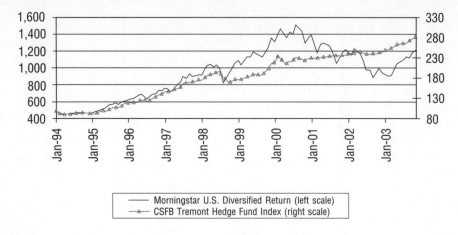

Fund	Volatility	1 Year	3 Year	5 Year	10 Year
CSFB/Tremont Hedge Fund Index	8.48%	15.46%	7.50%	9.96%	11.11%
Morningstar U.S. Diversified Return	16.28%	32.79%	−2.49%	3.29%	10.41%

Figure 21.2 CSFB Tremont Hedge Fund Index versus Morningstar U.S. Diversified Return

Source: Raw data from Credit Suisse First Boston Tremont Index LLC and Morningstar, Inc.

That brings us to the one of the more important questions when analyzing funds of funds: Which is the better management style—active or passive management?

Taking Charge or Along for the Ride?

In 2001, Morgan Stanley published a white paper on investing in funds of hedge funds. The research essentially concluded that since no one knows the future, and therefore one cannot know in advance which styles are going to do better than any others, it is best to have exposure to all styles. Since "every dog has its day," the odds are that some of those styles will be doing well, at least on a relative basis. The report showed, using historical returns, that doing this gives an overall return that is reasonable over time, and does so with very little volatility.

If you combine this strategy with selecting above-average managers within each style, you should be able to have an above-average fund of funds. There is a certain logic to this argument, and it certainly should serve to dampen volatility. There are a number of funds of funds that use such an approach. The Morgan Stanley model suggests 40 to 50 such funds is about the number of funds needed to smooth out returns and give proper diversification.

That same year, Alexander Ineichen of UBS Warburg[2] delivered a 134-page report entitled: "The Search for Alpha Continues—Do Fund of Hedge Funds Managers Add Value?" This report concluded that people should search for fund of funds managers who bring an edge to the evaluation process, but also should recognize that different objectives as to risk and return parameters would lead managers to create different allocation models. Fund managers who were more interested in capital preservation would allocate to lower-risk strategies and those who looked for higher returns would allocate to higher-risk strategies.

That dispersion of returns among styles can be quite large. The Alternative Asset Center (www.aa-center.net) has a very good fund of funds index. (See Table 21.3) Let me offer a few comments on their data.

First, notice that returns are not consistent. Investing in a fund of hedge funds is not investment nirvana. Second, there is a clear bias in the average fund of funds. Look at the high return years. They correspond with the bull market. That means that most funds of funds are "long-biased" the broad stock market.

Second, in other charts on the Alternative Asset Center web site, it is clear that the difference from the top 10 percent funds to the bottom 10 percent is significant. It averaged over 2 percent per month in 2003. In some years, like 1998, the difference can be as much as 5 percent per month. Of course, a fund can be in the top 10 percent in one month and the bottom 10 percent the next. In fact, it makes sense that this would be true, as to be in the best or worst group, the manager is probably seeking higher returns and is thus exposed to more volatility.

The UBS Warburg study just cited shows a chart of the steadiest fund of funds compared with the most volatile from 1995 through mid-2001. They roughly end up in the same place.

Now, let me describe a study by Standard & Poor's done on 446 funds of funds beginning in 1999. Of these, 112 funds fit into the top 25 percent or quartile for that year. The next year just 27 funds were still able to be in the top quartile, yet 51 of the previously best-performing group slipped into the worst quartile in 2000.

From 27 top quartile funds, we find that just three made the top quartile the next year (2001), and four years later (2002) there was just one fund that had been in the top quartile of funds of funds for four years running. Each year, almost double the number of funds dropped to the lowest quartile as remained in the top quartile.

Table 21.3 AAC Fund of Hedge Funds Benchmark

	Jan	Feb	Mar	Apr	May	Jun	Jul	Aug	Sep	Oct	Nov	Dec	YTD
2003	0.76%	0.54%	-0.02%	1.11%	1.90%	0.63%	0.07%	0.66%	1.17%	1.84%	0.32%	0.90%	10.34%
2002	0.45%	-0.15%	0.75%	0.55%	0.56%	-0.66%	-1.01%	0.42%	-0.25%	-0.37%	0.70%	0.79%	1.78%
2001	1.62%	0.16%	0.08%	0.54%	0.97%	0.11%	-0.15%	0.58%	-0.86%	0.78%	0.34%	0.88%	5.14%
2000	1.36%	5.01%	0.50%	-1.73%	-0.37%	1.92%	0.37%	2.23%	-0.14%	-0.30%	-0.62%	1.55%	10.05%
1999	1.32%	-0.01%	1.95%	3.06%	0.83%	2.77%	0.89%	0.26%	0.42%	1.00%	4.26%	5.19%	24.11%
1998	-0.22%	2.06%	3.03%	0.47%	-0.31%	0.08%	-0.12%	-5.06%	-0.87%	-0.58%	1.74%	1.87%	1.88%
1997	2.96%	1.67%	-0.27%	0.36%	2.26%	2.35%	4.12%	0.10%	2.55%	-0.86%	0.14%	1.53%	18.12%
1996	2.90%	0.17%	1.20%	2.67%	1.44%	0.57%	-1.48%	1.56%	1.57%	1.95%	2.53%	0.93%	17.15%

Choosing a Fund of Funds Manager

So does that mean choosing a better than average fund of funds manager is simply random luck? No, not at all.

Some would argue that the studies we have discussed suggest picking a more static fund of funds style, like that suggested in the Morgan Stanley study, is the way to go. Since all returns seems to regress to the mean over time, choose a fund whose target is the mean or slightly better. For some investors, that might be indeed the right approach. If your desire is to diversify your portfolio and to minimize volatility, that approach might be appropriate.

This approach is somewhat like investing in the S&P 500 index. Properly executed, you should get somewhere near the average.

However, you are not making use of the inherent advantage of the hedge fund marketplace, and that is the relative inefficiency of the markets. Figure 21.3 is from the UBS study. Notice the wide range of returns of hedge funds.

Quoting from the study, "Given that the hedge fund industry is opaque, i.e. inefficient, the more experienced and skilled fund of funds managers should have an edge over the less experienced and skilled. Given the high dispersion of returns between managers, hedge fund selection is most likely a value-added proposition.[3]

What that means is that there is the potential for fund of funds managers to add alpha because of their experience, relationships, and hedge

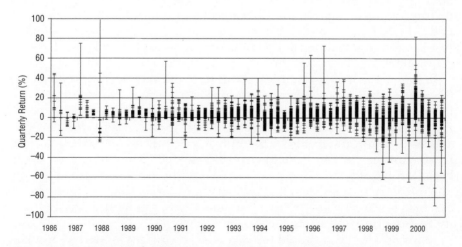

Figure 21.3   Dispersion of Fund of Funds Returns (1986–2000, Quarterly Returns)
Source: UBS (raw data from Quellos).

fund selection process. In this context, I do not refer to returns that are better than the S&P 500, but returns that are better than the hedge fund industry average or those of their peers.

So what does all this say as to how investors should choose and evaluate fund of funds managers? I think there are two clear implications.

1. Investors should look for managers whose clear intent and style reflects their own personal portfolio needs.
2. Investors should look for managers who demonstrate the ability to find, assess, and choose hedge funds that are best of breed.

There are fund of funds managers who by design target returns in the 6 to 8 percent range with very little volatility (whether they achieve it is, of course, another matter). While that may seem perfectly reasonable to some investors, others may want higher returns and are willing to take more risk and the occasional significant drawdown. Choosing a manager who does not meet with your original objectives will soon result in your looking for another manager.

Second, as Ineichen noted, experience and skill count in a game where there is as much clear inefficiency as there is in hedge fund selection. Running a fund of funds is not a game for rookies. Managers should have some serious familiarity with the hedge fund market, as well as research capability.

All that means that choosing a manager simply on past recent performance with the expectation of that performance continuing is probably not a good way to select a manager. If that is the model, then I expect that in the future Dalbar will do a study on fund of funds investors and find they do not make what the average fund of funds makes for the precise same reason mutual fund investors underperform: They chase recent returns.

In looking at managers, think about how well they actually understand the strategies in which they are investing (or are they just looking at performance numbers?); how well they understand the relationship between the investment strategy and the actual performance; and whether they appear to be on the inside of the industry or just use a database to find funds. Are they set up to market or to research? They should be doing both, but usually the same person won't do both. How thorough is the due diligence process? Finally, it goes without saying that you want to find a manager who is your "partner," someone you can trust to do the right thing. Integrity in a private business is everything.

In my opinion, you should find a manager who "fits" you, both from an objective style and because you believe in the manager. I would suggest, barring some new event or information, to stay with that manager for at least three years, and then reevaluate.

A good fund of funds should be the cornerstone of hedge fund investing for all but the largest institutions, which can in effect create their own fund of funds.

Rydex SPhinX

This chapter wouldn't be complete without mentioning the introduction last October by Rydex of a mutual fund that is essentially a fund of hedge funds. It is called the SPhinX Fund, and it invests in the S&P Hedge Fund Index. (Thus the odd spelling of SPhinX—**S&P H**edge Fund **In**de**x**.) Rydex has pushed the fund of fund's camel nose under the mass market tent with its introduction of the SPhinX Fund. This will open a floodgate of similar funds. Within a few years the world of hedge funds may be open to everyone, as it should be.

Basically, Rydex is exploiting a sort of loophole in the rules. Mutual funds can invest in indexes. S&P created an investable hedge fund index. This index is comprised of 40 different hedge funds across nine different strategies. These nine strategies make up three subindexes called the S&P Arbitrage Index, the S&P Event-Driven Index, and the S&P Directional/Tactical Index. Each of the subindexes has three of the nine strategies.

There was no attempt made to represent the entire hedge fund universe or to include all funds. S&P specifically excluded long-only strategies, emerging market funds, and Regulation D strategies (which makes sense, given what it is trying to do).

Starting with a universe of between 1,500 and 3,500 funds in those nine strategies, S&P eliminated small funds, funds that were closed, and funds that are not focused on one strategy, to come down to the 40 chosen funds.

Then S&P allocated exactly one-third of the Hedge Fund Index to each of these subindexes, and fixed amounts within each subindex to the specific funds.

Then, they worked with an investment platform called PlusFunds to create separate managed accounts for each of those subfunds, and that allows them to mark to market (price) on a daily basis, which is a requirement for mutual funds.

The funds they have chosen are large (average $665 million in assets), are well staffed, and have been in existence for some time. If you have been involved in the hedge fund world, they are recognizable names.

The fund is available to accredited investors, and can be purchased directly from Rydex or through Schwab and other similar firms. Or, if you are not an accredited investor, if you have an account managed by a registered investment advisor he can make the investment for you as part of his regular investment advice, after assessing your suitability for investing in the fund.

This is the first of many such funds. There are other firms that are now creating their own hedge fund indexes. There will soon be numerous subindexes as well, and then you will be able to invest in each of those as separate funds.

Probably the chief criticism of these funds will also be one of the main virtues. Because they have to create an artificial and investable index in order to create the mutual fund, they will be limited to established funds with good track records and which also have significant investment capacity. Is this good or bad for investors? Investors in these funds will by and large be smaller investors who should be taking less risk. Large investors will likely still seek the smaller private funds that have the ability to find and allocate to more niche strategies, which should give them an edge.

That being said, the Rydex fund charges only 1.95 percent. Do these other funds have enough edge to overcome what will for many be higher fees? Will the smaller fund managers have the clout that an S&P and its large brethren have in getting to the mainstream hedge funds? S&P has done a very solid job of choosing managers and diversifying risk. My bet is the fund will be successful and will spawn scores of competitors.

Eventually, the barriers to investing in hedge funds will come down. That can only be good for investors.

A Few More Facts

Before we leave this fund of hedge funds discussion, let's look at a few basic concepts.

Fund of Funds Structure

A fund of hedge funds is similar in concept to a mutual fund. The mutual fund pools money to invest in multiple stocks or bonds, while the fund of hedge funds pools money to invest in multiple hedge fund managers. A manager of a fund of hedge funds can drop or add hedge funds in the fund based on his own strategy and due diligence. The manager can diversify across managers in one strategy or multiple ones.

Some funds of funds will invest in more than 100 funds, in almost every conceivable strategy. Some will invest in as few as three, with all of the underlying funds being in narrowly focused strategies. While the reason for the former is fairly obvious, a more narrowly focused fund makes sense when you like a particular type of strategy (say convertible arbitrage) and want to limit your specific manager risk. I would expect to see certain investable indexes created of these more narrow strategies within the next few years.

Fees

The range of the fees that a fund of hedge funds might charge is all over the board. Some charge a flat 1 percent of money under management and no incentive fee (or portion of the profits). Others charge no management fee and charge only an incentive fee, sometimes as high as 25 percent. More than likely the funds will charge in the ranges of a management fee of 1 to 2 percent and 10 to 20 percent of the profits.

These are fees on top of the underlying hedge fund fees. However, the individual investor is sacrificing these fees for the benefits mentioned earlier. Professional money management and due diligence come at a price, but the price may be less than the risk of too little diversification or not enough proper due diligence.

A Few Thoughts on the Risk in a Fund of Funds

Typically I find that investors look at past performance and track records when choosing funds. They probably ask fewer questions for a fund of funds than they do with a single manager fund, thinking there is less risk. That is not always the case.

As I mentioned earlier, investing in a fund of funds is not nirvana. There are some risks you should ask about when looking at a fund of funds.

First, I would always ask how and when leverage is being used. If it is, is the leverage applied across the board to all funds on an equal basis, or only to selected funds? For instance, one legitimate use of such selective leverage might be to increase the returns of funds that use lower-volatility strategies and to not do so with higher-risk funds. But what if there is serious overleverage in just one or two hot funds, which have provided all the apparent returns without showing any obvious risk, waiting to show up when you invest?

Also, some funds of funds use as much as four times leverage. While this might not statistically increase the risk all that much on a fund that contained 75 different, equally weighted funds, it might be disastrous for a fund with only 10 target funds. (If one fund imploded, it could drop the value of the fund of funds by 40 percent.)

Make sure you know what are the largest percentage holdings of a fund of funds. There is nothing wrong (and indeed it might be exactly what you want) with a fund of funds that has 30 to 40 percent invested in a single fund, but you need to know that before you invest.

It may be that a fund's fine performance is due to one or two outstanding investments. Are these funds still taking money? Was part of the performance of the fund built on the track records of funds in which it can no longer invest, or which have since returned money?

The track records of some funds of funds may look steady, but if they are concentrated in just one strategy, then you have strategy risk. If that is what you are seeking, then that may be a good thing. But that is significantly different from a fund of funds like the SPhinX fund, which equally weights nine different strategies with 40 funds.

As with all hedge funds, you want to know about cash controls, independent administrators and auditors, and references.

As an observation, not all fund of funds managers will reveal the specific funds in which they are invested, for good reason. If you work hard to find that special manager, why share that with your competitors, especially if he has limited capacity? But they should be willing to give you a percentage breakdown by strategy of the underlying investment portfolio.

In short, look under the hood before you buy.

Doing Your Due Diligence 22

It's not what we know that will cause problems for our investments.
It's what we don't know that always causes the disasters.

D ue diligence is the process of investigating a fund or investment opportunity before you invest. It is the most important element of the investment process but is often ignored by many investors.

Although much of the material in this chapter is technical, it is important information that will help you understand all your investments, not just hedge funds, so I urge you to keep reading.

"Hedge fund investors don't always understand what they're investing in. According to a study by Prince & Associates, three-fourths of the 384 affluent hedge fund investors surveyed didn't know their hedge fund's investment style or if they used leverage. And according to the study, those who didn't know, didn't want to know. But it makes for good cocktail chatter. Just pass the shrimp, please."[1]

In nearly every case of hedge fund fraud, the investors simply did not do their homework. That's exactly why conducting a due diligence process like the one I describe in this chapter is so valuable.

If you go through the process, it is much more likely you will end up with a fund or manager that is a match for your goals and fits into your investment philosophy. You won't be having to jump from fund to fund, manager to manager, chasing last year's earnings. You will know what to expect, and won't get nervous when the occasional drawdown occurs. You will also have an idea of what situations—and not your emotions—will cause you to exit the fund.

This chapter focuses on the due diligence process for hedge funds, but the principles are the same for mutual funds or investment managers. Many of the questions that may focus specifically on hedge funds have their corollaries when looking at investment managers and mutual funds.

Finding a good hedge fund is not easy, in part because there is no central source for listing funds. There are at least 6,000 hedge funds and private pools by the latest estimates, and some knowledgeable industry analysts now put that number at closer to 8,000. Less than a third are in the public databases. (A third of the hedge funds in my fund of funds do not list themselves in the public databases.)

There are a variety of styles among hedge funds. Finding the style that is right for your investment needs is critical. Some hedge funds managers are good and some are just lucky. You do *not* want to invest in the lucky one, as luck always runs out, typically just after you invest. There is any number of ways that managers can hide problems in their management styles. It is important to uncover them before you invest. Hedge funds are businesses. The business side of the fund is just as important as the investment side. Are the managers good businessmen as well as smart investors?

The Due Diligence Process

Institutional investors, family offices, and investment advisors like myself usually have a lengthy list of questions we ask prospective funds and managers. These questions are designed to give us the information we need to evaluate the fund. Further, they help us decide between funds that are similar in style and performance. There are hundreds of market neutral and long-short equity hedge funds. Choosing one or another can be difficult.

As an example, I might want a 15 to 20 percent exposure to convertible arbitrage in my fund. There are scores of such funds, and a number of them may make it through the initial screening rounds. On the surface, the funds may look alike. They may even have similar trading styles. What would make me choose one fund over another? Which fund has the best edge? In many cases, it comes down to comfort levels. How much confidence do I have that my money (and that of my clients!) is being managed well and is safe?

While writing this chapter, I sent an e-mail to a number of my friends in the hedge fund community, and asked them to send me their due diligence questionnaires. I also asked a number of hedge funds to send me some of the questionnaires they get that they thought were particularly good. As you might suspect, the majority of the questions were similar. But what was interesting to me were the differences.

Most of the forms had one or two sets of questions designed to ferret out a particular set of issues or problems. My deep suspicion is that these differences were brought about by the authors having experienced an unpleasant relationship, and the questions were designed to avoid that problem in the future. I must confess that my own forms were not an exception to this rule.

I began to compile and organize the questions into one due diligence document. I was amazed at the length of the document as I finished. I decided I must cut the number of questions down, as they numbered over 100, and many were multipart.

The problem was, however, that as I reviewed the document over a few weeks, each piece of information was important, and gave further insight into the company or comfort about the safety of the money invested.

The questions are designed to give us insight into the fund on several different levels. The most important thing to understand about a fund is "Why" it makes money. If you cannot understand the "Why" of a fund, you should not be investing. This is the critical question that will help you understand what the dominant factor in performance of the fund is: skill or luck. As I stated earlier, luck always runs out, typically just after you invest. More funds are based on luck or random chance than you might think, but I can guarantee you no fund manager will admit it, and most of them would be insulted if you said so. Genius is a rising market, and good performance has persuaded more than a few managers they are geniuses. Avoiding such genius is crucial to capital preservation. Finding true investment ability (genius or not) is the secret to capital growth.

The next most important question is "How" the fund makes money. What are the strategies and systems used, and what is the risk taken?

If you can get a good feeling about those two questions, then you follow up with the more mundane but critical questions of "Who," operational issues, structure, safety of assets, and, of course, performance.

Rather than try to creatively present these questions, I will simply list them, along with comments on the ones that are not obvious. As you read through this list, think about the investments you already have.

Remember, too, that having the answers to these questions is not enough to truly evaluate a fund. Whenever possible, I want to visit with the management of the fund at their offices. I want to get to know the people who will be managing my money.

I will not invest with someone I don't like or if there is some question left unresolved in my mind, even if it is only intuition. No matter how good the track record looks, or how compelling the story, I simply walk away.

That doesn't mean I have to get warm and cuddly feelings. I am not expecting to be their best friend. On the contrary, it is quite possible that I will someday have to redeem my money from them, and getting too close can make that process difficult. In general, it is better to keep the relationship on a positive professional basis. (That being said, most of the people I deal with are genuinely nice and a pleasure to be with.)

I am a pretty easygoing guy. Like Will Rogers, I have never met a man I didn't like. Many of the best traders and managers are not "people" persons, or they may be intensely iconoclastic, shy, or introverted. But they are still nice people with good ethics and standards. I always try to give everyone the benefit of the doubt.

But sometimes after meeting a potential manager, I develop a sense that this is not a person with whom I want to do business. Something just doesn't feel right, even though I cannot always put a finger on it. It is always a wise thing to "go with your gut." That is advice, by the way, that is given and followed by many professionals in my position.

Unfortunately, there is nothing like a standard due diligence form. Frankly, if you are a smaller investor, the chances of you getting a fund to answer all these questions is slim. But it is likely they have similar forms, and many of them will send you one of the forms they have filled out. If you are using a consultant or a fund of funds to do your due diligence on your behalf, it might be useful to see what form they are using.

(My comments are in italics so as to distinguish them from the questions.)

DUE DILIGENCE QUESTIONNAIRE

A. General Information

1. Company Name:
2. Fund(s) or Program(s) Name(s):
3. Offshore/Domestic Sister Fund:
4. Manager(s):
   Address(es):
5. Primary Contact(s):
6. Phone:
7. Fax:
8. E-Mail/Web Site Address:

B. Business Structure

1. Describe the origins and history of the company. Who were the founders of the company, and are they still active? Are there any new principals? If relevant, describe the important events and experiences of management that give the company its "edge."

Every fund manager, almost without exception, will tell you they have a "proprietary system" that gives them their "edge" or ability to profitably trade. This question is the start of the process of trying to determine what their edge is. These funds are charging very high fees, and they should bring some edge, knowledge, or ability to the table that will truly add to their performance. Presumably you are looking at them because their performance is good. (We seldom look at funds with bad performance.)

You want to find a reason that their performance is good. More often than most of us would like to admit, good performance in a fund or investment has been a result of random chance and not because of good investment practice and skills. Their positive returns simply benefited from being in the right market at the right time. As an example, the literature for the Janus 20 technology mutual fund in which my wife had some of her money in the late 1990s told us their performance was due to their exceptional ability to analyze companies. When management was still telling her the same thing in 2001, it began to have a hollow sound.

Their returns had more to do with a bubble in technology stocks and a lack of diversification (which made them exceptionally risky) than any ability to pick stocks. They were in the right place at the right time. Mind you, there is nothing wrong with that. We are all trying to find the sweet spot. But they confused luck with skill, and didn't move when it became the wrong place. Many of the questions you will read here are designed to help us try to see whether we are dealing with luck or skill.

2. Describe the ownership structure of the company and its affiliated companies, including marketing arms (an organizational chart would be helpful). Include a description of the division of power and authority of the principals.

   This is designed to give you a feel for the organization. For instance, I generally like to see someone besides the manager doing the marketing. While I may talk with the manager at some point, if he is spending too much time marketing, he is not managing my money. I want to see staff in charge of compliance, administration, and operations, generally someone who is not responsible for trading or investing. These can be time-consuming activities, and if a manager is doing them all or a part of them, he is not focused on the most important thing, and that is making me money.

3. What is the length of the current business structure, and have there been any changes?

4. What is the number of decision makers? Who are they and what is their tenure? Who is on the investment committee? Who and how many research analysts are employed?

5. What are the primary sources of investment information/resources used by the firm, and how are they utilized? Are these provided by suppliers or paid for independently? Does the fund use consultants? Are they paid for by the fund or by the management firm?

   Does management create its own system, or do they rely on outside sources for trading direction? Some managers simply follow models developed by other managers, or follow trading services. How much discretion does a manager use if they employ such services? Funds of this type are not really adding value. Many brokerage firms supply costly information services in return for trading business. Later on, we will want to know at what level the fund is paying commissions.

6. Please provide biographies/resumes of the principals and key employees. (Please include current residence; past employers; colleges/universities attended; marital status/children, outside activities and organizations, etc.)

   How busy are the managers? You want to know something about their personal lives, especially in smaller organizations, because major changes in someone's life can have an impact on how they trade. Are there stabilizing factors in their lives like family or church? In conversations I like to know what they read for pleasure, what kind of activities they go to, where they spend vacations, and so on. You are trying to get to know the person and see if there is a balance. For large funds with dozens of traders and staff this is not as critical, but many (if not most) funds are smaller, and the behavior of key personnel can have a major impact on the fund.

7. How many are on staff (by division) and what is their background? (Trading desks, operations/administration, etc.)

8. Have you ever lost any key personnel and if so, why?

   In smaller firms, this can be a key question. The track record may be due to someone who is no longer with the firm. One of the warning signs I look for is the departure of key personnel. I once avoided a fund, which by all appearances was doing well, because the marketing director left just as the marketing was getting easy. No one could give me a good reason for his departure, and he was under an agreement not to speak. The fund later developed problems.

9. What plans, if any, are there if a key person was to become unavailable for an extended length of time? Are there any health problems among key personnel? How often do principals and key personnel have physicals?

10. Do all professionals in the firm have an exclusive contract with the firm? In what outside business activities are the principals and key employees engaged?

11. Summarize the turnover (by departures and new hires) of investment professionals for the past three years, by year.

12. Are the principals and staff investors in the fund? What is the approximate percentage of the principals' net worth invested in the fund?

    This is a very important question. I want to see if the managers have a large portion of their personal assets in the fund.

13. Are any of the principals or staff related? Does the firm do business with outside vendors with family connections?

    If there are family connections, then you need to ask about fees, costs, and so on. Since most funds have the investors pay the administrative costs, you want to make sure these are done at arm's-length negotiated fees.

14. Please describe the general principles for principal/employee compensation. Who in the firm receives incentives?

15. How direct is the relationship between compensation and power?

    These two questions are key. Many funds use a number of traders and analysts. If key personnel are not properly rewarded, they will eventually leave for greener pastures. Obviously, that's not a trend you want to see. But you also want to make certain that traders are not given an incentive to take large risks. Good trading talent is a rare thing, and needs to be nurtured.

16. Does the firm use outside (third-party) marketing firms? Are the terms for clients introduced by these firms different than those who come to the firm directly? Are outside marketers paid by annual flat fees or by a percentage of the income from the money they raise?

    It's all about the money. Let's say you are introduced by a third-party marketer who gets 25 percent of the fee income. When the fund gets close to capacity, the fund managers may be tempted to to forcibly redeem you and take money from another person from whom they get full fees. This also let's you know if management is open to negotiation on fees. While smaller investors have little ability to negotiate, larger funds and investors might be able to find some wiggle room, especially with newer funds.

17. What is the size of assets under management? What were the assets under management at the beginning of the last five years?

    a. Fund assets.   b. Strategy assets.   c. Total firm assets.

18. At what size will the fund/strategy stop accepting new money, and why will you stop at this level?

Is the fund growing too fast? How much new money can the fund actually put to work in any one given month? Is there a discernible negative correlation between growth and earnings? Growing too fast can seriously dilute earnings for some hedge fund strategies. Other strategies can only be effective at certain levels. When the funds grow beyond that level, they begin to dilute earnings. While this may allow the manager to make more money, it does not help the investor. Interestingly, if a manager has a large part of his own money in the fund, diluting earnings can cost him money, which is why you want to know how much they have in the fund.

19. What is the current client mix?

a. What is the approximate number of clients?

b. What is the mix between institutional, fund of funds, and individual accounts?

c. What is the mix between managed accounts and fund investments?

d. What is the percentage of assets controlled by your five biggest investors (or consultants, should they control/influence more than one investor)?

e. What percentage of your investors are onshore versus offshore?

f. What is the turnover of your investors?

Different investors may have different priorities. If one class dominates a fund, the temptation might be to skew the fund management to please those clients. If the fund is dominated by several large investors, how reliable and stable are they? Are they "hot money"? If a fund is susceptible to losing several large investors, it could seriously change the income structure of the fund manager. Having to let go employees and cut back on services could impair the fund severely. While this may not be an issue, if there is a large concentration among a few investors, you will want to closely watch assets under management on a monthly basis.

20. What are the current and next priorities for the firm (asset growth, increase/improvement in staffing, implementation of new trading strategies/programs, etc.)? How do you intend to make them happen, and who is responsible for implementation?

A hedge fund is a business. Every well-managed business has goals and priorities. Are the ones of the fund reasonable? Will they help the fund become more profitable?

21. Is the fund particularly advantageous or disadvantageous for tax-exempt investors or taxpaying investors?

C. Strategy Information

This section is quite critical. This is where we try to find out if the managers are gunslingers who have just been lucky or have a reproducible trading system. We are trying to find out if the track record was the result of a favorable trading climate, which will always change, or if the managers have a strategy for all seasons. If you want to keep from chasing the latest hot track record, only to find that the managers cool off when you get in the fund, this is where you must begin.

You can't know until you "look under the hood" if a strategy is right for your portfolio. Simply knowing that a fund is a convertible arbitrage or a fixed income fund is not enough. There are many ways to trade fixed income or convertible bonds. For instance, some fixed income funds are designed to make money when credit spreads are narrow and others prefer widening credit spreads. While the track records may even look similar, the underlying strategy can be as different as night and day. If you are putting together a portfolio of funds and want exposure to more than one fixed income fund, you will look for funds that have different trading strategies. Putting two funds in a portfolio that use the same strategy is not true diversification.

This section also let's me keep one of the basic rules for fund investing: never invest in a fund if you can't understand what they are doing, or if they won't explain what they do. Some investors are comfortable with "black boxes." I am not. Maybe it is the anecdotal evidence I have picked up over the years, but it seems like the funds which have the most problems are the ones with "black box" strategies.

Now I must confess that there are some strategies I simply cannot understand. While I can grasp the concepts generally, the details are simply out of my experience level. If everything else checks out, then I bring in an outside consultant or a friend who is experienced in that market and have them meet with the manager. I frequently find that the third party can explain the concepts to me.

1. Describe the trading approach or strategies used. If there is more than one approach used for the fund under review, please specify the differences between the various systems and upon what basis capital is allocated to each approach.

Some funds are one-trick ponies. For certain styles, that is good, and you want to make sure they stick to their knitting. Other types of funds need multiple trading strategies for different investment climates. An equity-

based hedge fund that never changes its strategy to conform to the volatility of the market is going to disappoint you in the future.

2. What trading/investment instruments are used?

3. What drives the performance?

Not knowing the correct answer to this question can cost you money. For instance, one of the steadiest high-performing hedge funds in the 1990s was a market timing fund. But after October 2000, its fund performance went flat.

The fund was very good throughout the years at avoiding large losses, and still is, but its particular system appears to need a bull market to actually make a profit. If your view is that we are a long way from the next bull market, the funds like this should be avoided. The difficulty is in spotting that trend (the need for a bull market) prior to its development.

If the performance is tied to certain types of economic environments or market volatility, then you have to ask yourself, how likely is it that that climate will continue in the future? Does the fund manager have a plan to adapt to new environments other than waiting for things to change? Does he have the demonstrated skill sets needed to function in a different type of investment climate, or will he be educating himself on your money?

4. Have there been any material changes to the investment approach used for the fund during the performance record period (reduced/increased leverage, new parameters, new markets)?

Many hedge fund managers are constantly tinkering with their trading systems. If there have been changes, you want to know why and for how long has the new, improved version been in place. You also want to know how the manager determined to make a change. Some changes, based on back-tested data, can produce wonderful theoretical results, only to have the climate change resulting in large losses. If changes, such as the use of leverage, are the result of a manager's discretion or "feel" for risk, you want to know what criteria is used to make that change, and how comfortable you are with the decision-making process.

5. How is money made or lost?

6. What is your firm's edge or expertise? What makes your strategy unique?

7. What percentage of trading does each strategy represent? (Give ranges if applicable.)

8. What percentage of trading is in nonlisted instruments?

9. What percentage of trading would you deem to be "illiquid" instruments?

   You want to make sure the liquidity of the fund's assets and their redemption policy are compatible. If investor's begin leaving a fund with a large portion of illiquid assets, you probably don't want to be left holding the bag.

10. What is the best market environment for your trading?

11. What conditions cause "normal" losses for you? Unusually "large" losses?

12. What would you consider to be an abnormal loss, and what would cause this to occur?

13. What efforts are made to limit the losses mentioned in questions #11 and #12? Is it automatic or discretionary?

14. How large of a loss can a position sustain before it will be closed out? Is there a risk control element in place at all times (i.e., a constant hedge of some amount)?

15. How many positions are typically in the portfolio?

16. How much capital can be allocated per position (to the best ideas)? What is the highest percentage of the capital that can/will be devoted to a single position?

17. What is the methodology to invest new assets relative to existing positions, and over what time frame do new assets get invested?

18. What process is employed for a withdrawal, redemption, or cutback in equity?

19. Is leverage used, and if so how much? How do you define/calculate leverage?

20. Will leverage be used to increase the position size of only certain positions, or is it allocated to all positions?

21. Please provide the maximum historical leverage, minimum historical leverage, maximum authorized leverage, and typical leverage employed. If leverage fluctuates, who determines the level of leverage at any one time and on what basis?

22. If applicable, please give the option adjusted spread, option adjusted duration, and option adjusted convexity of the portfolio, along with their target ranges.

23. How long would it take, with normal conditions, to liquidate the fund's entire portfolio, and what would be the effect on net asset value (NAV)?

24. Who are your primary lenders/sources of financing? Are you trading in the name of the fund with your source of financing?

25. Does the leverage create income subject to unrelated business income tax (UBIT)?

    This applies to pension funds and IRAs. These investors will need to use an offshore vehicle if they want to get into a fund that uses leverage.

26. Where do most of the trading/investment ideas come from?

27. Give a life process of a trade both profitable and unprofitable.

28. How long is the track record, and what is the historical monthly performance?

29. When does the track record begin?

    a. Is any of it pro forma? If so, give details as to how and on what basis the numbers were produced.

    b. Is all of it audited?

    c. Is it net of all fees?

30. Questions concerning volatility: Was an annual return generated by large gains in one or two months? Or was the annual gain spread across the period? Examine the peak to valley drawdowns. How long did it take you to recover? How volatile is the fund relative to its peers? If more volatile, please validate the excess risk. Why did a recovery occur? Did you change your strategy? Or did market conditions improve?

31. Questions concerning breadth: Did you turn an even profit in all issues, or has there been a concentration that accounted for the majority of the gains of the fund at any one time? What is the average number of investments in the portfolio? What is the breakdown in terms of long and short?

32. Questions concerning repetition: Is the fund's investment process easily repeatable, or did an isolated incident cause the fund to report good performance? What has to happen for the performance to be able to repeat (good analysis, availability of certain investment instruments, opportunities, etc.)?

33. What benchmark do you feel is most appropriate against which to measure performance? Why?

34. If a trading model or strategy is used, under what conditions do you override the model?

35. Please discuss the circumstances of the three largest drawdowns. Were there any changes in the overall strategy as a result?

36. Have there been changes in your trading strategy that would render a portion of your track record less meaningful to a current evaluation?

37. Who is responsible for executing the trades (provide name and experience) and do they have any discretion over the assets in the strategy?

38. Do you perform stress tests on the portfolio?

Risk Analysis (Please answer all applicable and/or relevant questions)

This is important, and not just for the obvious point that controlling risk is a key to good investing. Sometimes, when building a portfolio, you can take funds or managers who have such uniquely different approaches to a particular investment market that the combination of the two reduces risk. You can't determine this by just doing correlation analysis. You have to acquire a basic understanding of how a fund creates risk, and how it controls it.

Second, by understanding the nature of the risk, you can see how that risk corresponds to other types of risk in your portfolio. Different funds, with seemingly different investment strategies, may all have risk from a specific event, such as a widening credit spread or a rise in interest rates. It is only as you know the specific event risks of each fund in your portfolio that you can see if you are overexposed in your total portfolio,

As you ask these questions, you also want to find out how a manager deals with risk on a personal level. Is the manager a Cool Hand Luke or is he simply indifferent, trusting his models and analysis? If a manager does not have active risk controls in place, which he can clearly explain to you, avoid the fund like the plague.

1. How do you identify/quantify risk?

2. How do you control or manage risk?

3. Please describe the maximum, average range, and value as of (current date) for the portfolio gross long position (percent of portfolio assets).

4. Please describe the maximum, average range, and value as of (current date) for the portfolio gross short position (percent of portfolio assets).

5. Please describe the maximum, average range, and value as of (current date) for the portfolio net position (percent of portfolio assets).

Why the three questions? Because some funds could generate their returns on the long positions, but have more risk in their short positions. Depending on what they trade, if the market climate changed, you could be taking more risk with less opportunity for reward.

6. Please describe the maximum, average range, and value as of (current date) for the portfolio beta.

Beta is important, especially if we are in a long-term secular bear market. Beta is the statistic used to denote market correlation. Beta numbers range from 1 to –1. A beta of 1 means the fund performs exactly as the index against which it is measured. A beta of –1 means it performs in the exact opposite manner. A beta of 0 means there is no correlation between the fund and the index. In general, most investors want a low beta in a hedge fund. If you were looking for a high beta, you could probably find that in a mutual fund, with far lower fees.

You have to be careful with beta. I remember reading somewhere that a management group did an analysis of hundreds of varying economic indicators, looking for a reliable predictor of the markets. Supposedly, the most statistically reliable factor was the price of butter in Bangladesh. Beta is useful, but you need to determine why a low beta exists and that it is not just a random factor.

7. Please describe the maximum, average range, and value as of (current date) for the largest single position concentration (percent of portfolio assets).

8. Please describe the maximum, average range, and value as of (current date) for the country concentration (percent of portfolio assets).

9. Please describe the maximum, average range, and value as of (current date) for the sector net exposure (percent of portfolio assets).

10. Please describe the maximum, average range, and value as of (current date) for the number of long positions in the portfolio.

11. Please describe the maximum, average range, and value as of (current date) for the number of short positions in the portfolio.

12. Please describe the maximum, average range, and value as of (current date) for the annual portfolio turnover.

13. Please describe the maximum, average range, and value as of (current date) for the portfolio accounting leverage (total long and total short/contributed capital).

14. How do these levels compare over the past 12 months to the fund's historical exposure?

D. Product Characteristics

This is mostly about basics, but what you are looking for is the existence of something that is unusual. Is the auditor a small local CPA firm? Why a particular law firm? After a while, you start to see the same names, and that makes you comfortable.

In fact, I would rather see an audit from a firm like Arthur Bell or Rothstein, Kass than from a Big Four. The large firms often change lead partners, or send a different accountant every few years. I like to see boutique specialist firms who know what to look for when they audit a fund, and don't have a large personnel turnover.

When you call the lawyers, CPAs, administrators, and custodians, try to get the actual staff who work on the account. You might be surprised what you can find out about a fund and its history, how well they handle their paperwork and so on, just from talking with the people they hire. If you get a funny feeling in your conversation, it should raise a big red flag. If the fund has changed auditors or administrators recently, you want to know why, and you want to call the old firm.

1. Structure (LP, LLC, Ltd, master feeder, C.3.1, C.3.7, etc.).

2. Fees (management, incentive, hurdle rates, high water mark, other).

3. Subscription policy: minimums, timing, fees charged? Do you have specific terms or arrangements for funds of hedge funds? Family offices? Large investors? Are all investors in the fund charged the same fees?

In a study done by Infovest, 31 percent of hedge funds said they were negotiable on fees and 43.7 percent of funds of hedge funds said they were negotiable on fees. Mostly, the negotiated fees are for larger investors. But you want to ask.

4. Redemption policy: What would be the timing of repayment, and would there be any fees charged? Describe lockup period, notice periods, terms of payout, and so on.

5. Does the lockup period match the liquidity of the investments in the fund?

6. Are there any other fee structures, or business arrangements between the firm and/or the principals and employees and any other party, either directly or indirectly, involving rebates, and so on?

		Yes	No
7. a. Accepted investors:	U.S. Citizen	___	___
	U.S. Tax-Exempt Entity	___	___
	ERISA Accounts	___	___
	Foreign Entities	___	___
b. Suitability requirements:	Accredited	___	___
	Qualified Purchaser	___	___
	Superqualified	___	___

8. Auditor:

   Contact:

   Address:

   Phone:

9. Legal counsel:

   Contact:

   Address:

   Phone:

10. Prime broker and clearing:

    Contact:

    Address:

    Phone:

11. Custodian (if different than above):

    Contact:

    Address:

    Phone:

12. Offshore administrator:

    Contact:

    Address:

    Phone:

13. Explain your process for choosing your custodian, administrators, and prime brokers. Are there any soft-dollar arrangements? How long have you known and worked with them? Were there previous relationships with any of them?

14. What are the fees for the various parties listed above?

15. Explain your process for choosing your auditors. How long have you known and worked with them? Were there previous relationships with any of them? Does the same person perform the audit each year? Have there ever been any problems with the audits? Have you changed auditors? What are the fees?

16. How does the auditor track the fund's assets during an audit? (Follow the cash; reconciling each trade; confirmation of asset levels; verbal/written confirmation with custodian.)

E. Operations/Trading

A brilliant manager who can't follow through on the paperwork is a disaster in the making. As noted elsewhere, you want to know who is making the decision on how to value the funds' assets, and what methodology they use. Are there any potential conflicts of interest? And, of course, what disaster preparations and backup procedures are in place?

1. With what custodian/prime brokers are the assets of the fund maintained? Are all assets, including cash, held in custody with a third party? Explain how fund assets may be moved and invested. What are your policies and procedures to safeguard fund assets (third party signatures, multiple signatures, etc.)?

2. How do you assure that all accounts are traded pari passu (on an equal basis)?

3. Does the firm or any principal trade for its/their own account?

4. Will daily or weekly NAV estimates be provided upon request? Discuss accounting and reporting procedures. Does the administrator calculate the NAV? From whom does the administrator get the data (direct feed from the prime broker, multiple direct feeds, the manager, the prime broker confirmed by the manager, or other)?

5. Who prices your portfolio, and how is the valuation/pricing done (marked to market, independent valuation, pricing service, bid list)?

6. Is there subjective pricing (i.e., illiquid or thinly traded securities)? If so, who is responsible for establishing pricing? Describe the process.

7. For the purposes of providing estimates, how is valuation/pricing done (marked to market, independent valuation, pricing service, bid list)?

8. How soon after the end of the reporting period is the "final" month-end NAV provided?

9. List and provide samples of all reports and regular correspondence sent to your investors and the frequency with which they were sent.

10. How often are audits conducted? Were there any factors in the past that caused a variance?

11. When do K1's come out?

12. What transparency is available?

    a. Open position reports.

    b. Summary information.

    c. Dialogue only.

    d. Other/describe.

    e. None.

13. Explain what internal records (investor records, accounting records, etc.) are kept and in what form they are maintained. What security procedures are in place for these records?

14. How will "emergency" situations be handled? Do you have written emergency policies? Detail backup procedures.

    a. Loss of principal(s) or key personnel?

    b. Natural disasters such as power outages, destruction of offices, and so on?

    c. Is there an off-site facility for record storage and trading capability?

F. Daily Order Entry (if applicable)

1. Who determines what and when orders are placed? If unavailable, then who supervises order placement?

2. Who receives telephone confirmation on fills?

3. Are lines taped?

4. What is your procedure for handling execution errors?

5. Are written confirms received and reviewed? By whom?

6. Are term sheets for over-the-counter (OTC)/structured deals reviewed prior to entering the trade? If yes, by whom?

7. What information is received from brokers on a daily basis?

8. Are monthly brokerage statements received and reviewed? Are broker reconcilements prepared?

9. Describe all procedures (including timing), for processing a trade settlement and checkout.

   a. What controls are in place to protect against settlement risk?

   b. What procedures are in place to monitor unsettled trades?

10. What types of orders are placed to initiate positions (market, limit orders, stops, etc.)?

    a. How are split-price fills allocated across accounts?

    b. In the event of a partial fill, how would the allocations to multiple accounts be handled?

    c. How do you evaluate your methods for allocating positions and rotating split-price fills to determine that no account is favored by such procedure?

G. Compliance Section

1. Who handles compliance issues? Do you have an internal compliance officer?

2. Are registrations with any agencies required? If yes, which ones and are you properly registered?

3. Do you trade futures contracts? If yes what percentage? Are you registered with the Commodity Futures Trading Commission/National Futures Association (CFTC/NFA)? If not, please attach a copy of exemption request letter from CFTC/NFA.

4. Is there an independent monitor or an internal monitor to ensure that the terms of the fund's offering are being upheld, in terms of fair and equal fee distribution, fair and equal liquidity constraints, maintenance of the minimum investment, and maintenance of reporting timeliness?

5. What is the firm's policy and procedures regarding the trading of employees' personal and family-related accounts as well as the policy against "front-running"?

6. Are there or have there ever been any pending complaints, proceedings, disciplinary actions, or litigation against the firm, its advisor, its principals, associated persons, employees, or any firm managed by the advisor or its principals?

7. Explain circumstances surrounding any pending or threatened litigation or any unresolved customer complaint of any nature against the firm or any of its principals.

8. What relationships do you have that could be conceived as having the potential for a conflict of interest (brokers, accounting, auditors, sales reps, clients, or others)?

H. References and Legal Documents

References are key. Many analysts use the professional references given by the fund as a starting point. They ask the given references for other references they might think useful. On more than one occasion, I have found the second-level reference to be far more informative than the given references.

Not all funds will provide a list of other investors. They have to get permission to do so, and many investors simply do not want their names given out.

1. Could you please provide us with the names, addresses, and contact numbers of two persons who are currently invested in your fund?

2. Could you please provide us with at least three references for each of the principals, both personal and professional?

3. Could you please provide us with the following legal documents:

   a. Memorandum of association, prospectus, and subscription documents of the fund.

   b. Certificate of good standing for the fund.

   c. Latest audited financial statements for the fund.

   d. Articles of incorporation of your company.

Summary:

Simply getting responses to all of the preceding questions will not ensure that an investment in any given fund will be a success.

But, with the right answers, it greatly increases your chance of avoiding frauds or incompetence. The latter is more of a problem than the former, although incompetence rarely makes headlines, while fraud always does.

It is much more likely that you will pick funds that are suited to you both quantitatively (risk to reward) and qualitatively (suitability to your personal investing approach). Because you understand the investment, you won't make the mistakes most mutual fund investors make: buying after a run-up based purely on performance, selling based on emotions, and not understanding the realistic prospects for return and thus getting impatient.

All That Glitters, Etc. 23

A wise man will make more opportunities than he finds.

—Sir Francis Bacon (1561–1626)

While a secular bear market, rising interest rates, a Muddle Through Economy and a falling dollar may not be the best environment for the broad stock market and bonds, they do suggest other investment opportunities. In this chapter, I will examine some opportunities outside the traditional world of investments including gold, commodities, and real estate. I'll also offer a few comments on whether this is a good time to start your own business.

Why these topics? First, because I get so many letters from readers of my weekly e-letter asking me about my views on them. Second, they all offer a different way to play what I feel will be the coming trends. Rather than make specific suggestions which will be dated the moment the book is printed (buy this, sell that), I will discuss what I see as the general outlook for each of these areas, and then direct you elsewhere for further reading and study if you are so inclined.

I'll begin with gold since I'm asked about this commodity most often.

Gold was not selected arbitrarily by governments to be the monetary standard. Gold had developed for many centuries on the free market as the best money; as the commodity providing the most stable and desirable monetary medium.

—*Murray N. Rothbard*

For more than two thousand years gold's natural qualities made it man's universal medium of exchange. In contrast to political money, gold is honest money that survived the ages and will live on long after the political fiats of today have gone the way of all paper.

—Hans F. Sennholz

There can be no other criterion, no other standard than gold. Yes, gold which never changes, which can be shaped into ingots, bars, coins, which has no nationality and which is eternally and universally accepted as the unalterable fiduciary value par excellence.

—Charles De Gaulle

Few things stir the imagination as does gold. It seems to be somehow deeply imprinted into the psyche of the human race. Gerald Loeb noted that it seems to be the "most deeply rooted commercial instinct of the human race."

There are times I really wonder about this. It is, after all, simply a soft metal with few practical purposes. There are many metals more rare and more costly. There are many metals with more practical uses. But for some reason, for thousands of years, gold has been the one constant of commerce. Gold mined in Solomon's fabled mines is probably still being used today.

I know all the usual answers about why. Back in the 1980s, I wrote a newsletter on gold stocks that concentrated primarily on developing and junior mining companies. I read a great deal about gold, visited mines, attended mining conferences, and thoroughly enjoyed the experience. I have invested in a lot of mining stocks. During that time I saw the gold and mining stock market from the inside. Gold has been very, very good to me. I will tell you a few of the things I learned, and how I feel about gold today.

In the first place, I divide gold into two piles: "insurance" gold and "investment" gold. I feel strongly about insurance gold. I think everyone should own some gold.

Insurance gold is not an investment. It is not intended for sale or profit—ever. If you are buying something with no intention of selling, it is not an investment.

My fondest dream is that I will give what insurance gold I have to my grandchildren (assuming that one of my seven children actually has some kids) and that *they* will give it to *their* grandchildren. If that happens, nothing disastrous occurred in our lifetimes that caused us to part with the insurance gold.

I read a lot of history. Most of the time the world rocks along just fine. But then, out of the blue, something comes along and upsets the applecart. War, famine, invasion, disease, weather patterns, gunpowder; you know, the usual litany of suspects. But it is precisely because everything is going along so well that most people are unprepared. And 99 percent of the time, the unprepared have nothing to worry about. For most of the world the next day is much like the last one. It is for that 1 percent of the time when life deals you a terrible blow that you are glad you have insurance.

I have life insurance. I sincerely hope my great-grandchildren reap the benefits later rather than sooner. But I still pay the premiums every year, even though the doctor and my genes tell me I will live into my nineties. I buy health insurance, and usually my only visit to the doctor is for my annual allergy shot. But I still buy it.

I also think you should buy gold. I don't think your insurance gold should be 20 percent of your net worth, but you should have some. There is no set amount or percentage. It is what you feel comfortable with. My theory is that if there is really a crisis or disaster, then a little gold will go a long way.

First, let me state I am not a congenital gold bug. I became bearish on gold in the early 1990s. As late as November 1998 I wrote that I was not buying *investment* gold at that time.

But in February 2002, I turned bullish on gold as an investment, and I still am. I expect to remain so for some time.

I am bullish on gold because, as monetary theorists like Rothbard and Sennholz, quoted earlier, as well as the founder of the Austrian economics school Ludwig von Mises and his disciple, Nobel laureate F. A. von Hayek, have noted, gold is a currency.

I turned bearish on the dollar, and thus the world's "neutral" currency was ready to once again begin its rise. By neutral, I mean that if the entire world doubled the supply of currency tomorrow, the general price of gold in terms of the prices of the various currencies would double, but the buying power of gold would remain the same. I am sure you have seen the studies that show that a specific amount of gold will still buy a suit or a loaf of bread much as it did 100 or 200 years ago. While such specific studies are somewhat dubious in nature, the theory is more or less correct. Gold maintains a reasonable buying power over long periods of time. Since a currency is something we use to buy and sell assets, gold as an investment holds the position as a neutral currency, which, as Charles de Gaulle noted, cannot be manipulated by world governments.

On an interesting historical note, it was de Gaulle, the president of France, who in 1971 began to demand gold for France's dollars from the U.S. central bank. Since the French (and the rest of the world who would follow their lead) would eventually end up with all the gold in Fort Knox,

Nixon closed the "gold window." It was, as Bill Bonner noted in *Financial Reckoning Day*, the end of the gold standard and the beginning of the dollar standard. It was also the beginning of an explosive run in gold prices.

Now, in 2004, as the slide of the dollar has further to go (in my opinion), the potential for a rise in gold is significant. An approximately 10 percent drop in the trade-weighted dollar produced an approximately 40 to 45 percent rise in gold. Will another 10 to 20 percent drop in the trade weighted dollar mean a similar rise in gold?

That is impossible to say. There is no one to one connection between the amount of dollars in circulation and an ounce of gold. It is far more complex than some mere construct like that. Gold is actually a very thin market.

Richard Russell, writing in his *Dow Theory Letters* says that the total value of all the gold in the world is around $1.4 trillion. This sum includes the gold in central banks, in the jewelry boxes and buried in the backyard in every country, and of every person in the world. That is a fraction of world currency and net worth. There is just not much of the "barbarous relic," as John Maynard Keynes termed it. Could gold explode to the upside, creating another bubble as it did in the late 1970s? Given the emotional attachment to gold, it could. Then again, it could have an orderly rise.

What will be the eventual price of gold? Some think in the $500 range. Some suggest $3,000. I could give you 20 different charts and graphs from any number of analysts with their prediction on gold. They are all over the board. Some of them will be right. I simply have no way to know which one, and have no opinion, other than that the general direction of the price of gold is up, and will be so until the dollar stabilizes.

Until that time, it is my opinion that gold will be an excellent investment.

Taking Stock of Gold

Now gold stocks and all the related mining stocks can benefit significantly if gold is to rise. If gold were to move only 10 percent, correctly chosen gold stocks can jump enormously. Gold stocks give you some real leverage if you want to play in the gold stock world. The recent 45 percent rise in gold was accompanied by a 120 percent + rise in the Morningstar Precious Metals Index. Certain stocks, if you were lucky enough to own them, went much higher.

Here's why. If a company is mining gold and its costs are $280 to get the gold out of the ground, it is only making $20 an ounce if gold sells for $300. But if gold sells for $340, then the company makes $60 an ounce or three times what it makes at $300 gold. That is a 200 percent profit increase on just a 13 percent move in the gold price. At $400 gold, the profits rise 1,200 percent. There are many mining companies that have a cost of gold production very close to $300. Many mines in South Africa lose money at $300 gold. A small move in gold can make huge differences in the profitability of a company.

If there is not much gold in the world, relatively speaking, there is an even smaller amount of gold stocks. There is roughly total market capitalization of $120 billion of gold stocks. That is less than half Microsoft's market cap.

But notice I said *correctly chosen gold stocks*. There's the catch. There are lots of gold companies and promoters that are more interested in mining your money than in mining gold. They take advantage of our human fascination with the yellow metal to separate us from our hard-earned cash. The recent rise in gold is bringing out the usual suspects, promoting various holes in the ground as the greatest find since the King Solomon Mine.

The gold investment world is full of sharks, con artists, promoters, and thieves who are eager to prey on the rookie investors. On the other hand, the gold mining world also has some of the nicest, most honest people you will ever meet. There are some genuine businessmen who simply live for the thrill of extracting gold or other metals from the ground. Sometimes, you can just decide to invest in people rather than a particular stock. There are some mining company managers who are just winners no matter where they go. They will figure out how to get *something* profitable out of the ground. People who have invested in their projects long-term have always been happy.

The only way to invest in the gold world is to have a reliable guide who can distinguish between the "good" guys and the "bad" guys, and can also find out which companies have minable gold or serious prospects.

I have repeatedly said that the only way to invest is to either become very knowledgeable about an investment area, or to let a professional do it for you. That goes triple for the gold stock market! If you decide to use gold stocks as a way to profit from the drop in the dollar, it will do you no good to invest in the wrong stocks. You can't rely on most of the information or promotions you get in the mail on gold stocks. Much of the so-called "independent" analysis isn't independent and is financed by the companies themselves.

This is not a market in which to invest a few thousand dollars on a hot tip. You have better odds in Vegas. If you want to invest directly in gold stocks (rather than gold stock mutual funds), then you'll need to do some diligent research. You need to find some reliable gold stock newsletters and brokers to help you, attend gold conferences, and get a real feel for the gold mining world *before* you ever invest a penny! This is not a world for rookies or amateurs. If you are going to do it, and there is no reason not to if that is where you want to spend your research time, then be serious about it.

I list a number of web sites, books, and newsletters on gold and gold stock investing under "gold links" at my web site, www.2000wave.com.

Your Basic Commodities

Many of the large trends I have written about (the dollar, interest rates, the stock market, inflation, etc.) offer significant opportunities for investment. If you understand the risks and are prepared for them, this might be an area in which you can allocate some of your risk capital.

But before we explore how to invest in commodities, let me recommend how you do not do it.

Commodity industry executives have long said that about two-thirds of all individuals investors lose money in futures. Actually, the real number is probably a lot higher. In fact, one senior executive of one of the largest brokerage houses in the country once told a private group of industry insiders that fully 95 percent of their clients lost money.

When you look at the track records of the professional Commodity Trading Advisors (CTAs) who make their living every day in these markets, you realize how hard it is to win. It is not uncommon for even the best traders to have losing periods of 20 to 40 percent or more. The commodities futures markets are not for those with weak stomachs.

Do *not* attempt to trade futures on your own. I cannot make it any clearer than that. The odds are very high that *you will lose money*. The worst thing that can happen is that you make money on your first few trades and you decide to get serious about the commodity markets.

Don't let some broker you haven't met talk you into a guaranteed-to-win, always-been-in-the-money trade on heating oil or soybeans. Think about it. If the trader was that good, he would be managing big money and wouldn't have time to call you.

So Why Even Write about It?

While investing in commodities or futures on your own is a recipe for disaster, there are some reasonable ways to participate in these markets. More so than in any other area, if you want to invest in the commodity markets, in my opinion you need to find successful professionals to do it for you. I have been involved in the futures markets for 15 years. (I know a little of what I am talking about!)

(At this point, I should note that Millennium Wave Advisors, LLC (my firm) is registered with the National Futures Associations and the Commodity Futures Trading Commission. I am a CTA/CPO (Commodity Trading Advisor/Commodity Pool Operator) and I have a firm which is an IB (Introducing Broker). I do not recommend trades, make trades, or have a quote machine near my desk. I do not manage separate accounts. I do not do any retail business. I do not offer a trading service. The registrations are required for certain referral activities in which my firm participates.)

If you want to invest in the commodities futures world, I would suggest you do so by investing in a commodity pool (or if you are quite wealthy or aggressive or both, a separate managed account) rather than try and trade on your own. Even with a professional, the volatility and risk can be high.

Having said that, these funds can be useful in the diversification of certain types of portfolios. For those investors who want to try to profit from the eroding dollar and other macroeconomic situations, these funds may make sense. I am going to discuss the pros *and* cons and try to give you the tools to analyze for yourself whether this is an area of investment you should consider.

My first involvement in the investment management business was in 1989 as a consultant to a commodity fund. To this day, I get daily reports on commodity funds and traders. I have watched commodity funds go from being excellent investments for certain investors to so-so to boring (or worse) and back to good again. I have attended dozens of conferences on commodity funds and hedge funds over the years, meeting with more managers and funds than I can remember. There has been an evolution in management style in these funds over the past two decades.

Commodity funds, with some notable exceptions, have been performing well as of late, after a long dry spell. What has been the driver for this performance and is there reason to believe it can continue? (But keep in mind, past performance is not indicative of future results.)

What Are Global Macro Funds?

First of all, there are really two types of global macro commodity funds, which can be differentiated by their style of trading. One is discretionary (trend-predictive) and the other is systematic (trend-following). A discretionary fund generally relies on economic analysis and the ability of managers to predict events, such as a fall in the dollar or a rise in European interest rates. Systematic funds are basically trend-following funds of one form or another. A systematic fund waits for those events to begin happening and then invests as the trend develops.

Both types of funds focus on global macroeconomic changes. They can take positions on currencies, interest rates, commodities, and stocks anywhere and everywhere. While macro funds represent only about 9 percent of the hedge fund universe (*Source:* Hedge Fund Research, Inc., Zurich Capital Markets, and Parker Global Strategies LLC), they are the most well known category of funds. This is the style of fund that George Soros and Julian Robertson have made famous. They also represent the bulk of the spectacular problems in the hedge fund arena—Long-Term Capital Management and the recent Eifuku collapse.

While I think some of these discretionary funds will be among the best performers of this decade, I also think some of them will be among the worst. These are risky funds and should represent only a small portion of your portfolio, if any. Since most have $1,000,000 minimums, they are simply not appropriate for most of my readers.

On the other hand, systematic funds are far more interesting to me for the potential they offer.

What is the difference between a global macro hedge fund and a global macro commodity fund? Historically, a "pure" commodity fund traded only futures and was regulated by the Commodity Futures Trading Commission (CFTC) and to a lesser extent by the Securities and Exchange Commission (SEC). Today, there are still funds that offer a pure "commodity play," but in general, the differences between hedge and commodity funds have blurred, as now almost anything that moves is traded on some futures market somewhere, and many hedge funds use futures to hedge or diversify.

There are very few systematic global macro hedge funds that are open to U.S. investors and/or have minimums under $1,000,000. For that reason, I am going to confine the remarks in the rest of this chapter to systematic global commodity funds, which are readily available in the United States, often for very reasonable minimum investments for this type of investment vehicle.

Volatility, Volatility, Everything Is Volatility

The best way to understand commodity funds is to start with volatility. In the alternative investment world, macro funds, and especially trend-following commodity funds, are known as "long vol" or long volatility investments. By that, we mean if you think there is going to be a lot of volatility and large trends, then that is the environment in which these funds have historically performed very well. (Conversely, there are a number of environments where these funds do not do well such as flat markets with whipsawlike trends. And again, keep in mind that past performance is not indicative of future results.)

But by definition, trend-following funds are themselves going to be volatile. Let's examine why.

At the risk of oversimplifying, look at Figure 23.1. Your basic trend-following system will get in at point A, after the trend has started, and get out at point B, after the trend has reversed. This means the system will not be able to profit from the entire move as it does not get in at the beginning and that you are basically guaranteed a losing period at the end of the trend as a reversal is required to exit.

One common feature of many of such systems is that they cut their losing trades rather quickly and let winning trades ride. This is a wonderful thing when there are lengthy trends with large price movements such as illustrated in Figure 23.1. However, it can be painful when there are short trends with small movements and quick reversals (see Figure 23.2).

It is especially painful when there are numerous back-to-back short trends that reverse below the entry point quickly, resulting in potentially significant losses that can add up over time.

(Figures 23.1 and 23.2 are for illustrative purposes only and are not indicative of any fund's performance.)

Again, at the risk of oversimplification, you want to be "long vol" when there are prospects of large directional trends.

Managed Accounts Report (*MAR*) is a newsletter that tracks commodity traders. They calculate an index called the CISDM Trading Advisor Qualified Universe Index that is an average of the traders in their database. Figures 23.3 and 23.4 show how the index has done since 1983. (These figures are for illustrative purposes only and are not indicative of any fund's

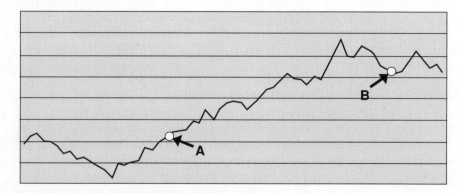

Figure 23.1   Trend-Following System in Long Trend

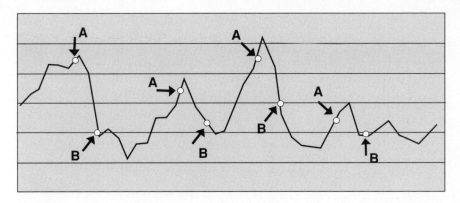

Figure 23.2 Trend-Following System in Short Trends

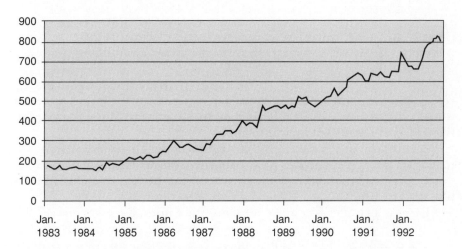

Figure 23.3 CISDM Trading Advisor Qualified Universe Index 1983–1992

performance. An investor cannot invest directly in an index. Moreover, indexes do not reflect commissions or fees that might be charged to a fund and which might materially affect the performance data presented.)

From 1983 to 1992, the index gained 15.9 percent (average annual return) with a 16.6 percent standard deviation. The track record for CTAs over the past 10 years has been spotty at best. While it has grown by 8.8 percent (average annual return) with an 8.9 percent standard deviation, if you look at the record, you will find that the bulk of the gains have come in short periods since 1993, as indicated by the arrows. During the

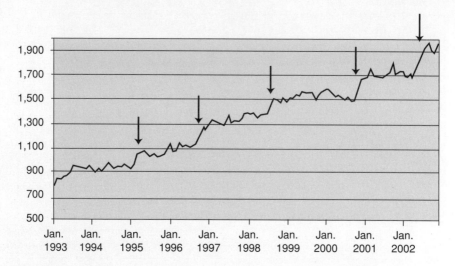

Figure 23.4 CISDM Trading Advisor Qualified Universe Index 1993–2002
Copyright © CISDM 2002. All rights reserved. Reproduced from www.marhedge.com.

rest of the time the index was treading water at best or losing money at worst. (Past results are not indicative of future results. There is a substantial risk of loss when trading futures.)

Recently, the index has picked up significantly. The question you have to ask is, "Is this just another one of those short bursts of growth between longer periods of disappointing returns, or is it the beginning of a period like 1983 to 1992?"

There is of course no way to peer into the future. How you answer that question depends on the assumptions you make. If you assume a continuation of or a return to the global macro environment that looks like 1993 to 2001, then your answer is that this is just a nice run, and we will soon see a return to a flat performance.

The recent good performance has been due largely to long runs in currencies (the rise in the euro, for example), energy, and metals. But primarily, it is the currencies.

In my opinion and for reasons I have written about at length, we could see a continuing drop in the dollar that could last for several years. This decline in the dollar will put pressure on commodity prices.

While there will be corrections in these markets accompanied by significant volatility, if I am right it is possible that this will produce sustained longer trends, which is precisely the type of environment in which global macro funds historically perform well. (Keep in mind that past results are not necessarily indicative of future results.)

And since most global macro funds are quite large, they need movements in areas where there is trading capacity. A large movement on coffee or cotton would not make a significant difference to the bottom line of most large funds, even if they caught the movement perfectly. They cannot get enough exposure in these small markets. The large funds concentrate in the financial and energy markets, as that is where the real potential is.

That being said, investing in such funds is not for the faint of heart. Even during the best periods of global macro commodity fund performance, there are serious losing periods. Because the MAR index is an average of numerous funds, it tends to understate the size of the losing periods. *In even the best funds, there have been and will be in the future losing periods of 25 percent or more. As I said earlier, trend-following funds by definition will have losing periods.*

Risks and More Risks

L et's talk about some of the risks associated with these funds. They generally are highly leveraged and performance can be volatile. There is no secondary market for the interests and, although they often have monthly or quarterly redemptions, there are often notice and other restrictions that apply to such redemptions that adversely affect their liquidity. In many cases, a portion of the trading occurs on foreign markets on which U.S. regulations do not apply. Many of these funds (particularly the futures funds) charge substantial fees and expenses. As a result, you should only consider allocating the high-risk portion of your portfolio to this class of investment.

How Do You Choose a Fund?

I n researching this chapter, I called my good friend Art Bell, whose CPA firm probably audits more commodities funds (and certainly many of the largest) than any other firm in the world. I met Art in 1990, as he audited the funds with which I worked. (Full disclosure requires me to point out that his firm audits my financial services companies and funds, as well as handles my personal tax work.)

We talked about the "state of the commodity fund world." He made two points which I pass on to you. First I asked him, "What is the single most important factor or difference between successful commodity funds and unsuccessful funds?" His answer was simple: "Research."

Successful firms today are using increasingly sophisticated math, have access to far more data and are aggressively searching for relationships and connections among the various data they collect. In addition, there is far more time spent on risk management and risk control than ever before. In evaluating a commodity fund, it is important to know how much time and effort they devote to research, and how they manage risk. It is especially important to know if management will override their risk management systems. One of the more famous blow-ups in the commodity fund world came as the manager of a very large fund became convinced that the Dow was extremely overvalued when it first reached 4,000 and refused to follow his system, which said to exit the short position as the Dow climbed much higher.

And that brings us to Bell's second observation: Many of the larger funds are currently targeting lower volatility and lower returns than they have in the past. In the 1980s, a number of funds had 30 percent plus years, and to be "competitive" in that arena meant that you had to target such returns. To get these numbers meant you had to use lots of leverage and take more aggressive risk. This meant many funds had serious volatility, and it was not unusual for a fund to blow up.

Recently, a number of large firms (billion-dollar plus) have taken the stance that less volatility makes more sense in today's environment. Their investors have told them they like steady performance as opposed to large swings in their accounts.

There are funds that still swing for the fence, but the overall trend is for larger funds to not be as aggressive. This does not mean they will not experience volatility. They most certainly will. It simply means they have adjusted their goals and risk parameters. (If, for example, they get a series of small losing trades, the overall result could be the same as one large loss.)

How do you choose a fund that may be right for you? For the largest portion of my readers, I would start with well-known and established names with longer track records. There are perhaps a half-dozen names that come to mind. You should also recognize that these funds are going to experience volatility, so this should be an investment you plan to keep over several years.

Nearly every major brokerage firm has access to these public funds. Most brokerage firms also have a number of private funds as well. Accredited investors also may be able to access certain of these private funds.

Should you invest after a losing period or during a winning period? The answer is that there is no way to know what the next few months of any fund performance will be. As you look back over track records, you can find times where a few losing months were followed by a few more losing months, and a few winning months were followed by even more winning months. In general, if you decide you want exposure to this market, then my suggestion is to choose the fund that fits your criteria and invest.

One last note: You will see as you look at the track records of these funds that their performance has come down over the past 15 years. A great deal of this is because many futures funds invest only a small portion of their capital in actual futures contracts. The rest is kept as margin in short-term interest-bearing treasury notes. When short-term rates were 8 to 10 percent, this could be a significant part of a fund's income. With rates at 1.5 percent, it does not make as much difference. Even if the funds achieved the exact same returns on their investments, the overall returns would be down due to the difference in interest rates. Conversely, if interest rates go back up, the funds will make more simply due to interest.

Getting Real

All real estate is local. The valuations depend on local conditions. Investing in downtown real estate of small, but once thriving, farming communities has not been particularly profitable. Values in downtown Manhattan have climbed through the ceiling. Small Park Avenue co-ops sell for millions while only a few miles away, spacious homes are available for a fraction of the co-op's price.

Location. Location. Location.

I can't comment on your specific location, but I can make a few remarks on the macro environment which will affect real estate values.

Besides location, what drives the nominal value of real estate? Inflation. Three percent inflation means that, all else being equal, a property will double in price in 24 years.

Serious fortunes have been made by many investors of all sizes who buy income real estate, leverage the property and hold it for years, letting their tenants in effect pay off the mortgage. What's the old line? The easiest way to make a million dollars is to borrow it and then pay it back.

I think real estate holds some very interesting opportunity over the next few years for long-term investors. It is possible to lock in reasonably low long-term rates. I think we will look back in a decade or two and see this as a once-in-a-lifetime opportunity. Thus one of the most significant costs of doing business in real estate is low.

Now rising rates will lower the value of real estate, and for a few years things might be bumpy. But if you have the right real estate with the ability to keep tenants, as long as you can service the debt, inflation will eventually be your friend.

Direct real estate investing requires a serious level of commitment and research (surprise, surprise). Whether buying single family homes as rental property, apartments, or commercial real estate, it takes management savvy and the ability to think about where the local economy and business will be over the next decade. Many investors use management firms, while others do it for themselves.

When's the best time to buy? It obviously depends on your location, but as with stocks, you want to buy when values are good. That may mean before an area becomes hot. For instance, certain retirement meccas may do very well as the top level of the boomer generation looks for just the right spot to spend the next phase of their lives, as well as their savings. Even during a recession, these areas may see prices continue to rise for both their residential and commercial real estate.

What will drive values down and create buying opportunities in other areas? A recession is the first thing that comes to mind. Investors with the fortitude to buy when times are tough generally get better values and lower rates. Patience is required.

The local bookstore is full of books on investing in real estate. If this area is of interest to you, become knowledgeable before you invest.

A Few Thoughts on Starting a New Business

We are facing a Muddle Through Economy. Author Michael Gerber tells us in *The E-Myth* (HarperCollins, 1988) that 80 percent of new businesses fail within five years. Why would you want to start a business given these odds?

You may have some very good reasons to start a business today. And, I wouldn't want anyone to say that I discouraged you just because things might be a little tougher than in the 1990s.

I have a confession. I am a serial entrepreneur. I have started more than my share of businesses and projects. Some have done pretty well, thank you, while others went down in flames. Starting any new venture is fraught with peril and difficulties, frustration and disappointment. But the rewards of making it work are immeasurable.

If you have a good idea or project or if you see a need and can profitably fill it (and enjoy doing so!), then I encourage you to jump in. Don't wait until times are perfect, because they never will be. Whenever you start, you will find multiple problems for which you did not plan.

Thomas Jefferson said, "Were we to be directed from Washington when to sow and when to reap, we should soon want bread." Waiting for someone to ring a bell that says it is a good time to start a business means you will probably miss opportunity. Study. Research. Plan. Then, with your awareness of potential problems, if you're still intent, go for it.

Starting (or buying) and growing a business remains the single best way to create wealth. If you plan well and grow, maybe yours will be one of those small-cap value companies that will be perfect for Bull's Eye investors. Good luck.

Bull's Eye Investing **24**

Every hunter knows that you don't shoot where the duck is, but where the duck is going to be. You've got to "lead the duck." If you aim where the duck is at the moment you shoot, you will always miss your target (unless the duck is flying very slowly or straight at you!).

Bull's Eye Investing attempts to apply that same principle to investing. In the previous 23 chapters, I have tried to help you target your investments toward where the market will be, not where it was.

To be a successful investor during the remainder of this decade, you'll have to change your behavior from what you did in the 1980s and 1990s. We started the recent bull market with high interest rates, very high inflation, and low stock market valuations. All the elements were in place to launch the greatest bull market in history.

Now we have the opposite environment. The stock market has high valuations, interest rates have nowhere to go but up, the dollar is dropping, and the twin deficits of trade imbalance and government debt stare us in the face. We face a long-term secular bear market as broad stock market valuations return to lower levels. The economic headwinds suggest a Muddle Through Economy.

In spite of the problems, we need to keep in mind a central fact: The U.S. economy will continue to grow. Throughout this book, I've stressed that the investment opportunities have changed from the ones you pursued over the previous two decades.

To use another hunting analogy, it is no longer deer season. It is time to hunt for something else and maybe even to hunt in a different place altogether, with different types of weapons and hunting gear. The basics will be the same. We are still hunting and will bring home our trophies—in this case it will be profits. We will just get them from a different source than we did last season.

It is an era of emphasizing absolute returns over relative returns. It is a period in which research and homework will be rewarded, rather than blind trust in an ever upward-spiraling market. *Bull's Eye Investing* is about seeking value and controlling risk and working with the trends rather than against them.

Now, let me with leave you with a few optimistic thoughts about the future.

The Nature of Change

My interest is in the future, because I am going to spend the rest of my life there.

—*Charles F. Kettering*

How well we deal with change is at the heart of the investment enterprise. As we have seen from our survey of the academic literature on the psychology of investing, the overwhelming conclusion you have is how consistently the broad class of investors (which does not include you or me, of course) assume that the current trend will continue long into the future.

Investors all too often rationalize their actions with the mantra of "this time it's different" or assume they will be able to nimbly react to or avoid the affects of the change when it happens. It never is and they hardly ever do.

My personal career path has been one of almost constant change. Yet it is but an echo of a million other entrepreneurs and businessmen and women. We all deal with change. In fact, the amount of change that I have had to deal with is rather unremarkable, in the grand scheme of things. There are millions—perhaps billions—of people who go through far more abrupt changes almost daily.

Some of the changes were forced upon me. Some of them I willingly embraced. I have told my friends on several of these changes that I hope this is the last time I have to reinvent myself. I succumb to the fantasy that most investors have: that the trend of today will continue. And yet, I know that this is not likely. The field in which I plow and reap is changing rapidly, and it is unlikely that in 10 years it will even look the same.

When I began 30 years ago, there was no fax, no overnight delivery, and phone service was expensive. Computers? Not until 20 years ago, and they were toys compared to today's machines. It cost a lot of money to deliver a newsletter up until just a few years ago. Now the marginal cost is almost nothing. One or one million is pretty much the same to me.

Research was a visit to the library and books and a few magazines and newsletters. Now I get scores of letters and articles every day delivered to my "mailbox," plus an almost infinite amount of data at my fingertips using something called Google. I have almost five gigabytes of research and articles stored from just the past few years on my computer, which I can search with a few keystrokes. To write an 8-to-10-page weekly letter like I do even 10 years ago would have taken a week to write and a month to research. Now I can access huge amounts of data each week and I write my weekly letter on a computer in about five hours on a Friday afternoon. (I've read that they will soon have pills that will help our memories. I am going to need them.)

International readers? Very few ever saw my musings in the past decade. Now I have thousands of international readers, often from some amazingly remote locations. My work may soon be translated into Chinese.

In short, the changes have been dramatic. At times, I complain, it has been hard to adjust. A lot of times those changes were just plain not fun. Some of them were very expensive lessons. Yet, I continue on down my current business path. But I know that change is coming. *Change is like a train. Either it can run over you or you can catch it to the future.*

But I can hear that peasant from China, as he follows an ox on the way to the city, telling me I can't even begin to imagine the speed of change. Think about the changes in China and Russia or other parts of the developing world in the past 10 years. My less-than-sainted dad last hitched a wagon to drive to town in the 1920s. He saw a man put on the moon with a slide rule, a yellow pad, and pencils 40 years later. That pace of change has only increased.

In 1967, the movie *The Graduate* was the hit of the season. We remember that famous scene where a young Benjamin Braddock (Dustin Hoffman) was told to seek a career in plastics. That was the rage at the time. But it turns out that was bad advice. More than 40 percent of jobs in plastics have disappeared since 1967.

And yet there has been plenty of job growth. There were clearly better opportunities than plastics. But in 1967, if asked where the jobs and opportunities were going to come from, the proper and correct answer would have been, "I don't know, but they will."

Princeton Professor Alan Krueger tells us a quarter of all workers are now in occupations that were not listed in the Census Bureau's occupation codes in 1967.[1]

Personal computers were yet a dream. AT&T was still a monopoly. Fiber optics? The Internet? Cell phones? Robotics? Biotech? Global positioning? Faxes? Video? MP3?

There is plenty of entrepreneurial activity in the world, and the future foundation for large companies which will reward their investors is even now being laid. Look at just a few examples from just one week's worth of announcements.* Will it be these firms or their competitors that become the next Microsoft or Amgen?

John Jorsett of *The Scotsman* reports,

A team of scientists has discovered a completely new way to make electricity from nothing more than flowing water. The breakthrough, the first new method of electricity production for 160 years, could provide free, clean energy for devices such as mobile phones and calculators. On a large scale, it could conceivably be used to feed power into the national grid. Dr. David Lynch, dean of the Faculty of Engineering at the University of Alberta in Canada, where the technology was developed, said: "The discovery of an entirely new way of producing power is an incredible fundamental research breakthrough that occurs once in a lifetime. . . . The system relies on the natural 'electrokinetic' effect of a fluid flowing over a solid surface. An interplay of forces results in a thin layer of water—where it meets the surface—with a net electric charge.[2]

From the AFP (Agence France-Presse):

French scientists using an innovative microscopic scanning technique say they have discovered that nerve cells almost buzz with molecular agitation when they communicate with each other. The work sheds light on how cells operate at the synapse. . . . But *nanotechnology*, harnessed to a video camera by French researchers, shows the receptors to be extraordinarily active and that they even move around dynamically on the membrane surface.

Ian Hoffman of the *Oakland Tribune* reports,

Defense scientists are on the cusp of what could be a military revolution—warfare at the speed of light. "We've made a quantum leap here," said Randy Buff, solid-state laser program manager for the U.S. Army's Space and Missile Defense Command. "We're anxious to get out there

---

*Thanks to Bill King of *The King Report* daily newsletter for these examples.

and do something." . . . By coaxing a huge power boost out of tiny laser diodes like those in CD players, scoreboards, and supermarket scanners, scientists are squeezing unprecedented power out of lasers made of exotic crystals. . . . The latest breed of solid-state lasers now are poised to break the dominance of giant, chemical gas-powered beams with compact, mobile weapons that can run off a Humvee's diesel engine or a jet fighter's turbine. Experts liken this evolution to the shift from 1950s vacuum tubes to the solid-state transistors now driving everything electronic.

The BBC's Ania Lichtarowicz reports,

Scientists in the United States have developed a new way of taking medicines which could improve the effectiveness of some treatments including HIV therapy. Swallowing pills could become a thing of the past. Writing in the journal *Nature Materials* they describe a drug-containing microchip which can be implanted in the body. This then releases the medication slowly so the patient no longer has to take any pills.

From the AP:

One minute Gary Formanek was hitting balls at an Oregon driving range. The next, he was lying on the ground, his left side paralyzed from a stroke. The only drug that treats strokes didn't help. So doctors snaked a tiny corkscrew into Formanek's brain and pulled out the stroke-causing clot. The device that saved Formanek from disability, if not death, is generating excitement among brain experts who say the novel technology might finally offer hope for the most devastating strokes. Called the MERCI Retriever, it's still experimental. But in early testing, it seems to restore blood flow in almost half of patients—people who couldn't be helped by today's only stroke-busting medication.

From *Science Daily*:

Chemists at Rice University have demonstrated that disordered assemblies of gold nanowires and conductive organic molecules can function as nonvolatile memory, one of the key components of computer chips. "A large part of the cost associated with creating integrated circuits comes from the painstaking precision required to ensure that each of the millions of circuits on the chip are placed in exactly the right spot," said lead researcher Jim Tour, an organic chemist at Rice. "Our research shows that ordered precision isn't a prerequisite for computing. It is possible to make memory circuits out of disordered systems."

USA Today reports that scientists have discovered a test that accurately predicts the likelihood of a heart attack for someone with chest pains, thus offering the potential for significantly lowering the death rate from the number one killer.

We're constantly reading about such new innovations, almost on a daily basis.

There are three significant areas of technology that hold tremendous promise in the next few decades.

The *computer and information revolutions* are barely into their fourth decade. The difference between the power and the cost of the computers of only 10 years ago, not to mention 40, is dramatic. The difference over the next 20 years is going to be even more so. The increased power combined with the decreased cost will allow for tremendous new cost-saving technologies. Also, as automation of assembly and manufacturing lines increases, we will have the ability to customize everything from clothes to cars to manufacturing equipment.

The *biotechnology revolution* has the potential to be every bit as powerful as the computer revolution has been, generating a wide array of new companies with technologies for extending our lives, preventing and healing diseases and more efficiently feeding and clothing us. There are many of us who are at midlife today who will live to see a robust 100 years. My children will be part of the first generation to celebrate the coming of two centuries, thanks to the life-enhancing and life-prolonging drugs and biotechnologies that lie just around the corner.

The *quantum revolution* (the way we think about the forces of the molecular world) will allow us to build increasingly smaller and cheaper machines, opening the way for a vast array of new technologies. Later in the third or fourth decades of the twenty-first century, fusion-powered electric plants will give us unlimited clean power at a fraction of the current cost. There are a number of new low-cost power sources that offer the potential to rival the internal combustion engine early in the next century. Plus, there are dozens of new developments in lasers, ceramics, and metals, which will not in and of themselves change the world as much as the above three revolutions, but do offer significant improvements to our quality of life.

I can't predict where the jobs and new investment opportunities will come from in the next 30 years. They're still being invented in the garages and labs around the planet. We can speculate, but I believe the future will surprise us. It is precisely these surprises that will create the largest opportunities.

It is the unique ability of Americans to deal with change that makes me an optimist about the future of my country. We are going to have to face some very difficult changes, which given the pace of change will be even larger than what we have already faced. But coping with change is in our DNA. It is what we do.

And the ability to deal with change is not an exclusively American trait. There are millions of Chinese, Indians, Europeans, Asians, and the rest of an increasingly free world creating new technologies and thinking about ways to make their lives better. Each nation and each culture will add to the quality of life and the increased pace of change.

Think of the changes that have been wrought by a handful of inventors over the past. Think about how more inventors have yielded ever more new products. And then think about how many more magnitudes of creativity, from small garages to the largest corporations, is even now being unleashed to develop new products and industries.

I am not certain about much, but I am certain about this: the future will be different than we think it will be today. We can plan and dream. But more than ever we need to think about Plan B and C and D. The odds are your personal world is going to change dramatically in the next 10 years. How you cope with the change, and even use it to make your life better, will be the measure of how well you thrive.

Through my free weekly letter, I hope I can be part of your "let's think about the future" for a long, long time. And I bet you we find the future far more fascinating and fun than we can even begin to imagine.

Appendix

Suggested Reading Material

Books

Let me suggest a few thought-provoking books for your library.

*Fooled by Randomness: The Hidden Role of Chance in the Markets and in Life by Nassim Nicholas Taleb

Simply one of the best books on risk and investing I have ever read. Taleb examines what randomness means in business and in life and why human beings are so prone to mistake dumb luck for consummate skill. I consider it essential reading for anyone who wants to be a better investor. In addition, it is a fun and well-written book. I highly recommend it. In fact, you should make this your next book purchase.

*Against the Gods: The Remarkable Story of Risk by Peter Bernstein

Peter Bernstein is one of God's gifts to investors, and is the dean of investment analysts. His credentials are too long to list. When he writes, pay attention.

Controlling risk is at the heart of investing. Understanding how humans view risk is critical to controlling the risk in your own world. Bernstein has written a comprehensive history of man's efforts to understand risk and probability, beginning with early gamblers in ancient Greece, continuing through the seventeenth-century French mathematicians Pascal and Fermat and up to modern chaos theory. Along the way he demonstrates that understanding risk underlies everything from game theory to bridge-building to winemaking. I found this book to be remarkably well written and an excellent study of how the world has come to view risk.

This is a book for serious investors and historians. This is a highly recommended book.

*Financial Reckoning Day by Bill Bonner and Addison Wiggin

This book went to #1 on the *New York Times* best-seller list. I think this is a book you should buy and read. What you will find is a book that goes to the heart of the controversy between Ludwig von Mises and John Maynard Keynes, two of the greatest economic minds of the twentieth century. Does imbalance lead to hard correction or can it be managed back to balance? Do "managing" imbalances lead to more imbalance and bigger problems, or does it make any correction easier than it would have been?

Comprehending this debate is central to understanding the ebb and flow of economies and markets. It will also point the astute investor to large trend investment opportunities (like the drop of the dollar, for instance). Bonner (and his co-author Addison Wiggin) lay out the case for the problems associated with imbalance. They make the case for the Austrian school of economics founded by Ludwig von Mises, but in a far more readable manner.

*Stock Cycles: Why Stocks Won't Beat Money Markets over the Next Twenty Years by Michael Alexander

This started as a self-published book, and is now making the mainstream. A well reasoned book on Kondratieff long wave theory, and other stock cycles, Alexander makes a powerful case for a long term secular bear. Read it. I wrote about it at length in Chapter 4.

*When Genius Failed: The Rise and Fall of Long-Term Capital Management by Roger Lowenstein

An analysis of the Long-Term Capital Management debacle of 1998 and one of the best-written books I have read in a long time. Completely fascinating from beginning to end. Read this and then *Fooled by Randomness* (above) to get a feel for how hard it is to choose money managers.

*Bull!: A History of the Boom, 1982–1999: What Drove the Breakneck Market—and What Every Investor Needs to Know about Financial Cycles by Maggie Mahar

If you don't know where you have been, how can you know where you are going? Well-written, thought-provoking, and interesting.

*Wall Street Meat by Andy Kessler

Want to know how Wall Street analysis really works, from someone who was inside the beast? Read this very funny, well-written, and quite informative book. Find out how Jack Grubman, Mary Meeker, Henry Blodgett, and Frank Quattrone did what they did. Warning: It is more than a little graphic. Not for anyone who gets nervous around four-letter words or investors who want to keep their illusions.

*Trendwatching: Don't Be Fooled by the Next Investment Fad, Mania, or Bubble by Ron Insana

There's always a bubble being created somewhere that you can ride. Insana goes into the history of bubbles and how to recognize them. Again, if you don't know where you've been, how can you figure out where you are going?

*The New Finance by Robert Haugen

This is a classic book on value investing and a devastating refutation of the random walk theory. It has recently been updated by Haugen. I keep it near my desk and refer to its charts and thoughts frequently. Again, this is one that all investors, from beginner to pro, should have in their libraries.

Newsletters and Web Sites

Let me confess. I am an information junkie. Each week I read hundreds of letters, articles, stories, books, reports, magazines, newspapers, and so on, and then sit down and write my own free weekly e-letter. You can subscribe to *Thoughts from the Frontline* at www.2000wave.com if you are not already getting it. I do this because my day job partially entails trying to discern future trends in the investment markets and then figuring out ways clients can benefit. The letter serves as a discipline for me to focus my thinking on what I really learned that week, which I would (or should!) write anyway. I am grateful to my publisher and his sponsors for making it available and thus free to you.

Many readers want to know some of my favorite sources for information, so let me suggest a few sources. They range from free to very expensive. Mind you, these are just a few of the more regular letters and reports, but it will give you a few ideas of where to go if you want to do some of your own direct research.

- First, subscribe to Richard Russell's *Dow Theory Letters* ($250 a year—www.dowtheoryletters.com). Richard is the dean of investment writers, starting his letter in 1958. He is now 79 and writes a daily letter on the markets and trends. But the reason to read him is the market wisdom that drips off his keyboard. He has seen it all. He has no ax to grind, no product to push, and nothing to sell. He writes every day because he likes it. He also recommends gold stocks and follows that market as well. Pay attention and learn, grasshopper.

- For actual and specific investment advice, you can go to www.pirateinvestor.com, where you can find the newsletters for Porter Stansberry and Dr. Steve Sjuggerud. They are hardworking writers and analysts. Their marketing promotions are a tad over the top (as are those of most subscription newsletters), but the actual content of the letters is quite good. Steve has a free weekly service called Investment U, which is a great place for someone to learn the basics. You can sign up on the site.

- Go to www.dailyreckoning.com. You can sign up for their free daily letter written by Bill Bonner and Addison Wiggin (called the *Daily Reckoning*) with essays from guest writers, including yours truly from time to time. You can click on the DR Marketplace and see the subscription letters they offer. I particularly like Lynn Carpenter at Fleet Street, who is a contrarian value investor. I also contribute an article for the letter from time to time. Dan Denning writes and edits a letter called *Strategic Investing* which makes me think and is worth the price. James Boric, whom I wrote about in Chapter 18, writes a letter called *Penny Stock Fortunes*, which seeks to find undervalued small-cap stocks. If you are looking for investment ideas in that space, it is worth the $59.

- My friend and former business partner Gary Halbert writes a well-written weekly letter, typically focused more on politics and how it affects your investments, as well as a wide-ranging variety of investment topics: www.profutures.com. Very thoughtful and balanced analysis.

- I get three letters every day that are intended for serious traders and funds. They are quite pricey, being at least several thousand a year. Basically, depending on the size of your firm or fund and distribution list, they negotiate the price. They do make some concession to individuals, but are still not cheap.

  1. Greg Weldon gets up by 3 A.M. and writes several newsletters a day, and is one of the smartest macro analysts I know. He writes a letter focused on metals called *Metal Monitor* (gold, nickel, etc.), which is a mere $250 a month for individuals, and another called *Money Monitor* ($500 and up a month and one of my favorite letters and a must-read). If you are running a fund, you need this letter. For a free trial subscription information call Bill Herron at 203-858-1459 or e-mail weldonfinancial@comcast.net.

  2. Dennis Gartman writes *The Gartman Letter*, which is a daily letter. Dennis gets up at 2 A.M., reads everything from everywhere and has

a four-page letter in my box by 6 A.M. telling me what happened while I was asleep, plus telling me what it will mean to the market and offering suggestions on how to trade the trends. He is balanced and savvy. I find it must reading and it helps that he is a good writer. You can contact them at dennis@thegartmanletter.com.

3. Bill King writes *The King Report* every day, which is again on my computer very early. King spends his time combing scores of publications for the interesting tidbits that will be the news and weaving them into an analysis of how the market will react. Typically larger institutions will subscribe for distribution to their managers. You can e-mail him at thekingreport@ramking sec.com for subscription details.

- The monthly Bank Credit Analyst, edited by Martin Barnes is one of the best and more reliable of economics letters. Barnes is one of the smartest analysts in the country. The firm does a number of letters, but I like the basic *U.S. Bank Credit Analyst* (bcaresearch.com).
- There are several very good analysts and writers who post their work for free on the Internet. First, Stephen Roach writes for Morgan Stanley every Monday and Friday. I never miss him. You can go to www.morganstanley.com, click on site directory, and then click Global Economic Forum. (I also have come to like much of the rest of their strategy team, as they make me think even when I disagree with them.)

  Bill Gross and Paul McCulley write a monthly letter at www.pimco.com. These guys sit on top of the largest pile of bonds in the world and write some of the most intriguing letters I know of. My only complaint is they only write once a month. Guys who write this well should be required to write more. Roach, McCulley, and Gross are required reading, and the price is right.
- On the international political front, every day I get a letter from www.stratfor.com, which is one of my favorite sources for geopolitical information. *Barron's* or somebody like that called them a mini-CIA. They do seem to get the news before it shows up on TV and in the paper. For $99, you can stay ahead of the news. No spin, no BS, no ads, just thought-provoking commentary and news summaries. Also, an odd but interesting site is www.debka.com. They seem to get some good scoops from time to time.
- My friend David Tice of the Prudent Bear Fund has a great web site. Regular writers Marshall Auerback and Doug Noland should be a staple part of your investment diet: www.prudentbear.com.
- My old friends at Phillips Publishing have a web site called www.investorplace.com. They offer several newsletters, but I like the contrarian approach of Richard Band. I have known Richard for

years, and he is a very steady no-nonsense New Englander and writes a very good letter. Doug Fabian edits a letter called *Successful Investing*. For those of you who are looking for advice on timing mutual funds or your 401(k), I would recommend this letter. It is a simple and basic moving average approach which will help you avoid the big losses and catch the uptrends. You can do it yourself (Doug pretty much explains all the details of what he does) or you can pay him a few bucks.

- How can I leave out Gary Shilling? You probably know him from *Forbes*, but he also writes a 40+-page letter every month, full of graphs and charts and insight, as well as the definitive book on deflation. You can find information at www.agaryshilling.com. The letter is $295 a year.

- For currency traders, my friend Chuck Butler of Everbank writes an excellent daily letter on the status of currencies. You can get him to add you to the list by e-mailing him at Chuck.Butler@EVERBANK.com. As an aside, the bank will open a CD account in just about any currency, including Chinese renminbi, which is why his focus is on currencies.

- Barry Ritholtz writes a twice-weekly free letter called the *Big Picture*. You probably see him a lot on TV. He is a very smart guy and thinks before he writes, which is not always the case for analysts. You can contact him at ritholtz@yahoo.com.

- I will give you one of my little secrets: my friend Mark Ford writes the excellent (and free) daily e-letter, *Early to Rise*. It focuses on business and marketing issues as well as personal goal-setting strategies, and so forth. It is like having your own personal life and business coach. *ETR* is one of my must-reads. You can get it at www.early-torise.com/SuccessStrategies.htm. Mark is one of the best marketing minds in the world.

- One wish: I get a daily, and very addictive, letter from Art Cashin (from UBS Warburg and on CNBC all the time). It is for the "trade" only. His bosses (read: the lawyers at UBS) should allow him to make it available to the public. There has got to be some way. When they finally wake up, I will let you know in my weekly letter.

Bond Information

As a registered investment advisor I receive daily bond offerings from TD Waterhouse Institutional Services. While this information says institutional, its purpose is to supply a list of bonds to sell to clients like you, my readers. Although that is not what I do in my business, many other brokers and registered investment advisors use this information, or information supplied by their firms, to help their clients.

Most people will be familiar with bond mutual funds and maybe government, municipal, and corporate bonds, but there is a broad array of choices in the marketplace. Table B.1 shows just a few from the list TD Waterhouse sent me on November 17, 2003. Two examples are given of each type of fixed income investment talked about in the following paragraphs, but there are usually 5 to 10 such examples in each category every day.

Certificates of Deposit (CDs)

The first offerings are certificates of deposit from around the country with maturities ranging from 3 months to 15 years. Here is an example of two. The CPN is coupon and what the investment yields, the MTY is maturity, and YTM is yield-to-maturity. Since these investments are sold at par or $100 the CPN and YTM are the same. As we will see, some bonds are already trading in the secondary market and have a price above premium or below discount to the par value of $100. In that case the CPN and YTM will be different numbers.

Table B.1 Sample Bond Choices

CDs

Term	Issue	CPN	MTY	Price	YTM
6 Month	Beal Bank	1.25%	2/27/2004	$100.00	1.25%
5 Year	Meridian Bank	3.70%	11/26/2008	$100.00	3.70%

Callable CDs

Term	Issue	CPN	MTY	Call	YTC
5.5 Year	Columbus B&T	4.100%	5/28/2009	11/28/2004	4.100%
15 Year	First Bank PR	5.750%	11/28/2018	5/28/2004	5.750%

Money Market Rates

Money Market Name	7 Day Yield
TD Waterhouse Bank	0.10%
CA Municipal Portfolio	0.39%

Municipals

Rating	Issue	CPN	MTY	Price	YTM	Worst Call	Call@	YTW
Aaa/AAA	NY MTA Rev	4.750%	11/15/2027	$ 99.73	4.77%	11/15/2012	$100.00	4.77%
A3/BBB	Cal St GO	5.250%	11/1/2027	$101.19	5.16%	11/1/2013	$100.00	5.10%

Agencies

Rating	Issue	CPN	MTY	Price	YTM	Call	Call@	YTC
AAA	FHLB	4.710%	8/11/2014	97.25	5.04%	2/11/2004	$100.00	7+%
AAA	FNMA	5.000%	11/3/2017	96.00	5.41%	5/3/2004	$100.00	7+%

Corporate Bonds

Rating	Issue	CPN	MTY	Price	YTM	Call	Call@	YTC
A1/A-	Suntrust Cap. Trust	7.900%	6/15/2027	$110.31	7.000%	Callable 07	$103.92	5.670%
Baa3/BBB	Motorola Inc.	7.600%	1/1/2007	$110.44	4.000%	N/A	N/A	N/A

Source: TD Waterhouse.

Callable Certificates of Deposit

The second offerings are callable CDs. These are CDs that can be called away before maturity by the institution which issued it. That is why the YTC, yield-to-call, could be a different number than the CPN.

Money Market Rates

Most of you should be familiar with money market accounts from your bank, brokerage account, or 401(k)s. On this day the seven-day yield varies from .10 percent to .39 percent, so as you can see not all money market accounts are created equally and some may be subject to taxes while others are tax exempt.

Municipals

Municipal bonds are issued by local, state, and municipal entities and have varying degrees of risk depending on the project funded and financial strength of the issuer. The ratings are done by third-party rating services like Standard & Poor's and Moody's. Here we have some examples where the bond is trading in the secondary market and the coupon and yield-to-maturity do not match. Worst call is the first date the issue can be called, the price it will be called at, which can sometimes be a premium to par, and the YTW, yield-to-worst.

Agencies

Agencies are bonds issued by government and quasi-government organizations like the Federal Home Loan Bank (FHLB), Fannie Mae (FNMA), and Freddie Mac (FHLMC). These notes are backed by a pool of mortgages otherwise known as a collateralized mortgage obligation (CMO). Another type of pooled note, called a collateralized debt obligation (CDO), is not an agency and an example is not shown, but the pool of debt might be credit card debt, auto loans, and bank loans.

Corporate Bonds

These are bonds issued by corporations and may have a callable feature, be insured against default, pay interest monthly, quarterly, semiannually, or annually. As with all bonds the details will be spelled out in the offering documentation. These details are called the covenants and they do not change until the bond is paid off by the issuer. As an example, think of all the details in a home mortgage that are detailed out when the loan is originated and do not change until the mortgage is paid off.

If you are going to be a direct buyer of bonds, and there is no reason that you cannot if you are willing to spend the time to learn, I would go to your local bookstore and pick up a book on bonds—that is, a book devoted to bond investing, not a chapter in a general book on investments. Also get a large bag of coffee.

Hedge Fund Industry Resources

Hedge Fund Industry Websites

Albourne Village
(U.K.-based, news, research, discussion board for alternative
    investments)
http://village.albourne.com

Alternative Asset Center
(Fund of hedge funds database, index, and book)
www.aa-center.net

Alternative Investment Management Association (AIMA)
(Global, not-for-profit trade association for hedge funds, managed
    futures, and managed currency funds)
www.aima.org

Alternative Investment Research Center
Cass Business School—City of London
(U.K. nonprofit academic research center, research)
www.cass.city.ac.uk/airc/index.html

Altvest
(Hedge fund database)
www.investorforce.com/#

Center for International Securities and Derivatives Markets (CISDM)
(Nonprofit academic research center, research, hedge fund and
managed futures database)
http://cisdm.som.umass.edu

Chartered Alternative Investment Analyst
(Alternative investment designation sponsored by the CISDM and
AIMA)
www.caia.org

CogentHedge.com
(Hedge fund database)
www.cogenthedge.com

Eurekahedge
(News, worldwide hedge fund and fund of hedge funds databases,
indexes)
www.eurekahedge.com

Evaluation Associates Capital Markets, Inc
(Consultant, hedge fund index)
www.eacm.com

FundFire
(News)
www.fundfire.com

Hedge Focus
(French-based, news, research)
www.hedgefocus.com

Hedge Fund Alert
(Weekly hedge fund publication)
www.hfalert.com

Hedge Fund Association
(International not-for-profit association of hedge fund managers and
service providers)
www.thehfa.org

Hedge Fund Center
(News, research, third-party providers)
www.hedgefundcenter.com

Hedge Fund Consistency Index Newsletter
(News and hedge fund database)
www.hedgefund-index.com

Hedge Fund Intelligence
(U.K.-based hedge fund publishing group, news, hedge fund
    databases)
www.hedgefundintelligence.com

Hedge Fund Marketing Alliance
(Industry information and links)
www.hedgefundmarketing.org

Hedge Fund Research
(Hedge fund database, hedge fund and fund of hedge funds indexes)
www.hedgefundresearch.com

Hedge Funds Review
(Monthly hedge fund magazine)
www.hedgefundsreview.com

Hedge Week
(Daily hedge fund news)
www.hedgemedia.com

HedgeCo.net
(News and hedge fund database)
www.hedgeco.net

HedgeFund.net
(News, hedge fund database)
www.hedgefund.net

HedgeFundNews.com
(News, research, hedge fund database)
www.hedgefundnews.com

HedgeIndex.com
(Credit Suisse First Boston/Tremont hedge fund indexes)
www.hedgeindex.com

HedgeWorld
(News, research, hedge fund database, service providers)
www.hedgeworld.com

Hennessee Group
(Hedge fund consultants, news, research, monthly publication)
www.hennesseegroup.com

Journal of Alternative Investments
(Institutional Investors quarterly academic journal)
www.iijai.com

MarHedge
(News, hedge fund and managed futures indexes)
www.marhedge.com

MSCI
(Hedge fund indexes)
www.msci.com/hedge

PerTrack 2000wave
(Software for analyzing third-party hedge fund databases)
www.pertrac2000.com

Standard & Poor's
(Hedge fund and commodity indexes)
www2.standardandpoors.com

Talent Hedge
(German-based, hedge fund indexes)
www.talenthedge.com

The Texas Hedge Fund Association
(News, research, links)
www.texashfa.org

Van Hedge Fund Advisors
(Hedge fund database and indexes)
www.vanhedge.com

For those who are interested and who qualify, I write a free letter on hedge funds and private offerings called the *Accredited Investor E-letter*. You must be an accredited investor (broadly defined as an investor with net worth of $1,000,000 or $200,000 annual income—see details at the web site.) You can go to www.accreditedinvestor.ws to subscribe to the letter and see complete details, including the risks in hedge funds. (I am a registered representative of and president/owner of Millennium Wave Securities, LLC, a National Association of Securities Dealers (NASD) member firm.

Hedge Fund Books

Anson, Mark J. P. *The Handbook of Alternative Assets.* New York: John Wiley & Sons, 2002.

Calamos, Nick P. *Convertible Arbitrage: Insights and Techniques for Successful Hedging.* Hoboken, NJ: John Wiley & Sons, 2003.

Ineichen, Alexander M. *Absolute Returns: The Risk and Opportunities of Hedge Fund Investing.* Hoboken, NJ: John Wiley & Sons, 2003.

Jobman, Darrell. *The Handbook of Alternative Investments.* New York: John Wiley & Sons, 2002.

McCrary, Stuart A. *How to Create and Manage a Hedge Fund.* New York: John Wiley & Sons, 2002.

Nicholas, Joseph G. *Investing in Hedge Funds: Strategies for the New Marketplace.* Princeton, NJ: Bloomberg Press, 1999.

Nicholas, Joseph G. *Market-Neutral Investing: Long/Short Hedge Fund Strategies.* Princeton, NJ: Bloomberg Press, 2000.

Owen, James. *The Prudent Investor's Guide to Hedge Funds.* New York: John Wiley & Sons, 2000.

Phillips, Kenneth S., and Ronald J. Surz. *Hedge Funds: Definitive Strategies and Techniques.* Hoboken, NJ: John Wiley & Sons, 2003.

Schneeweis, Tom, and Joseph F. Pescatore. *The Handbook of Alternative Investment Strategies.* New York: Institutional Investor, 1999.

Strachman, Daniel A. *Getting Started in Hedge Funds.* New York: John Wiley & Sons, 2000.

Warwick, Ben. *Searching for Alpha: The Quest for Exceptional Investment Performance.* New York: John Wiley & Sons, 2000.

Hedge Fund Conferences

There are several firms that promote hedge fund conferences of various types. Some are for "the trade" and might be of little use to those outside the business, but many are geared for investors. From time to time, I speak at some of their conferences. You will simply have to look at the material for individual conferences to determine which might apply to you. The web sites are:

MAR Hedge: www.marhedge.com
Infovest21: www.infovest21.com
Institute for International Research (click on Finance and
    Investments) www.iirusa.com
Financial Research Associates: www.frallc.com

Hedge Fund Net Worth Requirements: Why a Million Isn't Always Enough

Many high-net-worth investors believe that if they say they're worth more than $1,000,000, they will qualify to receive information on private offerings and hedge funds. However, this is a myth that continues to be perpetuated by many web sites and newspaper articles.

The attitude is "What I am worth is nobody's business but mine. I will reveal I have a net worth of more than $1,000,000, but don't want to say anything more. Just show me your information."

I understand that sentiment. I agree with it. But the rules surrounding private offerings don't. Unfortunately, it is not enough to simply be worth $1,000,000 in all cases to see information or invest in a private offering or hedge fund. Sometimes an individual has to be worth (or have investments worth) $1.5, $2, or $5 million, and in certain cases $25 million. Although the following is a generalization, I will briefly explain the reasons behind each of those numbers in a second. Before I start, you should know that the rules are complex. I'm not an attorney and can't give you legal advice. I'm simply trying to give you a sense of the issues involved and why being absolutely honest when you're completing the forms and questionnaires is in your best interest.

Briefly, here are the different levels and qualifications for individuals, and the types of offerings available to each. If you are investing through an entity like certain trusts, corporations, or partnerships there is a different set of requirements that are beyond this discussion.

Below $1,000,000. Just for the record, if you are a nonaccredited investor, it is technically possible for you to get into a small number of private offerings and even certain hedge funds, although it is highly unlikely you will ever find one for which you qualify. For example, if the fund does not charge an incentive fee (a performance-based fee), it is possible that a nonaccredited investor might qualify, if the investor has the knowledge and experience in business and investments sufficient to evaluate the merits and risks of the securities offered. It is more likely that you would qualify for a publicly registered fund, like a public futures fund. Further, the minimum investment amounts typically would require too high an investment. However, SEC-registered advisors and SEC-registered funds with incentive (or performance) fees must apply the higher standard for incentive fees, below.

Accredited Investor. Net worth must be in excess of $1,000,000 or annual income in excess of $200,000 for the previous two years with an expectation of an income of $200,000 in the current year. Net worth is calculated on the entire net worth of your assets, which is generally accepted to include your home and private businesses, assets, and so on. Different advisors can have varying standards as to what they accept as an asset for the purposes of determining if someone is an accredited investor. Most advisors or funds would not accept an investor whose entire net worth was in a primary home, even if equity in the home was more than $1,000,000. Often the question from the fund or advisor's point of view hinges on the liquidity of the investor and the nature of the private investments. If you invest jointly with your spouse the income requirement increases to a joint income of more than $300,000. There are other rules for entities that invest.

Some private funds have a minimum net worth requirement of $1,000,000. Some require more. There are a three primary reasons why some funds require higher levels—whether the fund (1) pays incentive fees to a registered investment advisor; (2) trades futures contracts as part of its portfolio; or (3) was structured using an exemption from investment company registration that permits it to take more than 99 beneficial owners.

Incentive Fees—Qualified Client. Net worth must be over $1,500,000. Net worth is again typically calculated on the entire net worth of your assets, including home and private businesses, assets, and so on, although different funds may have their own more restrictive standards.

Nearly all funds charge a management fee, which is usually figured as a percentage of assets under management. For instance, a 1 percent management fee on a $100,000 investment would be $1,000 per year.

An incentive fee is when the fund manager is paid a portion or a percentage of the profits generated over a specified period of time. Typically, that is 20 percent of the profits. If a $50,000,000 fund made 20 percent or $10,000,000 for the year (net of the management and other fees), the incentive fee would be $2,000,000. The investors would make $8,000,000 or 16 percent. (This example is for illustrative purposes only and does not represent the performance or fees of any fund.)

I have seen incentive fees as low as 5 percent on some funds and as high as 40 percent, and have heard of 50 percent incentive fees. There are items such as hurdles, high water marks, minimums, and so on that all can be part of the fee structure, but for now we are just concerned with how incentive fees impact who is able to invest.

If a fund is managed by a firm which is *not* a Registered Investment Advisor with the Securities and Exchange Commission or certain states with similar incentive fee rules, the fund can charge an incentive fee and take accredited investors. If the fund manager is a Registered Investment Advisor, the investor must be a qualified client, which is the next level. Funds that are managed by Registered Investment Advisors and charge an incentive fee are only available to qualified investors who have a net worth of more than $1,500,000.

Futures Contracts—Qualified Eligible Person (QEP). This applies to investors with liquid portfolios of over $2,000,000, with certain exceptions. The qualified eligible person (QEP) designation is for those persons who own securities (including commodity pool participations) of issuers with whom they are not affiliated and other investments of at least $2,000,000. This designation is primarily associated with commodity pools. This is not a net worth of all assets, but roughly is the value of investments.

Let's add some more confusion and some more to the alphabet soup. Some hedge fund managers are registered with the CFTC (Commodity Futures Trading Commission) as commodity pool operators (CPOs). They may not necessarily be primarily commodity traders, but, subject to certain exceptions, if they use futures (even just for hedging purposes) in their fund they are required to register with the CFTC.

As a CPO, a hedge fund manager is required to provide certain information and reports to investors that because of the nature of the requirements they may find cumbersome for a hedge fund to provide. The CFTC exempts CPOs from those requirements if the only persons they solicit are QEPs. To meet this standard, an individual investor must have $2,000,000 in investments OR have $200,000 in exchange-traded initial margin in a futures brokerage account or equivalent. You can combine these two components to qualify. For instance, you could have investments of $1,000,000 and also have a futures account with $100,000 in your account, which would allow you to qualify as a QEP.

This can admittedly be tricky. Some investments might qualify and others might not. If you are close to the minimums, your personal advisor will need to make a judgment.

Some funds of hedge funds are registered as commodity pools and some are not. Since many hedge funds use futures to hedge equity or bond positions or to diversify, it is not difficult for the manager of a fund of funds to have to register as a CPO. Pat McCarty, legal counsel for the CFTC, noted that 50 percent of the largest hedge funds are registered as commodity pool operators. Some hedge funds elect to follow the CFTC requirements, and others are willing to limit their potential market alternatives in order to forego the pleasure of dealing with CFTC rules.

More Than 100 Owners—Qualified Purchaser or QP. A fund that is limited to 99 accredited investors is a "3(c)(1)" fund. There is a certain type of fund that is available only to larger investors. This higher net worth requirement fund is called a "3(c)(7)" fund (from the section of the securities laws which provide the relevant exemption). This type of fund can have more than 99 investors and is usually limited to 499.

A qualified purchaser or QP is essentially a natural person or family organization with net investments of at least $5,000,000 or an institution with net investments of at least $25,000,000, with a lot of categories for partnerships, banks, insurance companies, and so on. A fund manager can have both types of funds, which essentially use the same strategy. Thus, there are a number of fund families that have funds with this higher net worth requirement. Often the fund for "smaller" investors is closed, or has a waiting list.

Arbitrary Requirements. Some fund managers may feel their strategy is suited for only certain types of investors, using their personal standard to determine net worth, sophistication, institutional status, and so on. It's their fund and their ballgame, so they get to make additional rules. Sometimes you can get them to relax those rules and sometimes they are quite firm.

The Bottom Line

If you want to find out about funds with higher net worth requirements as outlined here, you must meet the minimum net worth requirements. Let me be very clear that I am *not* suggesting you fudge or misrepresent your net worth. These standards were set to protect investors and should be strictly enforced. I *am* suggesting that it is in your interest to accurately represent your net worth.

Source Notes

1 Car Wreck, Traffic Jam, or Freeway?

1. Robert J. Shiller, *Irrational Exuberance* (Princeton, NJ: Princeton University Press, 2000), pp. 182–183.
2. Ibid., pp. 12–14.
3. Harry S. Dent Jr., *The Roaring 2000s: Building the Wealth and Lifestyle You Desire in the Greatest Boom in History* (New York: Simon & Schuster, 1998).
4. Cowles Foundation for Research in Economics at Yale University. Available from http://cowles.econ.yale.edu/default.htm.
5. John Y. Campbell and Robert J. Schiller, "Valuation Ratios and the Long-Run Stock Market Outlook: An Update," NBER Working Paper No. 8221 (2001).
6. John Geanakoplos, Michael Magill, and Martine Quinzii, "Demography and the Long-Run Predictability of the Stock Market." Cowles Foundation for Research in Economics at Yale University, Paper No. 1380 (August 2002), p. 3. Available from http://cowles.econ.yale.edu/P/cd/d13b/d1380.pdf.
7. Ibid.

3 The Trend Is Your Friend (Until It Isn't)

1. Sandra Ward, "After the Deluge," *Barron's*, Vol. 81, Issue 32 (August 6, 2001), p. 26 (3 pages).
2. Ibid.
3. Ben Stein and Phil DeMuth, *Yes, You Can Time the Market!* (Hoboken, NJ: John Wiley & Sons, 2003).
4. Hussman Econometrics study: www.hussman.net.
5. Ibid.
6. Chet Currier, "'Black Hole' Awaits in 2005, Analyst Says," *Rocky Mountain News* (January 16, 2004).

4   Catching the Next Wave

1. Michael A. Alexander, *Stock Cycles: Why Stocks Won't Beat Money Markets over the Next Twenty Years* (Lincoln, NE: iUniverse.com, 2000), p. 30.
2. Ibid., p. 40.
3. Ibid., p. 72.
4. Ibid., p. 74.
5. Ibid., pp. 101–102.
6. Ibid., p. 114.
7. Ibid., p. 150.
8. Ryan Mathews and Watts Wacker, *The Deviant's Advantage: How Fringe Ideas Create Mass Markets* (New York: Crown Business, 2002).
9. Mark Ford, *Early to Rise.* daily e-mail letter(www.earlytorise.com/Success Strategies.htm).

6   Financial Physics: Interconnected Relationships

1. The data employed throughout the analysis in Chapters 5 and 6 was procured or derived from various sources. For an index of the stock market and related information (earnings per share, price/earnings ratio, etc.), two series of data have been used. The first is the Dow Jones Industrial Average closing prices available from Dow Jones & Company. The second is the S&P 500 index data series available from Robert Shiller at http://aida.econ.yale.edu/~shiller/. The Shiller series has at least 100 years of history, has been reviewed extensively, and is generally recognized as valid and credible. The data is based on a methodology that is less subject to single-point distortions; it represents the average daily price for each month or year. Many analyses use a single period of time (i.e., the close on December 31), which can deliver distorted results by having a price that may not be representative of the price levels in the market during that year. The average daily price is a more consistent means to measure price levels of the year. For a more extensive discussion of the methodology, please refer to Professor Shiller's web site.

   The values for earnings per share for the S&P 500 index were also determined from Professor Shiller's web site. The methodology and assumptions are further explained in his books, *Market Volatility* and *Irrational Exuberance*. The price-earnings ratio reflects the average index value divided by the trailing 10-year average for earnings per share. As Professor Shiller explains, this method reduces the distortions that can occur during periods when earnings reports are temporarily distorted due to unique corporate or economic events. In the end, we accepted Professor Shiller's data series as it has been generally tested by time and review.

   The economic and market data also includes measures of the economy and interest rates. Gross domestic product is the chosen measure of overall economic output. There are two series for GDP: one that includes the effects of inflation, nominal GDP (GDP-N), and one that is reduced by inflation, real GDP (GDP-R). Data subsequent to 1929 was obtained from the Bureau of Economic Analysis. For the series prior to 1929, the data was developed by Nathan S. Balke and Robert J. Gordon (1989) and presented in the *Journal of Political Economy* ("The Estimator of Prewar Gross National Product: Methology and New Evidence," vol. 97(1), pp. 38–92). For interest rates, the series was developed from data included in *A History of Interest Rates*, Third Edition, by Sidney Homer and Richard Sylla to reflect the U.S. Treasury equivalent note with a constant 10-year maturity for periods from 1900 to 1989; subsequent data was obtained from the Federal Reserve Bank and other sources.

7   Risky Expectations

1. Robert D. Arnott and Peter L. Bernstein, "What Risk Premium Is 'Normal'?," *Financial Analysts Journal* (March/April 2002), pp. 64–85. Copyright © 2002, Association for Investment Management and Research. Reproduced and republished from *Financial Analysts Journal* with permission from the Association for Investment Management and Research. All rights reserved.
2. Ibid., p. 81.
3. Ibid.
4. Ibid.

8   Plausible Expectations: A Realistic Appraisal of the Prospects for Earnings Growth

1. Warren Buffett, Berkshire Hathaway's 1987 Chairman letter.
2. Bear, Stearns report, 2002.
3. I rely on the Bear, Stearns report for the pro forma earnings and options expenses. The rest is from Yahoo! Finance or company reports.
4. Jonathan Finer, "Pension Funds' New Realities Drag Profits Down," *Washington Post* (October 23, 2002).
5. Robert D. Arnott, private research paper.
6. Sue Kirchhoff, "Pension Squeeze," *Boston Globe* (October 25, 2002).
7. Louis K. C. Chan, Jason Karceski, and Josef Lakonishok, "The Level and Persistence of Growth Rates," *Journal of Finance* 58(2) (April 2003).
8. Ibid., pp. 4, 8, 11–12, 16–17, 26–27.
9. William J. Bernstein and Robert D. Arnott, "Earnings Growth: The Two Percent Dilution," *Financial Analysts Journal* (September/October 2003), pp. 47–55.
10. Ibid., p. 47.
11. Ibid., p. 47.
12. Ibid., p. 54.

9   Pension Fund Problems in Your Backyard

1. Dennis Cauchon, "W.Va. in Deepest Pension Peril," USAToday.com (August 3, 2003). Available from www.usatoday.com/news/washington/2003-08-03-w.va.-pension_x.htm.

2. Dennis Gartman, *The Gartman Letter* (October 27, 2003).
3. Cauchon, "W.Va. in Deepest Pension Peril."
4. See report by Parry Young, "U.S. Public Pensions Face Uncertain Times," Standard & Poor's (June 24, 2003). Available from www.nesgfoa.org/pdf/US%20Public%20Pensions%20Face%20Uncertain%20Times%206-24-03.pdf.

10 The Issue of Retirement in an Aging World: Is It Something in the Water?

1. Harry S. Dent Jr., *The Roaring 2000s: Building the Wealth and Lifestyle You Desire in the Greatest Boom in History* (New York: Simon & Schuster, 1998).
2. Robert D. Arnott and Anne Casscells, "Demographics and Capital Market Returns," *Financial Analysts Journal* (March/April 2003), pp. 20–29.
3. Centers for Medicare & Medicaid Services, "2002 Annual Report" (http://cms.hhs.gov/statistics/nhe/projections-2002/(1.ASP)).
4. "The Breaking Point," *Fortune* (March 3, 2003), pp. 104–112.
5. Roger G. Ibbotson and Rex A. Sinquefield, "Stocks, Bonds, Bills, and Inflation: Simulations of the Future (1976–2000)," *Journal of Business*, Vol. 49, Issue 3 (1976), pp. 313–338.
6. AdvisorSites, Inc., "What Will Stocks Return over the Next Twenty Years?" (July 16, 2002). Available at http://cgi.advisorsites.net/cgibin/articles/formatarticle.pl?domain=budrosandruhlin&type=fnews.
7. Employee Benefit Research Institute (EBRI): www.ebri.org/rcs/2003; American Savings Education Council (ASEC): www.asec.org; Matthew Greenwald and Associates, Inc.: www.greenwaldresearch.com.
8. See article by Nevin Adams, "Retirement Confidence Based on Shaky Assumptions?," Plan Sponsor (April 11, 2003), www.Plansponsor.com (www.plansponsor.com/pi_type11/?RECORD_ID=20241).

11 Demography Is Destiny

1. Martin Barnes, *The Bank Credit Analyst* (March 2003), © BCA Research 2003 (www.bcaresearch.com).
2. Richard Jackson and Neil Howe, "The 2003 Aging Vulnerability Index: An Assessment of the Capacity of Twelve Developed Countries to Meet the Aging Challenge," Center for Strategic and International Studies (CSIS) (March 2003). Available at www.csis.org/gai/aging_index.pdf.
3. Ibid., pp. 7, 8, 11.

12 King Dollar and the Guillotine

1. Caroline L. Freund, "Current Account Adjustment in Industrialized Countries," Board of Governors of the Federal Reserve System: International Finance Discussion Paper No. 692 (December 2000). Available at www.federalreserve.gov/pubs/ifdp/2000/692/ifdp692.pdf.

2. Stephen Roach, Morgan Stanley's "Stephen Roach Weekly Commentary." Available at www.morganstanley.com/GEFdata/digests/latest-digest.html.
3. Hans Sennholz, Ludwig von Mises Institute (www.mises.org).
4. Marshall Auerback of the Prudent Bear Fund.
5. A. Gary Shilling, *Insight* newsletter (www.agaryshilling.com).
6. Adrian Van Eck, *Money-Forecast Letter*.
7. Benjamin Fulford, "The Panic Spreads," *Forbes* (April 18, 2002).
8. Hans Sennholz, "Saving the Dollar from Destruction," Ludwig von Mises Institute (www.mises.org).
9. Ibid.
10. Ibid.

13   The Muddle Through Economy

1. Ben Bernanke speech, "Remarks by Governor Ben S. Bernanke at the Global Economic and Investment Outlook Conference," Carnegie Mellon University, Pittsburgh, Pennsylvania (November 6, 2003). Available at www.federalreserve.gov/BoardDocs/Speeches/2003/200311062/default.htm#fl1#fl1.
2. Stephen Moore, The Cato Institute (November 16, 2003, www.cato.org), published in the *Washington Times* (November 6, 2003).
3. Ibid.
4. Bruce Bartlett, "Manufacturing Is Not in Trouble," Commentary, August 18, 2003, National Center for Policy Analysis (www.ncpa.org).
5. Ibid.
6. Ibid.

14   Chairman Greenspan and the Shoot-Out at the OK Corral

1. Dennis Gartman, *The Gartman Letter* (November 22, 2002).
2. Remarks by Governor Ben S. Bernanke, "Deflation: Making Sure 'it' Doesn't Happen Here," before the National Economists Club, Washington, D.C. (November 21, 2002). Available at www.federalreserve.gov/BoardDocs/speeches/2002/20021121/default.htm.
3. Gartman, *The Gartman Letter* (November 22, 2002).
4. Bernanke, "Deflation."
5. Ibid.
6. Ibid.
7. Remarks by Chairman Alan Greenspan, "Monetary Policy under Uncertainty," at a symposium sponsored by the Federal Reserve Bank of Kansas City, Jackson Hole, Wyoming (August 29, 2003).www.federalreserve.gov/boarddocs/speeches/2003/20030829/default.htm.

15   Why Investors Fail: Analyzing Risk

1. Financial Research Corporation (www.frcnet.com), 1999.
2. See newsletter by Jeffrey A. Dunham, "Why Did Investors Earn 20% Less Than Their Mutual Fund Investments?," *Dunham & Associates Insight* (1st

Quarter 2002), p. 2. Available at www.dunham.com/Articles/Newsletter 03_2002.pdf.

3. Financial Research Corporation (www.frcnet.com), 1999.
4. David Dreman, "What Earnings Recovery?," *Forbes* (July 8, 2002), www.Forbes.com/global/2002/0708/065.html.
5. Ibid.
6. Louis K.C. Chan, Jason Karceski, and Josef Lakonishok, "The Level and Persistence of Growth Rates," National Bureau of Economic Research Working Paper No. w8282 (May 2001). Available at www.nber.org/papers/w8282.
7. Nassim Nicholas Taleb, *Fooled by Randomness: The Hidden Role of Chance in the Markets and in Life* (New York: Texere, 2001).
8. Ibid.
9. Dr. Gary Hirst, private research notes.
10. Financial Research Corporation (www.frcnet.com), 1999.
11. Gavin McQuill, "Investors Behaving Badly: An Analysis of Investor Trading Patterns in Mutual Funds," Financial Research Corporation (April 23, 2001), pp. 56–64.
12. Ibid., p. 64.

16 Taking Stock: The Fundamental Nature of Bull's Eye Investing

1. MarketScreen, available at www.marketscreen.com.
2. C. Heath and A. Tversky, "Preference and Belief: Ambiguity and Competence in Choice under Uncertainty," *Journal of Risk and Uncertainty* 28 (1991), pp. 4–28.
3. Robert J. Shiller, F. Kon-Ya, and Y. Tsutsui, "Why Did the Nikkei Crash? Expanding the Scope of Expectations Data Collection," *Review of Economics and Statistics* 78 (1996), pp. 156–164.
4. David N. Dreman and Eric A. Lufkin, "Investor Overreaction: Evidence That Its Basis Is Psychological," *Journal of Psychology and Financial Markets*, Special Edition (2000), p. 22.
5. David Dreman and Michael Berry, "Overreaction, Underreaction and the Low P/E Effect," *Financial Analysts Journal* (1995), pp. 21–30.
6. Eugene F. Fama and Kenneth R. French, "The Cross Section of Expected Stock Returns," *Journal of Finance*, Vol. 47, No. 2 (June 1992), pp. 427–465.
7. William Bernstein, "The Cross-Section of Expected Stock Returns: A Tenth Anniversary Reflection," *Efficient Frontier* (2002), www.efficientfrontier.com/ef/702/3FM-10.htm.
8. You can find information about Dan Ferris and *Extreme Value* November 2002 edition at www.pirateinvestor.com.

17 Bringing Out Your Inner Spock

1. Charles Mackay and Bernard M. Baruch, *Extraordinary Popular Delusions and the Madness of Crowds* (New York: Metro Books, 2002).

2. Jared Diamond, *Guns, Germs and Steel: The Fates of Human Societies* (New York: W. W. Norton & Company, 1999).

3. David Hirschleifer, "Investor Psychology and Asset Pricing," *Journal of Finance* 56 (2001).

4. R. Nisbett and T. Wilson, "Telling More Than We Can Know: Verbal Reports on Mental Processes," *Psychological Review* 84 (1977), pp. 231–259.

5. Leda Cosmides and John Tooby, "Cognitive Adaptations for Social Exchange," in J. Barkow, L. Cosmides, and J. Tooby (Eds.), *The Adapted Mind: Evolutionary Psychology and the Generation of Culture* (Oxford University Press, 1992), pp. 163–228.

6. Robert Trivers, *Social Evolution* (Menlo Park, CA: Benjamin/Cummings, 1985); "The Elements of a Scientific Theory of Self-Deception," *Annals of New York Academy of Sciences* 907 (2000), pp. 114–131.

7. S. E. Taylor and J. D. Brown, "Illusion and Well-Being: A Social Psychological Perspective on Mental Health," *Psychological Bulletin* 103, (1988), pp. 193–210.

8. Jonathan Freedman, *Happy People* (New York: Harcourt Brace Jovanovich, 1978).

9. Vicki S. Helgeson, and S. E. Taylor "Social Comparisons and Adjustment Among Cardiac Patients," *Journal of Applied Social Psychology* 23 (1993), pp. 1171–1185; J. V. Wood, S. E. Taylor, and R. R. Lichtman, "Social Comparison in Adjustment to Breast Cancer," *Journal of Personality and Social Psychology* 49 (1985), pp. 1169–1183; G. M. Reed, "Stress, Coping, and Psychological Adaptation in a Sample of Gay and Bisexual Men with AIDS," unpublished doctoral dissertation (University of California, Los Angeles, 1989).

10. Albert Wang, "Overconfidence, Investor Sentiment, and Evolution," *Journal of Financial Intermediation* 10 (2001), pp. 138–170.

11. Amos Tversky and Daniel Kahneman, "Judgement under Uncertainty: Heuristics and Biases," *Science* 185 (1974), pp. 1124–1131.

12. Daniel Kahneman and Amos Tversky, "On the Psychology of Prediction," *Psychology Review* 80 (1973), pp. 237–251.

13. S. Gadarowski, "Financial Press Coverage and Expected Stock Returns," Cornell University Working Paper (2001).

14. Gary Klein, *Sources of Power: How People Make Decisions* (Cambridge, MA: MIT Press, 1999).

15. Joseph Piotroski, "Value Investing: The Use of Historical Financial Statement Information to Separate Winners from Losers," *Journal of Accounting Research* 38 (Supplement) (2000). Also available from http://gsbwww.uchicago.edu/fac/joseph.piotroski/research.

16. Partha Mohanram, "Is Fundamental Analysis Effective for Growth Stocks?" (2003). Available from www.ssrn.com.
17. James Montier, *Behavioral Finance: Insights into Irrational Minds and Markets* (Hoboken, NJ: John Wiley & Sons, 2002).

18 The Value in Stocks

1. Thomas J. Stanley and William D. Danko, *The Millionaire Next Door: The Surprising Secrets of America's Wealthy* (Atlanta: Longstreet Press, 1996; New York: Pocket Books, 1998).
2. Adam Smith, *The Money Game*, (New York: Random House, 1976).

20 Hedge Funds 101: The Basics

1. Jeff Joseph, "Investing for Absolute Returns: The Rydex SPhinX Fund," Rydex Capital Partners I, LLC (October 2003).
2. Alfred Winslow Jones, "Fashions in Forecasting," *Fortune* (March 1949), pp. 86–91, 178–186.
3. Carol J. Loomis, "Hard Times Come to the Hedge Funds," *Fortune* (January 1970).
4. Ibid.
5. Ibid.
6. Beth Healy, "Colleges Turn to Hedge Funds," Boston Globe Online (April 16, 2003).
7. Bing Liang, "Hedge Funds: The Living and the Dead," *Journal of Financial and Quantitative Analysis* (September 2000).
8. Gaurav S. Amin and Harry M. Kat, "Hedge Fund Performance 1990–2000: Do the 'Money Machines' Really Add Value?," ISMA Center, University of Reading, Working Paper (December 6, 2001).
9. William Fung and David A. Hsieh, "Hedge Fund Benchmarks: Information Content and Biases," *Financial Analysts Journal* 58(1) (January/February 2002), p. 24.
10. Richard Elden, "The Evolution of the Hedge Fund Industry," *Journal of Global Financial Markets* 2(4) (Winter 2001).
11. Jean-Marc Vichard, "The Hedge Most Forgotten," Global Association of Risk Professionals, *GARP Risk Review* 9 (November/December 2000).
12. Todd E. Petzel, "Risk Management and Alternative Investments," Association for Investment Management and Research, Conference Proceedings: Hedge Fund Management (2002), pp. 27–31.
13. Jamie LaReau, "Investors Urged to Up Hedge Fund Due Diligence," *FundFire* (April 14, 2003), www.fundfire.com; information from white paper by Infovest21.
14. Fung and Hsieh, "Hedge Fund Benchmarks," p. 26.

15. Alexander M. Ineichen, "The Search for Alpha Continues: Do Fund of Hedge Funds Managers Add Value?," *UBS Warburg Global Alternative Investment Strategies* (September 2001).
16. Fung and Hsieh, "Hedge Fund Benchmarks," (2002) p. 30.

21 Investing in a Fund of Hedge Funds

1. Richard Elden, "The Evolution of the Hedge Fund Industry," *Journal of Global Financial Markets* 2(4) (Winter 2001).
2. Alexander M. Ineichen, "The Search for Alpha Continues: Do Fund of Hedge Funds Managers Add Value?," *UBS Warburg Global Alternative Investment Strategies* (September 2001).
3. Ibid., p. 38.

22 Doing Your Due Diligence

1. See article by Rich Peebles, "Market Summary: Bullish News Flops, Gold Romps," PrudentBear.com (May 28, 2002). Available at www.prudentbear.com/archive_comm_article.asp?category=Market+Summary&content_idx=12111.

24 Bull's Eye Investing

1. Dr. Alan Krueger, *New York Times* op-ed, November 13, 2003.

Bibliography

Alexander, Michael A. *Stock Cycles: Why Stocks Won't Beat Money Markets over the Next Twenty Years.* Lincoln, NE: iUniverse.com, 2000.

Amenc, Noel, and Lionel Martellini. "Portfolio Optimization and Hedge Fund Style Allocation Decisions." *Journal of Alternative Investments* (Fall 2002).

Amin, Gaurav S., and Harry M. Kat. "Hedge Fund Performance 1990–2000: Do the 'Money Machines' Really Add Value?" ISMA Center, University of Reading, Working Paper (December 6, 2001).

Amin, Gaurav S., and Harry M. Kat. "Welcome to the Dark Side: Hedge Fund Attrition and Survivorship Bias over the Period 1994–2001." ISMA Center, University of Reading, Working Paper (December 11, 2001).

Anson, Mark J. P. *The Handbook of Alternative Assets.* New York: John Wiley & Sons, 2002.

Arnott, Robert D. "The Role of Hedge Funds in a World of Lower Returns." Hedge Fund Strategies: A Global Outlook, *Institutional Investor* (Fall 2002).

Arnott, Robert D., and Anne Casscells. "Demographics and Capital Market Returns." *Financial Analysts Journal* (March/April 2003).

Arnott, Robert D., and Peter L. Bernstein. "What Risk Premium Is 'Normal'?" *Financial Analysts Journal* (March/April 2002).

Bartlett, Bruce. "Manufacturing Is Not in Trouble." Commentary: National Center for Policy Analysis (August 18, 2003) (www.ncpa.org).

Bernanke, Ben S. "Deflation: Making Sure 'It' Doesn't Happen Here." Remarks before the National Economists Club, Washington, D.C. (November 21, 2002).

Bernanke, Ben S. "Remarks by Governor Ben S. Bernanke at the Global Economic and Investment Outlook Conference." Carnegie Mellon University, Pittsburgh, Pennsylvania (November 6, 2003).

Bernstein, Peter L. *Against the Gods: The Remarkable Story of Risk.* New York: John Wiley & Sons, 1996.

Bernstein, William J., and Robert D. Arnott. "Earnings Growth: The Two Percent Dilution." *Financial Analysts Journal* (September/October 2003).

Bonner, William, with Addison Wiggin. *Financial Reckoning Day: Surviving the Soft Depression of the 21st Century.* Hoboken, NJ: John Wiley & Sons, 2003.

Brinson, Gary P., L. Randolph Hood, and Gilbert Beebower. "Determinants of Portfolio Performance." *Financial Analysts Journal* (July–August 1986).

Calamos, Nick P. *Convertible Arbitrage: Insights and Techniques for Successful Hedging.* Hoboken, NJ: John Wiley & Sons, 2003.

Cauchon, Dennis. "W.Va. in Deepest Pension Peril." USAToday.com (August 3, 2003).

Chan, Louis K. C., Jason Karceski, and Josef Lakonishok. "The Level and Persistence of Growth Rates." NBER Working Paper No. w8282 (May 2001); *Journal of Finance* 58(2) (April 2003).

Dent, Harry S., Jr. *The Roaring 2000s: Building the Wealth and Lifestyle You Desire in the Greatest Boom in History.* New York: Simon & Schuster, 1998.

Diamond, Dr. Jared. *Guns, Germs and Steel: The Fates of Human Societies.* New York: W. W. Norton & Company, 1999.

Dreman, David N., and Eric A. Lufkin. "Investor Overreaction: Evidence That Its Basis Is Psychological." *Journal of Psychology and Financial Markets*, Special Edition (2000).

Dunham, Jeffrey A. "Why Did Investors Earn 20% Less Than Their Mutual Fund Investments?" *Dunham & Associates Insight* (1st Quarter 2002).

Elden, Richard. "The Evolution of the Hedge Fund Industry." *Journal of Global Financial Markets* 2(4) (Winter 2001).

Fama, Eugene F., and Kenneth R. French. "The Cross Section of Expected Stock Returns." *Journal of Finance* 47(2) (June 1992).

Finer, Jonathan. "Pension Funds' New Realities Drag Profits Down." *Washington Post* (October 23, 2002).

Freund, Caroline L. "Current Account Adjustment in Industrialized Countries." Board of Governors of the Federal Reserve System: International Finance Discussion Paper No. 692 (December 2000).

Fung, William, and David A. Hsieh. "Hedge-Fund Benchmarks: Information Content and Biases." *Financial Analysts Journal* (January/February 2002).

Gadarowski, S. "Financial Press Coverage and Expected Stock Returns." Cornell University Working Paper (2001).

Geanakoplos, John, Michael Magill, and Martine Quinzii. "Demography and the Long-Run Predictability of the Stock Market." Cowles Foundation for Research in Economics at Yale University, Paper No. 1380 (August 2002).

Greenspan, Alan. "Monetary Policy under Uncertainty." Symposium sponsored by the Federal Reserve Bank of Kansas City, Jackson Hole, Wyoming (August 29, 2003).

Haugen, Robert A. *The New Finance: The Case against Efficient Markets.* 2nd ed. Upper Saddle River, NJ: Prentice Hall, 1999.

Healy, Beth. "Colleges Turn to Hedge Funds." Boston Globe Online (April 16, 2003).

Hirschleifer, D. "Investor Psychology and Asset Pricing." *Journal of Finance* 56 (2001).

Ibbotson, Roger G., and Rex A. Sinquefield. "Stocks, Bonds, Bills, and Inflation: Simulations of the Future (1976–2000)." *Journal of Business* 49(3) (1976): 313–338.

Ineichen, Alexander M. *Absolute Returns: The Risk and Opportunities of Hedge Fund Investing.* Hoboken, NJ: John Wiley & Sons, 2003.

Ineichen, Alexander M. "Hedge Funds: Bubble or New Paradigm?" *Journal of Global Financial Markets* (Winter 2001).

Ineichen, Alexander M. "The Myth of Hedge Funds." *Journal of Global Financial Markets* (Winter 2001).

Ineichen, Alexander M. "The Search for Alpha Continues: Do Fund of Hedge Funds Managers Add Value?" *UBS Warburg Global Alternative Investment Strategies* (September 2001).

Insana, Ron. *Trendwatching: Don't Be Fooled by the Next Investment Fad, Mania, or Bubble.* New York: HarperBusiness, 2002.

Jackson, Richard, and Neil Howe. "The 2003 Aging Vulnerability Index: An Assessment of the Capacity of Twelve Developed Countries to Meet the Aging Challenge." Center for Strategic and International Studies (CSIS) (March 2003).

Jacobs, Bruce I. "Controlled Risk Strategies." *ICFA Continuing Education: Alternative Investing.* Charlottesville, VA: Association for Investment Management and Research, 1998.

Jobman, Darrell. *The Handbook of Alternative Investments.* New York: John Wiley & Sons, 2002.

Jones, Alfred Winslow. "Fashions in Forecasting." *Fortune,* (March 1949).

Joseph, Jeff. "Investing for Absolute Returns: The Rydex SPhinX Fund." Rydex Capital Partners I, LLC (October 2003).

Kessler, Andy. *Wall Street Meat: My Narrow Escape from the Stock Market Grinder.* New York: HarperBusiness, 2003.

Kilka, Michael, and Martin Weber. "Home Bias in International Stock Return Expectations." *Journal of Psychology and Financial Markets,* Special Edition (2000).

Klein, Gary. *Sources of Power: How People Make Decisions.* Cambridge, MA: MIT Press, 1999.

LaReau, Jamie. "Investors Urged to Up Hedge Fund Due Diligence." *FundFire* (April 14, 2003) (www.fundfire.com).

Liang, Bing. "Hedge Funds: The Living and the Dead." *Journal of Financial and Quantitative Analysis* (September 2000).

Loomis, Carol J. "Hard Times Come to the Hedge Funds." *Fortune,* (January 1970).

Loomis, Carol J. "The Jones Nobody Can Keep Up With." *Fortune* (April 1966).

Lowenstein, Roger. *When Genius Failed: The Rise and Fall of Long-Term Capital Management.* New York: Random House, 2000.

Mackay, Charles, and Bernard M. Baruch. *Extraordinary Popular Delusions and the Madness of Crowds.* New York: Metro Books, 2002.

Mahar, Maggie. *Bull!: A History of the Boom, 1982–1999: What Drove the Breakneck Market—and What Every Investor Needs to Know about Financial Cycles.* New York: HarperBusiness, 2003.

Mathews, Ryan, and Watts Wacker. *The Deviant's Advantage: How Fringe Ideas Create Mass Markets.* New York: Crown Business, 2002.

McCrary, Stuart A. *How to Create & Manage a Hedge Fund.* New York: John Wiley & Sons, 2002.

McQuill, Gavin. "Investors Behaving Badly: An Analysis of Investor Trading Patterns in Mutual Funds." *Journal of Financial Planning* (November 2001).

Mohanram, Partha. "Is Fundamental Analysis Effective for Growth Stocks?" 2003. Available from www.ssrn.com.

Montier, James. *Behavioural Finance: Insights into Irrational Minds and Markets.* Hoboken, NJ: John Wiley & Sons, 2002.

Nicholas, Joseph G. *Investing in Hedge Funds: Strategies for the New Marketplace.* Princeton, NJ: Bloomberg Press, 1999.

Nicholas, Joseph G. *Market-Neutral Investing: Long/Short Hedge Fund Strategies.* Princeton, NJ: Bloomberg Press, 2000.

Patel, Sandeep A., Bhaskar Krishnan, and Jacqueline Meziani. "Addressing Risks in Hedge Fund Investments." Hedge Fund Strategies: A Global Outlook, *Institutional Investor* (Fall 2002).

Peebles, Rich. "Market Summary: Bullish News Flops, Gold Romps." Prudent-Bear.com (May 28, 2002).

Peskin, Michael W., Satish I. Anjilvel, Michael S. Urias, and Brian E. Boudreau. "Why Hedge Funds Make Sense." *Morgan Stanley Dean Witter: Quantitative Strategies* (November 2000).

Petzel, Todd E. "Risk Management and Alternative Investments." Association for Investment Management and Research, Conference Proceedings: Hedge Fund Management (2002).

Phillips, Kenneth S., and Ronald J. Surz. *Hedge Funds: Definitive Strategies and Techniques.* Hoboken, NJ: John Wiley & Sons, 2003.

Piotroski, Joseph. "Value Investing: The Use of Historical Financial Statement Information to Separate Winners from Losers." *Journal of Accounting Research* 38 (Supplement) (2000): 1–41.

Schneeweis, Tom, and Joseph F. Pescatore. *The Handbook of Alternative Investment Strategies.* New York: Institutional Investor, 1999.

Shiller, Robert J. *Irrational Exuberance.* Princeton, NJ: Princeton University Press, 2000.

Shiller, Robert J., F. Kon-Ya, and Y. Tsutsui. "Why Did the Nikkei Crash? Expanding the Scope of Expectations Data Collection." *Review of Economics and Statistics* 78 (1996).

Siegel, Jeremy J. *Stocks for the Long Run: The Definitive Guide to Financial Market Returns and Long-Term Investment Strategies.* New York: McGraw-Hill, 1998.

Singer, Brian D., Renato Staub, and Kevin Terhaar. "Determining the Appropriate Allocation to Alternative Investments." *Hedge Fund Management: AIMR Conference Proceedings* (2002).

Stein, Ben, and Phil DeMuth. *Yes, You Can Time the Market!* Hoboken, NJ: John Wiley & Sons, 2003.

Strachman, Daniel A. *Getting Started in Hedge Funds.* New York: John Wiley & Sons, 2000.

Taleb, Nassim Nicholas. *Fooled by Randomness: The Hidden Role of Chance in the Markets and in Life.* New York: Texere, 2001.

"2003 Wilshire Report on State Retirement Systems: Funding Levels and Asset Allocation." Wilshire Associates, Inc. (March 2003).

Vichard, Jean-Marc. "The Hedge Most Forgotten." *GARP Risk Review* 9 (November/December 2002).

Wang, Albert. "Overconfidence, Investor Sentiment, and Evolution." *Journal of Financial Intermediation* 10 (2001).

Warwick, Ben. *Searching for Alpha: The Quest for Exceptional Investment Performance.* New York: John Wiley & Sons, 2000.

"What Will Stocks Return over the Next Twenty Years?" AdvisorSites, Inc. (July 16, 2002).

Young, Parry. "U.S. Public Pensions Face Uncertain Times." Standard & Poor's (June 24, 2003).

About the Author

Who Is John Mauldin?

I often read a book and wonder about who the author is beyond the obligatory two or three paragraphs on the back flap. For those interested, I talked my publisher into letting me give you a little bit more of a personal history.

I am often asked how to become an investment writer/analyst. The answer is I do not know. My rather torturous trek is not a model for young aspirants. It seems that I subscribe to the Yogi Berra School of Career Paths: "I came to the fork in the road and I took it." Sometimes the path was obvious, and sometimes it was forced upon me. Change was not always welcome, but it has always been interesting.

I grew up working in a small print shop, setting type by hand and running small presses, as well as having the obligatory newspaper routes. I graduated from Rice University in 1972 and the Southwestern Baptist Theological Seminary in 1974. God not being willing to foist me on some poor unsuspecting church (what a disaster that would have been!), I ended up running a small family printing business. I grew it substantially and then we sold it in 1976. I eventually became somewhat of a direct mail guru back when direct mail was just beginning to be computerized. I started a company that printed checks and sold checkbooks through the mail, which allowed me to volunteer with a missionary outfit called Youth with a Mission for three years. During that period I did some consulting with an investment newsletter publisher. In 1981, I returned to the check printing company, where we developed a new technology for printing checks. When we introduced the prototype in 1982 at COMDEX (a large computer show) it was the fastest bit-mapping printer in the world—120 fully programmable pages a minute using magnetic toner, which was something in those days. It sold for $240,000 in 1982 dollars, if I remember correctly. I was fortunate (and forced) to sell out my interest at a very nice profit, as the largest investor wanted an older and more seasoned high-tech CEO. His mistake, my good fortune. That was my first (and last!) foray into the high-tech world. I then turned my attention to the investment publishing client (Dr. Gary North and the American Bureau of Economic Research), eventually buying a stake in the firm.

That was when Howard Ruff was the big dog on the block with 200,000 subscribers, Bill Bonner at Agora had a small office in a very rough neighborhood in Baltimore (it made me nervous to go there even during the day!), and Tom Phillips was only a few years from his kitchen table. The investment newsletter publishing community, while competitive, worked closely together, sharing tips and secrets, as it was to everyone's benefit to grow the total market.

Even though I had an emphasis on economics at Rice, this was really my introduction to the investment world. It was at that time I was introduced to Ludwig von Mises and Murray Rothbard and gained an appreciation for the Austrian school of economics. (I actually met with Nobel laureate Friedrich Hayek, author of the seminal *Road to Serfdom*, in Austria; he was in his late 80s at the time.) I helped a lot of subscribers get in the cellular telephone lotteries, and our personal partnerships ended up winning a few. I banged around in Africa attempting to get some cellular licenses there (l-o-o-o-ng story), trying to make lightning strike twice.

I also looked at hundreds of investment ideas and managers. I read voraciously and began to get some glimmer of the field. I soon realized there was more money to be made in managing money than writing about it. I formed a partnership with Gary Halbert of ProFutures in the late 1980s and we began to offer a variety of funds and managers to clients, helping build that firm into a quite respectable venture. Rather than directly managing money, we managed managers, so to speak. We emphasized alternative managers, market timers, asset allocation, commodity funds, and hedge funds. I had begun to write under my own name in the late 1990s and was meeting with some small success, and I enjoyed it enormously.

I sold out to Gary in 1999 (a very friendly transaction) as I wanted to pursue some different directions. In addition to writing, I wanted to begin to manage money on my own. In my previous business, I looked over the shoulders of some of the better market timers, watching them at their trade.

I had been introduced to a money management and market timing system developed in the late 1970s using money flow indicators that had a very good track record. The gentleman who had done the work was retired and looking for someone to use his system. I spent a great deal of money having it independently verified and then bought the system.

I found out as much about myself as I did about market timing. What I found out was that I did not have the emotional personality (the stomach?) to directly time the markets with someone else's money. I could do it with mine and not lose sleep. But when it was a client's, I simply worried too much over each move of the tape. It bordered on obsession, although some members of my family might say I had a hazy idea about where the border was. Even with a mechanical system, I could not relax. My wife says the best day of our marriage was when I sent the client money back.

I can watch another manager trade and not blink, and I thoroughly enjoy the process of finding and monitoring investment managers and funds. Thus I returned to doing what I knew and enjoyed best, which was finding money managers for my clients, with an emphasis on hedge funds and alternative managers. I will say that I believe the experience helped make me a better judge of investment talent.

During this time (late 2000) I put my newsletter on this new thing called the Internet, starting with a thousand or so readers. It began to grow surprisingly quickly. Today my publisher sends the letter out to well over 1,500,000 readers each week.

What I now do every day is one of the most fun things I could ever imagine doing. I am insatiably curious about the future. I want to know what is around the Curve in the Road. My passion is to try to understand the worlds of economics and investment, politics and science, and how they all may come together in the future. I read anything and everything that interests me and then write about it. I get to analyze the investment approaches of some of the smartest (and most interesting) people one could ever hope to meet. I have the opportunity to travel to lots of fun places. And amazingly I make a living at it. I get paid to read and think and talk to interesting people (which includes you when we finally get to meet). What a deal!

The letter was first a passion. I simply love the discipline of writing. It forces me to think. I did not realize just how large it would become, or what a focus of my business life.

By early 2002 it was clear that my small firm could not handle the potential business without serious restructuring. I had built a few businesses with lots of employees before. I knew what it would take. To add more staff, researchers, salespeople, and so on would take time away from the reading, research, manager analysis, writing, speaking, and client conversations that I really enjoyed.

I decided to develop a series of strategic relationships with other firms that would allow me to do what I do best and what I enjoy doing. In essence, I direct investors interested in my ideas to these firms; they do the sales and share in the due diligence and research responsibilities, and we divide up any income that is generated.

For those who are interested and who qualify, I write a free letter on hedge funds and private offerings called the *Accredited Investor E-letter*. You must be an accredited investor (broadly defined as having a net worth of $1,000,000 or $200,000 annual income—see details at the web site). You can go to www.accreditedinvestor.ws to subscribe to the letter and see complete details, including the risks in hedge funds. (I am president of Millennium Wave Securities, LLC, a NASD-registered broker-dealer.)

A Few More Details from the Official Bio

John is a Fort Worth, Texas, businessman, married to his wife Eunice (his favorite Canadian export) and the father of seven children ranging in age from 9 through 26, five of whom are adopted.

He was chief executive officer of the American Bureau of Economic Research, Inc., a publisher of newsletters and books on various investment topics, from 1982 to 1987. He was one of the founders of Adopting Children Together Inc., the largest adoption support group in Texas. He currently serves on the board of directors of the International Reconciliation Coalition and the International Children's Relief Fund. He is also a member of the Knights of Malta, and has served on the executive committee of the Republican Party of Texas.

He is a frequent contributor to numerous publications, and guest on TV and radio shows as well as quoted widely in the press.

John is the president of Millennium Wave Advisors, LLC (MWA), an investment advisory firm registered in multiple states. MWA is also a Commodity Pool Operator (CPO) and a Commodity Trading Advisor (CTA) registered with the Commodity Futures Trading Commission (CFTC), as well as an Introducing Broker (IB). He is also the president and a Registered Representative of Millennium Wave Securities, LLC, which is a member of the NASD.

For those seeking John's personal and business references, pictures of his family, or further information, we would refer you to www.john mauldin.com.

Index